MW00626692

THE MEU

Marine Expeditionary Unit

SMARTbook

Guide to Battle Staff Operations & the Rapid Response Planning Process

The Lightning Press

Norman M. Wade

The Lightning Press

2227 Arrowhead Blvd.
Lakeland, FL 33813
24-hour Voicemail/Fax/Order: 1-800-997-8827
E-mail: SMARTbooks@TheLightningPress.com
www.TheLightningPress.com

The Marine Expeditionary Unit (MEU) SMARTbook

Guide to Battle Staff Operations & the Rapid Response Planning Process

ISBN: 978-1-935886-18-1

Special recognition goes to the command, staff and Marines of the 15th Marine Expeditionary Unit. Thank you for what you and other servicemembers do for our Nation each and everyday. Hooah!

Photos. Courtesy Department of Defense and the Military Services.

Printed and bound in the United States of America.

Preface

The Marine Expedtionary Unit (MEU) SMARTbook is designed to be a reference for MEU and PHIBRON Commanders, MEU and PHIBRON staffs and the commanders and staffs of the Major Subordinate Elements (MSE) and Naval Support Elements (NSE) of the ARG-MEU team.

The Marine Corps Planning Process (MCPP) is the basis for MEU staff planning. Planning is the art and science of envisioning a desired future and laying out effective ways of bringing it about. In war, planning can be essential to the ability to seize the initiative. In order to seize the initiative, we must be able to anticipate events and act purposefully and effectively before the enemy can. Planning mitigates crises by dealing with crisis situations before they reach crisis proportions.

The Rapid Response Planning Process (R2P2) is an accelerated execution of MCPP geared to Crisis Action Planning. The R2P2 process allows the MEU/PHIBRON to anticipate potential missions, create a set of standardized responses through analytical decision-making, and rehearse their responses to achieve full capability within six hours of receipt of a warning or execute order.

Rapid planning requires extensive training in the techniques and procedures associated with R2P2. It requires standardized, detailed, parallel, and concurrent command and staff actions using Standard Operating Procedures (SOPs) that are understood by all members of the unit.

The Marine Expedtionary Unit (MEU) SMARTbook helps to generate tempo and staff synergy in time-compressed situations through the use of "playbooks" for rapid planning and templates for efficient briefings.

This planning handbook is based primarily on 15th MEU's staff SOP, although the material and concepts are applicable to all MEUs. When examples or unit specific references are made, they refer to the 15th MEU.

SMARTbooks - The Essentials of Warfighting!

Recognized as a doctrinal reference standard by military professionals around the world, SMARTbooks are designed with all levels of Soldiers, Sailors, Airmen, Marines and Civilians in mind.

SMARTbooks can be used as quick reference guides during actual tactical combat operations, as study guides at military education and professional development courses, and as lesson plans and checklists in support of training. Serving a generation of warfighters, military reference SMARTbooks have become "mission-essential" around the world. Visit **www.TheLightningPress.com** for complete details!

Design, Composition and Production Services

The Lightning Press offers design, composition and production services for those units wishing their own tactical SOP, handbooks, and other doctrinal support materials. With ten separate books currently in circulation, we have authored and published more than 25 military doctrinal reference books in the SMARTbook military reference series over the past 18 years. This Marine Expeditionary Unit (MEU) SMARTbook can be edited, customized and reproduced with unit-specific material for any MEU or similar type unit.

References

The following references are useful in conjunction with The Marine Expeditionary Unit (MEU) SMARTbook. All references are considered public domain, available to the general public, and designated as "approved for public release; distribution is unlimited." The Marine Expeditionary Unit (MEU) SMARTbook does not contain classified or sensitive material restricted from public release.

Marine Corps Warfighting Publications (MCWP)

MCWP 2-1	Intelligence Operations
MCWP 2-15.3	Ground Reconnaissance
MCWP 3-1	Ground Combat Operations
MCWP 3-2	Aviation Operations
MCWP 3-11.2	Marine Rifle Squad (w/CH1)
MCWP 3-11.3	Scouting and Patrolling
MCWP 3-11.4	Helicopterborne Operations
MCWP 3-13	Employment of Amphibious Assault Vehicles (AAVs)
MCWP 3-14.1	Light Armored Vehicle -25 Gunnery and Employment
MCWP 3-15.5	MAGTF Antiarmor Operations
MCWP 3-16	Fires Support Coordination In The Ground Combat Element
MCWP 3-17.1	River-Crossing Operations
MCWP 3-17.3	MAGTF Breaching Operations
MCWP 3-24	Assault Support
MCWP 3-31.5	Ship-To-Shore Movement
MCWP 3-33.1	Marine Air-Ground Task Force Civil-Military Operations
MCWP 3-33.2	Civil Disturbances
MCWP 3-33.5	Counterinsurgency Operations
MCWP 3-33.8	Multi-Service TTP For Conducting Peace Operations
MCWP 3-35.3	Military Operations On Urbanized Terrain (MOUT)
MCWP 3-35.4	Doctrine For Navy/Marine Corps Joint Riverine Operations
MCWP 3-40.4	Marine Air-Ground Task Force Information Operations
MCWP 3-43.1	Raid Operations
MCWP 4-11.3G	Unit Embarkation Handbook
MCWP 4-11	Tactical-Level Logistics
MCWP 5-1	Marine Corps Planning Process
MCWP 5-11.1	MAGTF Aviation Planning
MCWP 5-12.1	The Commander's Handbook On The Law Of Naval Operations
MCWP 6-11	Leading Marines

Table of Contents

Chap 1

MEU Overview & Staff Functions

MEU Overview & Staff Organization

I. Mission of the U.S. Marine Corps....1-1
II. Organization and Structure....1-1
A. Headquarters, U.S. Marines Corps....1-1
B. Operating Forces....1-1
C. Marine Corps Reserve....1-7
D. Supporting Establishment....1-7
III. Marine Air/Ground Task Force (MAGTF)....1-3
IV. Types of MAGTFs (MEF, MEB, MEU, SPMAGTF)....1-4
A. Marine Expeditionary Force (MEF)....1-4
B. Marine Expeditionary Brigade (MEB)....1-5
C. Marine Expeditionary Unit (MEU)....1-6
D. Special Marine Air/Ground Task Force (SPMAGTF)....1-6
V. The MEU Cycle....1-7
VI. Key MEU Billets and Personnel....1-8
VII. List of MEUs....1-10

I. Administration (MEU S-1)....1-11
Mission....1-11
Organization....1-11
Capabilities and Functional Areas....1-11
Operation and Execution Support....1-13
I. MEU Finance and Disbursing (DISBO)....1-14
II. MEU Public Affairs (PAO)....1-17
A. Logistical Support to Media Operations....1-19
B. Standing Public Affairs Guidance....1-20
C. DOD Principles of Information....1-21
E. DOD Media Guidelines....1-21
F. Incident/Accident/Casualty Reporting....1-23
III. Religious Ministries Programs (Chaplain)....1-24
- The Chaplain's Role ISO MEU Operations....1-25
IV. MEU Headquarters Commandant (HQCMT)....1-26
V. MEU Staff Judge Advocate (SJA)....1-27
A. Legal Assistance....1-28
B. Legal Considerations During Operations....1-30

II. Intelligence (MEU S-2)....1-31
Mission....1-31
Organization....1-31
I. The Nature Of MEU Intelligence....1-32
II. Two Basic Objectives of Intelligence....1-32
III. Intelligence Requirements....1-33
IV. Intelligence Concept Of Operations....1-34

V. Combat Intelligence Center (CIC) 1-36
- Surveillance & Reconnaissance Center (SARC) 1-37
VI. Intelligence Communications Systems....1-36
VII. MSE Intelligence Section Integration 1-38

III. Operations (MEU S-3)....1-39
Mission....1-39
Organization 1-39
I. MAGTF Planning 1-40
A. Training and Exercise Employment Plan (TEEP) 1-40
B. Battle Rhythm and Scheme of Maneuver (SOM)....1-41
C. Battle Update Brief (BUB)....1-41
D. Operations and Intelligence Brief (Ops/Intel)....1-41
II. Command and Control (Landing Force Operations Center)....1-42

III(a). MEU Force Fires....1-43
I. Fires Organization 1-43
A. MEU / PHIBRON Fire Support Agencies 1-43
B. PHIBRON Supporting Arms Coordination Center....1-43
C. MEU Force Fires Coordination Center 1-43
D. BLT Fire Support Coordination Center (FSCC) 1-44
II. MEU/PHIBRON Air Agencies....1-44
A. Navy Tactical Air Control Center (TACC) 1-44
B. Marine Air Control Group (MACG) Air Support Element (ASE) 1-44
III. MEU Fires Operating Procedures....1-45
IV. MEU Fires Personnel 1-46
V. SACC/FFCC Manning 1-49
VI. Fire Mission Tracking (SACC/FFCC) 1-50
VII. MEU Targeting....1-52
VIII. Fires in the Rapid Response Planning Process (R2P2)....1-54
IX. MEU Fires Communications....1-56

III(b). Air Operations 1-57
Mission....1-57
Six Functions of Marine Aviation....1-57
I. Responsibilities Afloat....1-58
II. Pre-Deployment Responsibilities....1-59
IV. The Air Plan 1-60
V. Air Combat Element of the MEU....1-62

III(c). Chemical, Biological, Radiological, and Nuclear Defense (CBRND) 1-63
I. Readiness Objectives....1-63
II. Responsibilities....1-64
A. Command Responsibilities 1-64
B. Staff Responsibilities....1-64
C. Battalion Landing Team (BLT) 1-67
D. Aviation Combat Element (ACE)....1-67
E. Combat Logistics Battalion (CLB)....1-68
III. CBRND Team Organization....1-69
IV. Training and Readiness....1-70
- Mission Oriented Protective Posture (MOPP)....1-71
A. Individual Standards 1-70
B. Unit Standards 1-70
C. Unit Training....1-72
V. CBRND Operations and Defensive Procedures....1-72
A. CBRN Attack Alarm/Warning System 1-72
B. Communications 1-72

C. CBRND Alert Conditions 1-72
D. Evacuation Procedures (Suspected Chemical & Biological Samples) ... 1-73
VI. CBRN Reporting 1-74
VII. ECBRN Force 1-77
A. Capability/limitations 1-76
B. Organization 1-76
C. Training 1-77
D. Equipment 1-77
E. Embarkation 1-77
F. ECBRN Force Employment 1-78
VIII. CBRN References 1-80

III(d). Antiterrorism/Force Protection and Military Police Detachment (AT/FP) 1-81
- Antiterrorism/Force Protection Officer 1-81
- MP Detachment 1-81
I. Antiterrorism and Force Protection (AT/FP) 1-82
- AT/FP Concept of Operations 1-83
- AT/FP Considerations 1-84
A. Phase I (Preparation) 1-82
B. Phase Two (Incident Response) 1-87
C. Phase Three (Recovery) 1-87
II. Law Enforcement Operations 1-88
A. Probable Cause 1-89
B. Assumptions 1-89
C. Body Views and Intrusions 1-90
D. Search and Seizure 1-91
III. MEU Criminal Investigations Division (CID) 1-90
- Investigative Procedures 1-93

III(e). Combat Camera 1-95
Mission 1-95
I. Concept of Operations 1-95
II. MEU COMCAM Responsibilities 1-96
III. Role of Combat Camera 1-97
IV. COMCAM Sections 1-98
V. Training 1-100

IV. Logistics (MEU S-4) 1-101
Mission 1-101
I. Logistics Planning Concepts 1-102
- Concept of Logistics Support 1-103
A. Planning Sequence 1-102
B. Internal MEU Logistics Coordination 1-104
C. Logistic Support Requests (LSR) 1-104
- Logistics Reporting Requirements 1-105
II. Supply 1-106
A. Force Activity Designator (FAD) 1-107
B. Contracted Services 1-107
C. Naval Logistics Integration (NLI) 1-107
D. Class of Supply Requirements 1-108
III. Maintenance 1-110
A. Echelon of Maintenance 1-110
B. MIMMS / GCSS-MC 1-110
C. Maintenance Reconciliation & Reporting 1-111
D. MEU Maintenance Management Officer (MMO) 1-112
E. Funding Responsibility 1-112

IV. Ammunition ... 1-112
A. Ammunition Expenditure Reports ... 1-112
B. Ground Ammunition Request Process ... 1-113
C. Aviation Ammunition ... 1-114
V. Embarkation ... 1-116
A. Embarkation Planning ... 1-116
- Navy Embarkation Personnel ... 1-117
- Embarkation Duties and Responsibilities ... 1-118
B. Embarkation Plans and Orders ... 1-116
- Serial Assignment Tables (SAT) ... 1-121
C. Execution of Embarkation Operations ... 1-120
D. Personnel (PAX), Mail & Cargo (PMC) ... 1-122

VI. Communications (MEU S-6) ... 1-123
Mission ... 1-123
I. Typical Missions ... 1-124
A. Wideband / Ground Mobile Forces (GMF) ... 1-124
B. Ashore Single Channel Radio Operations ... 1-124
II. Afloat Operations ... 1-127
III. Capabilities/Primary Equipment ... 1-128
IV. External Interfacing ... 1-130

Chap 2 Mission Planning (R2P2, CAP, ORM)

I. Rapid Response Planning Process (R2P2) ... 2-1
I. R2P2 Overview ... 2-3
II. R2P2 Sequence/Timeline ... 2-4
III. Daily Operations/Intelligence Brief ... 2-6
IV. Actions Prior to Rapid Planning ... 2-8

II. Crisis Action Planning (CAP) ... 2-9
The Crisis Action Team ... 2-9
A. MEU CAT ... 2-9
B. The Battle Staff ... 2-9
C. Mission Commander ... 2-10
D. Assault Force Commander (AFC) ... 2-12
E. Mission Planning Cell (MPC) ... 2-12
Tenets of the Marine Corps Planning Process ... 2-11
Briefing File Management ... 2-12
Marine Corps Planning Process (An Overview) ... 2-14
I. MEU Commander's Initial Orientation (CIO) ... 2-16
- Commander's Battlespace Area Evaluation (CBAE) ... 2-17
A. Understanding of Battlespace (Where are we?) ... 2-16
B. Definition of Problem (Where do we need to go?) ... 2-16
C. Initial Vision for Success (How are we going to get there?) ... 2-16
II. Receipt of Mission ... 2-18
III. Conduct Problem Framing ... 2-19
- CAT I / Problem Framing Brief Guide ... 2-21

IV. Course of Action (COA Development) 2-22
- Staff Preferences 2-23
- Staff Estimates/Considerations 2-24
- CAT II / COA Brief Guide 2-26
V. Commander's Decision 2-28
VI. Reconnaissance and Surveillance (R&S) Planning 2-28
- R&S CONOPS/COA Brief Guide 2-29
- R&S Confirmation Brief Guide 2-30
VII. Detailed Planning 2-33
VIII. Confirmation Brief 2-32
- Confirmation Brief Attendees 2-33
- Confirmation Brief Guide 2-34
IX. SMARTPACK 2-38

III. Operational Risk Management (ORM) 2-39
ORM Process 2-39
ME Commander ORM 2-40

Chap 3 Mission Essential Tasks

Mission Essential Tasks Overview 3-1
Mission Matrix 3-1
Purposes of Operations 3-2

I. Noncombatant Evacuation Operations (NEO) 3-3
NEO Considerations 3-4
NEO Dilemmas 3-5
NEO Planning Guidance 3-6
NEO Rules of Engagement 3-8

II. Humanitarian Assistance/Disaster Relief (HA/DR) 3-9
Humanitarian Assistance (HA) Operations Planning Guidance 3-10

III. Reconnaissance & Surveillance (R&S) 3-13
Reconnaissance Fundamentals 3-14

IV. Information Operations (IO) 3-15
Information Operations (IO) Capabilities 3-15
MEU IO Considerations 3-15

V. Consequence Management Operations 3-17
Consequence Management Assumptions 3-18

VI. Amphibious Raid Planning 3-19
Amphibious Operations Primary Decisions 3-21
Amphibious Raid Considerations 3-22

VII. Airfield Seizure Planning 3-23

VIII. Limited Duration Small Scale Raid 3-25

IX. Visit, Board,Search, Seizure (VBSS) 3-27

Chap 4

Standing Missions

Standing Missions Overview........4-1
I. Alert Status for Standing Missions........4-1
II. Standing Mission Briefs........4-2

I. Tactical Recovery of Aircraft & Personnel (TRAP)........4-3
I. TRAP Zones........4-3
II. TRAP Levels........4-3
III. TRAP Zones & Levels........4-4
IV. TRAP Determination........4-6
V. TRAP Determination Brief Guide........4-8

II. Mass Casualty Recovery Team (MCRT)........4-9
I. Definition........4-9
II. Mission........4-9
III. Responsibilities........4-9
IV. Casualty Routing & Triage........4-10

Chap 5

MEU Liaison & Survey Elements

I. Forward Command Element (FCE)........5-1
FCE Task Organization........5-2
FCE Brief........5-4

II. Humanitarian Assistance Survey Team (HAST)........5-5
HAST Task Organization........5-7
HAST Assessment Questions........5-8
HAST Brief (Ward Room)........5-10

III. MAGTF Consequence Management (CBRN)........5-11
The MAGTF Consequence Management CBRN Equipment Set........5-11
AMEMB/Host Nation Support........5-11
Team Organization & Equipment........5-12

Chap 6

Appendices & Reference

A. Marshalling Area Control Officer (MACO) Checklist 6-1
B. Reception Plan Checklist 6-3
C. Checklist for Phasing Control 6-5
I. Ashore 6-5
II. Afloat 6-9
D. Aircraft Reference & Specifications 6-13
Basic Capabilities of ACE Aircraft 6-13
CH-46E Sea Knight 6-14
CH-53E Super Stallion 6-16
UH-1Y 6-18
AH-1Z Viper 6-20
AV-8B 6-22
KC-130J 6-24
MV-22B Osprey 6-26
E. Air Operations Quick Reference 6-29
I. Aircraft Embark Procedures 6-29
II. Aircraft Disembark Procedures 6-30
III. Aircraft Marking Plan 6-31
IV. Air Operations Requirements 6-32
V. Bump Plan (& Passenger Load Limits) 6-33
VI. Air Launch/Recovery Requirements 6-34
VII. Weather Minimum Mission Planning Chart 6-36
VIII. Rotary-Wing Over Water Flight Matrix 6-36
IX. Over Water Flight 6-37
X. AV-8B Currency 6-38
XI. Helicopter Currency (T/M/S) 6-40
F. Authorization to Fly Civilians/Foreign Nationals 6-41
Extended Civilian Flight Clearance 6-44
G. Diplomatic Clearances 6-45
Example Dip Clearance 6-45
Block Dip Clearance for Exercises 6-46
H. Signal Plan & Communications 6-49
I. Signal Plan 6-49
II. Waterborne Signals 6-49
III. R&S No Communication Plan 6-50
I. Missing Marine/Sailor Plan 6-51
J. Critical Thresholds & Sea State Chart 6-53
K. Daily Read Board & Rapid Request Form 6-55
L. Naming Conventions 6-57
Table 1. Unit Tag Names 6-58
Table 2. Geometry Names 6-59
Table 3. Fire Plan and Future Plan Names 6-60
M. Watch Information 6-61
N. Daily Meetings 6-63
O. Major Marine Corps Ground Equipment 6-64

Chap 7

Execution Checklists

Execution Checklists Overview 7-1

Naming Conventions for Execution Checklists 7-2
I. Amphibious Raid (Helo) 7-3
- Brief by Exception (applicable to all execution checklists) 7-3
II. Long Range Helo Raid 7-4
III. Amphibious Raid (Mech) 7-5
IV. Amphibious Raid (Motor) 7-5
V. FCE/NEO 7-6
VI. HAST/HADR 7-7
VII. CBRN 7-8
VIII. Mass Casualties 7-8
IX. Direct Action 7-9
X. Maritime Raid Force 7-9
XI. Reconnaissance & Surveillance (R&S)
a. R&S I - Rock Bands 7-10
b. R&S II - Female Names 7-10
c. R&S III - Musical Instruments 7-10
XII. Tactical Recovery of Aircraft & Personnel (TRAP)
a. TRAP (Air) 7-11
b. TRAP (Surface) 7-12

Chap 8

Abbreviations, Acronyms & Glossary

I. Abbreviations & Acronyms 8-1

II. Glossary 8-5

Chap 1

Marine Expeditionary Unit (MEU) Overview

Ref: NWC 3153K, Joint Military Operations Reference Guide (Jul '09), chap. 3 and www.usmc.mil.

The Marine Corps is organized as a general purpose "force in readiness" to support national needs. Deploying for combat as a combined-arms Marine Air/Ground Task Force (MAGTF), the Marine Corps provides the Nation with a responsive force that can conduct operations across the spectrum of conflict. The Marine Corps' most important responsibility is to win the nation's battles.

I. Mission of the U.S. Marine Corps

The primary mission, as stated in the National Security Act of 1947, "…is to provide Fleet Marine Forces of combined arms together with supporting air components, for service with the fleet..." This act also states that the Marine Corps minimum peacetime structure shall consist of "…not less than three combat divisions and three aircraft wings, and such other land combat, aviation and other services as may be organic therein…" In addition, the Marine Corps maintains a fourth Marine division and aircraft wing in reserve.

II. Organization and Structure

The Marine Corps is divided into four broad categories:

A. Headquarters, U.S. Marine Corps

Headquarters, U.S. Marine Corps (HQMC) consists of the Commandant of the Marine Corps and those staff agencies that advise and assist him in discharging his responsibilities prescribed by law and higher authority. The Commandant is directly responsible to the Secretary of the Navy for the total performance of the Marine Corps. This includes the administration, discipline, internal organization, training, requirements, efficiency, and readiness of the service.

Also, as the Commandant is a member of the Joint Chiefs of Staff, HQMC supports him in his interaction with the Joint Staff. The Commandant is also responsible for the operation of the Marine Corps material support system.

B. Operating Forces

Operating forces — the heart of the Marine Corps — comprise the forward presence, crisis response, and combat power that the Corps makes available to U.S. unified combatant commanders. The Marine Corps has established three permanent combatant-level service components in support of unified commands with significant Marine forces assigned: U.S. Marine Corps Forces Command (MARFORCOM), U.S. Marine Corps Forces Pacific (MARFORPAC), and U.S. Marine Corps Forces, Special Operations Command (MARSOC). The Commander, MARFORCOM is assigned to the Commander, U.S. Joint Forces Command (JFCOM). He provides the 2d Marine Expeditionary Force (II MEF) and other unique capabilities to JFCOM. Likewise, the Commander, MARFORPAC is assigned to the Commander, U.S. Pacific Command. He provides I and III MEFs to PACOM. The Commander, MARSOC is assigned to the Commander, Special Operations Command (SOCOM). He provides assigned forces to SOCOM. These assignments reflect the peacetime disposition of Marine Corps forces.

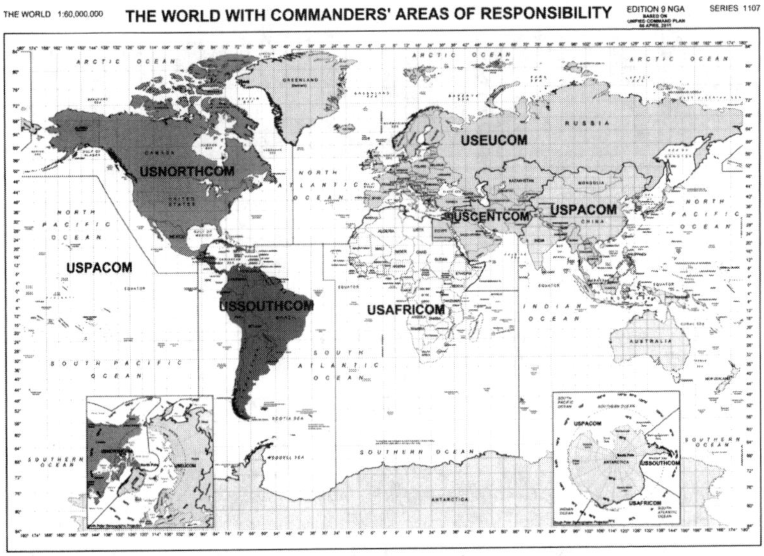

THE WORLD 1:60,000,000 **THE WORLD WITH COMMANDERS' AREAS OF RESPONSIBILITY** EDITION 9 NGA SERIES 1107

Marine forces are apportioned to the remaining geographic combatant commands — the U.S. Southern Command (SOUTHCOM); U.S. Northern Command (NORTHCOM); U.S. European Command (EUCOM); U.S. Central Command (CENTCOM); U.S. Africa Command (AFRICOM); and U.S. Forces Korea (USFK) for contingency planning, and are provided to these commands when directed by the Secretary of Defense. Listed below are the Marine Corps service component headquarters.

- **Marine Forces Command (MARFORCOM).** Located in Norfolk, VA and commanded by a three-star general. Commander, MARFORCOM provides the II Marine Expeditionary Force (MEF) and activated Marine Forces Reserve units to the Commander, USJFCOM.
- **Marine Forces Pacific (MARFORPAC).** Located at Camp H.M. Smith, HI and commanded by a three-star general. Commander, MARFORPAC provides I and III MEFs to Commander, USPACOM.
- **Marine Forces, Special Operations Command (MARSOC).** Located at Camp Lejeune, NC and currently commanded by a two-star general. Commander, MARSOC provides assigned forces to Commander, USSOCOM.
- Other Service Component Commands. The Marine Corps maintains a service component headquarters with U.S. Central Command, U.S. European Command, U.S. Southern Command, U.S. Africa Command, and U.S. Northern Command. Marine forces are apportioned, but not assigned to these unified geographic commands.
- **Marine Forces Central Command (MARCENT).** A three-star headquarters located in Tampa, FL. Commander, MARCENT also serves as Commanding General, I MEF, located at Camp Pendleton, CA.
- **Marine Forces European Command (MARFOREUR).** A one or two-star headquarters located in Stuttgart, Germany.
- **Marine Forces Southern Command (MARFORSOUTH).** A one or two-star headquarters located in Miami, FL.
- **Marine Forces Africa Command (MARFORAF).** A one or two-star headquarters currently located in Stuttgart, Germany. Commander, MARFORAF also commands MARFOREUR.
- **Marines Forces Northern Command (MARFORNORTH).** A three-star headquarters located in New Orleans, LA. Commander, MARFORNORTH also commands Marine Forces Reserve.

III. Marine Air/Ground Task Force (MAGTF)

Ref: NWC 3153K, Joint Military Operations Reference Guide (Jul '09), pp. 77-78.

The MAGTF is a balanced, air-ground combined arms task organization of Marine Corps forces under a single commander, structured to accomplish a specific mission or a number of missions across the range of military operations (ROMO).

MAGTFs are flexible, task-organized forces that are capable of responding rapidly to a broad range of combat, crisis, and conflict situations. MAGTFs vary in size and capability according to the mission, threat, and operating environment. The MAGTF is primarily organized and equipped to conduct amphibious operations as part of naval expeditionary forces. MAGTFs are also capable of sustained combat or peace operations ashore.

Each MAGTF, regardless of size or mission, has the same basic structure. A MAGTF consists of four core elements: Command, Aviation, Ground, and Logistics Combat Element. As the Ground Combat Element grows in size, the Aviation, Logistics, and Command elements typically become larger.

There are four basic MAGTF organizations: Marine Expeditionary Force (MEF), Marine Expeditionary Brigade (MEB), Marine Expeditionary Unit (MEU), and Special Purpose MAGTFs (SPMAGTF).

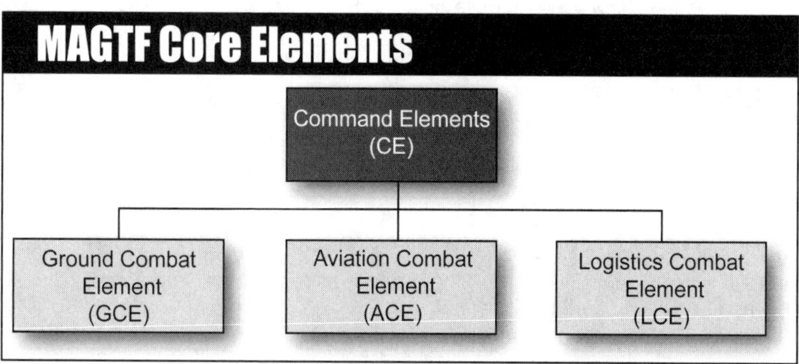

Ref: NWC 3153K, Joint Military Operations Guide, fig. 18, p. 77.

1. Command Element (CE)

The CE contains the MAGTF headquarters and other units that provide intelligence, communication, and administrative support. The CE is scalable and task organized to provide the command, control, communications, computers, intelligence, and joint interoperability necessary for effective planning and execution of operations.

2. Ground Combat Element (GCE)

The GCE is task organized to conduct ground operations to support the MAGTF mission. This element includes infantry, artillery, reconnaissance, armor, light armor, assault amphibian, engineer, and other forces, as needed. The GCE can vary in size and composition.

3. Aviation Combat Element (ACE)

The ACE conducts offensive and defensive air operations and is task organized to perform those functions of Marine aviation required to support the MAGTF mission.

4. Logistics Combat Element (LCE)

The LCE is task organized to provide the full range of combat service support functions and capabilities necessary to maintain the continued readiness and sustainability of the MAGTF as a whole. The LCE may vary in size and composition.

IV. Types of MAGTFs (MEF, MEB, MEU, SPMAGTF)

Ref: NWC 3153K, Joint Military Operations Reference Guide (Jul '09), pp. 78-82.

There are four basic MAGTF organizations: Marine Expeditionary Force (MEF), Marine Expeditionary Brigade (MEB), Marine Expeditionary Unit (MEU), and Special Purpose MAGTFs (SPMAGTF).

MAGTF SIZE (Largest to Smallest)	ELEMENT		
	GCE	ACE	LCE
Marine Expeditionary Force (MEF)	Marine Division (MARDIV)	Marine Aircraft Wing (MAW)	Marine Logistics Group (MLG)
Marine Expeditionary Brigade (MEB)	Marine Regiment (RLT or RCT)	Marine Aircraft Group (MAG)	Combat Logistics Regiment (CLR)
Marine Expeditionary Unit (MEU)	Battalion Landing Team (BLT)	Reinforced Helicopter/Fixed Wing Squadron	Combat Logistics Battalion (CLB)
Special Purpose MAGTF (SPMAGTF)	Elements of a MARDIV	Elements of a MAW	Elements of a MLG

A. Marine Expeditionary Force (MEF)

The MEF is the largest standing MAGTF and the principal Marine Corps war fighting organization. It is capable of missions across the range of military operations through amphibious and sustained operations ashore in any environment. Each MEF is comprised of a Command Element (CE), Marine Division (GCE), Marine Aircraft Wing (ACE), and a Marine Logistics Group (LCE). The three standing MEFs provide a reservoir of capabilities and combat power from which all smaller MAGTFs are formed. There are three standing MEFs: I MEF, II MEF, and III MEF.

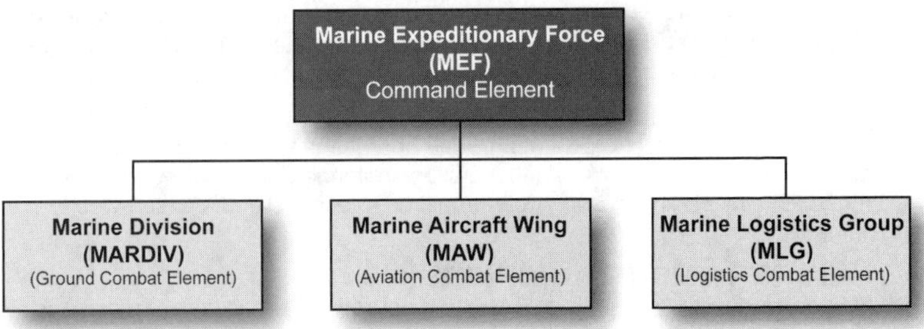

Each MEF is commanded by either a Lieutenant General or Major General and consists of anywhere from 20,000 to 90,000 personnel. A MEF generally deploys on U.S. Navy amphibious ships with support from Military Sealift Command (MSC) and Maritime Pre-positioned Force (MPF) vessels, as well as Air Mobility Command (AMC). A MEF deploys with 60 days of supplies for sustained operations ashore.

I Marine Expeditionary Force (I MEF)

Headquartered at Camp Pendleton, CA; units located in California and Arizona:

- 1st Marine Division (1st MARDIV) - Camp Pendleton, CA
- 3rd Marine Aircraft Wing (3rd MAW) - Miramar San Diego, CA
- 1st Marine Logistics Group (1st MLG) – Camp Pendleton, CA

II Marine Expeditionary Force (II MEF)

Headquartered at Camp Lejeune, NC; units located in North and South Carolina:

- 2nd Marine Division (2nd MARDIV) - Camp Lejeune, NC
- 2nd Marine Aircraft Wing (2nd MAW) - Cherry Point, NC
- 2nd Marine Logistics Group (2nd MLG) - Camp Lejeune, NC

III Marine Expeditionary Force (III MEF)

Headquartered in Okinawa, Japan; units located in Hawaii and Japan:

- 3rd Marine Division (3rd MARDIV) - Okinawa, Japan
- 1st Marine Aircraft Wing (1st MAW) - Okinawa, Japan
- 3rd Marine Logistics Group (3rd MLG) - Okinawa, Japan

B. Marine Expeditionary Brigade (MEB)

The MEB is a medium sized non-standing MAGTF that is task organized to respond to a full range of crises, from forcible entry to humanitarian assistance. MEBs are not standing organizations that are formed only in times of need. An example is post 9/11; the 4th MEB and 2nd MEB were formed to respond to combat and peacekeeping contingencies in Afghanistan and Iraq.

A MEB is commanded by a Brigadier General or Major General and consists of anywhere from 3,000 to 20,000 personnel. It also generally deploys on U.S. Navy amphibious ships with support from MSC and MPF vessels. It deploys with 30 days of supplies for sustained operations ashore.

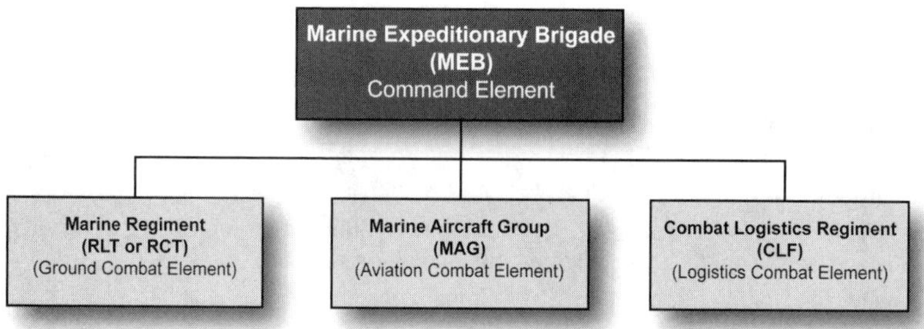

Marine Expeditionary Brigade elements consist of:

- Command Element (CE)
- Ground Combat Element (GCE) = Marine Regiment (RLT or RCT)
- Aviation Combat Element (ACE) = Marine Aircraft Group (MAG)
- Logistics Combat Element (LCE) = Combat Logistics Regiment (CLR)

Continued on next page

Types of MAGTFs (Continued)

Ref: NWC 3153K, Joint Military Operations Reference Guide (Jul '09), pp. 78-82.

Continued from previous page

C. Marine Expeditionary Unit (MEU)

The standard forward deployed Marine expeditionary organization. A MEU is task organized to be a forward deployed presence and designed to be the "first on the scene" force. A MEU is capable of a wide range of small scale contingencies, to include:

- Amphibious raids/limited objective attacks
- Noncombatant evacuation operations (NEO)
- Security operations /Counter-Intelligence operations
- Tactical recovery of aircraft and/or personnel (TRAP)
- Humanitarian/civic action operations

Prior to deployment, a MEU undergoes an intensive six-month training program, focusing on its conventional and maritime operations missions. The training culminates with a thorough evaluation and certification. In addition to possessing conventional capabilities, a MEU, when augmented with a Marine Special Operations Company (MSOC) provided by MARSOC, may be designated as a MEU (Special Operations Capable) or MEU(SOC). A MEU is commanded by a Colonel and consists of anywhere from 1,500 to 3,000 personnel. MEUs typically deploy for six-month deployments aboard U.S. Navy amphibious ships. They deploy with 15 days of supplies for sustained operations ashore.

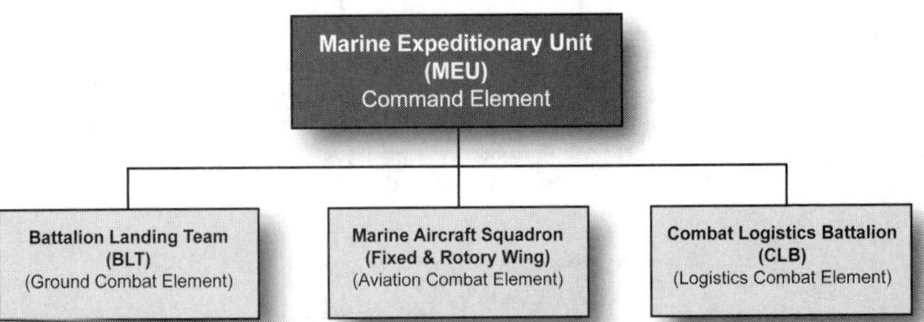

MEU elements consist of:

- Command Element (CE)
- Ground Combat Element (GCE) = Battalion Landing Team (BLT)
- Aviation Combat Element (ACE) = Composite Marine Squadron (Rotary wing with a complement of fixed wing aircraft, depending on mission)
- Logistics Combat Element (LCE) = Combat Logistics Battalion (CLB)

Continued from previous page

D. Special Marine Air/Ground Task Force (SPMAGTF)

The SPMAGTF is a non-standing MAGTF temporarily formed to conduct a specific mission. It is normally formed when a standing MAGTF is unavailable or inappropriate. Their designation derives from the mission they are assigned, the location in which they will operate, or the name of the operation in which they will participate. (i.e., SPMAGTF Somalia, SPMAGTF Katrina etc.). These MAGTFs vary in size and composition based on the individual mission. As with the MEU, the SPMAGTF may be the forward element of a larger MAGTF. Regardless of size, all MAGTFs are "expeditionary" forces. An expeditionary force is a capability, vice a structure. Any size MAGTF could be referred to as a Marine "expeditionary" capability.

C. Marine Corps Reserve

The United States Marine Corps Reserve (MARFORRES) is responsible for providing trained units and qualified individuals to be mobilized for active duty in time of war, national emergency, or contingency operations, and provide personnel and operational tempo relief for active component forces in peacetime. MARFORRES, like the active forces, consists of a combined arms force with balanced ground, aviation, and combat service support units. MARFORRES is organized under the Commander, MARFORRES. Their headquarters is located in New Orleans, LA.

D. Supporting Establishment

Marine Corps bases and stations — often referred to as the "fifth element" of the MAGTF — comprise the personnel, bases, and activities that support the Marine Corps' operating forces. This infrastructure consists primarily of 15 major bases and stations in the United States and Japan, as well as the personnel, equipment, and facilities required to operate them. These bases and stations fall under several regional commands to include Marine Corps Installations-East (MCI-East), MCI-West, and MCI-Pacific.

The supporting establishment also includes the Marine Corps Logistics Command (MCLC) and Training and Education Command (TECOM). Additionally, the supporting establishment includes civilian activities and agencies that support Marine forces.

V. The MEU Cycle

Each MEU follows a similar work-up/deployment cycle.

Phase 1: Interim / Build-Up Period

Upon completion of a deployment, the Marine Expeditionary Unit remains in a stand-by status for approximately one month, prepared to respond to events around the world. Following this period, the MEU "stands down," releasing its MSEs and retaining only its Command Element. The stand-down period provides the Command Element a chance to rotate select personnel and begin planning for the addition of newly assigned MSEs and the next round of work-up training. When the MSEs are received, the stand-down ends and the six-months of intense pre-deployment training begins.

Phase 2: Work-Up Period

Training during the six-month work-up period is often referred to as "crawl, walk, run." The Marines and Sailors progress through curriculum and exercises that teach individual, small unit, and unit tactics while integrating the separate MEU elements into a cohesive, flexible and powerful force. The work-up period includes training in the following areas: Amphibious Operations, Mechanized and Helicopter-borne Raids, Noncombatant Evacuation Operations, Humanitarian Assistance, and Urban Operations. Exercises conducted during the work-up period include: ESG - MEU Integration Training (ESGINT), Training in an Urban Environment Exercise (TRUEX), Composite Training Unit Exercise (COMPTUEX), and the MEU Certification Exercise (CERTEX).

Phase 3: Deployment

Following the work-up, the MEU deploys for six months as a self-sustaining force that the combatant commanders can direct to accomplish a variety of special operations and conventional missions in their areas of responsibility.

The missions may include:

- Conventional Operations (Amphibious Assaults and Raids)
- Tactical Recovery of Aircraft and Personnel (TRAP)
- Humanitarian Assistance / Disaster Relief (HA/DR)
- Non-Combatant Evacuation Operations (NEO)
- Security Operations
- Peace Enforcement
- Reconnaissance and Surveillance
- Airfield/Port Seizure

VI. Key MEU Billets and Personnel

COMPHIBRON Three	
Commodore	Captain (0-6)
Chief Staff Officer	Captain (0-6)
Master Chief	Chief Petty Officer (E-9)
Intelligence Officer N-2	
Material/Logistics Officer N-4	
Operations Officer N-3	
Communications Officer N-6	
TACRON OIC	
CATF Surgeon	
Combat Cargo Officer	
NBG OIC	
Supporting Arms Coordinator	
Vessel Personnel	
LHA Commanding Officer	
LHA Executive Officer	
LHA Operations Officer	
LHA Combat Cargo Officer	
LSD Commanding Officer	
LSD Executive Officer	
LSD Operations Officer	
LSD CCO	
LPD Commanding Officer	
LPD Executive Officer	
LPD Operations Officer	
LPD CCO	
MEU Command Element (CE)	
Commanding Officer	
Executive Officer	
Sergeant Major	
S-1/Adjutant	
HQCMDT	
Public Affairs Officer	
Staff Judge Advocate	
Chaplain	
Disbursing Officer	
S-2/Intelligence Officer	
Asst Intelligence Officer	
HUMINT Exploitation Team OIC	
RadBn OIC	
RadBn Asst OIC	
S-3/Operations Officer	
Asst Operations Officer	
Air Officer	
Asst Air Officer	
C-130 Planner	
CBRN Defense Officer	
Fires Officer	
Target Information Officer	
Force Protection Officer	
S-4/Logistics Officer	
Assistant Logistics Officer	
Supply Officer	
Embarkation Officer	
Medical Planner	
S-6/Communications Officer	
Asst Communications Officer	
JTF Enabler OIC	
Battalion Landing Team (BLT)	
Commanding Officer	
Executive Officer	
Sergeant Major	
H&S Company	
Executive Officer	
S-1/Adjutant	
Chaplain	
S-2/Intelligence Officer	
Scout Sniper Platoon Commander	
S-3/Operations Officer	
Assistant Operations Officer	
Air Officer	
FAC #1	
FAC #2	
Fires Liaison Officer	
Gunner	
CBRN Defense Officer	

S-4/Logistics Officer	
Maintenance Management Officer	
Supply Officer	
Embarkation Officer	
Surgeon	
Motor Transport Officer	
S-6/Communications Officer	
Company A	
Executive Officer	
1st Platoon Commander	
2d Platoon Commander	
3d Platoon Commander	
Weapons Platoon Commander	
Company B	
Executive Officer	
1st Platoon Commander	
2d Platoon Commander	
3d Platoon Commander	
Weapons Platoon Commander	
Company C	
Executive Officer	
1st Platoon Commander	
2d Platoon Commander	
3d Platoon Commander	
Weapons Platoon Commander	
Weapons Company	
Executive Officer	
81 mm Mortar Platoon Commander	
CAAT A	
CAAT B	
Artillery Battery Commander	
Executive Officer	
LAR Platoon Commander	
BLT Recon Plt Commander	
CEB Platoon Commander	
AAV Platoon Commander	
Tank Platoon Commander	
Marine Medium Helicopter Squadron (Rein)	
Commanding Officer	
Executive Officer	
Sergeant Major	
S-1/Adjutant	
Flight Surgeon	
Administration Officer	
S-2/Intelligence Officer	
S-3/Operations Officer	
AOPSO	
S-4/OIC	
S-4A/Embark	
S-6/Commincation Officer	
DOSS	
CH-46E ASO	
CH-46E NATOPS	
Ground Safety Officer	
Maintenance Officer	
AAMO	
CH-46E MMCO	
Airframes OIC	
Avionics OIC	
CH-46E F/L O	
Ordnance OIC	
Q/A OIC	
Combat Logistics Battalion (CLB)	
Commanding Officer	
Executive Officer	
Sergeant Major	
Operations Officer	
Asst Ops Officer	
Logistics Officer	
Asst Logistics Officer	
Communications Officer	
Engineer OIC	
Trans Support OIC	
Supply OIC	
Maintenance OIC	
Health Svcs Support Det OIC	
Dental Officer	
Medical Officer	

VII. List of MEUs

West Coast MEUs

West Coast MEUs fall under I Marine Expeditionary Force, and their main area of operations includes the western Pacific and Indian oceans (to include the Persian Gulf).

Official Name	Insignia	Headquarters
11th Marine Expeditionary Unit		Marine Corps Base Camp Pendleton, California
13th Marine Expeditionary Unit		Marine Corps Base Camp Pendleton, California
15th Marine Expeditionary Unit		Marine Corps Base Camp Pendleton, California

East Coast MEUs

East Coast MEUs fall under II Marine Expeditionary Force and maintain presence in the Atlantic Ocean and Mediterranean Sea.

Official Name	Insignia	Headquarters
22nd Marine Expeditionary Unit		Marine Corps Base Camp Lejeune, North Carolina
24th Marine Expeditionary Unit		Marine Corps Base Camp Lejeune, North Carolina
26th Marine Expeditionary Unit		Marine Corps Base Camp Lejeune, North Carolina

Japan MEU

The 31st MEU is the only permanently forward-deployed MEU, maintaining a presence in the Pacific Ocean at all times as part of III Marine Expeditionary Force.

Official Name	Insignia	Headquarters
31st Marine Expeditionary Unit		Marine Corps Base Camp Smedley D. Butler, Okinawa, Japan

I. Administration (MEU S-1)

Mission

The mission of the MEU S-1 is to coordinate timely and accurate administrative support for the Commanding Officer and all personnel assigned or attached to the MEU across the four functions of administration (general, personnel, manpower, and operational) in order to enhance the readiness and operational capabilities of the MEU and ensure success across the full range of military operations.

Organization

The administrative section operates under the staff cognizance of the Adjutant, a primary staff officer to the Commanding Officer and coordinates actions and issues through the MEU Executive Officer.

The MEU S-1 Section is comprised of the Adjutant, Administrative Chief, and four Administrative Clerks. Upon composite, a Marine Administrative Reach-back Cell (MARC) of a Personnel Chief and five Personnel Clerks, a Postal Detachment of a Postal Chief and four Postal Clerks, and a Disbursing Detachment of a Disbursing Officer and five Finance Marines will augment the section.

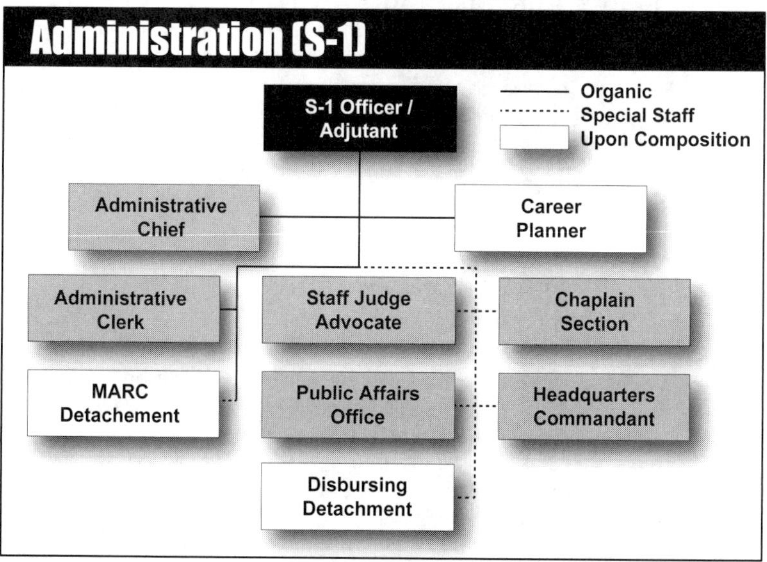

Capabilities and Functional Areas

The administrative section will provide administrative support in four functional areas of Marine Corps Administration outlined below.

General Administration

General Administration encompasses administrative and office management functions that provide direct support to the Commander. The following areas fall under general administration:

- Correspondence Management
- Directives Control Point

- Postal Affairs
- Legal Administration
- Military Awards
- Casualty Affairs
- Records Management
- Performance Evaluation Management
- Voting Assistance
- Forms and Reports Management

Personnel Administration

Personnel Administration encompasses those areas or tasks that generally deal with a Marine's administrative reporting requirements, including elements that affect a Marine's pay, compensation, promotion, and items existing in personnel records and systems. The following are administrative tasks within the MEU fall under personnel administration:

- Check in/out
- Separation and Retirement
- Promotions
- Transfers
- Temporary Additional Duty Travel
- Pay and Entitlements
- Processing Personnel Action Requests (PARs)

Manpower Administration

Manpower Administration includes optimally managing and allocating personnel throughout the MEU. Manpower Administration encompasses the following:

- Table of Organization Management
- Assignment and Staffing
- Personnel Strength Reporting
- Command Sponsorship Program
- Career Management
- Personnel Accountability Reporting
- Disability/Limited Duty Management
- Transition Assistance Management

Operational Administration

Operational Administration includes those administrative requirements that exist solely to support MEU operations and exercises and will take place mainly during or just prior to deployment. Operational Administration for the MEU includes:

- Operation Plan (OPLAN) Annex E Development
- Personnel Statistics Reporting
- Personnel Tempo Reporting
- Casualty Reporting and Tracking
- Combat Replacements
- Time-Phase-Force-Deployment-Data (TPFDD) Reporting
- Emergency Leave Procedures
- OPT/Staff Estimate for MCPP and R2P2
- Personnel Theater and Country Clearance Management
- Official Passport and Visa Management
- OPREP-3 Serious Incident Reporting (SIR)
- MEU Movement and Reporting Procedures
- Finance and Disbursing
- Morale, Welfare, and Recreation

Operation and Execution Support

The MEU administrative section will provide the Commanding Officer support in all four of the above functional areas, ensuring timely and accurate processing of administrative requirements and reporting accountability of personnel at all times. General, Personnel, and Manpower Administration are continuous whether in garrison or deployed and will be executed in accordance with established directives. Just prior to and during deployment, the administrative section plays an important role in the function of Operational Administration.

The Annex E to the OPLAN will cover specific administrative support during deployment. The primary focus of the administration section during deployment is to ensure that accurate and timely accountability of personnel is reported. During Joint or Combined Operations, the MEU S-1 will also be prepared to join and account for personnel from other services and/or countries; combined operations bring an even greater accountability challenge. The following information and guidance is provided to assist in accurate and timely reporting.

Personnel Reporting

Personnel accountability reports are required daily. The Personnel Status Report will be submitted to the MEU S-1 no later than 0900 and 2100 while embarked aboard ship or while executing an exercise/operation. When in garrison, the Personnel Status Report is due NLT 0800.

Casualty Reporting

Casualty reporting will be done in strict compliance with the current edition of MCO 3040.4 (MARCORCASASTPRO) or, when performing Joint Operations, with Joint Operations SOPs. At E-30 (30 days prior to deployment), each MSE in the MEU will receive the release authority for Personnel Casualty Reports (PCRs) for members of their command. At that time, MSEs, when faced with a PCR, will draft the PCR and submit it to the MSE commander for review and approval. The MSE S-1 will then submit the PCR to HQMC Casualty Branch using the Defense Casualty Information Processing System-Forward (DCIPS-Forward) 8.0 and courtesy copy the MEU Commanding Officer, MEU Executive Officer, and the MEU S-1.

MEU Movements

Prior to and upon completion of any administrative or tactical movement, the MSE will ensure stick leaders have sufficient copies of the stick manifest to provide combat cargo, the landing craft or helicopter, the MSE S-1, and COC ashore (if applicable). MSE Administrative Sections will provide manifests to the MEU S-1. During the initial deployment phase of an exercise or operation, Major Subordinate Elements (MSEs) are required to provide personnel updates every 2 hours to the MEU S-1.

Reports will be provided every 2 hours until all movement has stopped and all personnel are accounted for ashore. When the Command Element deploys ashore, updates will be submitted to the MEU S-1 via the MEU COC. When the Command Element remains on board ship, reports will be submitted to the MEU S-1 via the Landing Force Operation Center (LFOC) Watch Officer. Updates on movements are provided no more than every 2 hours until movement is complete.

I. MEU Finance and Disbursing (DISBO)

The Disbursing Officer is responsible to the MEU Commanding Office for all public funds assigned, timely and accurate pay, disbursements, and contract payments for any goods or services the MEU may incur.

Mission

The mission of the MEU Disbursing Section is to provide expeditionary disbursing support via flexible, responsive, and accurate customer service that reflects the highest standards of accountability and professionalism.

Organization

The disbursing section operates under the staff cognizance of the Disbursing Officer (a Special Staff Officer to the Commanding Officer) and coordinates actions and issues through the MEU Executive Officer. The disbursing section is comprised of the Disbursing Officer, Disbursing Chief, and three (3) Disbursing Clerks.

Capabilities and Functional Areas

Capabilities that the MEU Commander has through the Disbursing section include:

- Contract Payments – working in conjunction with the S4 Officer, Fiscal Officer, and Contracting Officer, the Disbursing Officer can pay contracts for services and goods procured by the MEU Commander.
- Foreign Claims Payments – working in conjunction with the MEU Staff Judge Advocate, the Disbursing Officer can make foreign claims payments.
- Split Pay
- Casual Pay
- Savings Deposit Program Allotments/Collections
- Marine Cash Program management
- Check Cashing

Pay Matters

The Disbursing section is responsible for advising on all pay matters regarding the Marines assigned to the CE and MSEs. The Disbursing section will advise the appropriate Administrative (S-1) section on all requests to make payments or adjust pay records to correct the Marine's pay account. MSE Commanding Officers will submit request via a NAVMC 11116 to IPAC for any bona fide corrections needed. MSE Commanders will designate a SNCO or Officer on each ship the responsibility of alerting the Disbursing Officer and the appropriate S-1 Officer of any pay (or other disbursing problems) problems for embarked Marines aboard that ship.

Travel Matters

Travel and shore patrol claims will be processed through the Defense Travel System (DTS). Travel advances will be requested through DTS and paid 3 days after the request has been approved. It is the Marine's responsibility to settle travel claims by submitting a travel voucher in DTS; assistance can be obtained through the travelers unit S-1. All travel vouchers should be submitted within 5 working days after travel is complete. All Officers and SNCOs are required by the Commandant of the Marine Corps to possess a Government Travel Charge Card (GTCC). S-1s will ensure that all frequent travelers (defined as all Officers, SNCOs, or sergeants and below that travel more than once a year on TAD orders) have the current charge card and appropriate Personal Identification Number (PIN) prior to departing CONUS on deployment. Personnel falling in the frequent traveler status will be denied travel advances, as the U.S. Government requires them to use the Charge Card.

Vendor Payments

The Fiscal Officer is responsible for paying bills incurred by the MEU (vendor payments). These include: IMPAC charge cards, contracts, aircraft landing fees, etc. There are numerous restraints for payments, based on the goods purchased or services contracted, so strict adherence to the DoD Financial Management Regulations Volumes 5 and 10 (DoD FMR Vols 5 & 10) will be enforced. All contracts and appropriate completed paperwork will come from the Contracting Officer via the MEU S-4 Officer, to the Fiscal Officer. The payments will be made in accordance with the above references. Most payments will be made by U.S. Government check. Every attempt should be made to ensure that all contracts be made payable in U.S. funds as the Disbursing Officer is not allowed to carry foreign currency, and the restrictions on obtaining foreign currency from Department of the Treasury approved banks in foreign countries are severe. Any bills to be paid in cash on foreign shores need to have the MEU Commander's authorization. Once he is satisfied that security of his funds is adequate, the payments can be made. 48 hours notice is required to get appropriate funds available and security arrangements set in place.

Check Cashing

The Disbursing Officer will appoint Agent Cashiers to cash checks. The MEU Commander will publish a Check Cashing Policy prior to each float that will be enforced by the Disbursing Officer and the Agent Cashiers. This policy will provide general guidelines; check limits, and other restrictions on the check cashing privileges of MEU personnel. MSE Commanders have the authority to make the policy more restrictive if desired, but must follow the overall guidelines set forth by the MEU Commander. Personnel will be able to cash checks during hours designated in the policy published by the MEU Commander. Uniform of the day or proper civilian attire, in liberty ports, is required to cash checks (no PT gear). ID cards will be required for ALL PERSONNEL, officers and enlisted, in accordance with DoD FMR Vol 5. Checks returned to the Disbursing Officer will be handled in accordance with the DoD FMR Vol 5 and the policy set by the MEU Commander. A letter will be drafted to the MSE Commander informing them of the bad check. Check cashing privileges will be restricted or revoked in accordance with the MEU CO's policy. The Disbursing Officer will immediately check the amount of the bad check from the Marine's pay. Bad checks by Navy personnel will be sent to the Navy Disbursing Officer for restitution. Check cashing can be done in the field, if necessary.

Split Pay/Navy Cash

Split Pay is available to deployed Marines. This provides them with a set amount per payday that is available through the individual's Marine cash card regardless of the ship they are embarked within the ESG. The amount is up to the individual, but must be in $5 increments. All ships in the fleet are equipped with Navy Cash K-80 machines (cashless ATMs). The Disbursing Officer is responsible for the enrollment and issuing of Marine cash cards to every Marine and Sailor within the MEU. Individuals can link their Marine cash cards to their personal bank account in order to transfer funds. If a Marine cross-decks to another ship, he will be able to access his cash card on the new ship. Marine cash cards will be issued during the at-sea training periods. Personnel losing or over drawing their cards will be required to report to the disbursing office where individuals will be handled in accordance with the Marine cash policy letter. Personnel must clear their accounts prior to debarking the ship upon conclusion of the deployment. A date will be set to close accounts prior to the conclusion of the deployment. Any funds left on the cash card will require the individual to contact Navy Cash in order to have funds transferred back to their personal bank account.

Field Operations

The Disbursing section normally deploys to the field when extended operations ashore are expected, or when the entire MEU is ashore. The MEU Commander will determine when there is a requirement for disbursing operations ashore. Security will be provided in accordance within DoD FMR Vol 5 guidelines. A secure area with restricted access is the basic requirement. A method of securing the disbursing office safes to an immovable object and an armed guard are also required. The Disbursing section will be co-located with the MEU Command Operations Center (COC) in a separate tent, but within the wire perimeter. This provides a roving guard outside and Disbursing personnel can provide an interior guard to guard the safes. This also provides access by the MEU CO, MEU S-4 and MEU S-1 to the Disbursing Officer to take care of any issues regarding vendor payments, casual pay, etc. If check cashing or casual pay is required in remote locations, transportation of disbursing personnel will be provided. Adequate security should accompany the personnel assigned the task of cashing checks and conducting other disbursement payments. If it is necessary to remain overnight, security must be provided to safeguard the public funds. In the event of imminent capture or the threat of being overrun by hostile forces, destruction of negotiable instruments will be carried out in accordance with DoD FMR Vol 5 requirements. This will be accomplished by burning (if practicable), or shredding and then burial. If possible, a list of monetary serial numbers will be maintained and returned to the Federal Reserve by any means available.

Security Requirements Aboard Ship

The DoD FMR Vol 5a states security requirements for a Disbursing Office. All ships of the LHD or LHA class have a dedicated troop disbursing office that will meet the requirements stated in the reference. A secured area with restricted access (with a cage or other barrier to perform business), and which can also be locked and/or alarmed when no one is present, is required. Safes with the ability to resist tampering need to be in the office to hold public funds and other negotiable instruments. Embarkation and debarkation are best accomplished by helicopter. The risk of security compromise is less than that of a movement by landing craft. The chances of an intentional attempt to steal negotiable instruments should be minimized at all times.

II. MEU Public Affairs (PAO)

Public Affairs (PA) activities for the MEU will be conducted in accordance with the current public affairs policy and regulations. During MEU deployment public affairs activities will also be regulated by public affairs guidance (PAG) from the applicable Unified/Fleet/Joint Task Force Commander(s).

Mission

The mission of the MEU Public Affairs Officer (PAO) is to provide timely and accurate information to better the public and individual Marine's understanding of the MEU mission, organization, capabilities and utility as an instrument available to the National Command Authority.

Organization

The PA detachment operates under the staff cognizance of the Public Affairs Officer (PAO), a special staff officer for the Commanding Officer. The PAO has direct access to the Commanding Officer; however, he coordinates all PA actions and issues with the MEU Executive Officer.

The PA detachment is normally comprised of the PAO, the PA Chief and two Combat Correspondents.

Functions

Command Information

The MEU PAO is responsible for:

- Writing and disseminating photos/video and stories to Marine Corps, DOD and public media outlets to include newspapers, magazines and websites
- Maintaining the MEU website
- Establishing a Unit Information Officer (UIO) program for all MSEs of the MEU
- Establishing and updating a Fleet Home Town News release program via the Digital Video Imagery Distribution System (DVIDS)
- Archiving all MEU press releases, news clips, photographs, and video productions for historical purposes

Social Media

The Commanding Officer reserves the right to utilize social media to disseminate information to the public. The MEU PAO is responsible for the management, appearance, functionality and content of the commands social media site(s). Information that is not appropriate for release to the public will not be posted on the commands social media site. Information that is not appropriate for release includes the following:

- Graphic, obscene, explicit or racial comments or submissions or comments that are abusive, hateful or intended to defame anyone or any organization are not authorized.
- Solicitations or advertisements are not authorized. This includes promotion or endorsement of any financial, commercial or non-governmental agency. Similarly, attempts to defame or defraud any financial, commercial or non-governmental agency are not authorized.
- Comments that suggest or encourage illegal activity are not authorized.

Additionally, the appearance of external links on this site does not constitute official endorsement on behalf of the U.S. Marine Corps or Department of Defense.

External Media Relations

The MEU PAO will facilitate the Commander's ability to conduct operational and/or tactical missions without being distracted by unnecessary contacts with military journalists and/or civilian news media, while maximizing these assets to achieve the command's PA mission. Professional news media representatives will be admitted to attend MEU events only with approval from the PAO. Requests for public dissemination of information concerning command activities will be referred to the MEU PAO. In accordance with current directives, the PAO will release routine, command-related information directly to the press. When dealing with sensitive matters, the PAO will consult with staff officers, the XO and the CO as appropriate before releasing the information. The MEU PAO is responsible for the following tasks:

- Act as the command's official spokesperson when engaging news media representatives (NMRS) and news affiliated agencies.
- Determine the number of local media outlets, host nation sensitivities, reporter/outlets profiles, and interests or agendas with United States Information Agency representatives located at U.S. embassies in foreign countries.
- Write Annex F to operations orders
- Write and disseminate public affairs guidance to commanders
- Write and disseminate press releases
- Respond to all media queries
- Coordinate and conduct press conferences
- Coordinate interviews and media days
- Coordinate media aviation requests
- Coordinate static displays for media and civilian interest
- Conduct media escorts
- Provide press information packages to educate the media on MEU operations
- Prepare Marines for media encounters by providing talking points

Community Relations

Community Relations (COMREL) is under that staff cognizance of the PAO and Department of Defense (DoD) Directives. COMREL includes any official interaction with members of the civilian community or community organizations involving MEU commitments such as participation in parades, visits, speaking engagements, volunteer events while at home or abroad.

Unit Information Officer (UIO)

Each MSE will appoint a UIO, E-6 or above, who will serve as the primary point of contact for the PA section. UIO Duties include the following tasks:

- Responsible for briefing PA matters when the PAO cannot be present
- Submit a comprehensive, monthly report to the PAO identifying significant unit events. Events will be considered for coverage by civilian or military media representatives
- Coordinate with the PAO to arrange for press, civic, and other official tours
- Facilitate media interviews with unit personnel and escort media representatives visiting the unit in accordance with guidance provided by the PAO
- Review the content and coordinate the management of unit websites. This Public Affairs Office must review all information posted to MSE websites
- Write stories highlighting the efforts of Marines within each MSE. Submit stories to the PAO for publication to various media outlets
- Provide unit photographs to the MEU PA section for DoD media outlets
- Act as the primary cruise book coordinator for your MSE. Submit photographs and cutline information per the timeline identified by the MEU PA section
- Act as the primary Tiger Cruise coordinator for the MSE
- Maintain up-to-date unit histories and biographies of all principal command

A. Logistical Support to Media Operations

Facilities. If billeting and messing facilities are commercially available, military services will, in general, not be available to visiting NMR. Request from NMR for these services will be considered on a case-by-case basis and if granted, provided on a reimbursable basis.

NMR Travel. NMR arriving by commercial means should be inoculated IAW the laws of the host nation. NMR entering on military aircraft will be required to have the same inoculations as the military forces participating in the operation. It is the NMRs responsibility to get the required immunizations.

Simulated Rank. NMR will be afforded the privileges of an officer in the rank of O-4 for messing, billeting and transportation.

Communications. Where possible, NMR will rely on commercial electronic communications assets to transmit their material. In the event commercial electronic assets are not available, commanders will permit the use of selected non-commercial communications systems (voice, FAX, and message) with a priority procedure or via expedited air and ground transportation, as appropriate, on a not-to-interfere basis. When commercial transportation means are not available for use by the NMR, video and audiotapes and still photographic film will be transported via expedited air or ground transportation as appropriate. When directed, commanders will support media with access to hard copy message capability or INMARSAT phones to file on a priority basis.

Courier flights. If available, such flights may be used for transporting NMR news media products to/from MEU units.

Transportation. Under conditions of independent and open media coverage, NMR are responsible for procuring their own transportation. Commanders are authorized to permit NMR to ride on military vehicles and aircraft whenever feasible on a not-to-interfere basis, when such travel is in connection with assignments to cover the operation or when commercial transportation is restricted in the area.

Equipment. Sponsoring commands will provide NMR with the type of equipment considered appropriate for the situation (e.g. 782 gear, flak jacket, Kevlar helmet, etc.) Appropriate training to use equipment will also be the responsibility of the sponsor. Medical: Emergency medical support will be provided to NMR as needed. Routine medical care is the responsibility of the NMR.

Medical. Emergency medical support will be provided to NMR as needed. Routine medical care is the responsibility of the NMR.

Media Casualties:

- NMRs may receive military medical care when commercial sources are not available or practical, on a non-reimbursable basis, as long as the NMR's condition did not exist previously.
- In the case of an injury or death of a NMR, the sponsoring news organization will be notified through military channels.
- A NMR covering military operations, if wounded or killed, will be treated with the same priority as a service member.
- Notifying next of kin of NMRs who are determined to be seriously ill, wounded, killed or missing is the responsibility of the news organization, not the military. The initial release of the name of a seriously ill, wounded, killed or missing NMR is the responsibility of the news organization as well. After the initial release, military PA's may release the name if asked.

B. Standing Public Affairs Guidance

While media are present in a unit's area of operation, it is the responsibility of the unit commanders and their staffs to offer assistance. This includes assistance with interviews, briefings, transportation and communications. Again, unit commanders and staff should not allow the media access to information that could prove harmful to operations and the security of the unit's personnel or mission. Security review is at the source. The characteristics of the military and global information environments essentially render field media censorship impractical as well as nearly impossible. All individuals must be responsible for protecting sensitive information.

Commanders will ensure their personnel are thoroughly briefed on their rights and responsibilities before speaking to the media.

When dealing with members of the media, personnel should be open, honest and forthright; and allow common sense and operational security to be their guide. Service members should be advised of the following:

- As our best spokespeople, they are encouraged to talk to NMRs, but each has the individual right not to do so.
- They must exercise care to protect classified information and preserve operational security. (Specific public affairs guidance will be provided to delineate what is releasable and non-releasable. For example, exact numbers and locations of troops and equipment and rules of engagement (ROE) are normally not releasable.)
- If classified or sensitive information is inadvertently released through words or photography, you are not authorized to confiscate film, audio/video tapes or NMR's notes. Report the incident by the quickest means possible to the unit commander or public affairs officer.
- Never lie to a NMR. If necessary, simply decline to answer the question.
- NMRs should be treated with courtesy and respect.
- Service members should be reminded that, with few exceptions, NMRs are trying to do their jobs and report the news. They want to be accurate and get the story "right." Within security constraints, we should help them get it "right."
- Service members should talk about matters within their area of responsibility, expertise and personal experience (stay in your lane).
- Avoid speculation (answering hypothetical "what if" questions).
- When stating a personal opinion, clearly state it as such.
- All discussions with NMRs will be "on the record."
- There is nothing wrong with admitting that you don't know the answer to a question. If time permits, try to find the information requested.
- If you are unsure whether requested information is releasable, say so. Again, if time permits, try to find out.
- Respect host nation sensitivities.
- When speaking to NMRs while in uniform, you represent not only yourself, but your fellow service members, your unit, your service, and the United States as well.
- Do not give out specific locations of friendly forces. Giving general locations such as the Arabian Gulf Region or the USS George Washington is acceptable.
- Do not discuss future operations.
- Do not be parochial to your branch of service. Stress the teamwork involved in combining the unique capabilities of each branch of service.
- When asked a question - take your time before answering. Make sure you understand what the NMR is asking (if not, ask for clarification). Formulate the answer in your head and then respond.

C. DOD Principles of Information

DOD Principles of Information are contained in DOD directive 5122.5, Change 1. They chart the course for all DOD Public Affairs activities, and apply to the full continuum of day-to-day activities and operations. It is the commander's responsibility to ensure that all planning for military activities and operations efficiently and effectively achieve the goals set by these principles. Timely and accurate information will be made available so that the public, Congress and the news media may assess and understand the facts about national security, defense strategy and on-going joint and unilateral operations. Requests for information from organizations and private citizens will be answered in a timely manner. In carrying out this policy, the following principles of information apply:

- Information will be made fully available, consistent with statutory requirements, unless its release is precluded by current and valid security classification. The provisions of the Freedom of Information Act and the Privacy Act will be complied with in both letter and spirit.
- A free flow of general and military information will be made available, without censorship or propaganda, to the men and women of the Armed Forces and their family members.
- Information will not be classified or otherwise withheld to protect the government from criticism or embarrassment.
- Information will be withheld only when disclosure would adversely affect national and operational security or threaten the safety or privacy of the men and women of the Armed Forces.
- The Department's obligation to provide the public with information on its major programs and operations may require detailed public affairs planning and coordination within the Department and with other government agencies. The sole purpose of such activity is to expedite the flow of information to the public; propaganda or publicity designed to sway or direct public opinion will not be included in Department of Defense public affairs programs.

D. DOD Media Guidelines

The DOD Media Guidelines, issues as Change 3 to DOD Directive 5122.5, provide the following guidelines for coverage of DOD combat operations:

- Open and independent reporting will be the principal means of coverage of U.S. military operations.
- Pools are not to serve as the standard means of covering U.S. military operations. Pools may sometimes provide the only feasible means of early access to a military operation. Pools should be as large as possible and disbanded at the earliest opportunity – within 24 to 36 hours when possible. The arrival of early access pools will not cancel the principle of independent coverage for journalists already in the area.
- Even under conditions of open coverage, pools may be appropriate for specific events, such as those at extremely remote locations or where space is limited.
- Journalists in a combat zone will be credentialed by the U.S. military and will be required to abide by a clear set of military security ground rules that protect U.S. forces and their operations. Violation of the ground rules can result in suspension of credentials and expulsion from the combat zone of the journalists involved. News organizations will make their best efforts to assign experienced journalists to combat operations and then make them familiar with U.S. military operations.
- Journalists will be provided access to all major military units. Special operations restriction may limit access in some cases.
- Military public affairs officers should act as liaisons but should not interfere with the reporting process.
- Under conditions of open coverage, field commanders will permit journalists to ride on military vehicles and aircraft whenever feasible. The military will be responsible for the transportation of pools.
- Consistent with its capabilities, the military will supply PAOs with facilities to enable timely, secure compatible transmission of pool material and will make these facilities available whenever possible for filing independent coverage. In cases when government facilities are unavailable, journalists will, as always, file by any other means available. The military will not ban communications systems operated by news media organizations, but electromagnetic operational security in battlefield situations may require limited restrictions on the use of such systems.
- These principles will apply as well to the operations of the standing DOD National Media Pool system.

Publicity, Casualties and Incidents

The Marine Corps is a source of news, and the news media will inevitably obtain and publish material concerning the Marine Corps that they consider newsworthy and of interest to the public. To insure that news reports are timely and accurate, and that good relationships with news media prevail, it is the policy of the MEU to initiate official releases or otherwise inform the news media of favorable or unfavorable unclassified activities or incidents that are newsworthy. Advising the news media promptly and keeping them informed on high visibility situations helps to prevent sensationalizing and misrepresenting the facts.

MSE's and cognizant staff will notify the Public Affairs Office immediately of any accidents, incidents, or disturbances that involve individuals of the command or on incidents that may result in local, national or international reaction or press interest. Such occurrences include but are not limited to:

- Accidents/incidents which cause casualties or extensive damage to civilian or military property
- Disease of potential epidemic significance
- Serious crimes or incidents which may arouse public or congressional interest
- Civil disorders
- Natural disasters occurrences such as earthquakes, storms, tidal waves, fires etc.

See facing page for discussion of incident/accident/casualty reporting.

Coordination with Information Operations

PA efforts in Information Operations are directed towards US and Coalition forces and US and international media. The MEU PAO will coordinate with the MEU IO Officer to ensure PA operations are synchronized with other members of the IO cell to ensure an Information Operations unity of effort with a focus on planning and "speaking with one voice." Other cell members include Command and Control Warfare (C2W), Civil Affairs (CA) and Military Information Support Operation (MISO).

Coordination with Command and Control Warfare (C2W)

PA will support C2W by developing information products to protect Marines and Sailors against the effects of dis-information or misinformation.

Coordination with Civil Affairs (CA)

MEU PA will support CA by providing accurate, timely and balanced information to the public. PA will coordinate with CA to verify facts and the validity of information. Public messages, statements or information campaigns must be de-conflicted prior to release.

Coordination with Military Information Support Operations (MISO)

MISO are directed toward local populations and adversary forces. PA and MISO may use the same communications media to communicate essentially the same messages to different audiences. The mission of PA is to inform the American and international public. The mission of MISO is to influence adversaries and local populations. It remains important to preserve the separation between of PA and MISO in order to maintain the credibility of PA spokespersons and products. MISO issues that may negatively impact on PA operations should be brought to the attention of the MEU CO.

Coordination with Combat Camera

Combat Camera is an asset whose mission is to support on-scene commanders and decision-makers. The on-scene commander has the responsibility to provide the media timely, high quality imagery when the media access to military operations is limited. In meeting these requirements, combat camera assets will provide unclassified still and video products to the PAO throughout the operation for possible PA use and public release.

E. Incident/Accident/Casualty Reporting

Following the declaration of an accident or an incident, the MEU PAO will notify higher headquarters via the OPREP-3 reporting system. This report will include assessment of the Public Affairs impact of the situation. The following are typical assessments:

- No media interest anticipated.
- Names and affiliation of media (if at the scene).
- Anticipate press interest. Proposed release and questions to follow.

By IMMEDIATE precedence message, the PAO will submit a proposed press release providing the information that is authorized to be released at that time.

The action addressee on the proposed press release message should be the commander to whom the MEU is OPCON. Info address should include the respective Combatant Commander as appropriate, as well as CMC (DivPA), and CHINFO. Additionally, the units that are affected should be included. The information included in the press release is dependent upon a myriad of different variables of given situation, and each accident/incident must be dealt with on a case-by-case basis. The PAO will be guided by current orders and directives, guidance from the respective Unified/Fleet/JTF commander, and the MEU CO.

If the incident occurs ashore or in adjacent waters of a foreign country, info addressees will include the appropriate U.S. Country Team Agency (e.g., AMEMBASSY, USDAO, AMCONCUL, etc).

When possible the initial release and follow-on releases should contain the following information: type of incident, where it occurred, time, number killed, missing or injured, status of the situation, units involved.

Guidelines

Information shall be withheld from the media when:

- Disclosure would adversely affect national security
- It would threaten the safety or privacy of U.S. Government personnel or their families
- It would violate the privacy of the citizens of the U.S.
- If it is contrary to law
- When an incident/accident is currently under investigation

Additionally, names of deceased will be withheld until 24 hours after next-of-kin (NOK) has been officially notified. In releases dealing with aircraft mishaps involving small detachments, releasing the name of the assigned afloat unit can alarm family members. The following applies:

- If the accident occurs at sea, the initial release will not be made until the primary and secondary NOK have been notified.
- If a statement must be made prior to NOK notification, the initial release will not name the unit involved except as one assigned to a larger command (e.g., COMMARFORCOM, COMSEVENTHFLT or COMFIFTHFLT).

Information Release Authority

- In CONUS, the MEU PAO will coordinate with the I MEF Public Affairs Office when releasing information pertaining to accident/incidents.
- While MEU is serving as the Landing Force within the Navy Fleet, the respective Fleet is the releasing authority for all accidents and incidents.
- The Combatant Command is the releasing authority for all information concerning accidents/incidents involving the MEU while it is operating within its respective AOR.

III. Religious Ministries Programs (Chaplain)

Mission

For religious ministries in the 15th MEU is to develop and implement the 15th MEU religious ministries program, to provide technical supervision and support for Major Subordinate Element (MSE) religious ministries, and to provide Command Officer and MEU staff advisory on religious and ethical issues impacting on the Unit and its operations, family readiness, troop morale, and troop well-being.

Organization

- Initiate, implement and coordinate religious ministry objectives within the 15th MEU AOR.
- Provide supervision to those chaplains and RPs assigned within the 15th MEU to ensure adequate religious ministries are provided.
- Oversee the religious ministries of the 15th MEU to ensure the provision of appropriate coverage among various faith groups, drawing upon available chaplains and lay leader assets.
- Participate in the 15th MEU staff action, with particular emphasis on provision of troop religious support needs, religious and cultural influences in areas of operations, family readiness, and general troop well being. Within staff processes, to develop and publish Religious Ministry Support Plans, as outlined in reference (e), for inclusion in operation/exercise plans.
- Serve as the primary liaison to the I MEF Chaplain in matters relating to religious ministry, and chaplains and RPs assigned to the 15th MEU.

Capabilities

- Religious Ministry Teams (RMTs) are assigned and may be altered to meet denominational requirements.
- Every effort should be made to ensure proper faith group representation and religious coverage. The MEU Chaplain will ensure an adequate number of Lay Eucharistic Ministers and Lay Leaders are trained to provide faith group representation for all faiths.
- The MEU chaplain may rotate to various ships/units when it does not conflict with primary ministry to MEU personnel and in concurrence with the Commanding Officer. The MEU Chaplain will operationally report to the MEU Commander and keep the I MEF Chaplain and/or Senior Area of Responsibility Command Chaplain informed via periodic ministry reports.
- The CRP will be evaluated as a part of the MEU certification process.

See facing page for discussion of the chaplain's role in relation to MEU and combat operations.

The Chaplain's Role ISO MEU Operations

Detailed Planning and Coordination through pre-mission briefings and rehearsals for all personnel. The goal is mission execution within six hours following receipt of a warning order. It is mandatory for the chaplain to be prepared to deploy to the field in support of assigned missions on short notice.

Survivability. As a principle staff officer, the chaplain is not easily replaced, and the impact upon morale can be significant if he or she is lost in combat. Nevertheless, chaplains are required by their very nature to be at risk and to be where the Marines need them the most. Prudence dictates a well-thought-out response to the heat of the moment and that the chaplain be a source of calming strength. The chaplain can be also most effective supporting the wounded and dying, traditionally in cooperation with Navy corpsmen.

Mobility and Speed. This demands a high degree of personal readiness and physical stamina to ensure the chaplain and his/her assistant are assets vice liabilities.

Audacity. Audacity achieved by a willingness to accept a certain amount of risk is possible because of the high level of integrated training and unity cohesiveness common in Marine Corps units. Chaplains serving Marine Corps units traditionally have been renowned for their selfless support during combat operations.

Religious Program Specialist Training. The RP's primary duty during combat operations is to secure transportation and to provide security for the chaplain. All RPs must secure and maintain current licensing for HMMWVs. Weapons qualifications as appropriate to their grade. T/O weapon for E5 and below is the M-16 service rifle and E6 and above will carry a M9 service pistol. RPs will attend Block I and II Training.

Combat Operations

Combat operations conducted by the 15th MEU include a variety of missions. Chaplains must be capable of supporting training operations during peacetime, contingency, and wartime operations. This requirement significantly impacts on organizations, material and training for 15th MEU chaplains.

Although not considered an ordinary role, chaplains can be called on to support special operations missions in a limited manner conducive to their role as chaplain, and cognizant of the requirements for noncombatants as described in the 1949 Geneva Conventions.

The 15th MEU is tasked to execute a variety of historical and special operations capable missions involving all assets of the MEU coordinated under one commander. Missions are planned using either deliberate or rapid planning processes. This environment demands flexibility, resourcefulness, speed, precision and reasoned audacity from every member, which significantly impacts the chaplain's role and readiness requirements.

Deliberate preparation involves meticulous planning, evaluation, rehearsal and coordination prior to execution. The chaplain must attend in an advisory capacity as a principle staff officer all planning sessions, and prudently intervene if appropriate.

Crisis response planning relies on the level of training and readiness of the MEU to plan and execute a mission with a six hour window. Operations planned in this manner demand the utmost in individual and collective proficiency from the MEU unit. They are conducted when there is little time for lengthy deliberate planning or rehearsals, and rely on standardized operating procedures developed by the MEU and its elements. A chaplain's effectiveness and usefulness in these operations are contingent upon his/her physical stamina, skill enhancement through prior training, and availability to the unit.

IV. MEU Headquarters Commandant (HQCMT)

Mission

The mission of the 15th MEU Headquarters Commandant (HQCMDT) is to manage the living conditions and working space conditions of the MEU. The smooth operation of field Command Posts or other living and work spaces that the MEU personnel occupy is critical to overall mission success.

Organization

The HQCMDT section operates under the staff cognizance of the MEU Executive Officer (XO), a primary assistant to the Commander of Troops when embark aboard ship. The HQCMDT section is comprised of two enlisted Marines, (1) MSgt, and (1) NCO (Barracks Manager).

Responsibilities on Ship and in Garrison

- The HQCMDT section will assist the Commander of Troops with the distribution of all personnel requirements by the Navy, across the MEU Command Element (CE) and Major Subordinate Elements (MSE) on board the big deck ship.
- The HQCMDT section is the point of contact (POC) for any discrepancy of enlisted living spaces and work spaces on board the ship. He is also the POC for all Fleet Assistance Program (FAP) Marine requirements by the Navy.
- The HQCMDT is the point of contact for all working parties and any port call requirements of Marines by the Navy.
- On ship the HQCMDT coordinates all living spaces for any enlisted personnel coming on board for temporary or permanent time. If personnel coming on board belong to one of the MSE's that person will be placed in that MSE living space if racks spaces are available.
- Prior to embarking the ship the MSE's will report counts of all personnel boarding for that evolution in order to assign FAP requirements to all MSE's, and Command Element sections.
- Prior to deployment the HQCMDT will assist all MSE representatives with the pickup, return and issuing of all MCCS gear provided to the MEU.
- In garrison the HQCMDT is responsible for any maintenance issues in the barracks and the Command Post (CP). All billeting issues of single and geographical bachelor Marines are coordinated through the HQCMDT section. All working party requirements needed by the 21 Area Commanders are assigned to the CE staff sections by the HQCMDT.

Operations/Exercises

The HQCMDT is responsible for the set up of all tents and the security of the Command Operation Center (COC). When the COC is operational, the HQCMDT will have Marines assigned from each of the staff sections of the CE in order to set up a guard force for the security of the COC area.

If the MEU is relocated from ship to shore, the HQCMDT becomes the Camp Commandant (CMCMDT) and is responsible for all living spaces and requirements of personnel to maintain the camp ground running smoothly in order to maintain mission capable.

In the event a camp ground needs to be established or occupied, the MSE's and CE sections will provide personnel to assist the CMCMDT.

Command Element Movements

Prior to the beginning of any tactical or administrative movement, the MSE's need to coordinate with the HQCMDT in order to adjust the FAP requirements for all those left behind.

V. MEU Staff Judge Advocate (SJA)

The Staff Judge Advocate (SJA) is the principal legal advisor to the MEU Commanding Officer on matters pertaining to operational, criminal, administrative and environmental law. Additionally, the SJA is a licensed attorney who can assist Marines and Sailors assigned or attached to the MEU with personal legal problems that are not disciplinary in nature. Such legal areas may include family law (adoption, child custody, child support, divorce, separation), consumer law, estate planning (wills & powers of attorney), and landlord-tenant law.

Mission

The mission of the MEU SJA is to provide timely, efficient, and appropriate legal advice to the MEU Commanding Officer, and the Marines and Sailors assigned to the MEU in order to promote force readiness and support MAGTF operations ashore and afloat.

Operational Law

Operational law refers to the laws and regulations – both domestic and international – that address Law of War and Rules of Engagement (ROE) issues that arise in MAGTF operations. This area includes treaties, international agreements and applicable customary international law. For instance:

- **I-IV Geneva Conventions of 1949** - Establishes protections for categories of individuals affected by international armed conflict.
- **Hague Convention of 1907** - Establishes Means & Methods of Warfare, such as tactics, weapons, and targeting decisions.
- **Chemical Weapons Convention of 1993** - Establishes restrictions/bans on certain chemical weapons and describes legal parameters for use of Riot Control Agents (RCA).

The SJA is available to provide instruction in areas concerning the Law of War, ROE, and Escalation of Force procedures.

Administrative Law

Administrative law refers to those laws that govern various administrative functions in the Marine Corps, the typical inquiries and investigations likely to arise in a deployed environment as well as other administrative functions such as claims, separations and retirement.

Military Justice

The term Military Justice refers to the administration of the rules and regulations established by the U.S. Congress in the creation of the Uniform Code of Military Justice. The purpose of military law is to promote justice, maintain good order and discipline in the armed forces, promote efficiency and effectiveness in the military establishment, and thereby strengthen the national security of the United States.

Legal Assistance

Legal Assistance refers to personal legal services provided to Marines, Sailors, and their families by military attorneys. These services may include advice, document preparation, research and limited representation in various disputes. Full-time Legal Assistance attorneys located at Marine Corps Bases and Stations around the world are permitted to enter into confidential communications with the Marine or Sailor seeking assistance.

Except for emergency cases arising during deployment, legal assistance issues should be handled through your local Marine Corps Base or Marine Corps Air Station Legal Assistance Office.

See following page (1-28) for further discussion.

A. Legal Assistance

Wills

A Will is a document which specifies property / asset division for a decedent. If a service member expires without a Will, state statutes of descent and distribution establish the order in which relatives inherit the decedent's possessions. These statutes differ from state to state but the general order is:

- Spouse and natural or adopted children and their descendents
- Parents
- Brothers and sisters and their descendents

If a service member obtains a will, then he or she dictates the distribution of property/assets. A determination regarding the need for a will depends on a variety of things such as personal preferences, finances, and the presence of dependents. It is likely in your best interests to obtain a will if you are married, have children, or possess significant assets. You may not need a will if you've never married, have no children, and possess limited assets as long as you are comfortable with your assets passing under the laws of your state of residence.

SGLI and Insurance

The individuals that are to receive insurance benefits, including Service members' Group Life Insurance (SGLI), are designated in the SGLI Election and Certificate completed by each Marine or Sailor. Ensure that this information is updated, especially if the owner of the policy has recently had significant events in their life such as divorce, marriage, or the birth of a child. When selecting SGLI beneficiaries be aware that SGLI and any additional insurance do not pass by will.

Powers of Attorney

A power of attorney (POA) is a written instrument whereby one person, as the principal, appoints another to act as his or her agent, giving them the authority to perform certain acts on their behalf. POAs are useful when a service member may have to conduct business while they are deployed that normally requires their physical presence or personal action. Such things could include buying or selling vehicles, handling financial accounts, managing cable, phone and power bills, and managing property. These are just a few examples. The two basic types of POAs are described below.

General Power of Attorney

- A general power of attorney gives another person, the agent, all of the principal's power to contract and act on their behalf.
- The agent can cash checks, sign leases, arrange shipment of household goods, and do any other action within the power or authority of the principal.
- Since a general power of attorney confers unlimited power to the agent, general powers of attorney are discouraged if a special power of attorney will be adequate.

Special Power of Attorney

- A special power of attorney authorizes only specific powers to the agent.
- This specific power or powers which are granted are specifically listed in the document and limit the agent to just those items.

POAs are subject to abuse; individuals obtaining POAs are advised to provide a PAO to only trustworthy and responsible individuals. Military POAs are valid in all fifty states; however, businesses and individuals are not required to recognize a particular POA. If you have a requirement for someone to handle your affairs while deployed, it's recommended that you check with the organizations that provide your services prior to deployment.

Required Legal Reports

Regulatory reporting requirements and mandatory CCIRs require the 15th MEU to capture certain events and generate reports to higher (i.e. allegations of hazing, safety mishaps, etc.). A sample 15th MEU Legal Report will be provided to the legal officer assigned to each MSE. This report describes particular legal actions and their disposition.

MSEs are required to submit a weekly legal report at the end of each week and a monthly legal report to the MEU SJA by the end of each month. The report includes:

- Non-judicial Punishment
- Courts-Martial
- Administrative Separations
- Investigations
- Liberty Risk Assignments
- Unauthorized Absences
- Civilian and Military Confinement
- Appellate Leave
- Non-support Complaints (per Legal Admin Manual Chapter 15)
- Congressional Interest Inquiries

Legal Considerations During Operations

See following page (p. 1-20) for discussion of standing rules of engagement (SROE) and the law of armed conflict.

Operational law (OPLAW) issues and considerations are pervasive throughout the planning and conduct of operations in the maritime domain.

OPLAW is a term used to capture a wide variety of legal and policy considerations that directly impact the employment of military force across the ROMO. OPLAW as it pertains to the maritime domain is frequently subdivided into three major components: Law of the Sea, Law of Armed Conflict, and ROE. Underpinning these three broad categories is a legal and policy framework that includes: domestic, foreign, and international law (which comprises treaty and customary law as well as United Nations Security Council Resolutions), bilateral and multilateral agreements, domestic policy, military policy, Joint and DOD regulations, and service regulations.

A more thorough discussion of these issues can be found in NWP 1-14M/MCWP 5-12.1, "The Commander's Handbook on the Law of Naval Operations."

B. Legal Considerations During Operations

Standing Rules of Engagement (ROE)

I always have the right and obligation to defend myself, unit and other U.S. Forces against hostile acts and demonstrations of hostile intent.

- A hostile act is an attack or other use of force against U.S. forces, e.g. firing on U.S. forces, throwing rocks at U.S. forces, or force used to impede the mission or duties of U.S. forces. Hostile intent is the threat of imminent attack; e.g. loaded weapon pointed at U.S. forces.
- If I, or other U.S. Forces, may be killed or seriously injured due to the actions of another, I may immediately use deadly force.
- If time and circumstances permit, I will attempt to control the situation without the use of force, e.g. verbal warnings or demonstrations of force.
- If the use of force is required, I will use only that degree of force necessary to stop the attack or eliminate the threat.
- If a force or group has been declared hostile, I may engage that force without observing a hostile act or hostile intent.
- I will use no more force than is necessary to accomplish the mission.
- When dealing with civilians, I will treat them with respect.

Law of Armed Conflict

- Don't attack noncombatants. Fight only hostile forces. All persons participating in military operations or activities are combatants. Remember that only combatants may be targeted.
- Destroy no more than required by your mission. Attack only military targets. Do not attack, mistreat, or harm wounded hostile forces or hostile forces who surrender.
- Use only the minimum force necessary, appropriate, and proportionate to accomplish the mission.
- Don't alter your weapons to increase the suffering of hostile forces.
- Don't attack churches, mosques, art museums, orphanages, historical monuments or cultural sites.
- Don't attack medical personnel, facilities, equipment, vehicles, ships, or aircraft protected by the Red Cross, Red Crescent, or Red Star of David.
- Collect and care for the wounded, sick, and shipwrecked, whether friend or foe.
- Let hostile forces surrender.
- Treat all captives and detainees humanely. Don't use coercion in questioning captives or detainees.
- Treat all civilians, particularly women, children, and the elderly, humanely and with respect.
- Provide medical care for sick and wounded captives, and safeguard them from the dangers of combat.
- Report all war crimes immediately. Remember, you may not order, or be ordered to commit, a violation the Law of War.

Chap 1

II. Intelligence (MEU S-2)

Mission

Plan, coordinate, manage, and perform Intelligence, Surveillance, and Reconnaissance (ISR) operations to anticipate, detect, define and evaluate threat capabilities and operating environment in order to provide the Marine Expeditionary Unit (MEU) with timely, accurate intelligence relevant to planning and execution of assigned missions in support of the Commander's decision-making process by reducing uncertainty about the hostile situation to a reasonable level, as well as to assist in protecting friendly forces through counterintelligence.

MEU Intelligence Organization

The MEU S-2 Section is composed of the Command Element (CE) Intelligence Staff and five detachments (dets) – one Radio Battalion Det (working Signals Intelligence (SIGINT)) and four Intelligence Battalion detachments (consisting of the Imagery Intelligence (IMINT) Platoon (IIP) Det; HUMINT Exploitation Team (HET); Topographic (TOPO) Det; and Ground Sensor Platoon (GSP) Det). The MEU S-2 also tasks and oversees the collection operations of any and all organic reconnaissance and surveillance elements attached to the CE.

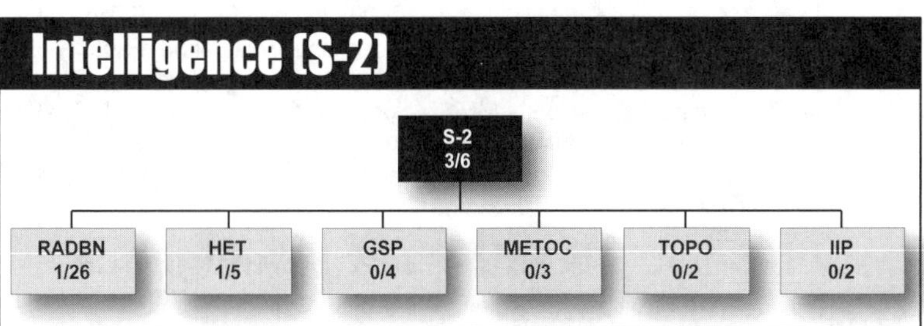

The MEU CE table of organization (T/O) normally has seven intelligence professionals (2/5) permanently assigned to the intelligence section. As composite date nears and the S-2 receives its various attachments, the S-2 T/O will increase to approximately 5/48; giving the MEU a very robust intelligence capability which provides the Commander analyzed intelligence across the spectrum of intelligence disciplines (HUMINT, SIGINT, etc).

Billet	Rank	MOS	Quantity
S-2 Officer	MAJ	0202	1
Assistant S-2 Officer	CAPT	0202	1
S-2 Chief	MSGT	0231	1
S-2 Analyst	LCPL-SGT	0231	3
S-2 System Administrator	LCPL/CPL	2551	1

The MEU Intelligence Section is responsible for focusing and orchestrating the effort of the MEU intelligence effort. Dedicated sections describing each discipline's mission, personnel, and equipment in detail are included in the following sections of this SOP.

I. The Nature Of MEU Intelligence

Today's threat environment requires accurate, actionable intelligence. By nature of its mission the MEU operates in a high-optempo, dynamic environment that can rapidly change from minute to minute. The MEU S-2 will incorporate all available intelligence assets (organic, adjacent, and higher) to support MEU operations, planning, and situational awareness by analyzing all-source intelligence to provide time sensitive analysis and production to the Commander. The end state is to enhance the Commander's situational awareness and decision-making process. To do this, MEU intelligence will follow the Joint Intelligence Process ensuring proper collection, analysis, production, and dissemination.

As a Combatant Commander's (COCOM) force in readiness, the MEU must integrate its intelligence capabilities and processes with the COCOM and the rest of the Intelligence Community (IC) to reduce the Commander's uncertainty. Intelligence drives operations, as much as an operation guides the focus of intelligence. As such, the Intelligence Section must operate under a proactive premise in order to assess the geopolitical, military, and threat environment, while maintaining a high level of situational awareness of MEU operations and plans. This proactive nature will allow us to identify indications and warnings (I&W) of potentially destabilizing events to which the MEU may have to respond.

Sometimes the smallest observation or battlefield detail gathered at the lowest level can have a significant impact on the conduct of MEU operations, but without the information being reported the MEU can lose the opportunity to increase our understanding of the environment. Intelligence within the MEU must move in two directions — both upward to the Commander and down to the individual Marines. To that end, every Marine is a collector of information, regardless of rank or station.

The bottom line remains that intelligence dissemination must be robust enough to support the MEU Commander both in his decision making process and the MEU planning process, as well as the MEU Major Subordinate Elements (MSEs) and the Marines that deserve information about their environment. As a result, every Marine needs to report unusual or noteworthy incidents to assist in removing the uncertainty that the MEU operates in.

II. Two Basic Objectives of Intelligence

- Reduce the Commander's uncertainty by providing accurate, timely and relevant knowledge about an adversary and the surrounding environment
- Assist in protecting friendly forces through counterintelligence

1. Reduce Uncertainty

Intelligence reduces battlefield uncertainty by identifying and evaluating existing conditions and enemy capability, estimating possible enemy courses of action, aiding in identifying friendly vulnerabilities an enemy may attempt to exploit, and assisting in developing and evaluating friendly courses of action (i.e. Red Cell). Intelligence thus plays a significant role throughout the planning and conduct of MEU operations at all levels and this requires a combined effort by all intelligence assets within the MEU.

Counterintelligence is "Information gathered and activities conducted to protect against espionage, other intelligence activities, sabotage, or assassinations conducted by or on behalf of foreign governments or elements thereof, foreign organizations, foreign persons, or international terrorist activities" (JP 1-02). The MEU Human Intelligence (HUMINT) Exploitation Team (HET) plays a central role in gathering information about adversarial elements and foreign governments, in coordination with other elements within the MEU, conducting activities to ensure appropriate force protection.

2. Protect Friendly Forces

Assist in protecting friendly forces through counterintelligence.

III. Intelligence Requirements

For the MEU intelligence process to operate more effectively, all MEU intelligence elements must synchronize their efforts and integrate into a common process or system. Integration prevents unnecessary duplication and facilitates an efficient intelligence cycle. The requirement for accurate and timely intelligence starts at the beginning of the planning process—indeed, it can form the very basis of the planning process—while additional intelligence requirements continue to manifest through execution. To ensure success, we separate the intelligence requirements into the following categories:

- Planning / Shaping
- Operational
- Transition

1. Planning/Shaping Intelligence Requirements

Long before the conduct of operations, MEU intelligence sections must consider planning and shaping preparations. Planning requirements include identifying known and likely areas of employment in order to stockpile mapping, charting, geodesy and imagery (MCG&I) products which facilitates the commencement of intelligence preparation of the battlefield. Additionally, intelligence should build command situational awareness through the production and dissemination of geopolitical, regional, country orientation, cultural, and threat briefs which are focused on the enemy and the operational environment.

The MEU S-2 Section will hold at least weekly intelligence coordination meetings when in garrison and aboard ship called the "Intelligence Synchronization Meeting" on the MEU S-2 calendar and battle rhythm. All MEU S-2 attachments and MSE intelligence sections are expected to provide representatives to this meeting; additionally, the Amphibious Readiness Group (ARG) N-2 and ship's intelligence Officer (SIO) will be invited to attend.

2. Operational Intelligence Requirements

During the conduct of operations, intelligence reporting must rapidly move in both directions. This includes intelligence reporting and finished intelligence products from higher to lower echelons, as well as Requests for Information (RFI) and mission debriefings from lower to higher echelons. In order to accomplish the timely movement of information, MEU intelligence must have the means to provide I&W directly to supported tactical units, as well as the integration of intelligence into the Command Operations Center (COC).

CE units and Staff, as well as MSEs need to submit deliberate RFIs electronically via the web enabled RFI system whenever possible. Tactical units being employed also need to provide mission reports and debriefs to the CE S-2 Section in a timely manner to allow the information to be analyzed and incorporated into the intelligence estimates.

3. Transition Intelligence Requirements

Intelligence gathering and analysis doesn't stop at the completion of an operation; instead, this merely begins the process of analyzing the environment and preparing for future operations. Critical to the improvement to MEU intelligence is the review of intelligence processes and practices used during planning and the execution of operations. Specifically, the compilation and group discussion of detailed After Action Reports (AARs) that capture lessons learned (which identify obstacles or issues that created friction in the intelligence process, along with realistic, practical corrective actions that can mitigate or reduce any friction points) are vital to the successful transition and continuation of the intelligence cycle.

IV. Intelligence Concept Of Operations

The MEU S-2 will provide all-source intelligence support to facilitate the MEU Staff planning process and the success of the MEU's Major Subordinate Elements (MSEs) and Maritime Raid Force (MRF) Platoon. Intelligence personnel from the Command Element (CE), Battalion Landing Team (BLT), Aviation Combat Element (ACE), Combat Logistics Battalion (CLB), MRF platoon, Amphibious Squadron (PHIBRON), and the Ship's Intelligence Section will all share the responsibility of providing integrated intelligence support to the Amphibious Readiness Group (ARG)/MEU. Intelligence tasking, collections, processing, analysis and dissemination will be conducted in accordance with this standard operating procedure (SOP) and respective theater and national intelligence agencies. The MEU S-2 will ensure timely, tactically relevant intelligence support to mission planning and execution.

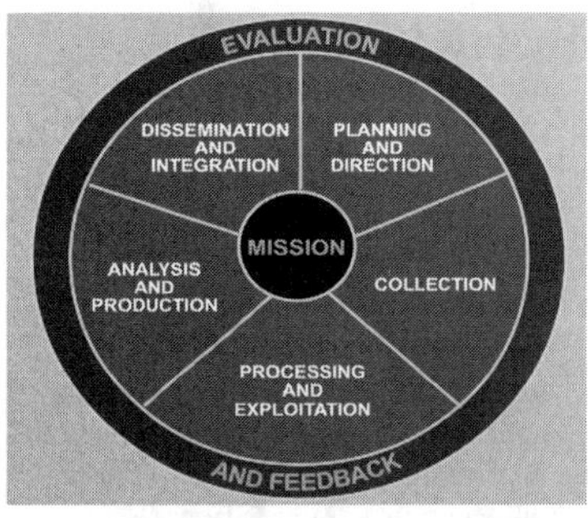

The Intelligence Process

"The sole criterion for good intelligence is whether it provides sufficient knowledge regarding the environment and an understanding of the enemy's capabilities, limitations, and intentions to effectively support the commander's planning and decision-making."

- MCDP 2

Requests for Information

Intelligence requests for information (RFI) will be coordinated with and fall into the greater MEU RFI process. Any member of the MEU Staff and/or MSE S-2 shop can send any intelligence RFIs to the MEU S-2. However, all MSE intelligence RFIs should be sent to the MEU S-2 through their own local S-2 shop (i.e. a BLT Company should send their RFI through the BLT S-2). Any element/organization requesting intelligence information from the MEU S-2 should submit their request either through the MEU RFI Management Tool or directly to the MEU S-2 via the Intel RFI Tool. However, for time critical RFIs the MEU S-2 will accept an RFI by any means possible.

The MEU S-2 will decide how best to service any and all RFIs - the S-2 will answer the RFI with the current information available, submit the RFI to Higher Headquarters (HHQ) or the intelligence community (IC), and/or convert the RFI into an intelligence requirement (IR) and enter the IR(s) into the intelligence collection plan (ICP). Only the MEU S-2 will submit an RFI to theater and/or national intelligence organizations/agencies. Direct Liaison Authority (DIRLAUTH) with outside intelligence organizations/agencies or HHQ Intelligence Centers is not authorized – this is to ensure that the MEU S-2 retains situational awareness on all intelligence requirements, as well as ensures that all MEU requirements are properly prioritized. Additionally, the MEU S-2 will validate, prioritize, and coordinate all MEU requirements in accordance with the MEU Commander's guidance.

Production

The MEU S-2 will serve as the functional manager for MEU intelligence production. Intelligence Production Requirements (IPRs) can be submitted by any member of the MEU Staff and/or MSE S-2 shop via the RFI process. All MSE IPRs should be sent to the MEU S-2 through their own local S-2 shop (i.e. a BLT Company should send their IPR through the BLT S-2). This will ensure the MSE S-2 Sections have an opportunity to service the request, prioritize multiple requests coming from their command, as well as maintain situational awareness of their command's requirements.

All finished MEU intelligence products will be prepared in accordance with the Department of Defense (DoD) intelligence standards and use the proper classification markings. If there is a gap identified in our intelligence, the MEU S-2 will serve as the liaison between the MEU and theater and/or national intelligence production centers to see if they are able to fill the intelligence gap. Additionally, the MEU S-2 will prioritize and coordinate all MEU production requirements in accordance with the MEU Commander's guidance, and utilize the national Intelligence Community (IC) and theater area of responsibility (AOR) production processes and centers when necessary. If all other intelligence organizations, to include the IC, cannot answer our RFI, the MEU S-2 will internally task the MEU Collections Manager with the intelligence requirement.

Collections

A synchronized collection management process will facilitate the collection of 15th MEU priorities and help mitigate resource competition. Organic, theater, and national collections will be coordinated, requested, and tasked by the MEU S-2 in accordance with the MEU Commander's priorities and intent. The MSE S-2 sections will submit their intelligence collection requirements (ICR) in priority order to the MEU S-2 for further MEU prioritizing and tasking. The following intelligence disciplines are utilized to provide the MEU an all-source intelligence approach: Geospatial Intelligence (GEOINT); Human Intelligence (HUMINT) - this includes the MEU Reconnaissance assets; Open Source Intelligence (OSINT); Measurement and Signature Intelligence (MASINT); and Signals Intelligence (SIGINT). The MEU Collection Manager (CM) will also request theater and national collection when our own organic collection assets are unable to fully cover the MEU requirement. All intelligence operations, whether ground or air, will be coordinated with the MEU S-3. The MEU S-2 CM will plan, coordinate, synchronize, and deconflict the intelligence collection plan (ICP) to ensure as many intelligence collection requirements (ICRs) and specific information requirements (SIRs) are being covered as possible, while ensuring the ICP is tied directly to the MEU priorities as directed by the Commander.

The MEU CM will chair a MEU Collections Synchronization Board to be held as needed and in conjunction with any ARG/MEU Collection Board. All stake holders, to include the MSEs and Staff should send representatives to the board prepared to discuss their priority collection requirements. Agenda items covered in the board will be collection assets available (organic, theater, and national), MEU priorities, the ICP, to include the named areas of interest (NAIs) and targeted areas of interest (TAIs) being covered over the next 24 hours or to the next Collection Board.

Dissemination

The dissemination of intelligence is one of the most critical phases of the intelligence cycle – without a good dissemination process intelligence becomes the proverbial "self-licking ice-cream cone." To prevent this, the MEU will use both the "push" and "pull" methods for product dissemination. Priority for dissemination for any one given product will always be the requesting unit. However, unit priority will be set by the Commander's guidance (i.e. main effort vs. supporting elements).

The primary method for intelligence dissemination will be the "push" method. The MEU S-2 will create distribution lists for all standard production, as well as create new distribution lists for ad hoc production. This will ensure the widest dissemination of products; allowing units the option to use a product for their own planning, that they themselves didn't think to request. Intelligence units will minimize the dissemination of single source reports as much as possible, and instead tie multi-source reports into a more informative all-source finished product whenever possible.

The MEU S-2 will also create a web depository to hang products to allow individuals to search and "pull" from – this is meant more for those that know a product was created and would like to quickly look for a product in the MEU intelligence archive. If one were not sure if an intelligence product was previously created or is very limited in time, it would be best for that person/unit to submit an RFI into the MEU S-2 and allow the S-2 to search the intelligence database of finished products.

V. Combat Intelligence Center (CIC)

The Combat Intelligence Center (CIC) is the overarching intelligence operations center established within the MEU to provide centralized direction for the collection, analysis, production, and dissemination efforts of organic and supporting intelligence assets, and ensures that these efforts remain focused on satisfying the Commander's PIRs that are essential to mission success. The CIC reviews and assesses threat related data and then compiles the information in a format that is quickly understood by those needing the information. This provides a common understanding of the threat within the designated MEU battlespace. The CIC is also responsible for developing, monitoring, and updating priority information requirements and RFIs in a timely manner in response to priority information requirements and RFIs of the MEU Commander, Staff, and MSEs. In addition to the collection, production, analysis, and dissemination functions that the CIC is responsible for directing, the CIC also supports the Landing Force Operations Center (LFOC) and MEU forces with any I&W of imminent threats.

The MEU CIC will be located onboard the main MEU CE vessel afloat and is the S-2 Section's main work area, as well as the main work area for all intelligence attachments. This will allow all the intelligence disciplines to collaborate and add to the overall intelligence collections, analysis, and production of the MEU. It also will assist in a much higher state of situational awareness by all intelligence personnel. If and when the MEU CO transitions his command and control (C2) ashore the CIC too will transfer ashore.

The MEU CIC is divided into three sections – the Surveillance and Reconnaissance Cell (SARC), the Production and Analysis (P&A) Cell, and the Intelligence Operations (Intel Ops) Cell.

See facing page for further discussion of these sections.

VI. Intelligence Communications Systems

The MEU S-2 will ensure adequate intelligence communication systems are available for requisite intelligence feeds, data and product dissemination. This effort is synchronized with and assisted by the MEU S-6 and appropriate theater intelligence centers. MSE S-2s operating detached from the MEU will coordinate intelligence specific communications with the MEU S-2 and appropriate S-6. Effective bandwidth rates will be justified based on mission, throughput and associated metrics. The following intelligence communications assets are employed to ensure intelligence production and analytical support to the MEU:

- Trojan Spirit (Light)
- Global Broadcast Service (GBS)
- Secret Internet Protocol Routing Network (SIPRNET)
- Joint Worldwide Intelligence Communication System (JWICS)
- Theater Specific Communications (CENTRIX)

These systems will be the CIC backbone on which MEU Intelligence rides and will be required both on ship and ashore. The analysts will need to be closely tied to area subject matter experts (SMEs) to ensure that the MEU is seeing the problem set from all sides and views.

Equipment

MEU S-2 equipment capabilities cover the entire intelligence spectrum (HUMINT, IMINT, MASINT, SIGINT, GEOINT and OSINT). Though not all inclusive, the MEU S-2 employs the following systems and applications to satisfy planning and execution of MEU missions: Global Command and Control System-Maritime (GCCS-M), Command and Control Personal Computer (C2PC), Falcon View, Joint Deployable Intelligence Support System (JDISS), Intelligence Analysis System (IAS), Image

Surveillance & Reconnaissance Center (SARC)

The SARC is responsible for coordinating and supervising the execution of the integrated organic, attached, and direct support intelligence, counter-intelligence (CI) and reconnaissance collection operations. The cell will also conduct detailed intelligence collection planning and coordination with the MSEs and ARG planners, with emphasis on ensuring understanding of the collection plan and specified intelligence reporting criteria. The SARC will also ensure the MEU LFOC and MSEs are apprised of ongoing intelligence, CI, and reconnaissance operations. The SARC should not be confused with the Reconnaissance Operations Center (ROC). Lastly, the SARC will receive routine and time-sensitive intelligence reports from deployed collection elements; cross-cueing among intelligence collectors, as appropriate; and the rapid dissemination of intelligence reports to MAGTF C2 nodes and others in accordance with standing PIRs/IRs, intelligence reporting criteria and dissemination plan, and the current tactical situation.

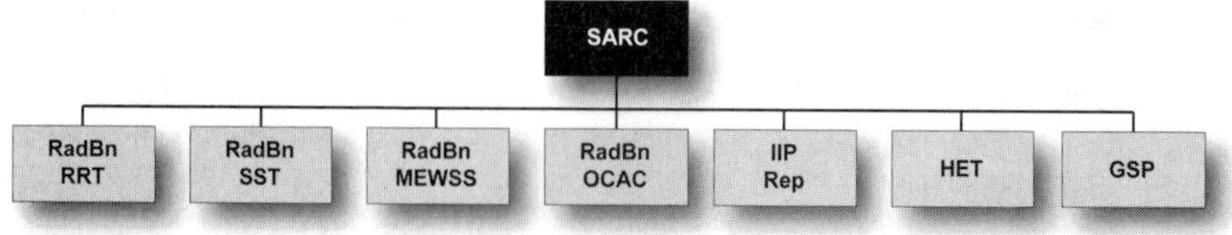

P&A Cell

The P&A Cell is responsible for managing and supervising the MEU's all-source intelligence processing and production efforts; this includes the fusion of the various intelligence disciplines to create intelligence briefs, estimates, order of battle, IPB products, target intelligence packages, and the battle damage assessments from mission reports (MISREPS). The P&A Cell is also responsible for managing the MEU intelligence databases, files, workbooks, and country studies. The P&A Cell OIC with guidance from Intel Ops will prioritize production requirements, as well as plan and maintain imagery, mapping, and topographic resources and other intelligence references. With the assistance of the intelligence system administrator the P&A Cell will also administer, integrate, operate, and maintain intelligence processing and production systems, unclassified general service and sensitive compartmented information systems; e.g., the intelligence analysis system or the image product library.

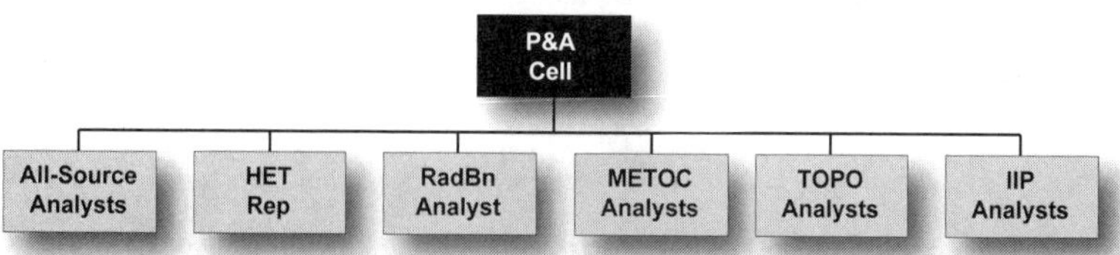

Intel Ops Cell

The Intel Ops Cell's primary responsibility is running intelligence operations and MEU support. The cell acts as the main conduit to the MEU Staff for all planning and any issues that may arise with intelligence support and services; this also includes the planning, directing, and supervising of the Red Cell during wargaming. Any Intel representatives within the LFOC also fall within the Intel Ops Cell. The provided PIR recommendations given by the P&A CELL are reviewed and updated for the MEU CO. All IRs are validated and prioritized. Intel Ops assigns intelligence tasks, as well as gives guidance to the SARC and P&A Cell. The intelligence system administrators (SysAdmin), to include the RadBn SysAdmin Marines, are also an element of the Intel Ops Cell. These SysAdmin Marines are responsible for the C4 systems within the CIC, to include the liaising necessary with the S-6 and/or N6.

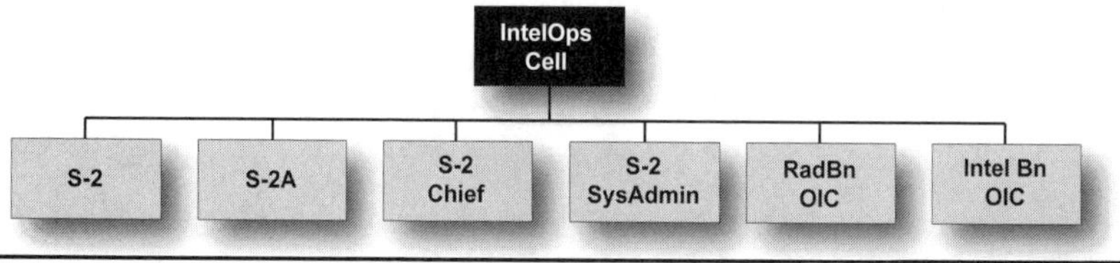

Product Library (IPL), Tactical Exploitation Group Remote Workstation and Windows Platform, Mapping Remote Replication System and DTAMS. Additionally, various intelligence databases from various sources (both classified and unclassified) assist the analysts in the exploitation of information and finished intelligence. Some of these databases include: the Department of Defense's Combined Enterprise Regional Information Exchange (CENTRIX), the Modernized Integrated Database (MIDB), Infrastructure Intelligence Portal (GEMINI), the USMC Intelligence Portal, the Web-Based Access Retrieval Portal (WARP), the USMC Imagery Reachback Site (IRS) for National Imagery, NGA's Geospatial Intelligence Portal, and the Marine Corps Intelligence Agency's (MCIA) Geographically Linked Intelligence Dissemination Environment for geospatial mapping data.

VII. MSE Intelligence Section Integration

Intelligence personnel from the MSEs serve as subject matter experts for their respective MSE. They are full mission partners in the Intelligence process and although they directly support their local commander's planning cycle, they also operate under the direction of the MEU S-2. This concept focuses the intelligence effort and maximizes available assets. MSE S-2s will coordinate and monitor the level of their personnel's integration in the CIC in balance with the needs of their commander. Each of the MSE S-2s retain basic unique staff responsibilities such as publications and files maintenance, security clearance program handling, and Mapping Charting and Geodesy (MC&G) maintenance and storage for their commands. The intent is to clearly define intelligence requirements based on the mission(s) while maintaining an ability to surge available assets when required.

MSE S-2s will maintain requisite automated data processing (ADP) hardware/software to ensure interoperability with the MEU intelligence section. MSE S-2s will ensure the MEU S-2 is aware of hardware/software configurations, discrepancies and new technical acquisitions to ensure maximum interoperability.

MSE S-2s are required to ensure tactical reporting is disseminated to the MEU S-2 (i.e Debriefs, SPOTREPS, MISREPS, etc.). The MEU S-2 SOP Appendix N outlines the various reports required to facilitate MEU intelligence dissemination. This requirement extends to handheld tactical photography as well. MSE S-2s are required to notify the MEU S-2 of opportunities for handheld photo collection. Camera inventories and specific technical optics are available to the MSEs. Photographic collection and dissemination is in accordance with the MEU S-2 SOP Appendix O. MSE S-2s will ensure standard annotations, format and image compression.

Command and Staff Relations

Per MCDP-2 (Intelligence), effective intelligence is an inherent and essential responsibility of the command. As the executive agent for intelligence, the MEU S-2 will ensure all MSE S-2s maintain direct access to MEU S-2 capabilities in order to support their Commander(s). Concurrently, MSE S-2s must integrate their capabilities with the MEU S-2 to establish the strongest intelligence support possible. This relationship necessitates mutual support.

III. Operations (MEU S-3)

Mission

Provide a forward deployed, flexible sea-based MAGTF capable of conducting AMPHIB OPS, crisis response and limited contingency operations, to include enabling the introduction of follow on forces, and, designated special operations, IOT support the theater requirements of GCC.

Organization

The MEU S-3 is traditionally the largest section when composited. Upon composition, the MEU S-3 gains an Air and Naval Gunfire Liaison Company (ANGLICO) Supporting Arms Liaison Team (SALT), a Military Police (MP) Detachment, a Force Recon Platoon (FORECON), and a Low Altitude Air Defense (LAAD) Detachment. In everything the MEU does the Operations section takes the lead in the planning and execution.

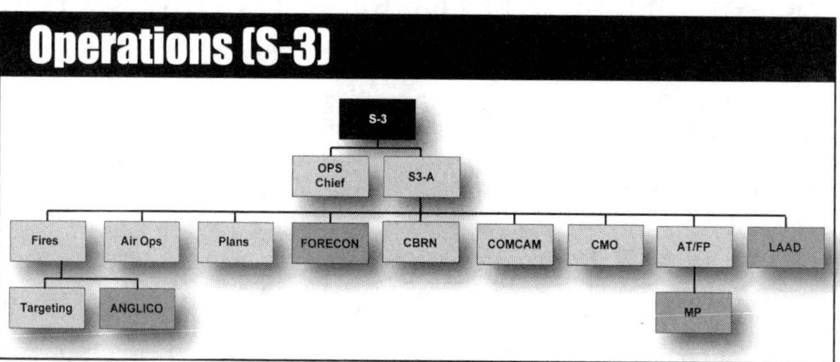

Example S-3 Billet Breakdown		
Operations Officer	1 × LtCol	0302
Operations Chief	1 × MGySgt	0369
Assistant Operations Officer	1 × Major	0302
Fires Support Officer	1 × Major	0802
Targeting Officer	1 × Captain	0802
Fires Chief	1 × SSgt	0861
Fires NCO	2 × Sgt-Cpl	0861
Air Officer	1 × Major	75XX
Assistant Air Officer	1 × Captain	75XX
MAGTF Plans Chief	1 × GySgt-Sgt	0511
MAGTF Plans NCO	2 × Sgt-Pvt	0511
CBRN OIC	1 × CWO3	5702
CBRN Chief	1 × SSgt	5711
ATFP Officer	1 × Captain	
Combat Camera Chief	1 x GySgt	
Combat Camera Marines	2 × Sgt-Pvt	
Civil Military Operations Officer	1 x Major	
Civil Military Operations Chief	1 x GySgt-SSgt	

I. MAGTF Planning

The MEU Operations section develops the planning for all training during formal and informal PTP, exercises, operations and events that the MEU participates in before, during and post deployment. Through the production of Fragmentary Orders (FRAGO), Operations Orders (OPORD), and Letters of Intent (LOI) the S-3 directs the movements of the MEU within the guidance and intent of the Commanding Officer.

Prior to deployment, the S-3 pieces together the requirements of the Higher Head Quarters (HHQ) with the MEU Commander's intent. The schedules and training requirements of each MSE and subset unit are synchronized with the Training and Exercise Employment Plan (TEEP) during Pre-deployment Training Plan (PTP). The MEU S-3 works hand in hand with each MSE S-3 to ensure all units within the MEU meet the standards of the MEF Order for the MEU PTP. In addition to the TEEP, the MEU S-3 produces and controls the Battle Rhythm and Weekly Scheme of Maneuver (SOM).

During deployment the MEU S-3 works to maintain the accuracy of the TEEP by including all Theater Security Cooperation (TSC) Events and Exercises. Within each Combatant Command (COCOM) the MEU is responsible for participating in TSC events with partner nations. As these events and exercises are added to the MEU TEEP the MEU S-3 will assign officers from the Operations Section to plan, coordinate, and supervise the MSE's involvement in each TSC.

A. Training and Exercise Employment Plan (TEEP)

The TEEP is a long term planning document developed and maintained by the MEU S-3 in order to track planning and training deadlines both during deployment and during PTP. The TEEP includes all the events for each element within the Command Element as well as each Major Subordinate Element. During PTP, the TEEP guides the MEU planning process to efficiently allocated resources for mission objectives . This coupled with the Commander's Operational Priorities establishes the planning priorities across the MEU.

JANUARY 2012																															
E-DAY																															
WEEKDAY	SUN	MON	TUE	WED	THU	FRI	SAT	SUN	MON	TUE	WED	THU	FRI	SAT	SUN	MON	TUE	WED	THU	FRI	SAT	SUN	MON	TUE	WED	THU	FRI	SAT	SUN	MON	TUE
DAY	1	2	3	4	5	6	7	8	9	10	11	12	13	14	15	16	17	18	19	20	21	22	23	24	25	26	27	28	29	30	31
15TH MEU CE									IRON FIST PREP WEEK							IRON FIST 2012															
	GCCS-MC CUTOVER PROCESS													GCSS-MC DATA TRANSFER																	
									PRTP	FISCAL INSP.																					
RADBN			INTEL BN - II TI						RADBN JLTI																						
INTEL BN				FORECON JLTI																											
FORCE RECON																															
ANGLICO																															
SECFOR																															
BLT 3/5						MWTC 12-1																									
HMM-364 (REIN)			MACG MMT JLTI						MACG COMM JLTI																						
			MACG HQ, ASE JLTI						MWSS FUELS JLTI																						
			LAAD JLTI						MWSS CRASH/FIRE JLTI																						
CLB-15																															
PHIBRON									ITT I																					ITT II	
LHA																															
LSD																															
LPD																															
SOTG HQ																															
SOTG ASLT CLIMBE																															
SOTG RAIDS BRANC																															
SOTG SPECIAL TRAINING																														CQT	
SOTG AT SEA																															

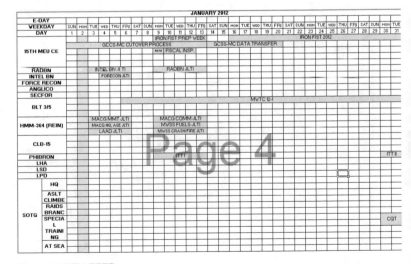

Example MEU TEEP

In order to maintain version control, all MSE and attachments submit their schedules to the MEU S-3. The MAGTF Plans Chief supervises the production and accuracy of the TEEP in the regular training meetings.

B. Battle Rhythm and Scheme of Maneuver (SOM)

The Battle Rhythm is a weekly or monthly document that directs the reoccurring events that the MEU participates in. The SOM is the weekly schedule for the MEU. Both the SOM and the Battle Rhythm are produced year round by the Operations Section regardless of deployment status.

Used daily, the Battle Rhythm depicts the routine meetings and requirements within the MEU. It is briefed during the Commander's Battle Update Brief / Operations and Intelligence Brief as a reminder of daily and weekly requirements. It does not depict every event, just those events that cross staff and unit boundaries. It also includes the daily and weekly reports (Situation Reports (SITREPS), Personnel Statistics (PERSTATS), etc).

C. Battle Update Brief (BUB)

While in garrison and deployed, the MEU S-3 holds the Commander's BUB as determined in the Battle Rhythm. While on ship it is coordinated and synched with the battle rhythm of the PHIBRON Staff but typically the meeting is held in the morning. The BUB provides the MEU Staff and MSE Commander's an opportunity to inform the Commander of his "standing" information requirements. Although not Commander's Critical Information Requirements (CCIR), the Commander requires information on a wide variety of topics and issues. The topics may include but are not limited to:

- Intelligence Updates(present situation, emerging threats, wx)
- Operational Updates (geographical depictions, adjacent units, etc)
- Training Readiness
- Medical Readiness
- Dental Readiness
- PERSTATS
- Maintenance Readiness
- Fiscal
- Communications Status

MSE Commander's also have specific information requirements to present during the BUB. Based on the situation and environment, the Commander may establish specific information requirements. If so, the Operations Officer (BUB lead) should disseminate the requirement to the appropriate staff sections or MSE.

D. Operations and Intelligence Brief (Ops/Intel)

Almost identical to the BUB, the Ops/Intel Brief occurs only while afloat/deployed and typically a few times a week. The "administrative" and "repetitive" items are eliminated—(Family Readiness, Fiscal, Dental Readiness, etc) in what becomes a shortened version of the BUB. Also, rather than MSE Commanders briefing templated material per BUB requirements, MSE Commander's have an opportunity for comments.

See pp. 2-6 to 2-7 for further discussion and briefing template for a daily operations/ intelligence brief.

II. Command and Control

While deployed the MEU S-3 coordinates the MEU movements and operations from two areas. Ashore the operations section resides in the Combat Operations Center (COC). While at sea the operations section resides in the Landing Force Operation Center (LFOC).

Landing Force Operations Center (LFOC)

Aboard Navy shipping the MEU S-3 occupies the LFOC. The setup of the LFOC is determined by the Operations Chief through the guidance of the Operations Officer and the MEU Commander. The Operations Chief runs the LFOC and controls its operation and upkeep. Within the LFOC the S-3 will appoint a Watch Officer (WO) and Watch Chief (WC) to serve as the OIC and SNCOIC of the LFOC while the MEU is conducting operations. The WO relays information to the CO and makes decisions on behalf of the CO as are necessary.

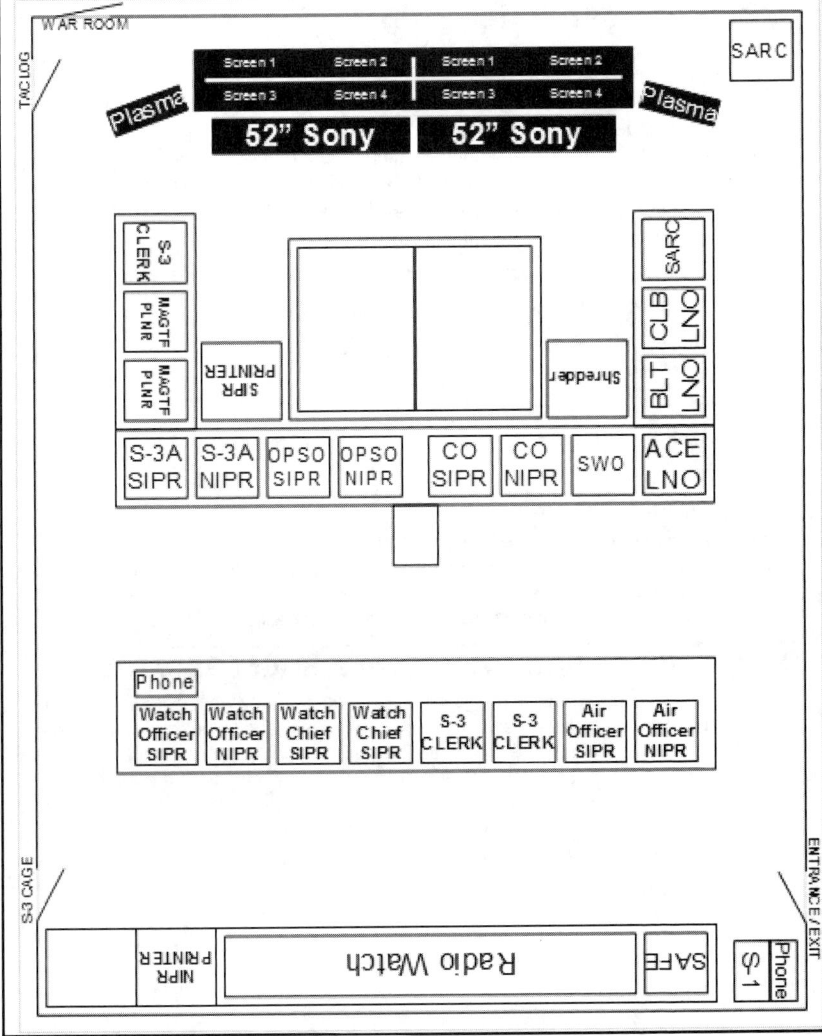

(S-3 Operations) III(a). MEU Force Fires

As defined in JP 1-02, fire support is fires that directly support land, maritime, amphibious, and special operations forces (SOF) to engage enemy forces, combat formations, and facilities in pursuit of tactical and operational objectives. Fire support coordination involves the planning and delivery of fires in support of MEU operations. MEU operations run the full spectrum of conflict, from providing humanitarian assistance to sustained combat operations ashore. Regardless of mission, the MEU will develop a fully integrated concept of fires that employs each asset with maximum effectiveness in support of the scheme of maneuver. Accurate and timely planning for, and prosecution of fires, requires detailed coordination, information exchange, and a thorough understanding of roles and responsibilities across the MEU and Navy Amphibious Squadron (PHIBRON). The mission of MEU Force Fires is plan, coordinate, and execute the efficient use of all supporting arms in support of MAGTF operations ashore and afloat.

I. Fires Organization

A. MEU / PHIBRON Fire Support Agencies

The composition and structure of MEU fires agencies is built around three principal organizations; the PHIBRON Supporting Arms Coordination Center (SACC) when afloat, the MEU Force Fires Coordination Center (FFCC) when ashore, and the Battalion Landing Team (BLT) Fire Support Coordination Center (FSCC).

B. PHIBRON Supporting Arms Coordination Center

The SACC is a single location onboard the amphibious command ship (LHD or LHA) in which all communication facilities, personnel, and various intelligence inputs incident to the coordination of fire support are centralized. The SACC exercises overall coordination and control of supporting arms assets during amphibious operations until responsibility for the coordination and control of fires is passed ashore. Fire support planners from both the PHIBRON and MEU Command Element (CE) staffs form the SACC. The SACC may also serve as the operations center for PHIBRON Tomahawk Land Attack Missile (TLAM) planning and execution.

- Once the MEU FFCC is established ashore and has assumed responsibility for the coordination of artillery, NSFS, and air support, the SACC assumes a standby and monitoring status.
- In accordance with JP 3-02, the designated commander may choose either the PHIBRON Supporting Arms Coordinator (SAC) or MEU Force Fires Coordinator (FFC) to supervise the SACC during mission planning and execution based upon the supported/supporting relationship.

C. MEU Force Fires Coordination Center

The MEU FFCC plans, coordinates, and executes lethal and nonlethal fires in support of the MEU commander's concept of operations. The FFCC is the senior fire support coordination agency, and the MEU CE staff provides the nucleus for this organization. FFCC is task organized to conduct fire support planning, targeting, maintain communications and situational awareness, liaise with external agencies, and coordinate fire support matters that impact the MAGTF as a whole. FFCC provides apportionment and allocation guidance of available fire support assets to subordinate elements in support of MEU operations.

- When embarked aboard ship the MEU FFCC and PHIBRON SACC form a cohesive, single agency that plans and integrates all fires for MEU/PHIBRON operations. SACC/FFCC works closely with the MEU Landing Force Operations Center (LFOC) during MEU operations to provide continuous reporting on the status of fire support systems, fire support coordination measures and geometries, fire mission processing.
- FFCC maintains control of fires for the entire MEU battle space until the BLT FSCC is established and ready to assume control of fires within their own battle space ashore
- When the MEU deploys ashore the FFCC will be positioned in the COC to allow for efficient coordination with the air, intelligence and current operations sections. The MEU FFCC coordinates with external, adjacent and subordinate fire support agencies to ensure the efficient planning and employment of supporting arms. The FFCC focus is on the deep battle and will control all fires within the MEU AO with the exception of the BLT AO.

D. BLT Fire Support Coordination Center (FSCC)

The BLT FSCC accomplishes fire support coordination and planning for the Ground Combat Element (GCE). Once established ashore, the FSCC is the focal point for fire support planning and integration with the ground commander's scheme of maneuver, communications, and control of fires within the BLT battle space. While afloat, FSCC personnel assist in fire support and mission planning and may augment the FFCC. Personnel assignment, setup, and operation of the BLT FSCC will be conducted IAW MCWP 3-16, this SOP, and applicable BLT SOPs.

II. MEU/PHIBRON Air Agencies

A. Navy Tactical Air Control Center (TACC)

The Navy TACC is staffed by members of the Tactical Air Control Squadron (TACRON) and is the primary navy air control agency for the planning, coordination, and direction of aviation support during amphibious operations. TACRON provides guidance, coordination and liaison to the SACC for the integration of aviation assets. Detailed discussion of the roles, responsibilities and components of the Navy TACC is provided in MCWP 3-31.6.

B. Marine Air Control Group (MACG) Air Support Element (ASE)

When operating from ashore, the ASE functions as the MEU Direct Air Support Center (DASC), providing procedural control of aircraft operating in support of the MAGTF. The ASE receives and processes joint tactical air requests (JTARs) and assault support requests (ASRs), coordinates scheduled and on call air support, assigns control of aircraft to specific controllers (BLT AirO, FAC, FAC(A), etc.), routes aircraft through the AO and provides aircrew with advisory information such as active gun target lines, control measures and enemy activity. The MEU ASE will collocate with the senior MAGTF fires agency ashore (FFCC/FSCC).

III. MEU Fires Operating Procedures

The following procedures will be used for coordinating planned and immediate fire support requests. Actual order of the procedures is based on message routing and approval procedures.

MEU Fires Operating Procedures

	Event/Task	Procedures
1	Receive fire support request (voice or digital)	☐ Radio or AFATDS operator records mission data on CFF card and passes card to fires chief
2	Plot Target	☐ Enter target location in EMT/AFATDS and plot on FFCC situation map (1:50,000) ☐ Hang CFF card above situation map ☐ Verify if target being attacked affects friendly units, violates or requires additional FSCMs
3	Consult Attack Guidance Matrix	☐ Extract appropriate attack guidance ☐ Determine desired effects and recommended munitions taking into account ROE, priority of missions, and available assets.
4	Conduct Necessary Coordination	☐ Coordinate fire mission internally to time the delivery of fires, coordinate gun target line/airspace, etc. ☐ When appropriate, contact lower, adjacent and higher FFCC/FSCC(s) ☐ TIO relays received fire mission data to LFOC and MEU S-2 via mIRC for informational purposes
5	Clear Fires	☐ FFCC passes mission approval/clearance to the appropriate firing agency and/or observer. ☐ *Positive clearance is the standard for all 15th MEU fire mission requests.*
6	Complete the Mission	☐ Monitor progress of the mission (aircraft routing, shifts or corrections, etc.) ☐ Record BDA on CFF card ☐ TIO relays RREMS/BDA to LFOC and MEU S-2 ☐ Shift priority targets as required ☐ Remove CFF card from situation map ☐ Fires chief records mission data in Fires Journal

IV. MEU Fires Personnel

During MEU mission planning and execution the SACC/FFCC will be activated and staffed by appropriate members of the MEU and PHIBRON staffs. The following section identifies personnel and assigned duties.

A. MEU Fire Support Officer (FSO)

The MEU FSO serves as the MAGTF Force Fires Coordinator and is the senior fire support representative to the MEU Commander for the planning, coordination and execution of fire support. FSO duties and responsibilities include:

- Reviewing major subordinate element (MSE) fire support plans and ensuring MSEs have adequate support
- Coordinating and disseminating battlefield geometry.
- Advising the MEU CO and S-3 on capabilities, limitations, and employment of fires
- Planning and coordinating fires in support of MEU operations to destroy or substantially degrade enemy operational capabilities and facilitate maneuver
- Developing and implementing fire support coordination measures in support of MEU operations
- Resolving fire support conflicts
- Publishing fire support plans and orders, to include Appendix 19 during deliberate planning or concept of fires briefs during crisis action planning
- Planning for and managing the MEU Fires and Effects Coordination Cell (FECC)

B. MEU Target Information Officer (TIO)

The TIO is assigned to the CE S-3 section and performs targeting and collateral damage assessments in support of MEU operations. The MEU TIO serves as the operations representative for planning and nomination of targets. His duties require close coordination with S-2/N-2, SJA, S-3, FSO, and other interested parties involved in target planning. Duties and responsibilities include:

- Selecting targets and matching appropriate responses to them, taking account of operational requirements and MEU/PHIBRON capabilities
- Tracking fire mission processing and updating the intelligence picture with effects achieved on targets
- Performing collateral damage estimation on planned targets, developing and distributing target lists, attack guidance matrices and target bulletins in support of MEU/PHIBRON operations
- Submitting MEU target nomination requests and field collateral damage estimations to higher headquarters
- Receiving and disseminating target intelligence updates
- Obtaining and disseminating No Strike List (NSL) targets within the MEU area of operations and nominating NSL targets to higher headquarters, as appropriate

C. MEU Air Officer / Assistant Air Officer (AirO/AAirO)

The AirO and AAirO are assigned to the MEU CE S-3 section and provide aviation expertise to the FFCC/SACC. When activated, the MEU AirO or AAirO will serve in the SACC or FFCC. AirO/AAirO fire support duties include:

- Reviewing and processing air support requests (ASRs) and joint tactical air requests (JTARs) from subordinate units to ensure adequate attack of targets, avoid duplication in the attack of targets, and protect friendly units
- Establishing liaison with the ACE, the GCE air officer, and the air officers of

higher and adjacent headquarters regarding air support and airspace management

- Preparing and publishing, in coordination with the MEU FSO, aviation fires planning documents to include Special Instructions (SPINS) and Annex W (Aviation) to the MAGTF OPORD
- Planning and disseminating, in coordination with the MEU FSO, air control measures in support of MEU operations
- Monitoring the tactical air request (TAR) net in the SACC/FFCC for information, or clearance if required, on immediate ASRs and JTARs
- Supervising and coordinating Tactical Air Control Party (TACP) activities
- Coordinating for, and advising the SAC and FSO on the employment of OAS

D. MEU Assistant Fire Support Officer (AFSO)

The AFSO serves in the MEU S-3 and is a troop list augmentee sourced from within I MEF during MEU composition. The AFSO assists in the planning and execution of fires, serves as the senior MEU fires representative in the absence of the FSO, and establishes and supervises the FFCC watch rotation during 24-hour operations.

E. MEU Force Fires Chief

The MEU Force Fires Chief is the senior 0861 Marine Artillery Scout Observer that is assigned to the MEU CE S-3 section. His duties include:

- Planning for, establishing and managing the SACC/FFCC
- Receiving and processing fire mission requests via voice and/or digital means
- Tracking fire mission processing and updating the MEU/PHIBRON common operational picture (COP) with Command and Control Personal Computer (C2PC)
- Supervising the production, dissemination, and management of MEU fire support related planning documents and products
- Training PHIBRON and MEU personnel in tactics, techniques, and procedures for the employment of supporting arms
- Establishing the SACC/FFCC watch bill in coordination with the FSO and PHIBRON SACC leadership

F. PHIBRON Supporting Arms Coordinator (SAC)

The SAC is charged with coordinating overall fire delivery of supporting arms and exercising general supervision over the activities of the SACC. This individual is assigned to the PHIBRON staff and may also be assigned as the PHIBRON TLAM Strike Officer. SAC duties and responsibilities include:

- Preparing, modifying, coordinating, and executing fire support plans
- Safely delivering offensive air support in coordination with NSFS
- Developing, engaging, and record keeping of enemy targets
- Coordinating NSFS support for MEU/PHIBRON operations
- Developing and assigning NSFS assets to Fire Support Areas (FSAs) and/or Fire Support Stations (FSSs)
- Delivering all PHIBRON supporting fires in a safe and timely manner

G. PHIBRON Supporting Arms Chief

The Supporting Arms Chief assists in setup and daily operation of the SACC and is the PHIBRON counterpart to the MEU Force Fires Chief. This billet is typically assigned to the PHIBRON TLAM Strike Chief. Duties and responsibilities include:

- Planning for, establishing and managing the SACC
- Receiving and processing fire mission requests via voice and/or digital means

- Tracking fire mission processing and updating the PHIBRON common operational picture (COP) with Command and Control Personal Computer (C2PC)
- Establishing and scheduling SACC watch bill requirements for PHIBRON personnel
- Training PHIBRON personnel in tactics, techniques, and procedures for the employment of supporting arms
- Coordinating NSFS support for MEU/PHIBRON operations

H. PHIBRON Naval Surface Fire Support Control Officer/ Liaison

Cruisers and destroyers assigned to the PHIBRON typically provide liaison officers to the PHIBRON staff that serve aboard the flag ship. These individuals coordinate and communicate NSFS support requirements in support of MEU/PHIBRON operations. During mission planning and execution these individuals work closely with the SAC and FSO to provide estimates of supportability and guidance for the employment of NSFS.

I. Tactical Air Control Squadron (TACRON) Air Support Coordinator (ASC)

TACRON is the navy counterpart to the MEU Marine Air Control Group (MACG) detachment, and executes overall cognizance of aviation activities afloat in support of MEU/PHIBRON operations. TACRON is assigned a USMC aviator who serves as the ASC. The TACRON LNO coordinates his efforts with the MEU AirO / AAirO and establishes a watch rotation for continuous representation by the ASC or MEU AirO during full SACC manning with 24-hour operations. Duties include:

- Coordinating for, and advising the SAC and FSO on the employment of OAS
- Receiving and processing ASRs and JTARs
- Coordinating with the AirO/AAirO for MEU aviation support to PHIBRON operations
- Coordinating external aviation support requirements for MEU/PHIBRON operations
- Monitoring the tactical air request (TAR) net in the SACC/FFCC for information, or clearance if required, on immediate ASRs and JTARs
- Providing tactical air direction of assigned aircraft

J. Target Intelligence Representatives (when assigned)

See section IV for guidance on the relationship between MEU/PHIBRON intelligence representatives and the SACC/FFCC.

K. BLT Fire Support Representatives

When conducting operations from afloat, and/or prior to amphibious offload of the BLT FSCC, the BLT commander may assign fire support representatives to the SACC/FFCC to maintain situational awareness, assist in the development of fire support plans, and advise the SAC and FSO on the capabilities and employment of BLT fire support assets. BLT liaison may include the Fire Support Coordinator (FSC), 81mm LNO, artillery LNO, BLT AirO, and Naval Gunfire Liaison Officer (NGLO).

Coordination and Control

SACC/FFCC is a dynamic environment, with representation and manning coming from various sections, units and detachments from the MEU and PHIBRON. Upon activation, personnel assigned to SACC/FFCC will fall under the staff supervision of the MEU FSO or PHIBRON SAC.

V. SACC/FFCC Manning

SACC/FFCC will be established and manned pursuant to mission tasking of MEU forces that requires the planning, coordination and execution of supporting arms. All SACC/FFCC personnel will report to the FSO upon receipt of a warning order or announcement of R2P2 CAT I.

Full Manning

SACC/FFCC will maintain a full manning status during periods of peak operational activity as determined by the PHIBRON SAC or MEU FSO. Full manning requires 24-hour operations with 12-hour shifts for all personnel. The SAC and FSO will establish a watch schedule based upon available personnel, anticipated periods of peak activity, and concurrent mission planning requirements. The full manning roster includes:

- MEU Fire Support Officer
- PHIBRON Supporting Arms Coordinator/Strike Officer
- MEU Assistant Fire Support Officer (if staffed)
- MEU Target Information Officer
- TACRON or ASE (DASC)
- MEU Air Officer / Assistant Air Officer
- MEU Force Fires Chief
- MEU AFATDS operator(s)
- PHIBRON Operations Specialist(s) assigned to SACC
- PHIBRON Strike Chief
- Radio Operators (MEU and PHIBRON)
- BLT FSCC Liaison Officer (when assigned)
- NSFS Liaison Officer(s) (when assigned)
- MEU Intelligence Analyst(s) (when assigned)

Reduced Manning

During extended operations or periods of reduced operational activity, SACC/FFCC may go into a reduced status at the discretion of the SAC and FSO. During periods of reduced-manning status, all SACC/FFCC members not on duty will be in a 15-minute standby status. Watch rotations will ensure a 24-hour presence with at least one representative from the following sections:

- MEU Fires
- PHIBRON SAC/Strike
- Aviation (TACRON, ASE or AirO)
- Radio operators and AFATDS operators (as required)
- MEU Intelligence Analyst(s) (when assigned)

Net Controllers/Radio Operators

Due to the requirement for 24-hour communications upon SACC/FFCC activation, the FSO and SAC will coordinate assignment of necessary radio operators/net controllers with their respective and communications officers.

SACC/FFCC Record Keeping

The SAC/FSO will ensure that appropriate records are maintained during all periods of SACC/FFCC activation. Information will include, but is not limited to:

- A log of significant events, missions fired, and combat reporting
- All pre-planned schedules of fire
- All NSFS request forms
- All JTARs
- All fire support or operational related message traffic

VI. Fire Mission Tracking (SACC/FFCC)

Each fire mission will be tracked both digitally and manually within the SACC/FFCC.

SACC/FFCC Situation Board

Status boards and map overlays serve as the primary means for ensuring safe, timely coordination of supporting arms. SACC/FFCC will maintain the fires situation board with associated 1:50,000 map(s), overlays and pertinent documents at all times.

Call For Fire (CFF) Cards

Fire mission data will initially be recorded to a pre-formatted CFF card appropriate to the type of mission request (i.e. arty, mortars, CAS, NSFS). The AFATDS operator will input the data from the CFF card into EMT/AFATDS and then hand the card to the Fires Chief to suspend above the situation map by rope (550 cord) and alligator clip. All active fire missions will have an associated CFF card suspended above the situation map. Upon completion of the mission, RREMS/BDA will be recorded to the CFF card and withdrawn from the situation map. The TIO will report RREMS/BDA data to the LFOC and MEU S-2 via mIRC chat.

Manual procedures include plotting the target location on the situation map with a push-pin and displaying gun target lines (GTL). Depending upon the asset utilized for attack of a target, a string will be tied between the firing unit location (i.e. Battery position with a push-pin attached to the grid location) and the target, used to depict the general GTL. This line will be maintained until completion of the mission, indicating an active GTL. Upon end of mission the target push-pin and GTL string will be removed from the situation map. **Automated** processing of fire missions in EMT/AFATDS will be conducted in accordance with system parameters for initiating, approving, and ending fire missions.

Control, Clearance and Approval of Fires

Guidance disseminated in the planning phases of a MEU operation or mission determines the routing and approval process for requests for fire. Factors taken into consideration include the communications net structure, expected volume of traffic, and the training level of FiST(s), SACC/FFCC, FSCC and the supporting arms agencies. The following paragraphs describe the types of control and approval methods, and standing MEU policy.

- **Control**. The two methods for processing fire mission requests are centralized and decentralized control. Centralized control requires that all requests for fires be submitted to the FFCC/SACC or FSCC for approval first and then be submitted to the appropriate supporting arm. Requests for fire support are sent by the observer directly to the supporting arm in decentralized control. The supporting arm processes the fire mission while SACC/FFCC/FSCC concurrently coordinates, clears, modifies or denies the observers request. Decentralized control requires the observer maintain communications with both the supporting arm and SACC/FFCC/FSCC.
- **Clearance and Approval**. The two methods for clearing fire mission requests are positive and passive approval. Positive clearance requires the SACC/FFCC or FSCC to transmit approval or denial of a fire mission request to the firing agency. Firing agencies (NSFS, CAS, artillery and mortars) and observers must wait for the SACC/FFCC or FSCC to grant approval prior to executing a fire mission under positive clearance. Passive approval (silence is consent) does not require a formal transmission from the SACC/FFCC or FSCC prior to engaging a target. The supporting arm and observer assume clearance unless the SACC/FFCC or FSCC denies the mission. Passive clearance may only be used in conjunction with decentralized control.

The MEU standard for controlling fires is decentralized control and positive clearance by the SACC/FFCC or FSCC.

During raids or similar MEU mission sets in which only one friendly element deploys ashore (i.e. company raid), the MEU commander may grant deviations to this standard and allow the on-scene commander's fire support entity (i.e. company FiST) to exercise control and clearance of fires within their objective area. This is especially suitable to long range raids in which limitations on communications ranges prohibit the SACC/FFCC from hearing traffic between an observer and CAS aircraft. The MEU FSO will brief responsibilities for the control and approval of fires, by phase, during each R2P2 confirmation brief.

Timing the Delivery of Fires

MCWP 3-16 identifies three techniques for timing the delivery of fires; Synchronization, Elapsed Time, and Event-Oriented. These techniques must be well-understood and practiced by all units/agencies involved in fire support in order to ensure the timely and accurate delivery of supporting arms. Synchronization is the preferred and primary method used by 15th MEU fire supporters. The MEU standard is Universal Time, coincident with the Zulu time zone. Units/agencies can independently access an automated, continuous broadcast of time, by use of HF radio (frequencies 10,000, 15,000, or 25,000), by telephoning the Naval Observatory, DSN 312.762.1401 (current as of 30 Jan 09), or from a Universal Time broadcast in conjunction with a GPS signal. Each R2P2 confirmation brief will conclude with a Zulu time hack for all personnel.

Passage of Control of Fires

During the initial phases of an amphibious operation, or MEU missions launched and controlled from afloat (i.e. company raid), SACC will maintain control of fires or will delegate control. Before going ashore the BLT FSC will receive a final update in the SACC concerning fire support coordination and the status of supporting arms.

Once the BLT FSCC is established ashore (when applicable) and can best accomplish the coordination and control of supporting arms for those forces, responsibility for the coordination and control of supporting arms will be passed from SACC to the FSCC following the checklist outlined in Appendix E. The MEU FFCC, once established ashore (when applicable) may resume control of fires outside the BLT AO for extended MAGTF operations ashore.

SACC remains activated and continues to monitor all required nets and fire mission processing throughout the period that fires are controlled ashore. Additionally, the SACC must be ready to reassume control of fires at any time. Reasons might include loss of effective communications by the BLT ashore, or enemy action which renders the BLT FSCC ineffective. In such cases close coordination of the change is required as soon as possible.

Fire Support Coordination Measures

Fire support coordination measures serve as the primary aid for the timely and safe delivery of supporting arms fires. Authority for the approval/establishment of fire support coordination measures within the MEU/PHIBRON operations area during unilateral MEU/PHIBRON operations will be in accordance with appendix H of this SOP. Joint or combined operations may require additional coordination for establishment of FSCMs. FFCC will promulgate guidance on such requirements for joint/combined operations and will serve as the principal coordination element with higher and adjacent agencies. 15th MEU forces will plan and utilize FSCMs in accordance with MCWP 3-16 and JPub 3-09.

Supporting Arms Procedures

Planning factors for supporting arms in support of MEU operations may include organic and inorganic CAS, direct support and general support NSFS, organic, direct support and general support artillery, and organic infantry mortars. The MEU FSO and PHIBRON SAC will identify available assets and coordinate for external support for MEU/PHIBRON operations. Assignment of roles and support relationships (DS, GS, etc.) for available supporting arms to subordinate elements is the responsibility of the MEU FSO and will be outlined in the Appendix 19 or R2P2 confirmation brief. MEU procedures for employing supporting arms, as well as specified roles and responsibilities, will be in accordance with Chapter 6 and Appendix E, MCWP 3-31.6 (May 2004).

VII. MEU Targeting

The purpose of targeting is to select for attack those enemy installations, units or equipment most critical to the accomplishment of the MEU mission. Effective and efficient targeting relies upon close coordination across the MEU staff, particularly intelligence, operations and fire support. The MEU's only formal targeting structure consists of the Target Information Officer, an artillery officer assigned to the Operations section. He is supported in his efforts by staff members from the MEU and PHIBRON staffs as well as higher joint and/or coalition targeting agencies.

Land Component Targeting Cycle

MEU forces will use the land component targeting cycle, Decide – Detect – Deliver – Assess (D3A) for planning and execution of MEU targets. The D3A methodology facilitates the attack of the right target, with the right asset, at the right time. The targeting process supports the MEU commander's concept of operations and assists in matching friendly capabilities against enemy targets, and requires close coordination between the commander and key personnel (fire support, operations & planning, intelligence and targeting).

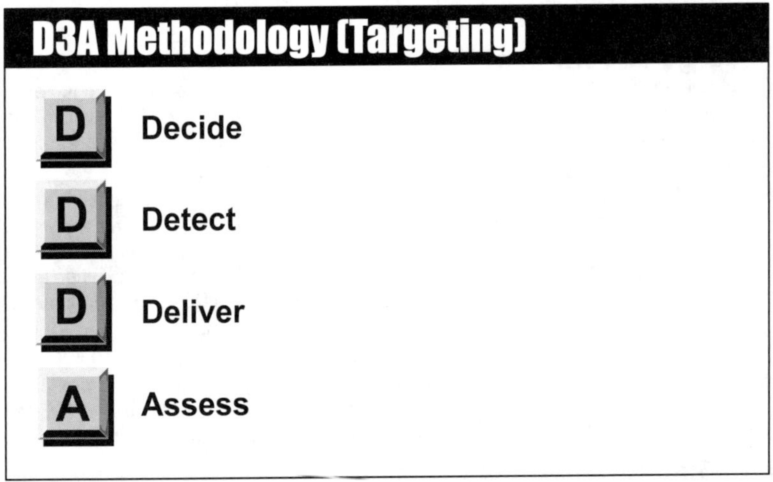

D3A Methodology (Targeting)
D
Decide
D
Detect
D
Deliver
A
Assess

For a more detailed discussion of D3A, roles, responsibilities and required outputs, see MCWP 3-16 and MCRP 3-16A.

Joint Intelligence Center (JIC)

When operating from ship, the Joint Intelligence Center (JIC) serves as the focal point for intelligence collection, analysis, production and reporting. The MEU targeting representative is the Target Intelligence Officer, normally an intelligence officer sourced from the MEU S-2 section. The Target Intelligence Officer is responsible for acquiring, analyzing, and processing all target intelligence data to determine possible effect, and to subsequently recommend targets to the TIO for engagement. Target intelligence information and updates are relayed to SACC/FFCC via the MEU S-2 section.

MEU Targeting Board

The MEU targeting board serves to develop and refine targeting priorities and disseminate target information in accordance with the MEU commander's objectives, guidance, and intent. This board also develops and nominates kinetic strike target packages for submission to higher headquarters when required. The MEU targeting board integrates with appropriate representatives from the PHIBRON staff when operating from afloat to comprise the Amphibious Force Targeting Board (AFTB), and is embedded within the MEU Fires and Effects Coordination Cell (FECC), discussed earlier.

Purpose/Tasks

- Develop/provide targeting guidance to the MEU and/or PHIBRON commander(s)
- Promulgate approved targeting guidance
- Prioritize available fire support and collection assets to targets
- Develop and recommend approval of the MEU/Amphibious Force Target List
- Review and integrate MEU/ARG operations, intelligence and targeting, efforts
- Develop targeting recommendations based upon current Rules of Engagement, Law of Armed Conflict, Public Affairs and Information Operations considerations.

Product Development/Outputs

The MEU Targeting Board/AFTB recommends and develops necessary planning documents in support of the mission. Depending upon the nature of planning (deliberate or crisis action), mission tasking, and time available, the targeting board drafts the High Payoff Target List (HPTL), High Value Target List (HVTL), Attack Guidance Matrix (AGM), Target Selection Standards (TSS), Target List, and appropriate kinetic strike request packages (discussed later in this section). MEU forces will utilize the consolidated AGM, HPTL, TSS matrix. The MEU Target List will include target number, location, description, and elevation. Once disseminated, the MEU Target List will be updated by MEU target bulletins.

Estimating Collateral Damage

The MEU TIO will perform field Collateral Damage Estimations (CDE) on all preplanned targets in support of MEU operations. CDE will be conducted in accordance with applicable theater directives and CJCSM 3160.01B (Aug 2007). Formal CDE requests will be submitted to higher headquarters in accordance with theater guidance. CDE calls for all planned targets will be briefed during R2P2 confirmation briefs or otherwise as directed during deliberate planning. Current U.S. Central Command (CENTCOM) theater guidance for targeting and collateral damage may be found on the CENTCOM CCJ2 Targets SIPR website, http://hqswebj2.centcom.smil.mil/targets.

No Strike List

SACC/FFCC will maintain and promulgate all applicable no strike lists (NSL) for the MEU area of operations.

VIII. Fires in the Rapid Response Planning Process (R2P2)

Accurate and timely fire support planning during MEU crisis action planning, known as R2P2, relies upon a common understanding of roles and responsibilities and close coordination across the MEU/PHIBRON. This section provides SOP playbook actions, briefing standards, and product development guidance to facilitate planning and execution of supporting arms and supplements the existing 15th MEU R2P2 SOP.

Organization for Planning

As time and circumstances permit, fire support personnel should make every effort to research and upload appropriate guidance provided by higher headquarters (i.e. NSL, CDE methodology, etc.) prior to commencement of R2P2. In most circumstances the MEU will receive indications and warnings or an initiating directive ahead of commencing R2P2.

MEU R2P2 Planning Timeline

The following timeline is provided from the MEU R2P2 SOP.

EVENT	*TIME (HR:MIN)*
RECEIPT OF MISSION / WARNING ORDER	(00:00 – 00:30)
FIRST CAT MEETING - MISSION ANALYSIS	(00:30 – 01:00)
COURSE OF ACTION DEVELOPMENT	(01:00 – 01:30)
SECOND CAT MEETING – COA SELECTION	(01:30 – 02:00)
DETAILED PLANNING	(02:00 – 04:00)
CONFIRMATION BRIEF	(04:00 – 05:00)
STAND-BY & ALTERNATE MISSION BRIEF (As Required)	(05:00 – 05:30)
FINAL INSPECTION/STAGE AIRCRAFT, BOATS, ETC.	(05:30 – 06:00)
EXECUTE (Launch of R&S or other elements as required)	(6 Hr mark)

CAT I and II Participation

The MEU FSO and TIO serve on the battle staff for R2P2 and will attend each CAT. During CAT I the FSO provides guidance to MEU assumptions/planning factors to facilitate detailed planning including whether any external fire support assets are available to support the mission. The FSO and TIO will be prepared to attend the mission commander's planning cell between CAT I and II to provide guidance on fire support asset availability, restrictions, and targeting considerations. The MEU FSO provides his estimate of supportability and preferred COA within CAT II. Once the MEU CO selects his preferred COA the battle staff and additional planners enter detailed planning.

R2P2 Detailed Planning

Immediately following the second CAT meeting, intelligence and operations planners from across the MAGTF will develop the initial mission synchronization matrix complete with phases, timelines and associated support. Fire support and aviation planners will provide on-station times for supporting arms as they apply to the mission commander's scheme of maneuver. Following CAT II, planners will commence detailed planning in their respective work spaces. SACC/FFCC serves as the central location for the integration of fire support planning and dissemination of fire support products across the MAGTF. Respective MSE fire support planners will maintain close contact with SACC/FFCC throughout detailed planning. The following table provides roles and responsibilities for fire support planning during R2P2. Essential to successful mission planning is close and continuous coordination between all agencies and planners.

Detailed Planning Reference Guide/Checklist

Action	FSO	TIO	AirO	FS Chief	BLT FSC	Co. FiST	SAC	ACE EFL
Develop MEU Essential Fire Support Tasks	P							
Develop Fire Support Timeline/Schedule	P	S	S		S	S	S	S
Coordinate external aviation FS assets	S		P					S
Coordinate external indirect FS assets	P				S			
Determine apportionment/allocation of available FS assets	P		S		S	S	S	S
Nominate RW/FW control measures (HAs, BPs, IPs, etc.)	X		S		S	S		P
Nominate NSFS FSA(s)/FSS(s)	X		S		S	S	P	
Nominate permissive control measures (CFL, BCL, etc.)	X P		S		S	S	S	S
Nominate restrictive control measures (NFA, RFA, etc.)	X P	S			S	S		
Nominate indirect fire positions (arty PAs, mortar positions, etc.)	X				P	S		
Incorporate No Strike List (NSL)	S	P		S				
Upload all above FSCMs to EMT/AFATDS	X	S		P				
Determine targeting approvals (deliberate and self defense)	X	P						
Determine control / approval of fires responsibilities	X P				S	S		S
Nominate MEU targets	X	P						
Weaponeer deliberate targets (JMEM, FAST-CD)		P						S
Perform Field CDE for deliberate targets		P						
Submit target nomination/kinetic strike requests to higher	X	P						
Publish MEU Target Bulletin	X	S		P				
Develop BLT FSEM (when MSN Cmndr)	S				X P	S		
Nominate BLT targets (when MSN Cmndr)	X	S			P	S		

X – Approval authority   P – Primary/lead agent   S – Supporting effort/input required

Confirmation Brief

For company-sized raids the Company FiST leader briefs this portion. If the BLT FSCC is being established ashore the BLT FSC may brief this portion as well. For MSOC missions the MSOC FAC briefs this portion. For other mission sets, this portion may be omitted or the on-scene fires observer may brief (i.e. FAC going ashore with a NEO force).

Confirmation Brief	
MEU FSO	MAGTF Essential Fire Support Task(s) Fire Support Apportionment/Allocation Fire Support Execution Matrix Fire Support Overlay - Graphical depiction of Obj Area on C2PC/EMT digital map - Restrictive FSCMs - Permissive FSCMs - Air Control Measures - NSFS FSA/FSS(s) and range fan - Artillery/mortar position areas and azimuth of fire - MAGTF Targets
MEU TIO	Targeting Approval Matrix (deliberate, fleeting, self defense) Deliberate Targets - Weaponeering (JMEM / FAST-CD) - Collateral Damage Estimation - Kneeboard target reference cards
Mission Commander Fires Planner*	Mission commander Concept of Fires Mission commander Fire Support Execution Matrix Fire Support Overlay Control of Fires by Phase FAC/JTAC Procedures Fire Support Nets/Frequencies
Escort Flight Lead / Strike Flight Lead	Type Escort / Follow-on missions Assets / Ordnance Load / Time on Station Fire Support Overlay Fire Support Nets/Frequencies Control of Fires by Phase Deliberate Targets

**For company-sized raids the Company FiST leader briefs this portion. If the BLT FSCC is being established ashore the BLT FSC may brief this portion as well. For MSOC missions the MSOC FAC briefs this portion. For other mission sets, this portion may be omitted or the on-scene fires observer may brief (i.e. FAC going ashore with a NEO force).*

IX. MEU Fires Communications

Physical Location of SACC/FFCC Communications Nets

When operating from ship, physical limitations of available radio nets available to the MEU/PHIBRON may prevent establishing communications across all doctrinal nets. During the planning phase of each exercise or operation, the SAC and FSO will closely coordinate with their respective communications officers to determine:

- SACC communications nets to be activated
- Specific physical locations of activated SACC nets
- Net Controller/Radio Operator requirements
- Specific frequency modulation and encryption equipment required to support SACC communications

Deviation from the standard SACC communications configuration will be announced to all fire support agencies.

Communications Nets

Net	Purpose	Net Control	Stations	Freq
Tactical Air Direction (TAD)	Direction of aircraft in CAS missions by a FAC/JTAC	DASC/ASE	DASC, SACC/ FFCC, FSCC, FACs, CAS acft	UHF/ VHF
Tactical Air Control Party Local (TACP(L))	Coordination between MEU/BLT AirO and FACs and approval/denial of CAS 9-lines	SACC/FFCC	MEU AirO, BLT AirO, FACs, FAC(A)s	UHF
Tactical Air Request (TAR/HR)	Request immediate air support	DASC/ASE	DASC, SACC/ FFCC, FSCC, FACs, HDC, TADC	HF
Naval Gunfire Air Spot (NGF AIR SPOT)	Request and adjust naval gunfire by FAC(A)	SACC/FFCC	SACC/ FFCC, FSCC, CG/DDGs, FAC(A)s	UHF
Naval Gunfire Ground Spot (NGF SPOT)	Request and adjust naval gunfire	SACC/FFCC	SACC/ FFCC, FSCC, CG/DDGs, FiSTs	HF
Naval Gunfire Coordination (NGF COORD)	Coordination between SACC/FFCC, FSCC, CG/DDGs, and NGLO	SACC/FFCC	SACC/ FFCC, FSCC, CG/DDGs, NGLO	HF
Landing Force Fire Support Coordination Net (LF FSC)	Coordination between SACC/FFCC, FSCC and fire support agencies	SACC/FFCC	SACC/ FFCC, FSCC, CG/DDGs	HF/ VHF
Artillery Conduct of Fire (ARTY COF)	To request and adjust artillery	MEU ARTY BTRY	SACC/ FFCC, FSCC, BTRY, FiSTs	VHF/ HF
Artillery Air Spot (ARTY AIR SPOT)	To request and adjust artillery by FAC(A)	MEU ARTY BTRY	SACC/ FFCC, FSCC, BTRY, FAC(A)s	VHF
Mortar Conduct of Fire (81s COF)	To request and adjust mortars	BLT 81s PLT	SACC/ FFCC, FSCC, BLT 81s PLT, FiSTs	VHF
15 MEU Fires mIRC Chat	Coordination and reporting between MEU/PHIBRON fire support and operations sections and other associated parties	SACC/FFCC	SACC/ FFCC, FSCC, CG/ DDGs, LFOC/COC, PHIBRON TFMOC	SIPR

NOTE: All units should plan for the use of encrypted radio networks. Understanding that secure communications may become unavailable, a contingency to operate in plain-text mode should be planned for as alternative means to communicate.

Chap 1

(S-3 Operations) III(b). Air Operations

See also App D: Aircraft Reference & Specifications, pp. 6-13 to 6-16 and App E: Air Operations Quick Reference, pp. 6-29 to 6-40.

Mission

Advise the Commanding Officer on the application and employment of MEU and non-MEU aviation assets for Air Reconnaissance, Anti-Air Warfare, Assault Support, Control of Aircraft and Missiles, Electronic Warfare, and Offensive Air Support in addition to coordinating the use of aviation assets during amphibious operations.

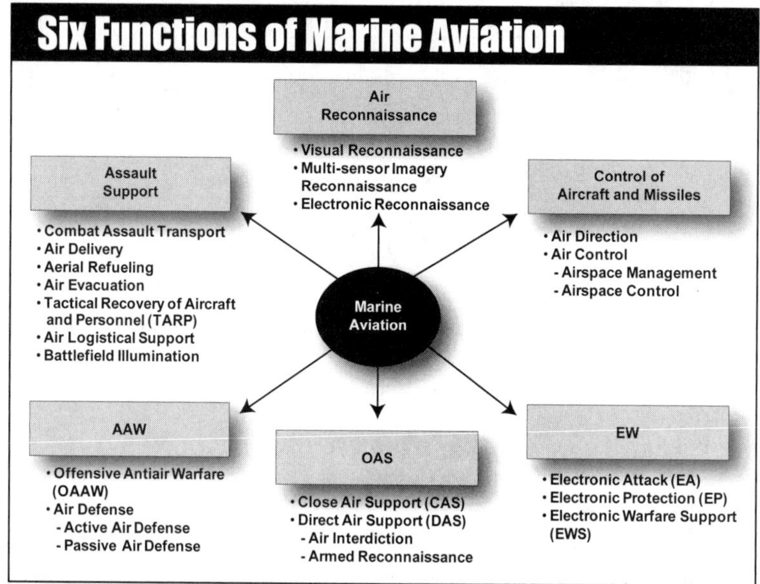

MEU Air Officers

The MEU Air Shop is comprised of two pilots/NFOs who are Tactical Air Control Party qualified, one being an O-4 and one being an O-3. Their primary responsibilities are to advise the CO and OpsO on all aviation issues, coordinate the use of organic and non-organic aviation assets for MEU operations, coordinated the training and employment of the MEU Air Combat Element (ACE), oversee JTAC/FAC currency and proficiency in the MEU, and serve as a member of the Supporting Arms Coordination Center (SACC) aboard ship.

The MEU Air Shop is a part of the Supporting Arms Coordination Center (SACC) aboard ship. See the Fires Cell section for a description of the SACC and fires integration during amphibious operations.

I. Responsibilities Afloat

The MEU Air Shop will have many duties in addition to those listed above. Once aboard ship, the primary job of the Air Shop is to coordinate and liaison with all the different entities on ship to efficiently and effectively employ ACE assets in accordance with the CO's guidance. Below is a list of the personnel involved in planning for use of aviation assets during amphibious missions:

Responsibilities Afloat

Aviation-Related Agency	Purpose
AIR COMBAT ELEMENT	Support MEU missions with aircraft and personnel
MEU AIR SHOP	Coordinate the employment of the ACE
BLT AIR OFFICER	Coordinate ACE assets for BLT missions
CLB OPERATIONS REP	Coordinate ACE assets for CLB missions
TACRON	ATO submission, TACRON Watch Officer, Foreign DIP clearance, Air Planning Board
HANDLER	Supervises the spotting of aircraft and loading of passengers and cargo
AIR BOSS	Oversees air operations on the ship
SHIP'S AIR OFFICER	Writes the ship's air plan, represents the ship's Operations Department
SAR DET REP	Coordinates necessary coverage by the ship's H-60 helicopters
METOC REP	Forecasts weather and sea state which will affect aviation operations
PHIBRON AIR OFFICER	Coordinates integration between PHIBRON and ACE operations

The Air Planning Board (APB)

The Air Officer will attend the daily Operations/Intelligence brief, the Current Operations brief (also known as BUBBAS), and the Air Planning Board (APB) daily. During the APB representatives from the above listed agencies will convene to coordinate mission requirements, training opportunities, and constraints for 24-, 48-, and 72-hour aviation forecasts. The end state of the APB, other than the efficient and effective use of ACE assets, is the daily Air Plan, usually written by the ship's Air Officer. The APB is chaired by a member of the TACRON. Inputs to the APB include but are not limited to mission requirements, aircraft maintenance readiness, aircrew currency, training opportunities, deck spotting and availability, PMC requests, airspace requirements, crew day limitations, ordnance load outs, deck opening and closing time, and commander's priorities. There are many competing interests at the APB. Therefore, everyone must realize that their priorities aren't necessarily everyone else's priorities.

II. Pre-Deployment Responsibilities

During pre-composite and formal Pre-Deployment Training Period (PTP), the MEU Air Officers have many responsibilities in addition to those mentioned in the above paragraphs. Prior to composite (prior to the MEU having an organic ACE), the MEU Air Officers will request air support from higher headquarters (MEF). This is done through the MEF FRAG process. In addition to the FRAG requests, the MEU Air Shop will have access to the range scheduling websites for the various ranges via the Range Facility Management Support System (RFMSS).

When composited, the MEU Air Shop is responsible for processing the Assault Support Requests (ASR) for the MEU. These ASRs will be submitted by designated operations personnel in each of the MSEs to the MEU Air Shop. The Air Officers will advise the MEU Operations Officer on the prioritization of the ASRs and will facilitate the allocation of ACE assets to fulfill all requests.

The MEU Air Shop will help to track ACE readiness with respect to aircraft maintenance, aircrew currency, and aircrew combat capability (ACC). The maintenance tracking is broken down into mission readiness status, aircraft modification, aircraft capability, and asset management. Aircrew currency will include but is not limited to pilot qualifications and currency for carrying troops over water (day/night), fast rope, NVG flight (HLL/LLL), external lifts, aerial refueling, and Deck Landing Qualification (DLQ). The different Type/Model/Series (TMS) aircraft have different expirations for their currency requirements; it is best to consult one of the SMEs in the various ACE detachments as they will closely monitor their own aircrew currency. The final and definitive source for the expiration of each type of qualifications is the Training and Readiness Manual for that particular TMS aircraft.

The MEU Air Shop is the senior TACP agency in the MEU. As such, all TACP training will be run through the MEU Air Shop. Since MSEs and other units will have JTACs and FACs, the MEU Air Shop will track currency requirements for TACP personnel from the BLT, ANGLICO, Force Reconnaissance, and the Air Shop itself. If a FAC or JTAC is near the expiration of his currency, the MEU Air Shop will advise the OpsO and CO of the situation and look to facilitate a TACP shoot to prevent that person from becoming unqualified. This may only require organic ACE assets but may require external CAS assets and/or coordinating with another unit to "piggy back" on a training opportunity. The MEU Air Shop may also be responsible for the tracking and procurement of various TACP gear based on the CO's discretion. This may include the following items:

Pre-Deployment Responsibilities

TACP ITEM	PURPOSE
PLDR	Designation of a target for laser-guided weapons
VECTOR/DAGR	Coordinate generation system (range, azimuth, position)
PSS/OFF	Software for mensurated grid generation
DPPDB	High-resolution map imagery
Binoculars	Visual magnification
IZLID	Infra-red target marking at night
Air panel	Easy visual acquisition of friendly forces
PAS-25	Thermal imager
Videoscout	Ability to have a real-time visual downlink with certain aerial sensors
Strikelink	Digital Close Air Support system
Rover	Ability to have a real-time visual downlink with certain aerial sensors

The MEU Air Shop is responsible for all message traffic with respect to embarking non-DOD personnel aboard ACE aircraft. In order to do this a message must be released to HQMC and notifying the proper agencies. MSEs will notify the Air Shop of an intent to embark non-DOD personnel with plenty of lead time (>30 days) in order for a message to be generated, released, and for HQMC to approve said passengers aboard ACE aircraft.

IV. The Air Plan

Below are some general rules applied to the production of the Air Plan:

Aircraft Spotting

- 30 minutes to spot and launch a CH-46E, AH-1W/Z, or UH-1N/Y
- 45 minutes to spot and launch a CH-53E
- 4 tow crews working at one time to move aircraft

Ordnance Planning

- 30 minutes to upload ordnance on a section of H-1s
- H-1s can't be loaded in the slash because it exceeds the max allowable towing weight
- H-1s will have to be spotted with the nose pointed out at a 30-45 degree angled when being loaded with ordnance (in case of ordnance cook-off and inadvertent firing)
- Cobras require the ship to go HERO 2 when the rounds are run through the gun feed chute during arming
- H-1s will need the Alpha Pattern when they come back from a shoot which will hold everyone in place until they land
- Harriers can be loaded in the slash
- If Harrier's return with forward firing ordnance they will have to land with the nose 30-45 degrees out, similar to the H-1s

Spread Spots

- A spread spot is a spot to put an aircraft on so that you can spread the blades to do maintenance
- CH-46Es will require one for any work on the rotor head
- CH-53s will require a spread spot to work on either the head or the tail

Below is an example of an air plan produced with the inputs from the Air Planning Board.

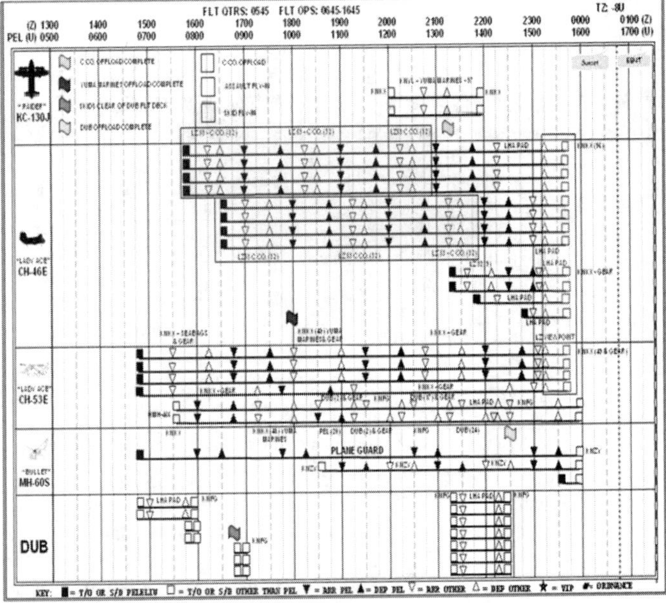

MEU aircraft will maintain different levels of alert status during mission readiness periods. Below is a description of some of the alert letters from the Assault Support Tactical SOP. This information is important because it factors into aircraft spotting, the deck cycle, and overall mission planning when utilizing any ACE asset. The ACE may have refinements to this SOP.

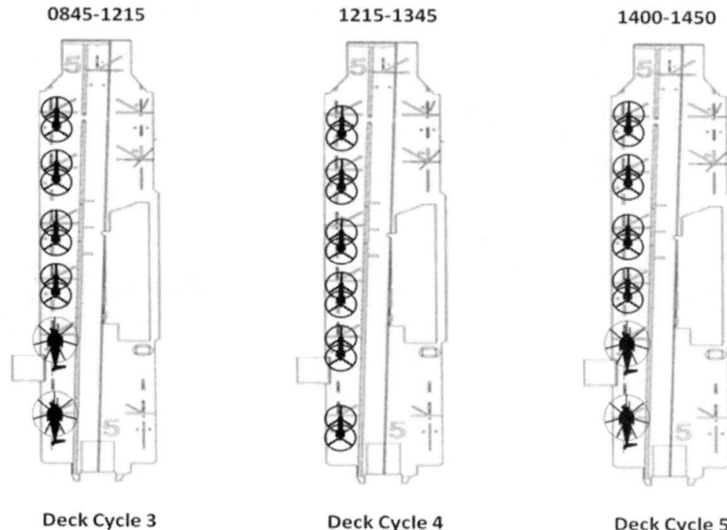

Example Deck Cycles on LHA/LHD (created from the Air Plan).

30-minute Strip Alert

Ordnance loaded, aircraft systems checks complete, aircraft signed off and preflighted. Aircraft will be turned, armed and op checked to include weapons systems and comm. checks. Once checked, de-arm and shutdown. Aircrews on standby in the ready room ready to respond to their aircraft immediately. Aircraft maintenance will not be performed on alert aircraft. Strip alert aircrew will have personal weapons and ammunition drawn prior to assuming the alert.

15 minute Strip Alert

Same as 30-minute strip alert with aircraft spotted, aircrew on the aircraft.

5 Minute Strip Alert

Aircraft turning, weapons and countermeasures armed, checklists complete. Aircraft are ready to launch – aircraft may refuel if required provided immediate fuel hose decoupling is possible.

V. Air Combat Element of the MEU

It is important to realize that the Air Shop is not in charge of the ACE but rather advises the MEU OpsO and CO on the ACE's employment. The typical MEU ACE composition is built around a Marine Medium Helicopter Squadron (HMM) and reinforced by a Marine Heavy Helicopter Squadron (HMH) detachment, Marine Light Attack Helicopter Squadron (HMLA) detachment, Marine Attack Squadron (VMA) detachment, Marine Aviation Logistics Squadron (MALS) detachment, Marine Wing Support Group (MWSG) detachment, Marine Air Control Group (MACG) detachment, Light Anti-Air Defense (LAAD) detachment, and a Marine Air Traffic Control Mobile Team (MMT) detachment.

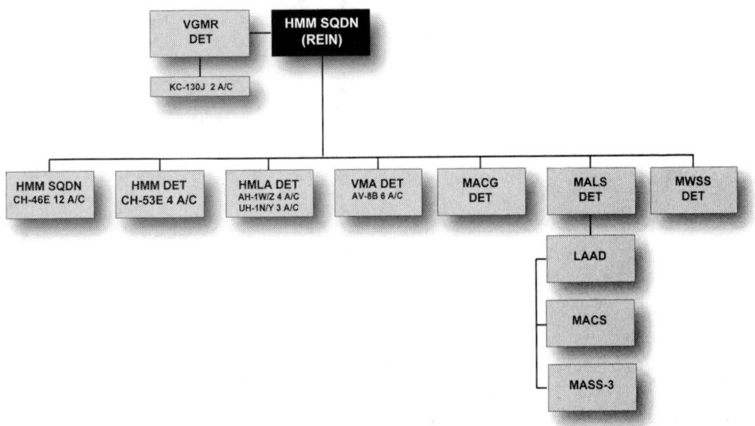

A typical ACE aircraft breakdown will look as follows:

- 12 x CH-46E Sea Knight helicopters (HMM)
- 6 x AV-8B Harrier II jets (VMM)
- 4 x CH-53E Super Stallion helicopters (HMH)
- 4 x AH-1W/Z Super Cobra helicopters (HMLA)
- 2-3 x UH-1N/Y Huey helicopters (HMLA)
- 2 x KC-130J Hercules cargo planes (VMGR)*

*KC-130Js from a VMGR squadron are tethered to the MEU. They will participate in MEU PTP but normally remain stateside on a 96-hour tether during deployment unless operations dictate otherwise.

See also App D: Aircraft Reference & Specifications, pp. 6-13 to 6-16 and App E: Air Operations Quick Reference, pp. 6-29 to 6-40.

Chap 1

(S-3 Operations) III(c). CBRND

Chemical, Biological, Radiological, and Nuclear Defense (CBRND)

CBRN Defense (CBRND) is concerned with mission accomplishment by limiting damage and casualties resulting from the employment of enemy nuclear weapons and/or employment of biological and chemical agents.

I. Readiness Objectives

Training

The objective of CBRND training is to provide commanders with trained personnel necessary to conduct operations in a CBRN environment. Readiness areas include:

- CBRND team training
- Individual and unit training
- Logistics
- CBRN reconnaissance
- Decontamination of equipment, vehicles, weapons and ambulatory/non-ambulatory personnel

Operations

Each MSE will have collective defense measures, planned and rehearsed, to include the ability to detect and evaluate hazards, the ability to react rapidly to those hazards, the ability to protect personnel and equipment, the ability to decontaminate itself and the ability to continue assigned missions. In addition:

- The CE will establish and maintain an CBRN Consequence Management (CBRN-CM) force capable of conducing assessments and reconnaissance of a chemical/biological incident site as established in this SOP
- The CLB, BLT and ACE augment the CBRN-CM force with unit 57XX personnel. The CLB will further augment the CBRN-CM force with EOD technicians when necessary
- Security and medical support will be provided by standing MEU elements within the MEU such as the Sparrow hawk and or Mass Casualty Team

Logistics

Each MSE will:

- Maintain T/E CBRN defense and CBRN-CM equipment in operational condition. Maintain an effective calibration program and ensure shelf life surveillance measures are practiced. Ensure all equipment is prepared for embarkation.
- Plan for immediate issue/distribution that will allow rapid access to CBRND equipment ashore or afloat
- At least one set of individual protective equipment (suit, boot covers, gloves, mask, spare filter and individual decontamination kit) will be embarked, along with all detection and decontamination gear. The second set of equipment will be forward deployed or remain behind in a fly away status based on the Commanding Officer's discretion.

II. Responsibilities

A. Command Responsibilities

Commanding Officers will ensure that all Marines are trained and equipped for CBRND operations IAW the 15 MEU Standing OPLAN and references.

B. Staff Responsibilities

Normal command functions and staff organization will be adhered to during the conduct of CBRND operations. CBRND is under the staff cognizance of the S-3. The following responsibilities and duties are generally assigned to primary and special staff officers with the MEU.

S-1

- Prepares and maintains CBRN casualty records, reports, and unit radiation dosage records in coordination with the medical officer and CBRN officer/NCO
- Coordinates radiation exposure status of subordinate organizations with the CBRN and Medical Officer's
- Determines straggler control measures
- Supervises graves registration
- Coordinates with the CBRN Officer and SJA for the handling of prisoners of war (POWs) in order to provide CBRN protective equipment and self-decontamination operations as specified in current international agreements and treaties

S-2

- Supervises the production and dissemination of intelligence in the following areas:
  - Enemy CBRN capabilities including production capabilities, weapons, and delivery systems
    - + Enemy CBRN defense equipment and training status
    - + Enemy intent to use CBRN weapons
- Initiates activities that degrade and counter the enemy's ability to acquire targets for CBRN attack
- Recommends CBRN reconnaissance of routes and areas
- Provide area meteorological conditions for use in predicting downwind hazards and determining its effect on the employment of CBRN weapons in the target area and its impact on friendly forces

S-3

- Prepares operation plans, orders, appendices, and annexes in accordance with the commander's guidance for CBRN operations.
- Considers the CBRN threat when determining the general location of the command post.
- Plans and coordinates CBRN defense training and inspections.
- Reviews and updates CBRN defense SOPs as well as training SOPs.
- Prepares and supervises the CBRN training program.
- Supervises training of CBRN monitor/survey teams, decontamination teams, and CBRN control center personnel.
- Inspects subordinate units' CBRN equipment.
- Activates the CBRN control center and coordinates its activities.
- Prepares and disseminates friendly force hazard predictions, minimum Mission Oriented Protective Posture (MOPP) recommendations, and effective downwind messages to subordinate units.

- Recommends required units, personnel, and equipment to conduct radiological/chemical surveys.
- Forwards CBRN reports and enemy CBRN attack alerts to higher, subordinate, and adjacent units or headquarters.
- Directs and supervises chemical detection, biological sampling, and radiological monitor/survey operations and reports within the unit.
- Ensures the preparation and promulgation of troop safety information.
- Supervise and direct the activities of the CBRND officer to include the following:
  - Advise the commander on CBRND readiness
  - Advise the commander on operational exposure guidance
  - Prepare the CBRND plans, orders, and instructions necessary to implement the commander's policies. This includes SOPs for CBRND, CBRN orders and annexes, and CBRN inspections.
  - Determine and recommend requirements for CBRN supplies and equipment
  - Estimate personnel, equipment, and supply requirements to support the CBRN appendix of the operation order
  - Coordinate and develop CBRND training exercises
  - Evaluate unit CBRND readiness
  - Supervise operation of the CBRN control center
  - Conduct and supervise CBRN equipment inspections
  - Provide recommendations for the training of the command and for the training of CBRN specialists. This includes formal school quotas.
  - Plan and make recommendations for decontamination functions
  - Supervise the training and activities of the MEU CBRND Chief to include the following:
    + Assist the CBRND Officer in the execution of his duties
    + Maintain the MEU Command Element's CBRND equipment
    + Ensure personnel are properly sized and issued an M50 field protective mask
    + Maintain the MEU CBRND technical publication library
    + Organize, train and perform duties as the SNCOIC of the MEU's CBRN-CM Force decontamination element
    + Conduct MEU Command Element individual and unit CBRND training

S-4

- Disperses and hardens logistic support facilities to reduce vulnerability to CBRN weapons
- Plans for increased transportation requirements due to the dispersion of units, increased demand for CBRN replacement equipment, and decontamination logistic requirements
- Ensures availability of CBRN defense equipment
- Develops plans to transport increased numbers of uncontaminated and contaminated casualties
- Plans for large-scale, thorough decontamination operations in response to an CBRN attack
- Prepares plans for and, when directed, supervises the construction and/or use of personnel shelters, decontamination sites, emergency power plants, and laundry facilities

- Coordinate with the ship for the reception of contaminated casualties/personnel in the event it is necessary to bring them aboard before decontamination is complete
- Coordinate with the ship for the decontamination of contaminated aircraft in the event decontamination ashore is not feasible

S-6

- Ensure all communications personnel are familiar with the CBRN warning and reporting system, specifically, format and precedence of CBRN 1-6 reports
- When provided adequate warning, ensure all communications equipment is covered by plastic or canvas in order to protect against contamination and reduce the decontamination effort
- Provide communications support for monitor/survey, decontamination and CBRN-CM operations as required

Medical Officer/Medical Planner

- Provide for treatment of CBRN casualties
- If required, supervise the inspection of food and water supplies for contamination and make determinations as to the possible salvage of contaminated food/water
- Coordinate with the CBRND Officer to monitor and evaluate nuclear radiation exposure history of subordinate units and advise the commander on the impact of additional exposure
- Direct the collection and processing of all biological samples
- Oversee periodic monitoring of all individual health records to ensure individual immunizations are up to date, and verify that personnel requiring optical inserts have them
- Ensure all medical personnel are trained in the treatment of CBRN casualties
- Ensure CBRN medications are obtained and made available for distribution in the event of a chemical threat; to include 3 atropine auto-injectors, 1 II PAM chloride injector and 1 CANA injector per Marine/Sailor
- Coordinate with the S-4 for the handling and movement of contaminated casualties
- Plan for and supervise the medical treatment of EPWs and civilian casualties who are exposed to CBRN agents

Maintenance Management Officer

- Supervise the management of the CBRND equipment maintenance management program
- Provide technical assistance and instruction in maintenance management matters pertaining to CBRND equipment
- Coordinate the input of all CBRND equipment into the Marine Corps Integrated Maintenance Management System (MIMMS) with the CBRN Officer
- Coordinate the maintenance management related programs; Operational Readiness Float (ORF), Quality Deficiency Reporting (QDR), Modification Control, Calibration Control, technical publication control, Corrosion and Wear Control Program Support for all CBRND equipment with the CBRND Officer.

Supply Officer

Coordinate acquisition, storage, control, issue, security, recovery and redistribution of all CBRND equipment and supplies with the S-4 and CBRND Officer.

C. Battalion Landing Team (BLT)

- Organize and train a battalion decontamination team.
- Organize and train battalion monitor/survey teams. Be prepared to conduct CBRN reconnaissance throughout the MEU's zone of operation.
- Interpret radiological information (fallout prediction, actual fallout, and monitor information).
- Appraise tactical significance of residual radiation areas.
- Coordinate with the medical officer to determine radiation effects on personnel.
- Interpret chemical information (chemical prediction and monitor/survey data).
- Coordinate the unit CBRN defense training program.
- Plan for immediate and operational decontamination of personnel and equipment.
- Supervise the procurement, issue, installation, and maintenance of unit CBRN equipment.
- Supervise the operation of the CBRN control center.
- Advise assignment of CBRN-trained personnel.
- Monitor employment of CBRND teams.
- Notify commanders if contaminated areas are within the area of operation.
- Supervise training and activities of the CBRN specialist to include the following:
  - Assist the CBRN officer in the execution of duties.
  - Assist the CBRN officer in ensuring that CBRN SOPs are up-to-date and effectively promulgated.
  - Maintain or assist in maintaining CBRN publications.
  - Recommend unit CBRN training requirements.
  - Provide direct supervision to the administration of the CBRN control center.
  - Plan CBRN monitor/survey (M/S) operations.

D. Aviation Combat Element (ACE)

- Organize and train a squadron decontamination team. Such team or teams will be proficient in decontaminating all aircraft types. Be prepared to establish a FARP/aircraft decontamination site in the event aircraft become contaminated.
- Be prepared to conduct aircraft decontamination aboard ship in the event decontamination ashore is not feasible
- Organize and train squadron M/S teams. Be prepared to conduct or support aerial surveys in the event of enemy or friendly use of nuclear weapons.
- Augment the CBRN-CM force with the squadron CBRN NCO
- Interpret radiological information (fallout prediction, actual fallout, and monitor information)
- Appraise tactical significance of residual radiation areas
- Coordinate with the medical officer to determine radiation effects on personnel
- Interpret chemical information (chemical prediction and M/S data)
- Coordinate the unit CBRND training program
- Plan for immediate and operational decontamination of personnel and equipment
- Supervise the procurement, issue, installation, and maintenance of unit CBRN equipment

- Supervise the operation of the CBRN control center
- Advise assignment of CBRN-trained personnel
- Monitor employment of CBRND teams
- Notify commanders if contaminated areas are within the area of operation
- Supervise training and activities of the CBRN specialist to include the following:
  - Assist the CBRN officer in the execution of duties
  - Assist the CBRN officer in ensuring that CBRN SOPs are up-to-date and effectively promulgated
  - Maintain or assist in maintaining CBRN publications
  - Recommend unit CBRN training requirements
  - Provide direct supervision to the administration of the CBRN control center
  - Plan CBRN M/S operations

E. Combat Logistics Battalion (CLB)

- Organize and train an CLB decontamination team
- Organize and train CLB M/S teams. Be prepared to conduct CBRN reconnaissance in your zone of operations
- Augment the CBRN-CM force with the CLB CBRN NCO and two EOD technicians
- Organize and train M/S teams IAW with Group SOPs. Be prepared to conduct CBRN reconnaissance in your area of operations
- Be prepared to construct thorough decontamination site(s)
- Interpret radiological information (fallout prediction, actual fallout, and monitor information)
- Appraise tactical significance of residual radiation areas
- Coordinate with the medical officer to determine radiation effects on personnel
- Interpret chemical information (chemical prediction and M/S data)
- Coordinate the unit CBRND training program
- Plan for immediate and operational decontamination of personnel and equipment
- Supervise the procurement, issue, installation, and maintenance of unit CBRN equipment
- Supervise the operation of the CBRN control center
- Advise assignment of CBRN-trained personnel
- Monitor employment of CBRND teams
- Notify commanders if contaminated areas are within the area of operation
- Supervise training and activities of the CBRN specialist to include the following:
  - Assist the CBRN officer in the execution of duties
  - Assist the CBRN officer in ensuring that CBRN SOPs are up-to-date and effectively promulgated
  - Maintain or assist in maintaining CBRN publications
  - Recommend unit CBRN training requirements
  - Provide direct supervision to the administration of the CBRN control center
  - Plan CBRN M/S operations

III. CBRND Team Organization

The ability of 15 MEU to function in an CBRN environment will depend primarily on individual preparedness and organized teams. This paragraph provides guidance and information on CBRND team assignments, organization, duties and equipment. All units will form, train and operationally equip these teams IAW this SOP. All units will, through proper screening, ensure that the most qualified (trained) personnel are used to fill team billets. Non-57XX CBRND Officers and NCOs will be school trained through the Division/MLG/Wing CBRND Platoons.

A. Control Center Teams

The MEU Command Element and the BLT will organize and train a CBRND control center team capable of performing the following tasks:

- Plans the employment of CBRN detectors and sensors
- Disseminates tasks of the M/S teams
- Disseminates overall unit CBRND guidance
- Coordinates troop safety considerations when friendly CBRN operations are planned
- Performs the computations needed to convert basic CBRN information into the required form, i.e. convert several CBRN-1 reports to an CBRN-2/3 report
- Plots and displays CBRN information
- Evaluates CBRN information
- Disseminates CBRN information

B. M/S Teams

1. Organization. Each MSE will organize and train M/S teams IAW parent command SOP's and directives. At a minimum, each MSE will have one M/S team, composed of two personnel, per area survey RADIAC meter rated by T/E or required by the MEU Unit Equipment Report (UER). In addition to these personnel, each MSE will be prepared to support M/S teams with drivers, radio operators and security personnel as required.

2. Training. Each team member should attend the appropriate CBRND course. In addition, at least 4 hours per quarter of team training should be conducted at the unit level to ensure proficiency.

3. Duties. M/S teams will be capable of performing the following duties:

- Operate for extended periods of time in protective clothing
- Conduct chemical agent detecting and surveying
- Conduct field biological sampling
- Conduct radiological monitoring and radiological surveys of contaminated areas, which includes operation of RADIAC instruments and individual dosimeters and properly utilizing radiological survey sheets and forms
- Submit M/S results up the chain of command utilizing the CBRN-4 report format

C. Decontamination Teams

1. Organization. All MSEs will organize and train decontamination teams IAW parent command SOP's, directives and this SOP.

2. Training. Each team member should attend the appropriate CBRND course given at Division/MLG/Wing Platoons. In addition, at least 4 hours per quarter of team training should be conducted at the unit level to ensure proficiency.

3. Duties. Each MSE will be prepared to perform operational and thorough decontamination independently or as part of a consolidated MEU effort.

IV. Training and Readiness

CBRND training will be conducted in as realistic a manner as possible. This paragraph prescribes standards of individual and unit readiness.

Proficiency Standards

Units and individuals within 15 MEU will attain proficiency as outlined below:

A. Individual Standards

General Objective. To achieve proficiency in individual protective measures necessary to survive an CBRN attack and accomplish assigned missions.

Specific Objectives. To attain and maintain proficiency in the individual training objectives as stated in the current edition of references (r) and (s) reproduced below:

Common standards applicable to all

- Identify NATO CBRN markers
- Maintain the field protective mask
- Don the field protective mask
- Don individual protective clothing to MOPP 4
- Perform basic functions while in MOPP 4
- Perform CBRN detection measures
- Decontaminate skin and personal equipment
- Conduct MOPP gear exchange
- React to a nuclear attack
- React to a chemical or biological attack
- Treat a chemical agent casualty
- Identify signs and symptoms of a Chem/Bio Attack

B. Unit Standards

General Objective. To develop and maintain the capability for mission accomplishment while under the threat of or actual CBRN attack.

Specific Objectives. To attain and maintain proficiency in the training objectives stated in the current, applicable edition of reference.

CBRND Team Training

MSE CBRND Officers and NCOs are responsible for the conduct and evaluation of team training.

Control Center Team

The MEU and BLT control center teams will be trained to the standards prescribed by the current, applicable edition of the references. Priority will be placed on fallout and chemical/biological hazard prediction, operational aspects, and basic reporting, recording and plotting procedures.

M/S Teams

M/S teams will be trained to the standards prescribed by the current, applicable edition of reference (t). This training will stress operational procedures under field conditions and will keep teams qualified to operate current RADIAC instruments, chemical agent detection devices and identification kits and biological sampling kits.

Decontamination Teams

Decontamination teams will be trained to the standards prescribed by the current, applicable edition of reference (t). This training will stress operational procedures under field conditions for both personnel and equipment decontamination.

Mission Oriented Protective Posture (MOPP)

Tactical situations, duty requirements and basic human needs will not permit personnel to remain totally protected against chemical or biological agents at all times. Implementation of MOPP allows options and compromises based on threat, temperature and workload to ensure accomplishment of the mission with minimum risk to personnel.

MOPP is a flexible system of protection for operations in a toxic chemical or biological environment. This system allows personnel to wear individual protective clothing and equipment consistent with the threat, work rate imposed by their mission, temperature and humidity without unacceptably degrading their efficiency from the effects of heat stress, psychological stress and other factors that affect the human senses.

The flexibility of MOPP is limited by the factors described below:

- Individuals will experience fatigue resulting from restricted airflow and increasing body temperatures. This increases the need for rest and sleep.
- Individuals will operate at decreased levels of efficiency, depending on prior training, proficiency and physical conditioning
- Individuals cannot attend to certain personal needs such as eating, caring for wounds, shaving, and elimination of body wastes

MOPP 0

- Over garment: Located in close proximity and ready for immediate use
- Over boots: Located in close proximity and ready for immediate use
- Mask/hood: Carried
- Gloves: Located in close proximity and ready for immediate use

MOPP I

- Over garment: Worn open or closed, based on the temperature
- Over boots: Carried
- Mask/hood: Carried
- Gloves: Carried

MOPP II

- Over garment: Worn open or closed based, on the temperature
- Over boots: Worn
- Mask/hood: Carried
- Gloves: Carried

MOPP III

- Over garment: Worn open or closed, based on the temperature
- Over boots: Worn
- Mask/hood: Worn, hood open or closed based on temperature
- Gloves: Carried

MOPP IV

- Over garment: Worn closed
- Over boots: Worn
- Mask/hood: Worn
- Gloves: Worn

Mask Only. Mask is worn in response to non-persistent agent. Suit, boot covers, and gloves not required.

MOPP Ready. Mask is stowed in carrier, carrier attached to body. One set of chemical protective gear is available within 2 hours. A second set is available within 6 hours.

B. Unit Training

CS/Mask Confidence Exercise

Each Marine will complete formal mask confidence training on an annual basis. This training will be conducted in accordance with MSE SOPs and safety regulations. The preferred method of conducting mask confidence training is in a field environment.

Integrated Training

When possible, CBRND training should be integrated into all phases of field training. CBRND will be exercised in a tactical scenario during a field exercise at least once annually.

V. CBRND Operations and Defensive Procedures

When intelligence indicates that enemy forces have CBRN weapons and have demonstrated the intent to employ those weapons, all indirect fire enemy attacks, particularly air and missile attacks, will be assumed to be CBRN attacks until they are proven otherwise.

A. CBRN Attack Alarm/Warning System

Local Alarms

All MSEs will establish an CBRND alarm system within their operating area. Local alarms will be in accordance with MSE SOPs and may include metal on metal, hand and arm signals, voice and wire. MSEs will ensure the alarms are understood up and down the chain of command. The vocal alarm is GAS or SPRAY.

General Warning

A general alarm will be passed over the radio when a CBRN attack is expected to involve a large area; when CBRN reports are received from higher headquarters or when intelligence indicates the likelihood of an imminent attack. Units under attack will initiate the alarm to adjacent units and to the MEU Command Post immediately. This warning will be sent through normal communications channels, using the CBRN-1 report format contained in this SOP.

All Clear

To preclude any unnecessary casualties following an CBRN attack, all units must request permission to conduct unmasking procedures from the Commanding Officer, 15 MEU. Once approval to unmask has been granted, the command ALL CLEAR will be given by the senior Marine present only after appropriate testing and unmasking procedures have been conducted. The command ALL CLEAR should not be passed over tactical radio nets; if however, it is necessary to do so, the receiving station should authenticate the sending station.

B. Communications

CBRND warning and reporting procedures do not require a dedicated communications system. Doctrinal tactical nets are sufficient.

C. CBRND Alert Conditions

CBRN Attack Probable

All intelligence indicates that an enemy CBRN attack is probable or imminent.

Warning. General warning.

Action:

- Activate control center, M/S and decontamination teams; CBRN Defense now becomes their primary duty.

- Ensure individual protective equipment, supplies and medications are distributed to all hands.
- Conduct pre-operational tests of all equipment.
- Take appropriate measures to protect food/water supplies and equipment from external contamination.
- MEU Commander will designate appropriate MOPP level.

CBRN Attack in Progress

Warning. Local alarms followed by CBRN-1 report to higher headquarters.

Action:

- Assume MOPP Level IV
- Initiate Individual Wipe down/Operator's Spray down as soon as practical but wait no longer than 5 minutes after the attack to conduct decontamination of contaminated skin
- Be alert for symptoms and perform self/first aid as necessary
- Continue with mission until directed otherwise

All Clear. Passed after selective unmasking procedures have been conducted and it has been determined that there is no longer an CBRN threat.

D. Evacuation Procedures for Suspected Chemical and Biological Samples

During the course of normal operations following a chemical or biological attack M/S teams may collect suspected samples containing chemical or biological contamination. Additionally, as a result of responding to a chemical or biological "incident" site, 15 MEU may be tasked with obtaining evidence or securing suspected weapons of mass destruction. In either case the following procedures will be utilized to evacuate the material to CONUS technical analysis laboratories or appropriate headquarters.

Once the sample is collected or secured, it will be packaged and marked in accordance with the procedures outlined in reference (f), CBRN Reconnaissance. Normally, the Navy EOD team assigned to the PHIBRON or the EOD team from the CLB will conduct packaging and sealing, if required.

Higher headquarters will be notified of the requirement to transfer suspected material. Higher headquarters will coordinate link up procedures between 15 MEU CBRND personnel and a Technical Escort or similar unit. Information required includes:

- Location of transfer point
- Call signs
- Frequencies
- Challenge and passwords
- Type of agent, if not specifically known, identify by biological or chemical
- Condition/quantity of material

Following procedures outlined in reference (g) for chain of custody procedures and documentation, 15 MEU CBRND personnel will transfer material to Technical Escort or similar unit for transportation to CONUS.

VI. CBRN Reporting

The CBRN Warning and Reporting System (CBRNWRS) consists of six reports. Each report is standardized by ATP 45/STANAG 2103 change 4, dated Jan 89 and the United States Message Text Format (USMTF). The U.S., NATO, British, Canadians and Australians use the same message formats.

CBRN Strike Serial Numbers

A four-character strike serial number will be assigned to each CBRN attack, which occurs in our zone of operations. The method for assigning these numbers is as follows:

- The first three numbers identify the sequential number of the attack against 15 MEU
- The last character identifies the type of attack. The letter N signifies a nuclear strike; the letter B signifies a biological attack; and the letter C signifies a chemical attack (i.e., strike serial number 002C is the second chemical attack reported in our zone of operations).

CBRN-1 Report

The CBRN-1 Report is used to provide early warning of CBRN attack and provide CBRN attack data utilized by the control center to compute hazard areas. The first time a CB weapon or nuclear weapon is used against friendly forces, the unit under attack or observing the attack will send the CBRN-1 report via FLASH precedence. All subsequent CBRN-1 reports, even if for a different attack, will be sent via IMMEDIATE precedence. When submitting CBRN-1 reports either lines Bravo and Charlie must be reported or line Foxtrot. All other lines are optional based on information available to the observer.

LINE	Chem/Bio	Nuclear
B	Location of observer	Location of observer
C	Azimuth from observer's position to attack	Azimuth from observer's position to attack
D	DTG of attack	DTG of detonation
E	DTG attack ended	N/A
F	Location of attack act or est	Location of attack act or est
G	Type of attack (means of delivery if known)	Type of attack
H	Type of agent P (persistent) NP (non-persistent)	Type of burst air, surface or subsurface
I	Number of munitions in the attack	N/A
J	N/A	Flash to bang time in sec
L	N/A H+5 minutes	Nuclear cloud width at
M	N/A	Stabilized cloud top or bottom angle at H+10 minutes

CBRN-2 Report

The CBRN-2 report is based on 1 or more CBRN-1 reports and is used to pass evaluated data of a particular CBRN attack to higher, adjacent and subordinate units.

LINE	Chem/Bio	Nuclear
A	Strike serial number	Strike serial number
D	DTG of attack	DTG of detonation
F	Location of attack act or est	Location of attack act or est
G	Type of attack (means of delivery if known)	Type of attack
H	Type of agent P (persistent) NP (non-persistent)	Type of burst air, surface or subsurface
N	N/A	Yield of weapon MT or KT
Y	Downwind direction of hazard and wind speed	N/A
ZA	Significant weather phenomenon	N/A

CBRN-3 Report

The CBRN control center uses the CBRN-2 report and the current weather/wind information to determine the downwind hazard or nuclear fallout area. This hazard area is then disseminated to all units who may be affected the hazard.

LINE	Chem/Bio	Nuclear
A	Strike serial number	Strike serial number
D	DTG of attack	DTG of detonation
F	Location of attack act or est	Location of attack act or est
H	Type of agent P (persistent) or NP (non-persistent)	Type of burst air, surface or subsurface
PA	Predicted hazard area coordinates (if wind speeds are less than 10 kmph, this item is 010, the radius of the hazard area in km)	N/A
PB	Duration of the hazard in attack and hazard areas	N/A
Y	Downwind direction of hazard and wind speed	Left and right radial lines of fallout area from GZ
Z	N/A	Effective wind speed, downwind distance of Zone 1, cloud radius.
ZA	Significant weather phenomenon	N/A

CBRN-4 Report

Actual contamination is reported using an CBRN-4 report. Separate CBRN-4 reports are plotted on the map to show where the hazard exists. For radiological contamination, CBRN-4 reports are also used to determine the rate at which the nuclear contamination is decaying (decreasing).

LINE	Chem/Bio	Nuclear
H	Type of agent	N/A
Q	Location of sample and type of sample	DTG of reading
R	N/A	Dose rate
S	DTG sample was taken	Location of reading

CBRN-5 Report

The CBRN-5 report is prepared from a plot of the actual area of contamination and consists of a series of grids that must be connected in order to visualize the contaminated area. This can be sent via radio; however, it is lengthy and is normally submitted via overlay. It can also be used to transmit the decay rate of fallout to units in the field.

LINE	Chem/Bio	Nuclear
A	Strike serial number	Strike serial number
D	DTG of attack	DTG of detonation
F	N/A	Location of attack act or est
H	Type of agent	N/A
O	N/A	Any other reference time when not H+1
S	DTG of sample	N/A
T	DTG of latest survey	H+1 DTG
U	N/A	1,000 cGyph contour line
V	N/A	300 cGyph contour line
W	N/A	100 cGyph contour line
X	Grids of area of actual contamination	20 cGyph contour line

CBRN-6 Report

The CBRN-6 report summarizes information concerning chemical or biological attacks and is prepared at the battalion level, but only when requested by higher headquarters. It is used as an intelligence tool to help determine enemy future intentions. It is written in narrative form, with as much information as possible under each line item.

LINE	
A	Strike serial number
R	Decay rate

VII. ECBRN Force

The purpose of the ECBRN force is to provide the MEU commander a method to protect the force. This is accomplished by utilizing a team of specially trained and equipped Marines to enter an area of suspected or actual contamination in order to determine the type and extent of contamination. With this information, decisions can be made whether or not existing CBRND equipment provides adequate protection for introduction of follow-on forces.

A. Capability/limitations

Capabilities

- Initial entry operations into a contaminated area
- Hazard assessment
- Initial detection and identification
- Sample collection
- Limited casualty extraction

Limitations

- If not on-scene during the incident, operations reduced to chemical/radiological detection and/or biological sampling.
- Not designed for large casualty extraction unless MOPP 4 (or less) is determined to be adequate protection.
- 12 SCBA limit "down range" time to approximately 45 minutes per 4-man team.
- Air bottle refill capability limited to 2 bottles in 45 minutes.

B. Organization

The ECBRN force capability is assigned to the CE. The majority of personnel will come from the MSC or platoon assigned by the MEU CO. It is highly desirable for all ECBRN Marines, except MOS 57XX, RTO and corpsmen to be assigned come from the same company/battery/platoon. It is also highly desirable for these Marines to be consolidated on the same ship as the equipment, normally the LHD/LHA. All MSEs to include the CE will augment the force. The ECBRN force will be organized as follows:

Command Element

- On scene commander (BLT CBRND Officer or CE CBRN Chief)
- GC/MS Operators (CLB and ACE CBRN NCOs)
- Comm section (1 BLT RTO)*
- EOD (2 CLB EOD technicians)
- Medical (2 BLT Corpsmen)

Reconnaissance Element

This element will be organized from the CE. The reconnaissance element will consist of 3 four-man teams, 1 hot zone coordinator and 1 cold zone coordinator for a total of fourteen. Each team will contain at least one NCO.

- Hot zone coordinator (1 Marine)
- Cold zone coordinator (1 Marine)
- Incident site assessors (1 team)
- Agent identifiers (2 teams)

Decontamination Element

The decontamination team will consist of 2 Marines led by a NCO.

Additional Support

- **Security.** If security is required, it will be provided by standing elements of the MEU such as the Sparrow Hawk or Bald Eagle forces. Security forces normally will not be required to secure the entire incident site. Security will typically be required for the CP/decontamination areas only. However, the situation will dictate the security requirements. Additionally, the security force can be used to extract casualties from the incident site provided the ECBRN force has determined that standard issue protective equipment is adequate.
- **Medical/Mass Casualty.** Normally, host nation medical facilities/transport should be used at an incident site. However, if the situation dictates, MEU medical triage/stabilization/treatment capabilities and/or casualty evacuation could be necessary. In either case treatment or evacuation by either host nation or MEU forces will occur in the cold zone upwind of the decontamination and/or CP area.

The MEU CBRND officer will normally remain aboard ESG shipping to provide reach-back support to the ECBRN force on the ground. Such support may include, but is not limited to:

- Research of materials discovered at the incident site
- Plume modeling
- Logistics
- Technical advice

C. Training

The TTPs and equipment used by the ECBRN force are largely unfamiliar to most Marines, even CBRN defense experts in the operating forces. Therefore, a standardized training package has been developed to bring the ECBRN force to a baseline of proficiency with the new equipment. This training package must be attended by all personnel identified in paragraph 5606(3)(a), (b) and (c) above. Due to the unique nature of the equipment and techniques, training is provided by already certified instructors at the MLG or Division Platoon level.

D. Equipment

Major items of ECBRN equipment are listed below:

36 Level B Protective Suits	18 Draeger PSS 7000 SCBA's
6 MultiRAE PLUS (PMG-50)	3 Quicksilver Sampling Kits
2 Draeger CMS	1 High Pressure Compressor (HPBAC)
36 Draeger PSS 7000 Air Cylinder's	1 Force Protection Line

E. Embarkation

The ECBRN equipment set comes with 4 quadcon containers in which to store and embark the equipment. The ECBRN equipment will not remain behind, nor be forward deployed. It will be embarked normally on the LHD/LHA.

F. ECBRN Force Employment

Alert Conditions

Alert conditions are common across all MEU missions. The table below outlines required actions by the ECBRN force for each alert condition:

Alert Status 180

Warning order issued

EQUIP DRAWN/BEGIN CHECKS

Weapons/Serialized gear drawn

Initial Inspections

Cross Deck

Alert Status 120

Ammo Issue to Plt Sgt

Comm Checks

Personnel Stage in Hangar Deck

Accountability

Rehearsals

Alert Status 60

Request Wpns Test Fire

Ammo Distributed

Wpns Test Fire

Final Inspection/rehearsal

Manifests to S-1 & Combat CESG

ECBRN OIC to LFOC

Mod Alert Status 60

Post Guard on Gear & return to berthing

Alert 30

Intel Updates

Stage on Ramp to Flight Deck

Planning Factors

- Is the contamination hazard known? If so, is it standard military agent, TIC, TIM, biological or radiological?
- What are the minimum standoff distances for the hazard or must maximum standoff be used?
- What is the wind direction/speed?
- Is the incident location known?
- Are there casualties, how many?
- Is on-scene medical treatment required?
- Is there a sufficient water supply available?
- What will be the disposition of contaminated waste? HN support or other U.S. government agency/contract?
- Is there a security threat? Terrorists/enemy?
- Are there any equipment or force limitations?
- ECBRN force/security/medical?
- How far from BLS/HLZ to initial staging area?
- How far from the staging area to the incident site?

Scheme of Maneuver

Ship-to-Shore

Large equipment footprint may preclude air only option. Requirement for vehicles may make surface option or surface/air option the only viable alternative unless HN or embassy provided vehicles are available.

Movement to Objective

No unique requirements from other missions unless distances require external vehicle support. Route security may be an issue.

Actions on Objective

1. Initial assessment team moves forward from the staging area in level B protection in order to establish a hotline.

2. Once the hotline is established reconnaissance teams begin suiting up and prepping detection equipment. The decontamination team sets up the decontamination line. The CP group establishes the command post and establishes communications. No one moves down range until the decontamination line is prepared to receive personnel. Once all elements are prepared, the incident site appears generally as depicted below:

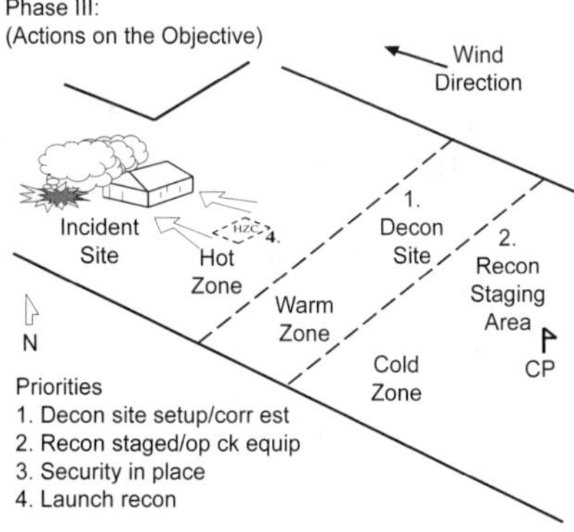

3. As reconnaissance teams move down range, they will check out with the hot zone coordinator, who will note the time in order to track air time. A backup team will remain at the CP, half-suited, ready to respond to the primary team if needed.

4. If the general location of the incident is known, the team will proceed to that point. If not known, the team will proceed on routes and search patterns determined during planning. Anytime the team enters a new area, structure or room they will submit a **LOCR report**.

1. **Location**: Where am I? Use the clock method when giving specific location inside a room. (The entry point to the room will always be 6 o'clock.)
2. **Observations**: Description of what I am seeing.
3. **Casualties**: Are there casualties, how many, living or dead, ambulatory non-ambulatory and symptoms.
4. **Equipment Readings**: PPM, Rad, Bars, LEL, O2.
5. Other immediate reporting require ments.
   a. First contact with casualties.
   b. Initial change in LEL and then any change more than 2%.
   c. Initial change in O2 level and then any change more than 2%.
   d. Any breach of the PPE.
   e. Secondary or improvised explosive device.
   f. Initial contact with contamination or any large change in the contamina tion level.
   g. Man down.

Search procedures

If multiple room building, a leapfrog method can be used to keep multiple teams in close proximity. If large open area, the team can be split accordingly utilizing any method of search as long as line of site can be maintained.

Marking Procedures

Device marking- one red chem light. One blue with red, denotes rendered safe device.

Withdrawal

No unique requirements from other missions unless distances require external vehicle support. Route security may be an issue.

Extract

Reverse of ship to shore.

Safety procedures

- Examine door for obvious hazards
- Monitor doors and windows for escaping gases
- Stand to the side of the door where there is no window if possible
- Ensure the body is well protected, open door slightly, and wait 5 seconds
- Examine room for obvious hazards.
- Hapsite team will not enter building until a safe LEL has been established

VIII. CBRN References

Joint Publications

JP 3-11 Joint Doctrine for Operations in an CBRN Environment

Marine Corps Publications

MCWP 3-37	MAGTF CBRN Defense Operations
MCWP 3-37.1	Chemical Operations, Fundamentals and Principals
MCWP 3-37.2	CBRN Protection
MCWP 3-37.3	CBRN Decontamination
MCWP 3-37.4	CBRN Reconnaissance
MCWP 3-37.4C	MTTP for CBRN Reconnaissance
MCWP 3-37.5	CBRN Defense of Fixed Sites, Ports and Airfields
MCRP 3-37A	CBRN Field Handbook
MCRP 3-37.1C	MTTP for Biological Surveillance
MCRP 3-37C	Flame and Riot Control Agents
MCRP 3-37.1A	MTTP for CBRN Vulnerability Analysis
MCRP 3-37.1B	Technical Aspects of Military Significant Chemical Agents and Compounds
MCRP 3-37.2A	Chemical and Biological Contamination Avoidance
MCRP 3-37.2B	Nuclear Contamination Avoidance
MCRP 3-37.2C	MTTP CBRN Aspects of Consequence Management
MCO 1510.89A	Individual Training Standards, Common Skills
MCO 1510.90	Individual Training Standards, Cpl - GySgt
MCO 3400.3E	SOP for CBRN Defense Training
MCO 1510.8A	MCCRES Vol VII, MAGTF Elements
MCO 1510.71B	Individual Training Standards for CBRN Defense Officers/ Specialists

Other Publications

(Secret)	Amphibious Operations in a Chem/Bio Threat Environment: Planners Handbook

(S-3 Operations) IIId. AT/FP

Antiterrorism/Force Protection and Military Police Detachment

It is essential that every member of this command be properly trained in Force Protection (FP) to prevent hostile actions against our personnel and physical assets. The MEU will implement Force Protection measures while on deployment during all phases of training on land, in port and while on liberty in order to provide personnel and equipment safety. The ultimate goal of force protection is to ensure no member of the MEU becomes the victim of a terrorist incident due to inadequate planning, training, knowledge or equipment.

Antiterrorism/Force Protection Officer

The AT/FP is an MP Officer who is specially trained to perform duties as the MEU Force Protection officer. This MP Officer is responsible to the commander. Tasks performed by the MEU Force Protection officer include the following:

- Develops unit plans to protect personnel and equipment and to preserve combat power
- Advises the commander on force protection issues
- Conducts vulnerability assessments of ports, points of embarkation or debarkation, and other forward areas while deployed and/or during predeployment site surveys
- Liaises with HN authorities, NCIS, and the Department of State for force protection measures abroad and to coordinate law enforcement matters while deployed
- Conducts MP training throughout the MAGTF (e.g., NLWs, detainee operations, evidence collection and handling, customs operations, level I antiterrorism awareness)
- Advises the commander on law enforcement and force protection matters during COA development and mission execution and develops MP support estimates of the situation for MAGTF operations
- Enhances unit preparedness through the identification, procurement, employment, and maintenance of force protection systems and equipment
- Supervises and coordinates MP assets and operations within the MEU
- Trains and/or supports HN, joint, and combined law enforcement activities
- Gathers and disseminates information within the MEU and submits police information and intelligence to the MEU S-2

MP Detachment

MP detachments provide specialized support to the MEU. The MP detachment is operationally controlled by the MEU command element through the MEU Force Protection officer. The MP detachment or cadre provides the MEU commander with force protection support capabilities, and the force protection officer suggests methods to detect and defeat the terrorist threat and plans and coordinates the MP operations. The MEU MP detachment is task-organized to provide the MAGTF commander capabilities in—

- MP support
- Interrogations
- NLW training and employment, per Marine Corps Warfighting Publication (MCWP) 3-15.8, MTTP for the Tactical Employment of Nonlethal Weapons (NLW)
- Force Protection planning and assessments
- Criminal investigations
- Accident investigations
- Physical security
- Tactical site exploitation
- Evidence collection and processing
- Forensics, and biometrics
- Protective services operations

I. Antiterrorism and Force Protection (AT/FP)

Background

Terrorists actively operate within the AORs that the 15th MEU will operate. Because of this, it is essential to protect the ability of the Commander to complete the mission through dedicated efforts to prevent and/or mitigate acts of terrorism against our personnel, our physical assets, and to preserve the integrity of our operations and combat power.

Mission

The 15th MEU conducts Antiterrorism/Force Protection (AT/FP) operations during all phases of training and operations afloat, ashore, and while in garrison in order to preserve the unit's capacity to complete the mission.

See facing page for an overview of AT/FP concept of operations.

A. Phase I (Preparation)

This phase consists of those actions taken to prevent terrorist attack, mitigate possible hazards and resulting losses, identify potential threats and countermeasures, and to prepare forces to respond and recover from an incident. During this phase, the following actions will be performed by Mission Assurance Personnel:

1. Develop Threat Assessments

Using all available unit information sources (S-2, HET) and inter-agency cooperation (NCIS), develop up-to-date assessments of potential terrorist, criminal, and foreign intelligence threats that may degrade the unit's ability to accomplish the mission. Threat Assessments will be developed for all sites used and/or inhabited by the unit during all phases of expeditionary operations and include ports, exercise locations, forward operations bases, bed down sites, APOE/SPOEs, logistics bases, and garrison locations. All threat assessments must be updated at least annually, or sooner based on changes in the situation. AT/FP personnel will maintain a file of current threat assessments within the MEU S-3.

2. Identify Critical Assets

AT/FP personnel will identify those assets belonging to the Commander that, if lost to a terrorist act, would prevent the unit from completing its mission. These assets will be identified and arranged to develop a list of Mission Essential Vulnerable Assets (MEVA) that will aid in the development of countermeasures and in the allocation of protection resources. This process will be performed in accordance with DOD Directive 2000.12.

3. Assess Vulnerabilities

Once potential and likely threats are identified along with assets that are essential to the mission, AT/FP personnel will determine what vulnerabilities exist. During this step, methods of mitigation will be determined that can be employed to reduce a particular vulnerability. Mitigation of vulnerabilities may be developed through

AT/FP Concept of Operations

AT/FP Operations are conducted in three phases:

AT/FP Concept of Operations

Phase One (Preparation)

Phase Two (Incident Response)

Phase Three (Recovery)

Phase One (Preparation)

This phase consists of those actions taken to prevent terrorist attack, mitigate possible hazards and resulting losses, identify potential threats and countermeasures, and to prepare forces to respond and recover from an incident. During this phase, the following actions will be performed by Mission Assurance Personnel:

1. Develop Threat Assessments
2. Identify Critical Assets
3. Assess Vulnerabilities
4. Conduct Site Surveys
5. Evaluate Residual Risks
6. AT/FP Planning
7. Training and Exercises
8. Establish a Force Protection Working Group

Phase Two (Incident Response)

This phase consists of those actions required to respond to an actual incident that places the unit's mission capability at risk. Such incidents include terrorist action, criminal activity, hazardous weather, and other threats against the unit that do not originate from a traditional adversary. During this phase, the following actions will be performed by AT/FP personnel:

1. Employ a Guard Force
2. Establish a Force Protection Posture
3. Employ a Response Force
4. Develop a Continuity of Operations Plan
5. Incident Reporting

Phase Three (Recovery)

1. Consequence Management
2. Restoration of Critical Infrastructure
3. Restoration of Support Structure
4. Disposal of Debris and Hazards
5. Reporting
6. After Action/Lessons Learned
7. Investigation

AT/FP Considerations

Arming of Security Personnel

All personnel performing security duties will be armed with appropriate quantities of ammunition. It may also be prudent for MSE commanders to arm key personnel such as officers and staff non-commissioned officers. All security personnel must be qualified with their weapon and fully trained on the applicable rules for deadly force and ROE. Under no circumstances will personnel carry weapons while in a liberty status. Security personnel, as detailed above, are under the operational control of the designated Guard OIC for each site.

Port Security

In some situations, the host nation will provide initial security of the port area for arrival of the ESG. However, each Commander of Troops (COT), in coordination with PHIBRON/MEU staffs, must be prepared to conduct close-in security of ships while in port. It is common the MEU may be required to augment ESG portside security due to manpower requirements.

Convoy Security

Convoy operations yield a two-fold danger. First, we are most vulnerable to attack when traveling on roads. Second, road and driving conditions are not the same as in the United States and may be almost as dangerous as encountering an enemy or terrorist attack. These two conditions require extensive planning and coordination for any ground movement. As such, certain conditions must be maintained:

- No tactical vehicle will travel alone. A minimum of two vehicles, each with armed assistant drivers and communications is required when traveling outside MEU/MSE forward operating bases.
- All convoys will have a designated convoy commander and movement will be coordinated by the MEU and MSE operations centers
- All personnel in tactical convoys will wear flak jackets and helmets
- All convoys will provide for security as required for mission accomplishment and as appropriate for the existing threat and conditions

Physical Security at CP/Bed-down Sites

Each MSE commander will ensure adequate security and countermeasures are established at each CP and logistics/bed-down site to include airfields utilized by the ACE. Commanders may adjust and expand measures as necessary. At a minimum, all CP/bed-down sites will have an established internal guard force with a roving patrol and an outer perimeter security force. The outer perimeter security force will include a vehicle checkpoint and a dismount point as well as crew served weapons positions to protect key/dangerous avenues of approach (if permitted by host nation conditions). A barrier plan that channelizes and restricts vehicle and foot movement will also be developed in order to protect vulnerable areas as well as provide blast mitigation at locations such as CP, billeting, chow hall, and ammo/weapons/vehicle/aircraft storage areas. As with any tactical operation, the following priority of work will be enforced when establishing sites:

- **Establish outer perimeter.** This is to include vehicle check/dismount points. Attention should be paid to locations and areas in the vicinity of the perimeter that may be favorable to enemy observation, direct fire, indirect fire, and consolidation. These locations should be included as areas of interest by follow-on security patrols. Attention must be paid to enemy capabilities. (For example, if the capabilities of the enemy include the employment of Indirect Fires using mortars with an effective range of 5km, patrol planning should consider methods to neutralize this threat by extending patrol routes to force the enemy out of effective employment range.)
- **Establish crew-served weapons positions (if required).** The use of common fundamentals such as mutually supporting fires, over watch, and effective fields of fire must be considered when placing crew-served weapons positions. In addition, communications means should also be planned to effective link positions with each other and throughout the guard force.
- **Establish inner perimeter security (guard force).** Ensure that guards are properly instructed on locations of Mission Essential Vulnerable Area (MEVAs) and other mission essential assets.
- **Conduct counter-mobility operations/construct obstacles and barriers.** Establish the use of barriers and channelizing effects to restrict the movement of potential threats along high avenues of approach, Entry Control Points (ECP)/Vehicle Control Point (VCP), and any other vulnerable area.

Physical Security at Exercise Sites

Some exercises may require certain elements to be geographically separated. For example, the BLT and CLB may be operating far forward of the ACE and MEU CE while conducting bilateral training. The same level of protection will be applied to units in the field away from CP/admin bed-down sites.

Subsistence Security

Units operating in the field shall subsist on U.S. rations only. Exceptions may be granted by the MEU Commander upon consultation with the MEU Medical officer for cases where contracted Host Nation support is available. Rations will be secured in a central location with appropriate barriers and guarded by the internal guard force or another organic element that is capable of providing constant security over this mission essential asset. Personnel shall use only authorized water from designated water distribution points.

MEVAs, Critical Assets and Infrastructure

Minimum requirements for assets required to be included in MEVA lists include the COC, JTF Enabler/Phoenix, TSCIF, Field Armory, ASP, FARP Sites, and Airfields.

Barrier Plans

Existing and planned barrier emplacements will be described by location, purpose, material, and execution. The incorporation of other assets such as sensors, surveillance, and guards will be further expanded upon if used by MSEs. It is essential that Barrier Plans not only enhance overall security and AT/FP posture, but most also work in concert with MEU operations and the overall mission.

Communications Plan

Any additional planning required to facilitate effective communications in support of AT/FP and force protection, such as personnel or equipment, will be included. In addition to this, a notification plan will be developed at the MSE level based on the environment and operational characteristics on the MEU's location. This will be particularly necessary as some elements of the MEU may be based at non-adjacent or nearby locations, making the timely notification of changes in threat and/or posture essential. To enhance communications efforts, a notification matrix will be developed by AT/FP personnel within the Command Element that shall be integrated at the MSE level. This allows the MEU to meet necessary reporting requirements to higher IAW with DOD policy (e.g. Mandatory reports to FBI Field Office; Department of State; Theater Commands; Blue Dart; OPREP, etc.).

Use of Force/ROE

All operations will include ROE and Use of Force instructions for guard and response forces as directed by higher. Particular attention will be paid to the use of Riot Control Agents (RCAs). The MEU Staff Judge Advocate is the point of contact for all ROE matters.

Random Anti-Terrorism Measures (RAMS)

AT/FP personnel will develop a RAM plan to implement random countermeasures during all operations. MSE's may integrate RAMs at the MSE level at their own discretion; however the implementation of RAMs above current Force Protection Postures must be reported to MEU AT/FP personnel within 24-hours.

Consequence Management (CBRNE/WMD)

A Consequence Management Team, specifically trained to identify and perform CM tasks, will be tasked to provide all-hazards CM capability to the MEU during operations.

High Risk Personnel

Any individuals that meet designation requirements will has protective service assets allocated as appropriate to provide an effective countermeasure to existing threats. The MEU AT/FP section will establish a Personal Security Detachment (PSD) in order to protect identified High Risk Personnel (HRP). The goal of a PSD mission is to protect the principle from all hazards, whether caused by personal design, accident, or negligence.

procedural changes, physical security enhancements, the addition of protective systems, or in the application of programmed solutions. The method for conducting the Vulnerability Assessment is in accordance with DOD Directive 2000.12 and must be performed on all sites that house critical assets or has an inhabited population of greater than 300 within 30 days of occupation. Vulnerabilities within the MEU will then be prioritized and reported via official means using the Department of Defense Core Vulnerabilities Assessment Management Program (CVAMP) within 120 days of completion of the initial vulnerability assessment. Only the MEU Command Element Mission Assurance Officer will be permitted to submit reports via this means.

4. Conduct Site Surveys

Prior to the arrival of the MEU to any site, AT/FP personnel are required to perform a Pre-Deployment Site Survey (PDSS) in order to develop an accurate situational picture of the operations area and to conduct preliminary coordination with security agencies (to include Host Nation Law Enforcement/Military). At a minimum, the MEU AT/FP Officer and/or Chief will participate in every PDSS and forming the Force Protection Advance Team (FPAT).

5. Evaluate Residual Risks

At the completion of the above steps, AT/FP Personnel will present to the Commander an analysis of residual risk taking into account threat, criticality, vulnerabilities, and mitigation measures. This is to allow the Commander to make effective risk decisions in order to guide future planning.

6. AT/FP Planning

While conducting operations, AT/FP personnel will participate in R2P2 and MCPP planning. This is to effectively integrate AT/FP planning into MEU operations. At least one member of the MEU's AT/FP team will participate in R2P2 and MCPP to include operational planning teams (OPTs).

7. Training and Exercises

Throughout the Preparation Phase, AT/FP personnel will conduct and/or coordinate for the comprehensive training of all MEU personnel to meet prescribed requirements as well as required due to changes in situation, threat, or mission. Included in this task is DOD and theater mandated training. Portions of this plan will be exercised by the unit throughout all phases of pre-deployment workup cycles and during operations when possible. AT/FP personnel will document all exercises separately to ensure the entire plan is exercised at least once annually.

8. Establish a Force Protection Working Group (FPWG)

The FPWG is established at E-Date and serves as a fusion cell to identify, discuss, and respond to matters pertaining to Force Protection. The working group will analyze current threat conditions as well as current operations to assist in identifying Force Protection requirements outside of those mandated by higher headquarters. In addition, the working group will assist in the sharing of information that may add in the effective planning and execution of AT/FP operations. All working group meetings will be added to the MEU Battle Rhythm and are chaired by the MEU AT/FP Officer. The MEU Force Protection Working Group consists of the following members:

- MEU S-3 Representative (AT/FP Officer)
- MEU S-2 Representative (SNCO and above)
- MEU S-4 Representative (SNCO and above)
- MEU HET Representative (SNCO and above)
- MEU SJA
- MEU Physical Security Chief (when staffed)
- MSE AT/FPOs
- PHIBRON/ESG FPO
- NCIS Special Agent Afloat

B. Phase Two (Incident Response)

This phase consists of those actions required to respond to an actual incident that places the unit's mission capability at risk. Such incidents include terrorist action, criminal activity, hazardous weather, and other threats against the unit that do not originate from a traditional adversary. During this phase, the following actions will be performed by AT/FP personnel:

1. Employ a Guard Force

During planning, the size and structure of a guard force, if required, will be developed. During this phase, the planned guard force will be implemented and integrated into the unit's site-specific AT/FP plan. The employment of the guard force may be under the cognizance of the MEU AT/FP Officer or the Headquarters Commandant as is appropriate. The guard force will be trained to prevent and respond to the existing threat as determined by AT/FP personnel.

2. Establish a Force Protection Posture

AT/FP personnel will make recommendations to the Commander on types of postures required to prevent, mitigate, and respond to current threats. In addition, changes may be recommended in response to changes in situation, threat, or mission. Once determined, the required Force Protection posture will be enacted by the guard force and will be considered in future planning.

3. Employ a Response Force

In situations where the unit must provide for its own emergency response, planning considerations will include provisions to establish a response force. These forces include Law Enforcement, EMS, Fire, as well as Quick Reaction Forces during tactical operations. Whereas the purpose of the guard force is prevention, the purpose of the response force is to rapidly mitigate damages/losses upon the initiation of an event. In many situations, these responsibilities can be delegated to other agencies as appropriate. AT/FP personnel will ensure specialized training where required.

4. Develop a Continuity of Operations Plan

AT/FP personnel will develop a Continuity of Operations Battle book, if one does not already exist for a preexisting site, that consolidates all resources, contact information, plans, sketches and other information in order to ensure mission accomplishment during an incident.

5. Incident Reporting

AT/FP personnel will ensure that all required reporting is conducted in accordance with regulations to include ancillary reporting to adjacent units and agencies.

C. Phase Three (Recovery)

This phase consists of those actions taken at the conclusion of an incident in order to return to normal operations. The below tasks are listed in order of precedence required to return the unit full mission capability.

1. Consequence Management

Specially trained personnel, designated as the MEU Consequence Management team, will conduct Consequence Management of those hazards (CBRNE, WMD) per the MEU's CBRNE Consequence Management protocol found in the CBRNE SOP.

2. Restoration of Critical Infrastructure

The second priority of recovery is the restoration of those assets that are critical infrastructure. These assets are time sensitive in nature as they are required to perform basic operations and is needed to complete any additional tasks. Critical Infrastructure restoration will be mitigated, where able, through the use of redundant systems.

3. Restoration of Support Structure

The third priority of recovery is the restoration of the support structure. This includes lines of communication, logistics routes, supply chains, and other resources required to support comprehensive unit operations. The restoration of these services will bring the unit to full mission capability.

4. Disposal of Debris and Hazards

Upon the restoration of all services that allow the unit to conduct full spectrum operations, efforts are then directed to the disposal of debris and/or hazards to return the area of operations to favorable conditions.

5. Reporting

Final incident reporting is made to include required follow-up reports to all agencies. This is accomplished across all functional areas. AT/FP operations will remain within the Recovery Phase until all reports are finalized.

6. After Action/Lessons Learned

The collection of lessons learned and the development of after action reports will be generated by AT/FP personnel to assist in future planning. This task may begin in this phase, but is not required to be complete to return to the unit to Phase One: Preparation.

7. Investigation

As required, the unit will perform investigations (command, criminal, et. al.) pertaining to the incident, its causes, and its impact on the unit's mission capability. The completion of this task is not required to return the unit to Phase One: Preparation.

II. Law Enforcement Operations

Title 10 of United States Code grants the commander the unique responsibility for maintaining good order and discipline. In addition, it grants Military Police the authority to execute Law Enforcement Operations to perform their duties to support the commander's mission. Aggressive law and order operations help the MAGTF commander maintain combat readiness and efficiency. MEU Military Police assist the commander in restricting or eliminating criminal activity by enforcing rules and regulations while not hindering the commander's ability to accomplish the tactical mission. Law and order operations include the following:

- Law Enforcement
- Criminal Investigations
- Accident Investigation
- Crime Prevention and Physical Security

MEU MPs conduct law and order operations within their authority and jurisdiction.

Authority

Authority is the lawful right of designated persons or agencies to exercise governmental power or control. MEU Military Police authority to enforce military law, order, and regulations is derived primarily from the Uniformed Code of Military Justice (UCMJ). Law Enforcement operations are executed under the direct authority of the MEU Commander and under the cognizance of the Mission Assurance Officer in order to prevent potential conflict of interest and provide proper oversight as prescribed by MCO 5580.2B (USMC Law Enforcement Manual).

- MEU Military Police have the authority to take appropriate action with persons subject to the UCMJ. Article 7b of the UCMJ and Rule 302 Manual for Courts-Martial give MP the authority to apprehend personnel subject to the UCMJ. Persons subject to the UCMJ are active duty military personnel, as well as some retired members, and other personnel listed in Article 2 of the UCMJ.

- MEU Military Police have no authority to apprehend civilians. However, civilians may be detained until they can be turned over to civilian authorities. Commanders and MEU Military Police are advised to consult with SJA concerning the circumstances warranting the detaining of persons not subject to the UCMJ.

Jurisdiction

Military jurisdiction is the extent of and limitation on the right to exercise authority and control over persons and offenses. Military jurisdiction is exercised through the application of military law, order, and regulations. The military has exclusive jurisdiction to try persons subject to the UCMJ. While conducting law and order operations MEU Military Police operate under various forms of jurisdiction:

- **Exclusive**. Under exclusive jurisdiction, the U.S. Government assumes sole jurisdiction over the designated area, i.e, military installations. In these areas the state has no authoritative merit.
- **Concurrent**. Concurrent jurisdiction exists when the U.S. Government and the state or local government exercise simultaneous authority over an area and either may assume investigative control.
- **Proprietary**. Proprietary Jurisdiction is when the jurisdiction belongs solely to the state (or other government). It applies in instances where the U.S. Government has ownership to an area but has not retained jurisdiction.

A. Probable Cause

Probable Cause (PC) to search exists when there is reasonable belief, based on believable information having a factual basis, that:

- A crime has been, is being, or is about to be committed
- The person, property, or evidence sought is located in the place or on the person to be searched
- PC information generally comes from:
  - Written Statements
  - Oral Statements communicated in person, or other means of communication
  - Information known by the authorizing official, i.e. the CO

Probable Cause to Apprehend

- A crime has been, is being, or is about to be committed; and
- The person to be apprehended is the person who committed the crime and is subject to the UCMJ

B. Assumptions

The following assumptions will be made until intelligence can provide an actual picture of the threat.

- MEU MP will deploy with the capability to accomplish the above stated missions. The MAGTF commander will establish mission priorities.
- If school trained investigators (criminal, accident, or MWD team) are not available, attempts should be made to provide these services by agreements with local military police units (Army, Navy, Marines, Air Force, Coast Guard) or host nation police agencies.
- MEU Military Police involvement in an incident/case are contingent on one of the following situation:
  - MSE Commander seeks MP assistance
  - An MP personally witnesses a criminal act
  - The MP receives a report of criminal activity
  - The senior MP assigns an MP asset to an investigation
  - When requested and coordinated by outside law enforcement agencies when appropriate and authorized by command

C. Body Views and Intrusions

Extraction of Body Fluids (Mil.R.Evid 312 & 313). The non-consensual extraction of body fluids (e.g., a blood sample) is permissible under two circumstances:

- Pursuant to a lawful search authorization; or
- Where circumstances show a clear indication that evidence of a crime will be found, and that there is reason to believe that the delay required to seek authorization could result in the destruction of evidence.

Involuntary extraction of body fluids will be conducted by a person with appropriate medical qualifications. Intrusion for Valid Medical Purposes (Mil.R.Evid 312(f)). Evidence or contraband obtained from an examination or intrusion conducted for a valid medical purpose may be seized and will be admissible in court-martial. Note. A chain of custody must be established and maintained. Self-incrimination. Protections of Article 31b. No person subject to the code shall:

- Compel any person to incriminate himself or to answer any questions the answer to which may tend to incriminate him.
- Advising them of their Article 31b Rights if subject to the UCMJ or appropriate Miranda Advisement.
- Compel any person to make a statement or produce evidence before a military tribunal if the statement or evidence is not material to the issue and may tend to degrade him.
- No statement obtained from any person in violation of this article, or through the use of coercion, unlawful influence, or unlawful inducement, may be received in evidence against him in trial by court-martial.
- All military person(s) suspected or accused of an offense will be advised of their rights under Article 31. This advisement will be recorded on a statement of suspect form.
- All civilian person(s) suspected or accused of an offense will be advised of their rights under the 5th Amendment.
- The MEU MP administering such rights will read it verbatim from a rights card or other authorized OPNAV document.

III. MEU Criminal Investigations Division (CID)

When staffed, the MEU possesses the organic capacity to conduct full-spectrum criminal investigations. The employment of CID personnel will be provided my MEF as available and requires coordination with the NCIS Special Agent Afloat while embarked upon the Expeditionary Strike Group (ESG). The CID mission encompasses several different roles during combat and contingency operations in order to support unit commanders:

- Criminal Investigations (Felony)
- Protective Services
- Crisis Negotiations
- Intelligence Gathering
- Criminal Investigations (Misdemeanor)
- Accident Investigation
- Crime Prevention and Physical Security

D. Search and Seizure

A search is a quest for incriminating evidence; an examination of a person or an area with the purpose to discover contraband or other evidence to be used in a criminal prosecution. Three factors must be present before the law of search and seizure will apply. Does the command activity constitute the following:

- A QUEST for evidence
- Conducted by a GOVERNMENT AGENT; and
- In an area where a REASONABLE EXPECTATION of privacy exists

A seizure is the taking possession of some item of evidence in conjunction with the investigation of criminal activity. The act of seizure is a separate and distinct act from search. On some occasions, the search is lawful and the seizure is not. Further, seizure must be accomplished by certain person(s).

Probable Cause (PC) searches based upon prior authorization (Military Rules of Evidence 315). Authorization to search an area may be granted by a "Neutral and Detached" commander who has jurisdiction of the area to be searched. As a rule, if that commander is involved in the evidence gathering process he is no longer neutral and detached.

Searches without prior authorization (Mil.R.Evid 315(g))

- **Exigency Search.** Permitted under circumstances demanding some immediate action to prevent the removal or disposal of property believed, on reasonable grounds, to be evidence of a crime.
- **Insufficient Time.** PC exists and there is reasonable belief that the time required to obtain authorization would result in the destruction, removal, or concealment of the property or evidence sought.
- **Lack of Communication (Mil.R.Evid 315(g)(2)).** PC exists and destruction, removal, or concealment of the property or evidence is a genuine concern, but communication with an authorizing official is precluded by military necessity.
- **Search of an Operable Vehicle (Mil.R.Evid 314(d)).** Two factors are controlling. First, a vehicle may easily be removed from the jurisdiction if a warrant or authorization were necessary; and second, the court recognizes a lesser "expectation of privacy" in automobiles. This rule also applies to aircraft, vessels, and tanks, as well as, automobiles and trucks.

Searches Not Requiring Probable Cause (Mil.R.Evid 314)

- **Searches Upon Entry to and Exit from U.S. Installations, Aircraft, and Vessels Abroad.** Commanders of such areas can authorize searches of person(s) or property to ensure the security, military fitness, or good order and discipline of the command.
- **Consent Searches (Mil.R.Evid 314(e)).** The owner or other person having control over the area to be searched consent to the search. If free and voluntary consent is given, no PC is required. A written consent form will be used.
- **Stop and Frisk (Mil.R.Evid 314(f)).** There are two elements to this rule. First the Stop; the MP has a reasonable suspicion to stop a person(s) for identification; second, should the MP making the stop have reasonable ground to fear for his/her life, a limited frisk or pat down of the person(s) outer-garments is permitted to determine if the person(s) is armed. Further, if the MP has no reason to fear his/her life, a frisk is not authorized.
- **Search Incident to a Lawful Apprehension (Mil.R.Evid 314(g)).** For this search to be admissible, the PC for apprehension must be valid. If there is PC, the MP may search the person and any place that person could reasonably reach.
- **Emergency Searches to Save Life or for Related Purposes (Mil.R.Evid 314(i)).** In emergency situations, searches conducted in an effort to render immediate medical aid, to obtain information that will assist in the rendering of such aid, or to prevent immediate or ongoing personal injury.
- **Plain View Seizure (Mil.R.Evid 316(d)(4)(C)).** When a government official is in a place where they have a lawful right to be, whether by invitation or official duty, evidence of a crime observed in plain view may be seized.

Criminal Investigations (Felony)

Investigating incidents with various violations contained within the punitive articles of the Uniform Code of Military Justice in the primary mission of CID. Attempts or conspiracy to commit an offense will be investigated with the same consideration as the actual offense. At a minimum, the following major criminal offenses will be investigated by CID. An attempt or conspiracy to commit the offense will receive the same consideration as an actual incident:

- Murder, manslaughter, negligent homicide, or unattended deaths
- Assaults which are aggravated through the use of a weapon or which require the victim to be treated or admitted at the hospital for lacerations requiring sutures and/or broken bones. Weapons include, but are not limited to, firearms, knives, sticks, bats, tire irons, glass bottles, and weapons, which could result in death or serious bodily injury.
- Rape, sodomy, and indecent assault
- Pandering or prostitution
- Robbery
- Forgery or fraud, excluding unauthorized use of telephone credit cards
- Arson, as determined by a fire marshal or where arson cannot be eliminated as a possible cause
- Extortion
- Drug offenses including theft of prescription drugs
- Burglary or housebreaking of an occupied residence or when the property stolen exceeds $250
- Black-market activities
- Larceny of government/private property valued in excess of $500 or a logical suspect has been determined. Additionally, all larcenies involving the theft of explosives, pyrotechnics or firearms
- Larceny of any police badge/credentials
- Child abuse as indicated after examination by a physician
- Child sex abuse involving suspected/actual child sex abuse to include carnal knowledge and indecent assault
- Suicides and attempts where self-inflicted injuries are of a serious nature requiring hospitalization or possible disability. Additionally, all attempts where the suspect has a secret or higher security clearance.
- Obscene telephone calls when there is a pattern or multiple calls
- Bomb Threats
- Worthless/insufficient funds checks in amounts exceeding $1000 when requested by command or when negotiated on a closed account
- Destruction of private/government property when damages exceed $500
- Request for assistance from local authorities or other investigative agencies involving the aforementioned crimes
- Violations of the law of land warfare
- Any crime, when directed by the senior MP

Protective Services

Although not a primary assignment, the MEU CID agent may be assigned as the lead on a personal protective detail for designated military and government officials.

Crisis Negotiations

During a crisis situation involving hostage(s) or barricaded suspects, the MEU CID agent may conduct negotiations with the suspect to resolve the incident.

Investigative Procedures

When initiating an investigation, the MEU CID agent follows a standard course of events:

Notifications

MEU MP should respond to the scene as appropriate and ascertain facts of the incident and provide crime scene security. Notification of MEU CID is determined by the seriousness of the incident.

Preliminary Investigations

Preliminary investigations are conducted to determine the scope of the incident and to collect the facts of the incident. This includes, but is not limited to, a crime scene examination, interviews of victims, witnesses, suspects, and the seizure of evidence.

Conducting Investigations

The investigation will be conducted utilizing the guidance set forth in the U.S. Army publication FM 19-20 (Law Enforcement Investigations).

Reporting Investigations

The MEU CID agent will generate a Report of Investigation (ROI) on investigations assumed by CID or investigations referred to the appropriate agency in accordance with the Marine Corps Law Enforcement Manual, Appendix B (Investigative Reporting Procedures). Additionally, the MEU CID agent will conduct the appropriate notification(s) to commands of the units involved in incidents.

Evidence Collection

Evidence seized as part of on-going investigations should be safeguarded and a proper chain of custody will be maintained. The evidence will be maintained until disposition of the evidence can be authorized by the adjudicative authority involved in the incident.

Testimony

The MEU CID agent may be required to testify at Courts-Martial and Non-Judicial Punishment (NJP) proceedings when requested.

Search Authority

During the course of an investigation, an investigator may make liaison with commanders and obtain command authorization for search & seizure of areas controlled by a specific battalion commanders or higher echelon authority. This authorization is based on probable cause, which is based on the fourth amendment of the Constitution.

Search Warrants

During the course of an investigation when leads surface outside the jurisdiction of the military, investigators may attempt to obtain a search warrant from local or federal authorities.

Liaison

Throughout the course of investigations, investigators make contact with a vast number of local, state, federal, military and international law enforcement agencies, to complete their investigations. Contact is also made with a variety of financial institutions and corporations.

Laboratory Analysis

Investigators have at their disposal several other government agencies, such as the U.S. Army and NCIS laboratories to conduct forensic analysis. These analyses include, but are not limited to, narcotics identification, latent print identification, trace evidence, serology analysis, firearm analysis, tool mark impression analysis, and questioned document analysis.

Polygraph Examinations

Further, CID may request NCIS to provide polygraph examinations as an investigative tool where available and when appropriate.

Intelligence Gathering

This is not a mission of CID; however, during the course of investigations, vast amounts of pertinent intelligence are obtained. This information may provide assistance to other sections within the military and government.

Criminal Investigations (Misdemeanor)

MEU Military Police will initially respond and conduct the preliminary investigation of all criminal incidents. Major criminal incidents will be referred to MEU CID Agent for investigation. The MEU CID agent is the principal criminal investigative agency during tactical operations. As determined by the local commander and applicable orders, all major criminal offenses will be referred to NCIS for investigation. MEU MP will investigate the crime, exhausting all leads and questioning all suspects. The investigating MEU MP officer will complete an incident complaint report and all required enclosures.

Accident Investigation

All vehicle accidents will be investigated provided they do not interfere with tactical or mission-essential operations. Accidents will be investigated by a school trained 5813 MP if available. The following vehicle accidents require an investigation regardless of vehicle type:

- Accidents resulting in a fatality
- Accidents involving host nation persons and/or property
- Accidents involving substantial vehicle damage and/or multiple vehicles
- Minor vehicle accidents do not require formal investigation, but will be reported when practical

If an accident investigator is not available and/or the Main Service Road (MSR) must be cleared quickly, a 5811 will complete an Incident Complaint Report (ICR). The Accident Investigator will:

- Assume investigative jurisdiction on all traffic accidents
- Coordinate with host nation authorities to obtain/exchange traffic accident information
- Obtain a Case Control Number (CCN) and maintain an administrative log of all cases
- Conduct investigations in accordance with applicable orders
- Weekly, provide the MEU Mission Assurance Officer with a written synopsis and courses of action for each on-going investigation and provide statistical data upon request

Crime Prevention and Physical Security

Crime prevention is accomplished by making units aware of the detrimental effects of criminal activity. The senior MP will provide commanders with instruction and information on recognizing, countering, and preventing criminal activities.

MEU Military Police will provide advice to unit commanders concerning security for rear area units, particularly those targets of interest to the enemy or criminal elements; e.g., CPs, arms and munitions storage areas, money facilities, command and control centers, and communication facilities.

(S-3 Operations) IIIe). Combat Camera

Mission

To provide guidance concerning the mission and capabilities for Combat Camera support within 15th Marine Expeditionary Unit (MEU). The potential value requires a determined effort to task, support, and obtain Combat Camera Imagery. This imagery provides commanders with an additional tool to ensure successful mission accomplishment.

- The mission of COMCAM forces is to provide Office of the Secretary of Defense (OSD), Chairman of the Joint Chiefs of Staff (CJCS), the Military Departments, combatant commands, and joint task forces (JTFs) with a directed imagery capability in support of operational and planning requirements through the full range of military operations.
- COMCAM forces perform unique and highly specialized missions with VIDOC capabilities supporting all phases of an operation or campaign. COMCAM teams are trained and equipped to access events and areas unavailable to other VI personnel or media representatives. COMCAM personnel maintain qualifications enabling them to operate with airborne forces, air crew, Special operations forces (SOF), and military divers. Their capabilities range from aerial photography to underwater photography. Furthermore, COMCAM teams have a technological capability for the timely transmission of images during fast-moving operations and support forward-operating maneuver elements.
- COMCAM imagery supports operational briefings, status reports, intelligence activities, information operations (IO), psychological operations (MISO), military deception, public affairs requirements, strategic communications, historical documentation, etc. Additionally, imagery is used to counter disinformation programs in support of sensitive operations.
- Combat reproduction supports these missions by giving the commander a high output reproduction capability. This capability is critical when dealing with missions that require mass reproduction of different and other mass production of printed material (i.e. orders, pamphlets), particularly when supporting IO and MISO.

I. Concept of Operations

The COMCAM unit will operate within the scope of all valid Department of Defense and Marine Corps orders and regulations in the accomplishment of its mission. COMCAM teams will be organized under the S-3 operations, or Information Operations section, during operations or exercises and in garrison situations to ensure imagery information and assets are available.

- 15th MEU COMCAM missions will be managed through the S-3, COMCAM Chief.
- The supported Joint Combatant Commander will deploy a Joint Combat Camera Management Team (JCCMT). Marine Corps Combat Camera may be tasked to provide COMCAM assets or be the executing agent for these teams.
- COMCAM teams deployed to support Combined, Joint Task Force (C/JTF) will be designated a JCCMT. When combined with other services' COMCAM personnel, the JCCMT will be assigned under the Joint Task Force Combined J-3 Operations (JTF C/J-3).
- COMCAM teams deploy with enough supplies to operate for a minimum of 45 days. Teams will receive re-supply if necessary.

II. MEU COMCAM Responsibilities

- Ensure directed COMCAM assets and products are provided during all phases of contingencies, operations, exercises and for garrison activities. COMCAM provides directed imagery capability to support situational awareness, evaluation of warfighting effectiveness, historical documentation, and other operational, and administrative requirements as directed.
- Provide Management of COMCAM equipment and technical oversight of all Visual Information (VI) equipment purchases in order to maximize interoperability, standardization and supportability

A. S-3

As per reference (c), the S-3 assigns to the Commanding officer, various production capabilities in photography, video, and other visual information arts. Accordingly, the S-3 is responsible for the supervision of all combat camera activities associated with the 15th MEU.

B. COMCAM Chief

The COMCAM Chief will provide staff oversight of COMCAM and serves as a battle staff/special staff officer who advises the commander on issues, capabilities and requirements pertaining to combat camera operations. The COMCAM Chief is normally assigned to the S-3 Section. The COMCAM Chief manages all assets to include Table of Organization and Equipment (T/O&E) and funding, and acts as the sponsor for augmentation tasking and request for forces from higher and adjacent commands to MSC. Additionally, the COMCAM Chief will develop the COMCAM annexes to operations/exercise orders.

C. Subordinate Element Missions

Subordinate Units

Any unit within attached to the 15th MEU will coordinate directly with S-3 for support COMCAM. This includes requests for Still and Video Camera Teams for field training and aboard aircraft. The COMCAM Chief will determine supportability per operational tempo, manpower availability, budget and internal training requirements.

Adjacent Units

Adjacent units can request support through COMCAM. Once the support is identified, COMCAM will work these requests directly with the units.

D. Coordinating Instructions

Higher Headquarters

COMCAM and printing support for higher command driven events shall be coordinated through COMCAM Chief.

Staff Judge Advocate and Copyright Laws

COMCAM is prohibited by law to copy, duplicate or reproduce any item protected by copyright. The only exceptions are identified under the "Fair Use Exception." COMCAM shall provide guidance to any customer requesting support on copyrighted materials.

Public Affairs

All imagery and products produced by COMCAM are public domain under U.S. Copyright law Title 17. However, COMCAM products and imagery will not be released to the public by any command or individual. The 15th MEU Commanding Officer will assign a releasing authority, normally the PAO.

III. Role of Combat Camera

Combat Camera (COMCAM) is a low-density, high-demand force enabler composed of highly trained Visual Information professionals prepared to deploy to the most austere operational environments at a moment's notice. Seasoned in the art of acquiring and using still and motion imagery, COMCAM forces provide the Secretary of Defense, Joint Chiefs of Staff, Combatant Commanders, Joint Task Forces and Services a directed imagery capability to support operational planning, intelligence, public affairs, information warfare, mission assessment, legal and countless other requirements during crises, contingencies and exercises around the globe.

As with combat operations, relative speed and concentration efforts are paramount so commanders and staff receive the imagery needed to plan missions and identify critical information. Still photo and video imagery of critical events help shape operation and strategic-level objectives and perception by presenting visual information as proof to reports and briefings. In today's global information environment, tactical events have strategic impact. Imagery acquired by Combat Camera personnel facilitates expedient decision making. It can also be a key element in maintaining public support. More importantly, COMCAM footage is often the only imagery of key events. Combat Camera capabilities significantly enhance/influence Information Operations (IO) by providing the skill sets in photography, videography, graphic design and reproduction that support IO missions and initiatives.

Types of Military Operations supported by Combat Camera

- Major Operations
- Homeland Defense
- Strikes
- Raids
- Show of Force
- Enforcement of Sanctions
- Protection of Shipping
- Freedom of Navigation
- Peace Operations
- Disaster Response
- Support to Insurgency
- Counterinsurgency Operations
- Combating Terrorism
- Noncombatant Evacuation Operations
- Recovery Operations
- Foreign Humanitarian Assistance
- Nation Assistance
- Arms Control and Disarmament
- Routine, Recurring Military Activities

Priorities of Support

The following is a general rule for priorities of support for the 15th MEU COMCAM unit:

- Operations, exercises and training
- Documentation of historically significant events
- Investigations, briefs, conferences, etc.
- Administrative photograph requirements; i.e., ISO Preps, passports, etc.

Support Examples

These include but are not limited to:

- Promotion photographs, local command boards, passports, visas and naturalizations
- Historical documentation, command/unit special events, after action/turnover imagery
- Legal support to include investigation imagery, forensic evidence, mishap documentation, land-use imagery (before and after)
- Operational and training support materials to include publications, handbooks, briefs, images/video for critiques
- Command level promotions, awards, and special recognition

IV. COMCAM Sections

The functional areas within the Combat Camera section will support 15th MEU with photographic, video, illustrative and reproduction assets and products in support of the commands or units mission requirements. Specific responsibilities include:

1. Still Photography

Operational imagery, studio type photography (promotion, local command board, passport, weight control photos, etc.) is accomplished by this facility. All official promotion board photos will be conduct at the local Base COMCAM unit with the exception of field promotion board photos.

- Digital acquisition/documentation
- Digital color and black & white printing from 2" X 2" passport to large format posters
- Scanning and photos
- Copy of imagery on compact disk (CD) and other media as required
- Interactive imagery CDs
- Photo Album collages for special events/historical documentation
- CD duplication
- Photographic restoration

2. Videography

- Digital video (DV) and audio acquisition on DV tapes and High-definition video (HDV)
- Digital video editing and production with special effects, titles, etc.
- Video duplication on Digital Video Disc (DVD)
- Video products provided on DVD with still imagery, audio & graphics
- Still to video transfer
- Multi-media products on CD/DVD with still imagery, audio & graphics

3. Graphics Arts

This includes desktop publishing, graphic arts, charts, and all duplication services (color and black and white)

- Rules of engagement, target, range and preventive maintenance cards
- Programs for special events
- Operation orders, maps, overlays, etc.
- Instructional and training materials
- Publications reproduction to CD

4. Reprographics

- Digital color press capabilities
- Reproduction of all classes of documentation (up to Secret)
- Reproduce local documents, SOP's, letterheads, etc.
- Reproduce documents of all sizes
- Color media

COMCAM will be the central control point for video and still imagery assets, to include specialized imagery acquisition equipment that may be required by units or commands.

COMCAM imagery will be forwarded as expeditiously as possible to the Defense Imagery Management Operations Center (DIMOC) and Combat Camera Imagery Management Unit (CCIMU) for further dissemination to other DOD agencies as required.

Organic COMCAM Support

COMCAM is budgeted to support 15th MEU with products for operational commitments, daily operations, historical documentation, and training requirements. The requesting unit will receive a minimum of three copies of the COMCAM product for Command Historical files. Larger requirements will be on a case-by-case or reimbursable basis and can be coordinated with the COMCAM Chief.

1. Photographic Products

- Printed photo albums are twenty pages or less. Most have multiple images in a collage/mosaic-type manner on each page
- Photo CDs are limited by file size to 650 megabytes. Images will be recorded to CD in a manner that allows the unit to print a good quality 8"x 10" image on a 300 dots per inch (DPI) or higher inkjet or laser printer. If possible, all significant images will be recorded onto the CD or DVD
- Electronic mail attachments can be forwarded for unlimited internal command distribution per the commander's guidance

2. Video Products

- Video productions of significant events shall be produced for 15th MEU and subordinate units per reference (c). All internal distribution will be provided on DVD or Video Compact Disc (VCD).
- Raw or unedited footage can be provided to the requesting unit for critique or historical documentation per the request
- Video duplication of a single event shall be limited to ten copies. Any request beyond ten copies will be accomplished on a reimbursable basis or by the customer supplying materials.

3. Graphic Arts

- **Proofreading**. Proofreading is the customer's responsibility. COMCAM will provide the customer a "draft" copy of any reprographic production before final production. Once the final product is approved for mass production any further changes will not be accepted unless approved by the COMCAM Chief.
- **Graphic Design & Desktop Publishing**. The Graphics section can produce training charts, enlarge maps, capture video/audio and edit desktop publishing.
- **Color Printing**. Advancements in technology have made it possible for color printing to be economical and are now the standard for reproduction.

4. Reprographics

Reprographics can reproduce large volume copies of operational plans and orders, training plans, administrative documents, etc.

5. Other Command Support

15th MEU COMCAM if directed by the 15th MEU Commanding Officer will provide units outside the 15th MEU with COMCAM support on a reimbursable basis or by providing the supplies and materials to accomplish the mission. COMCAM will provide the unit fiscal guidance for each request.

6. Classification Information

Classification or political sensitivity will not be used as a basis to deny operational documentation. COMCAM Marines are trained to properly label, handle and safeguard classified material.

- All COMCAM Marines will have at a minimum "Secret" level clearance or interim Secret clearance level status
- COMCAM is authorized to hold classified material over-night. Commands that require classified material support will submit their request through the S-3 Secondary Control Point (SCP).

Releasing Media

The 15th MEU Public Affairs Officer (PAO) will coordinate with the COMCAM Chief for unedited releasable video media (CD, DVD, etc) and still photography (digital or print) support for events to satisfy media requests, such as:

- Action shots of units involved in operations
- Unclassified military structures
- Initial force landings
- Unclassified Command Posts
- Unclassified press and VIP briefings
- Various types of equipment, especially new items
- Civil affairs, community relations, or humanitarian assistance or acts
- Accidents and incidents (after investigations are complete)
- Rescue, medical evacuations and medical care
- Interviews with commanders and personnel

5. Releasing Authority

The Personal Affairs Officer (PAO) will be the releasing authority for all imagery (video or still) given to outside media or other sources. The PAO will ensure that released imagery is unclassified and falls within standards for publicly released information. The 15th MEU PAO can delegate releasing authority to the COMCAM Chief at his/her discretion with the approval of the Commanding Officer of the 15th MEU.

V. Training

COMCAM is adaptive and provide fully qualified and equipped personnel to support sustained day/night operations. Their flexibility facilitates the tailoring of support for the full spectrum of operations including regional conflicts, small-scale contingencies, peacekeeping and foreign humanitarian relief operations.

Training Capabilities

- Video/Still Acquisition & Editing
- Production Development Layout & Design
- Imagery Transmission
- Large Scale Production
- Night Imagery Acquisition
- Aerial Imagery Acquisition
- Survival, Evasion, Resistance and Escape (SERE)
- Aircrew Qualified
- Visit, Board, Search and Seizure (VBSS)
- Helicopter Rope Suspension Technique (HRST)
- Special Operations Capability (SOC) Qualifications
- Raids Packages
- Maritime Interdiction Operations
- Close Quarters Combat
- Maritime Special Purpose Force (MSPF)
- Amphibious Reconnaissance
- Direct Action
- Tactical Recovery of Aircraft and Personnel
- High Risk Personnel (HRP)

Equipment

- 1- Combat Still Acquisition System (CSAS)
- 1- Combat Video Acquisition System (CVAS)
- 2- Visual Information Imagery Editing System (VIIES)
- 1- Canon 800mm DSLR Telephoto lens
- 1- Night Vision Acquisition System (NVAS)

IV. Logistics (MEU S-4)

Mission

To provide logistics, supply and embarkation coordination and in order to support all elements of the MEU. The MEU Logistics (S-4) Section will coordinate all MEU level logistics related requirements as well as assist each Major Subordinate Element (MSE) S-4 Section in planning and execution of their associated training/missions.

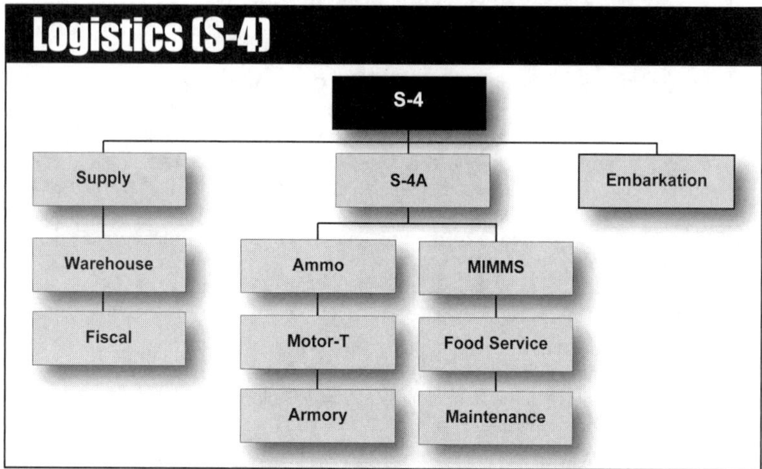

Command Element S-4 Section T/O			
Logistics Officer	Maj	0402	1
Assistant Logistics Officer	Capt	0402	1
Supply Officer	Capt	3002	1
Embarkation Officer	Capt	0430	1
Logistics Chief	MSgt	0491	1
Ammunition Chief	GySgt	2311	1
Embarkation Chief	SSgt	0431	1
Supply Chief	SSgt	3043	1
Warehouse Chief	SSgt	3051	1
Financial Management Chief	Sgt	3451	1
Embarkation Clerk	Sgt	0431	1
Motor Transport Operator	Sgt	3531	1
Motor Transport Mechanic	Sgt	3521	2
Maintenance Management NCO	Cpl	0411	1
Supply Clerk	Cpl	3043	1
Warehouse Clerk	Cpl	3051	1
Food Service Specialist	Cpl	3381	1
Infantry Weapons Repairer	Cpl	2111	1

Deployment Augmentation			
Contracting Officer (KO)	SSgt	3044	1
Financial Management Officer	1stLt	3404	1
Ammunition Technician	Cpl	2311	1
Logistics Planner	Capt – SSgt	04xx	1
Mess Chief	GySgt	3381	1
Maintenance Management Chief	SSgt	0411	1
Electrician	Sgt	1141	1
Generator Mechanic	Cpl	1142	1
Refrigeration Mechanic	LCpl	1161	1
Embarkation NCO	Cpl	0431	1

I. Logistics Planning Concepts

Certain basic concepts govern logistics/Combat Service Support (CSS) planning and operations. It is the application of these concepts that often produces conflict among the principles of CSS discussed in MCWP 4-1.

- Logistics/CSS planning will be concurrent and parallel with tactical planning to maximize support of the concept of operations
- Logistics/CSS planners must exploit organizational capabilities before requesting assistance from external sources
- To the greatest extent possible, the MAGTF commander must relieve combat and combat support units of CSS burdens
- The logistics/CSS system must be responsive, flexible, simple and economical. This requires application of the concepts of redundancy, austerity and centralization

Logistics/CSS Planner's Responsibilities

Throughout the planning for and execution of an operation, logistics officers must constantly re-evaluate support requirements. Continuously analyzing tactical and support operations, they identify and properly employ their resources to satisfy requirements. To provide responsive and sustained support, the operational logistician must anticipate requirements that exceed organic capabilities and forward timely requests for assistance to higher headquarters and/or external agencies to meet known shortfalls.

A. Planning Sequence

Following receipt of the initiating directive or warning order, logistics/CSS planning proceeds concurrently at all echelons throughout the MEU. The MEU concept of operations ashore is the basis for detailed CSS planning, which generally proceeds, in the following sequence:

Sequence of Planning

1. **Determination of overall requirements**
2. **Statement of requirements to higher authority**
3. **Allocation of resources and assignment of priorities**
4. **Preparation of detailed plans and orders**

Determination of overall requirements

Based on the MEU Commander's concept of operations, detailed CSS requirements are computed for each successive stage of the operation. Quantities and types of required equipment and supplies and other CSS needs are determined at the Major Subordinate Element (MSE) level and forwarded via the chain of command to the MEU S-4 for consolidation.

Sea basing

Normally, for MEU operations it is unnecessary to transfer substantial Landing Force supplies and CSS organizations ashore. Sea basing provides for limited CSS elements to become temporarily established ashore and allows for the majority of CSS assets to remain at sea and be sent ashore only when needed. When CSS is sea based, additional consideration must be devoted during the planning phase to ensure that CSS capabilities are balanced aboard those amphibious ships best suited to provide support. Additionally, sea basing increases helicopter support

Concept of Logistics Support

The effort of logistics support planning is focused on the requirements of the supported force in executing the Commander's operational plan. The objective of the Marine Expeditionary Unit (MEU) logistics planning effort is the integration of logistics sustainability with the firepower and mobility requirements of the Marine Air Ground Task Force (MAGTF). The focus of all logistics and supply personnel within the MEU is on the achievement of uninterrupted support within all Combat Service Support functional areas:

Logistics Support

1. Supply
2. Maintenance
3. Transportation
4. General Engineering
5. Health Services
6. Services

Major Subordinate Commands (MSC)

Major Subordinate Commands (MSC) will provide logistic support to deploying Major Subordinate Elements (MSE) in accordance with current I Marine Expeditionary Force (MEF) directives until composition of the MEU. Once composited, the Marine Expeditionary Unit (MEU) will continue to use I MEF as the primary source for all logistic support, to include funding throughout the deployment period. MEUs will be authorized to source logistic and supply support through local available sources within each theater of operation that the MEU transits. All funding for military or civilian contracted support will be the responsibility of the MEU and ultimately I MEF throughout the deployment period.

Combat Logistics Battalion (CLB)

The MEU Combat Logistics Battalion (CLB) will be the primary source of non-aviation logistic support following composition and during deployment. The Navy aviation supply/ maintenance departments organic to the LHA/LHD will be the primary source of logistic support for aviation-peculiar supplies. Supplies beyond the capabilities of the CLB will be requisitioned through the 1st MLG (if the items are readily available). Aviation peculiar supplies will be requisitioned through normal Navy channels by the senior Amphibious Ready Group (ARG) Supply Officer who normally resides aboard the LHA/LHD.

15 Days-Of-Supply (DOS)

The MEU will embark and maintain a minimum of 15 Days-Of-Supply (DOS) of all classes of supply unless specifically exempted by I MEF. It is at the discretion of the MEU Commander to determine the number of DOS of Class V(W) per DODIC to be embarked, not to exceed 15 DOS, unless authorized by CG, I MEF. Those supplies in Landing Force Operational Reserve Materiel (LFORM) will be counted towards this requirement. Embarkation of supplies and equipment will also be determined and/or prioritized based on the stowage space available aboard each ship of the ARG.

requirements since it involves an increased reliance on maintenance contact teams and replenishment by helicopter. In the event that air is not available, more time may be required to utilize landing craft to support operations ashore. This could take a substantial amount of time based on the location of the ship, availability of the landing craft, and sea state. Once the items are on the beach, transportation must be coordinated to move it to the unit requesting support.

B. Internal MEU Logistics Coordination

Following initial Mission Analysis, conducted by the Combined Action Team (CAT), each MSE will be assigned a role in planning and/or supporting the mission. During planning each MSEs S-4 should be monitoring and/or interacting with the primary mission MSE S-4 to provide any required support. Once support requirements associated to the mission have been identified, the primary MSE S-4 will coordinate directly with the MEU S-4. Logistics Support Requests (LSR) will be submitted to the MEU S-4 (Logistics Chief) for authorization and CLB tasking. Following approval and tasking by the MEU S-4, the CLB personnel aboard the respective ship will commence detailed coordination with the requesting MSE for delivery of necessary supplies.

C. Logistic Support Requests (LSR)

The LSR is a key document to ensure all proper information is obtained in relation to support requests and those requests are properly recorded. LSRs will be submitted for all classes of supply to include day-to-day operational requirements and/or port visits (i.e. rental vehicles/local cell phones). The LSR is normally filled out and submitted electronically, but can be printed and hand submitted as required. The requests can/will also support the maintenance of supply accounting to ensure both MSE and CE records are accurate.

While conducting ship-to-shore operations the MEU will coordinate logistics support through the Tactical-Logistics (TACLOG) agency. The LHA/D TACLOG will be the primary logistics coordination center for the Amphibious Ready Group (ARG). If the ARG is conducting split-ARG or "disaggregated" operations, then the individual ship (LPD/LSD) TACLOG will become the lead agency for the Landing Force (LF) organic to that ship. LF requests will be submitted through the Landing Force Support Party (LFSP) ashore, which is normally assigned to establish and manage the Beach Landing Site (BLS) and follow-on Beach Support Area (BSA). The LFSP will relay all requests to the TACLOG for movement of support materiel ashore. TACLOGs will maintain the current status of supplies aboard the ARG in support of the LF.

While executing operations ashore, the MEU S-4 (located within the MEU CP) will receive all support requests from the MSEs and coordinate with the MEU S-3 for appropriate MSE tasking to support necessary requirements. MSEs will submit requests, to include Rapid Requests, through their organic S-4 sections who will fill the requirement or pass it to the MEU if the requirement is beyond the MSEs organic capability to support.

Logistics Reporting Requirements

During field exercises/operations, the MEU will continue to maintain and track our logistical readiness. In order to maintain an up-to-date status of each MSE and CE for the MEU Commander, each MSE will submit a daily logistics report to the MEU S-4 either electronically or via the radio (MEU Command Net 2). The following report will be submitted daily when conducting field operations or while deployed:

15 MEU LOGISTICS SUMMARY REPORT		
FROM:	MSE (CALL SIGN IF VIA RADIO)	S-4 Comments:
TO:	MEU S-4 (CALL SIGN IF VIA RADIO)	
CLASSIFICATION:		
SUBJECT:	LOGISTICS SUMMARY	
A.	Rpt # _____ of _____	
B.	Location/Number of PAX:	Unit: ________ | PAX: _____ | Loc/Grid: __________
Remarks:		Unit: ________ | PAX: _____ | Loc/Grid: __________
		Unit: ________ | PAX: _____ | Loc/Grid: __________
C.	Class I (Chow):	Loc/Grid: __________ | DOS: __________
Remarks:		Loc/Grid: __________ | DOS: __________
		Loc/Grid: __________ | DOS: __________
D.	Class I (Water):	Loc/Grid: __________ | DOS: __________
Remarks:		Loc/Grid: __________ | DOS: __________
		Loc/Grid: __________ | DOS: __________
E.	Class I Critical Shortages:	Loc/Grid: ________ | Item: ________ | Qty: ______
F.	Class II Critical Shortages:	Loc/Grid: ________ | Item: ________ | Qty: ______
G.	Class III (Fuel):	Type: ______ | Loc/Grid: ______ | Gal: _____ | DOS: _____
Remarks:		Type: ______ | Loc/Grid: ______ | Gal: _____ | DOS: _____
		Type: ______ | Loc/Grid: ______ | Gal: _____ | DOS: _____
H.	Class III (Lube) Shortages:	Type: ______ | Required: ______ | Loc/Grid: ________
I.	Class IV Critical Shortages:	Type: ______ | Required: ______ | Loc/Grid: ________
J.	Class V(W) Shortages:	DODIC: _____ | Qty: ______ | Loc/Grid: ________
Remarks:		DODIC: _____ | Qty: ______ | Loc/Grid: ________
		DODIC: _____ | Qty: ______ | Loc/Grid: ________
K.	Class VI Critical Shortages:	Item: ______ | Qty: ______ | Loc/Grid: ________
L.	Class VII Shortages:	Item: ______ | Qty: ______ | Loc/Grid: ________
Remarks:		Item: ______ | Qty: ______ | Loc/Grid: ________
		Item: ______ | Qty: ______ | Loc/Grid: ________
M.	Class VIII Shortages:	Item: ______ | Qty: ______ | Loc/Grid: ________
Remarks:		Item: ______ | Qty: ______ | Loc/Grid: ________
		Item: ______ | Qty: ______ | Loc/Grid: ________
N.	Class IX Shortages:	Item: ______ | Qty: ______ | Loc/Grid: ________
Remarks:		Item: ______ | Qty: ______ | Loc/Grid: ________
		Item: ______ | Qty: ______ | Loc/Grid: ________
O.	Casualties Evacuated:	Qty: _____ | DTG: ______ (as of) | Loc/Grid: ________
P.	Casualties Awaiting Evac:	Qty: _____ | DTG: ______ (as of) | Loc/Grid: ________
Q.	Maint Cont Team (MCT):	TAMCN: ________ | Loc/Grid: __________
Remarks:		Maint Issue :
R.	Maint Deadlined Equip:	TAMCN: _____ | Type: ______ | Loc/Grid: _____ | DTG: ______
Remarks:		TAMCN: _____ | Type: ______ | Loc/Grid: _____ | DTG: ______
		TAMCN: _____ | Type: ______ | Loc/Grid: _____ | DTG: ______

Fig 4-3 Example Logistics Summary Report Form

II. Supply

Prior to composite, each Major Subordinate Command (MSC) is responsible for providing logistical/supply support to their Major Subordinate Elements (MSEs). While the MEU Commander can coordinate with each MSC as to the status of the MSEs scheduled to join the MEU, to include purchasing equipment/materiels prior to composition, the MEU does not have a supported/supporting relationship. Upon composition, those roles reverse and the MEU then becomes the higher headquarters (HHQ) for each MSE and attachment (i.e. Radio Battalion, Force Reconnaissance, etc). Therefore, each MSE must have a complete understanding of the MEU's business practices IOT properly interact, plan and support their individual element. As such, the following section will address the major issues associated to MEU supply operations in general. However, as every issue or situation can not be addressed, it is the responsibility of the MEU Logistics and Supply Officers to address unique situations as they occur and incorporate policies and procedures to rectify any gaps in support.

Forwarding of Repair Parts

When the MEU is deployed, 1st MLG (SMU) will forward all repair parts received for the CLB, to include SECREP shortfalls. A naval message will be sent to the MEU and the CLB stating by document number those items received and shipped by 1st MLG.

CLB Ashore

If the CLOC is not established ashore, the requesting S-4 will forward the request to the TACLOG. The TACLOG will then coordinate with the CLB TACLOG representative who in turn will task the CLB (afloat) to fill the requisition.

Requisition Management

The CLB will provide a recap of all resupply rapid requests filled during an exercise/operation, or weekly in the case of extended operations, to the supported unit Supply Officer so that fiscal visibility is maintained.

Use of Rapid Requests

Rapid Requests for supplies will only be submitted while in the field. Rapid requests will not be accepted by the CLB prior to the start of field exercises/operations ashore, nor will they be filled for units still embarked. Embarked units will requisition supplies using normal Marine Corps Asset Tracking Logistics and Supply Subsystems (ATLASS) procedures.

Open Purchase of Supplies

If an MSE Supply Officer determines that supplies cannot be obtained through the normal supply system, an open purchase request will be submitted to the MEU S-4, via the MEU Supply Officer. If the MEU S-4 concurs and the fiscal posture of the MEU allows, the request will be approved and forwarded to the ship's Supply Office for requisition. Items purchased ashore will require the establishment of contracted services. During field exercises and operations, these requests will be routed through the CLOC/TACLOG as required.

MSEs are not authorized to enter into agreements to purchase supplies or services on behalf of the 15th MEU from any unit, agency or vendor. Failure to abide by this procedure could cause the responsible individual to be personally liable for the cost of supplies or services rendered.

A. Force Activity Designator (FAD)

Elements of the MEU are in Force Activity Designator (FAD) II as provided for in the current edition of MCO 4400.16. As such, MEU elements are authorized to originate supply requisitions up to Priority 02. At E-90, 1st MLG will load committed code 02 for all MEU elements in accordance with the current edition of UM-4400.124. The following schedule will be used in establishing requisition priorities:

- **E-90**: Priority 02 for T/E mission-essential and deadlining/degrading mission essential repair parts. Priority 05 or 12, as appropriate for non-mission essential repair parts.
- **E-60**: Upgrade to Priority 02 non-mission essential T/E equipment deficiencies
- **E-30**: Upgrade all OPDEP back orders to Priority 02

B. Contracted Services

Request Process

If contracted services are required for field exercises/operations, exercise planners will identify these requirements to the MEU S-4 via their supporting S-4. Requirements should be identified on an open purchase request form and will contain a thorough justification. Requests will be reviewed by the MEU S-4 prior to being forwarded for purchasing action. Exercise planners are not authorized to enter into agreements to purchase supplies or services from anyone. Failure to abide by this procedure could cause the planner to be personally liable for the cost of such supplies or services.

Contingency Contracting Officer (KO)

As of 3 February 2011, I MEF has been directed that all west coast MEUs will be directly supported by a KO during both their deployment work up and deployment. The KO will join the MEU between E-180 and E-90 as MEF contracting personnel supports. The KO will fall under the direction of the MEU Supply Officer for coordination and establishment of all external support requirements.

C. Naval Logistics Integration (NLI)

Objective

The objective of NLI is to establish an integrated naval logistics capability that can operate seamlessly whether afloat or ashore, successfully supporting and sustaining naval operations unit in a joint warfighting environment.

Concept

NLI provides access and combines both Navy/Marine Corps logistics/supply agencies to provide greater depth of support. Prior to NLI initiatives, both the Navy and Marine Corps conducted support operations separately and only converged with regard to specific support areas (i.e. Marine aviation). Following establishment of NLI, all agencies to include Fleet Industrial Supply Centers (FISC), Priority Management Office (PMO), Husbanding Agencies and Global Distance Support Center (GDSC) services are now made available to support each service's requirements equally in greater support of the combined mission.

NLI/MEU Integration

The CLB Supply Officer is the primary MEU coordinator with regard to all NLI integration/support operations. As the CLB is assigned the mission of support the MEU, the additional support capabilities provide the CLB Supply Officer with increased ability to find and deliver required support items. While deployed, the CLB Supply Officer will work directly with the MEU Supply Officer (section) and MEU Logistics Officer to plan, coordinate and determine priorities prior to leveraging any NLI assets as some services (i.e. PMO) incur increased sourcing/delivery costs.

D. Class of Supply Requirements

The Landing Force Operational Reserve Material (LFORM) and Mission Load Allowance (MLA) stocks embarked aboard amphibious ships are for contingency purposes. Class III Bulk is an exception to this rule. In addition to those stocks, the CLB and/or other MEU elements will embark with the below listed supply blocks. Each class of supply represents anticipated requirements which fulfill operational/training requirements for the MEU while deployed.

Class I: Subsistence

Coordination for subsistence requires detailed planning and various lead times IOT ensure the right rations are available to support the mission/exercises. Early coordination between the MEU Food Service SNCOIC (S-4 Section) and the I MEF Food Service Officer (FSO) is essential; this ensures adequate support is provided in a timely manner.

- **Rations Embarkation Planning**. The MEU Food Service personnel (CE), in conjunction with the MEU S-4, will determine the number of DOS the MEU will embark aboard the ARG (in addition to LFORM). However, the goal of the MEU is to always load 15 DOS if possible (regardless of LFORM). The rations planning will be based off of anticipated training events both during PTP and while deployed. MEU Food Service personnel will coordinate with both the base and the MEU Embarkation Officer for both movement and loading of rations aboard ARG shipping. Every effort should be expended to ensure a mixture of rations is embarked to support the unit during deployments; this avoids excessive TOT cost and establishing large logistics pipelines from CONUS to support deployed units. Once embarked, the CLB will manage all rations and provide detailed usage reports to the MEU S-4 IOT maintain accountability. MSEs will submit an LSR to the MEU S-4 to request rations support.
- **Humanitarian Assistance/Disaster Relief (HA/DR) Support**. During deployments when HA/DR operations are conducted, Class I subsistence items cannot be used to feed affected personnel under these programs. Only military personnel, or United States citizens, can be supported. Approval for such feeding programs must be obtained in advance from HQMC/OSD. The use of subsistence supplies procured through Marine Corps MPMC subsistence in kind (SIK) funding is not permitted.

Class III: Petroleum, Oils, Lubricants (POL)

- **Bulk POL**. The MEU will submit requests to draw bulk fuel (JP-5/8 and MOGAS) from LFORM to the PHIBRON identifying priority, quantity, and sourcing ship(s). 1st Marine Logistics Group (MLG) is responsible for providing bulk MOGAS (unleaded fuel) storage containers as well as the initial LFORM POL quantities. The MEU will coordinate with both I MEF G-4 and the MLG for scheduling the movement and embarkation of the fuel.
- **Packaged POL**. A 15-day OPDEP block of selected POL (55-gallon drum or smaller) will be controlled and embarked by the CLB. It is recommended that Principal End Items (PEIs) be embarked with 15-40 weight oil in preparation for possible cold weather. This POL will be controlled and accounted for in the Consumable Class IX block and on the CLB LUBF. All MEU elements will identify, procure and deploy with adequate stocks to perform all preventive maintenance functions for the first 30-days of deployment. Care must be taken to ensure that annual PMs for major PEIs, whenever possible, are performed prior to deployment or deferred until post-deployment to eliminate the requirement to carry large amounts of POL. While deployed, replenishment will be provided by 1st MLG through available DSU outlets. Cold weather and other POL requirements will be submitted to the CLB NLT E-90.

Class V: Ammunition

See discussion later for ammunition (pp. 108-109) related information.

Class VIII: Medical Supplies

- **AMAL/ADAL Blocks**. The BLT will embark Authorized Medical Allowance List (AMAL) blocks customary to the establishment of an Aid Station with narcotics. The CLB will embark AMAL blocks customary to the establishment of an Aid Station with narcotics and enhanced shock, surgical and triage capabilities. Anti-malarial drugs will be ordered by the CLB prior to deployment based on number of personnel going into country and number of days in country. When requesting AMALS, specific consideration should be given to the treatment of NBC casualties and injuries likely in certain geographic locations. Additionally, the Authorized Dental Allowance List (ADAL) block will be embarked by the CLB. All blocks will be picked up from Medical Logistics Company, 1st MLG, according to timeline established by the CG, I MEF LOI for Deployment. Each MSE will deploy with 30-DOS of common "sick-call" items to be used during training exercises. Replenishment of the "sick-call" items will be through the CLB's OPDEP block. Additional replenishment stocks will be ordered from 1st MLG while deployed. While embarked, units will receive medical support from the ships.
- **Medical Funding Issues**. Title 10 funding for medical and dental supplies in support of MEDCAP/DENTCAP programs will be made available in accordance with CENTCOM Regulations 525-23. Operations, logistics, medical and fiscal personnel all need to ensure the planning and execution of medical/dental support operations are properly funded via the correct fiscal programs as U.S. military personnel support is funded separate from other operations designed to assist foreign personnel.

Class IX: Repair Parts

Prior to composition each MSE will continue to use order parts against their parent commands fiscal accounts. Once composited, each MSE will begin to order parts against the MEU's cost JON. In conjunction with MEU funding, the consumable Class IX block built and maintained by the CLB is a primary source of materiels. Once updated and established the Class IX block will be the primary (first) source used by the MEU to fill any and/or all repair part requirements. Using the block during PTP will help to verify usage rates as well as carrying individual parts within the block. During PTP and throughout deployment the CLB will be the main POC for contact between the MEU and the Sassy Management Unit (SMU) or Deployed Support Unit (DSU). Care must be exercised to ensure that the CLB embarks with its complete allowance. However, the block will be prioritized against other MEU requirements and if determined that the entire block can not be embarked, the MEU Commander will be briefed with regard to the potential risk that is assumed. All OPDEP block back orders will be upgraded to priority 02 NLT E-30. When the block is turned over to the CLB, a wall-to-wall inventory will be conducted prior to embarkation. It is recommended that the GCE, ACE and CLB conduct this inventory jointly IOT ensure that sufficient quantities and types of Class IX items are included in the block and to identify any deficiencies.

- **SECREPS**. The CLB will embark with a 30-day OPDEC block of SECREPS repair parts. This block will be replenished by 1st MLG during the pre-deployment phase.
- **PEB Items.** Pre-Expended Bin (PEB) items may be carried in the Class IX block, however it is necessary that each MEU element deploy with 30-60 days of PEB items since the PWR Generator Package will not normally factor in PEB items.
- **SL-3 Requirements**. All equipment must be l00% SL-3 complete when attaching to the MEU at composition per I MEF's SL-3 policy. Shortages must be procured from the parent command prior to embarkation. Ensure that requisitions are not submitted to the CLB which would either deplete the OPDEP block or require the requisition to be passed to 1st MLG. Requisitions for SL-3 components will not be submitted to the CLB unless the shortage can be directly attributed to a MEU related exercise. Only SL-3 components which deadline combat essential equipment will be requisitioned via an Equipment Repair Order (ERO).

III. Maintenance

The maintenance policies and procedures of a unit are normally not the focal point of discussion during breaks or out in the field. Maintenance is normally a last consideration in planning and usually left to the Maintenance Management Officer (MMO) and/or the Logistics Officer to track and maintain the overall maintenance effort. However, without an effective and understood maintenance plan, a units ability to execute its mission can be severely hindered if not compromised. Therefore, it is the responsibility from the Commanding Officer down to the most junior Marine to ensure the unit's equipment is properly maintained and cared for.

Publications

- All MSEs and attachments will report to the MEU with all of their appropriate publications on hand.
- All MSEs and maintenance personnel will refer to the 15th MEU Maintenance Management Standard Operating Procedures (MMSOP) for greater detail and direction regarding maintenance management actions.

A. Echelon of Maintenance

- MEU elements are authorized to perform maintenance in accordance with their mission statement. The CLB is authorized third echelon and limited fourth echelon maintenance. The MEU Commander may authorize limited third echelon maintenance capability to the BLT and the CE if the parent commands include third echelon repair men and tools with the detachments. Coordination must be made between the BLT, CE, and CLB concerning the limits of the third echelon maintenance to be done by the BLT and CE.
- The CLB Commander must coordinate with the Maintenance Support Officer, 1st MLG to ensure that fourth echelon maintenance limits are clearly defined

B. MIMMS / GCSS-MC

Marine Corps Integrated Maintenance Management System (MIMMS)

The Marine Corps is still currently using MIMMS as its primary maintenance management tool at the time this MEU order was re-written. Therefore, in order to provide adequate maintenance support while deployed, MEU elements must be fully trained in PC MIMMS as a Class I and Class II system. While the MEU Command Element's (CE) attachments/detachments (i.e. Radio Bn, ANGLICO, etc) will be absorbed into the CE's MIMMS coverage at composition, the MSEs will need to have multiple personnel available provide all necessary maintenance management coverage, especially while conducting split ARG operations. The 1st MLG MISCO is responsible to provide the training as required.

Global Combat Support System-Marine Corps (GCSS-MC)

The Marine Corps is currently transitioning to the GCSS-MC network to provide a more modern and capable requesting, tracking and reporting system. This new system will be fielded to the MEUs, and the rest of the Marine Corps, starting in Calendar Year (CY) 2011. This system will combine several separate systems (i.e. PC MIMMS, SASSY and ATLASS) into one system with the desired effect of streamlining support actions throughout the Corps. Aside from improving basic business practices, this system will provide increased visibility to commanders at all levels with regard equipment readiness. The 15th MEU is currently scheduled to complete the GCSS-MC migration and deploy with the system during Western Pacific (WESTPAC) 12-2. Once the transition is completed, this order and the MEU's MMSOP will need to be updated.

C. Maintenance Reconciliation & Reporting

Pre-Deployment

Upon composite of the MEU, each MSE will maintain their respective readiness data. Each MSE will report their MARES equipment readiness levels to the MEU in association with DRRS reporting. Also, the MEU S-4 will sponsor a bi-monthly maintenance meeting (scheduled via the TEEP) to review and discuss in-depth all maintenance related issues (not MARES specifically) affecting the entire MEU.

Deployment

Maintenance Meetings. During deployment the MEU will still be required to submit DRRS reports identifying the MEU's readiness. However, there will be an increased requirement to monitor and manage the MEU's overall maintenance stature to ensure mission accomplishment. This effort heavily relies on all logistics, supply and maintenance officers/personnel to understand the current and long-term readiness issues. Therefore, the MEU S-4 will coordinate and schedule the following maintenance related meetings to occur on the MEU's flag ship (LHA/D) while deployed:

- **MSE Reconciliation Meeting.** This meeting will be coordinated and managed by the CLB's Supply and Maintenance Officers and will occur once per week. The intent of this meeting is to identify and coordinate all required corrective actions with regard to each MSEs Daily Processing Report (DPR). This meeting is designed to ensure the CLB and MIMMS personnel are receiving each MSEs required reports, paperwork and cross-coordination.
- **MEU Maintenance Meeting.** This meeting will be coordinated and managed by the MEU S-4/S-4A and will occur once per week. The intent of this meeting is to provide the MEU Commanding/Executive Officer with a detailed briefing with regard to the MEU's overall maintenance readiness. Each MSE will brief their DPR and/or associated maintenance issues. In addition, the CLB Supply/Maintenance Officer will brief any related order/shipment/receiving issues associated to Class IX (repair parts).

Field Readiness Reporting. Daily Situation Reports (SitReps) will be submitted from all MSEs (attachments as required) to the MEU S-4 NLT 1800 daily detailing MARES reportable equipment, MEU designated equipment (in addition to MARES), current status of equipment, parts on order, and any amplifying information related to deadlined equipment.

Deadlined Equipment. Any equipment deadlined by the owning MSE or CLB will be immediately reported to the MEU S-4

- MSEs will establish a maintenance plan to ensure preventive maintenance and corrosion control is conducted throughout the deployment. Coordination will be conducted with the MEU S-4 to schedule required support (ventilation fans, stowage access issues, etc) to accomplished each MSEs plan.
- At a minimum, one maintenance stand-down period will be scheduled and conducted during the deployment.

Post-Deployment

Post-deployment reporting will be dominated by the JLTI process. The MEU will not specifically schedule any maintenance meetings outside the JLTI coordination effort. It should be expected that each MSE/attachment will be required to provide a representative to attend all MEF JLTI coordination meetings.

D. MEU Maintenance Management Officer (MMO)

The MEU MMO is responsible for ensuring that all MEU elements are using MIMMS procedures, that they understand the reconciliation process outlined in I MEF directives, and that weekly reconciliations are conducted once the CLB becomes the first source of third echelon repair. The MEU MMO is responsible for ensuring the accuracy of the readiness portion of the Weekly Situation Report; this is especially important while deployed. The MEU MMO is the coordinator of the MEU maintenance effort during the stand up period, maintenance standdowns, exercises, and the post-deployment phase. He is required to coordinate predeployment training and briefs with the MISCO and all element MMOs/MMCs and MM Clerks. This training should be scheduled at a minimum of two (2) different stages during the pre-deployment phase.

E. Funding Responsibility

Composition

During composition, the equipment being transferred from the MSCs to the MEU is the direct responsibility of the individual MSC (Division, MLG or MAW). They will be required to fund all necessary actions required to ensure the their equipment is condition code "A". If required, they will coordinate with the I MEF Comptroller for additional funding. However, it is generally in the MEU Commander's best interest to assist in any function to ensure the MSE is 100% mission capable at the time of composition.

Decomposition

Upon return from deployment, and the decomposition of the MEU MSEs, the MEU will generally be responsible for any funding requirements associated with returning the MSE's equipment to their parent command. However, the level of funding responsibility associated to the MEU will be based on the composition JLTI findings as well as I MEF's overall assessment of the decomposite JLTI process. The MEU will not be responsible for funding maintenance actions on equipment and/or items that were determined to be in disrepair upon joining the MEU at composition.

MEF Funding

Regardless, the MEF Comptroller will provide direct funding authorization to the applicable MSCs for the MSE's JLTI costs. The actual value of the direct funds transfer will be the average post-deployment JLTI maintenance costs of the last three MEUs. MSCs will provide total JLTI costs to I MEF G-4 and Comptroller within 30 days after transfer of equipment from the returning MEU to the MSC.

IV. Ammunition

Class V ammunitions are divided into two classes: Class V(A) aviation munitions and Class V(W) ground munitions. Although both classes of ammunition support MEU requirements, each has their own change of responsibility. The Navy, along with coordination from the ACE munitions officer, is responsible for the procurement, loading and management of aviation ammunition. Ground ammunition, to include the ACE's ground support elements (i.e. MACG det), is the management responsibility of the MEU S-4. Regardless of the responsible element, each ship's Weapons Department will coordinate and manage the overall ammunition requirements within the ARG as they will ultimately manage each ship's ammunition holds.

A. Ammunition Expenditure Reports

Upon completion of all scheduled training, the range OIC (assisted by the MSE Ammunitions Chief) will complete and submit an ammunition expenditure report to the MEU Ammunition Chief. The expenditure report will be submitted by MSEs to MEU S-4 NLT 24-hours following the completion of training. Follow-on ammunition issues will NOT be executed until the requesting MSE turns-in the previous ranges/training expenditure report. This will occur in both garrison as well as deployed.

B. Ground Ammunition Request Process

Prior to deployment, each MSE will submit their ammunition requests to the MEU Ammunition Chief for expenditure authorization and tracking purposes. The MEU Ammunition Chief, along with the MSE Ammunition Chief, will then coordinate with ASP personnel for staging and issue of requested ammunition. Once deployed, the CLB will assume the role of the ASP as they are assigned the responsibility of supporting all MEU requirements. The following figure depicts the ammunition request process while the MEU is deployed aboard the ARG:

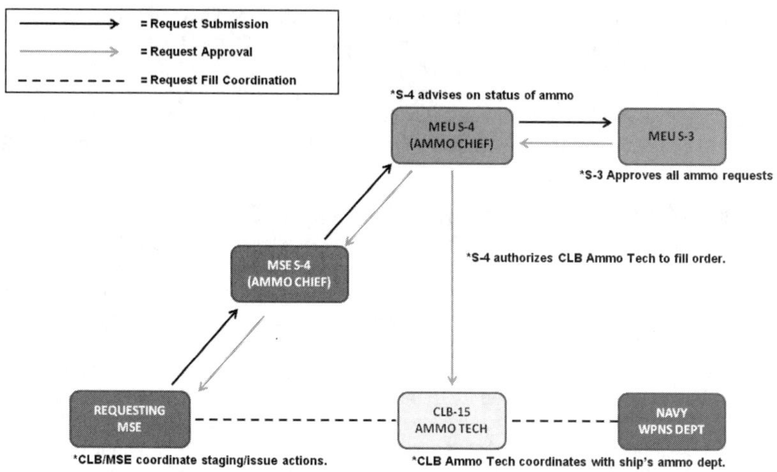

Example Flow chart for Ammunition Requests

C. Aviation Ammunition

Although the Air Combat Element (ACE) is part of the MAGTF, their maintenance and ammunition support is the responsibility of the Navy. Therefore, the MEU S-4 is not the primary agency to coordinate or manage the ACE's ammunition requirements. However, the MEU S-4 will monitor and influence (as required) the ACE's ammunition support IOT maintain situational awareness as well as ensure the support provided meets the expectations of the MEU Commander to accomplish all assigned missions.

Class V(A)

All aviation munition aboard the ARG is inventoried, stored, and maintained by the Ship's Weapons Department. The ACE's parent MALS Ordnance Officer (OrdO) submits, via naval message, the ACE's Non-Combat Expenditure Allocation (NCEA) to the ship IOT identify the requirements and allow for loading/storage planning. The ACE OrdO or SNOIC will ensure the NCEA is received by the Ship's Weapons Department and is supportable. If adjustments are required, then he will work with the ACE's parent MALS OrdO and Ship's Weapons OrdO.

Class V(A) Standard Training Package (STP)

The Standard Training Package (STP) and MLA are established by COMNAVSURFPAC ORDER 4080.1D and CGFMFPACO 4080.2D with amplifying instructions provided by CMC and/or COMMARFORPAC. The STP is aviation munitions positioned onboard the ship to be used for the ACE's training requirements. The STP munitions can only be used if they are supported in the ACE's NCEA. The ACE OrdO/SNCOIC will manage the ACE's NCEA and work with the Ship's Weapons Department to ensure only munitions on the ACE's NCEA are expended for training. They will ensure inventory, requisitioning, issue, receipt and expenditure reports are submitted and processed through the Ship's Weapons Department. The Ship's Weapons Department will submit Ammunition Transaction Reports (ATRs) IAW NAVSUP P-724 Conventional Ordnance Stockpile Management publication. He will work closely with the ACE's parent MALS OrdO and ACE OrdO on all changes to the NCEA and STP.

Mission Load Allowance (MLA)

Class V(A) munitions positioned on board ship as MLA are for contingency usage only. Only the numbered Fleet Commanders can authorize release of MLA for the ACE. The Ships Weapons Department will submit ATRs against the Ship's UIC vice the ACE MALS. Expenditures from the MLA do not count against the ACE's NCEA.

Class V(W)

It is imperative that all hands strive to maintain the maximum level of awareness regarding the accountability, storage, transportation, and safety of use for all Class V munitions. Each ship should have at least one Ammunition Technician (MOS 2311) from the CLB embarked to promote and maintain this awareness as well as manage all munitions in conjunction with the ship's weapons department.

Class V(W) Training Ammunition

Class V(W) training allowances are established by MCBul 8011 for PTP. The MEU S-4 Officer will actively manage all Class V(W) munitions allocations directed by the MEU S-3 and report to the I-MEF G-4 Ammo Officer. Embarked training ammunition allowances are established per COMNAVSURFPAC INST 4080 for MTA and LFORM.

- The MEU S-4 will manage training ammunition allowances. Some of the responsibilities will be delegated to the CLB pertaining to requisitioning, inventory and issue control. Expenditure reporting will be consolidated by the MEU S-4 and reported quarterly to I MEF AC/S G-4.

- Deploying units will embark or request prepositioning of Class V(W) above MTA allocation required for training exercises while deployed. Prepositioning of training assets will be coordinated with I MEF AC/S G-4 (Ammo) via naval message 90 days out from training. However, approval of requested allocations will be subject to I MEF's ability to supplement the request from within I MEF unit allocations.
- Identifying deploying units' Class V(W) training requirements is the responsibility of the deploying MEU's operations sections (to include all MSEs operations sections).
- Requests for prepositioning of training assets will be identified to the CG, I MEF AC/S G-4 (Ammo) NLT E-120 via naval message.
- Requests for prepositioning of training assets will be identified to the CG, I MEF AC/S G-4 (Ammo) NLT E-120 via naval message. This is a hard time-line due to the level of coordination required as well as actually physically moving the munitions from CONUS to CONUS or CONUS to OCONUS. During PTP evolutions the MEU S-4 will submit requisitions (MILSTRIP or DD Form 1348) for training ammunition to the supporting activity (e.g. Camp Pendleton, Ammunition Supply Point (ASP)). The MEU/CLB is responsible for coordinating the delivery of ammunition from the supporting ASP to the using unit.
- It is the deploying MEU's responsibility to make liaison with the PHIBRON to arrange for the onload of Class V(W) training ammunition from PTP allocations. On-load/off-load operations will normally be conducted via Vertical Replenishment (VERTREP) using helicopters from Landing Zone (LZ) Viewpoint on the coast of Camp Pendleton. MTA and LFORM are loaded per 4080 by NWS Fallbrook.
- Requests to embark ammunition over the shore line will be accomplished in accordance with BO P8000.2B. Requests must be endorsed by I MEF AC/S G-4 and cleared by the Explosives Safety office. The MEU Ammunition Chief will make all necessary liaisons as well as preparing all required documentation.

Contingency Ammunition

The quantities and types of Class V(W) materiel are based on the Combat Planning Factors (CPF's) established in the current edition of MCO 8010.1E (Class V(W) Planning Factors for Fleet Marine Force Combat Operations) and the personnel and weapons density of a MEU. The standard MEU Class V(W) LFORM package is found in the current edition of COMNAVSURFPACINST 4080.I and FMFPacO 4080.2.

- **Duties and Responsibilities.** Guidance for accountability and reporting of LFORM and MLA embarked aboard amphibious ships is contained in the current edition of COMNAVSURFPACINST 4080.I/FMFPacO 4080.2.
- **Withdrawal Authority.** Class V(W) LFORM assets may be released by numbered Fleet Commanders to embarked FMF units when required under actual combat or contingency conditions in accordance with the current edition of FMFPacO 4080.2. LFORM may also be used by the direction of the MEU Commander, without the approval of the numbered fleet commander (if time doesn't permit), to support real world contingency operations. Once LFORM ammunition has been used, a notification report will be submitted to the numbered fleet commander (a copy sent to I MEF G-4) detailing the situation followed by a munitions expenditure report (as required).

V. Embarkation

Due to the nature of deploying MEUs, embarkation readiness is a fundamental ingredient in the overall combat readiness of the MEU. This discussion is designed to clarify and add emphasis to doctrine, existing Navy/Marine Corps publications and procedures gained through the experience of several deployments.

See "Embarkation Duties and Responsibilities" on following pages for further discussion.

A. Embarkation Planning

- **Ship's Loading Characteristics Pamphlets (SLCP).** The SLCP is a written document that describes the ship's actual loading characteristics. It will contain information on berthing areas, cargo stowage areas, vehicle stowage areas and complete planning figures/diagrams of those areas. Each ship's SLCP is required to be officially updated following all modifications or adjustments to the ship's characteristics to ensure future units have the most accurate information when planning. Procurement of the SLCP is the responsibility of the MEU Embarkation Officer.
- **Organization For Embarkation/Assignment to Shipping (OEAS)**
  - **MEU Commander's Concept.** The first step in the embarkation process is determining the MEU Commander's desired concept for loading MEU equipment onboard the ARG. His assessments (CBAE) of mission priority, potential contingencies, equipment desires, tactical vs administrative loading, etc, should all be solidified prior to considering any other desires to include those of the MSE commanders.
  - **Ship Mix Considerations.** The ship mix of the ARG will have a significant effect on where certain units (i.e. Tanks) or cargo (Class IX block) will be embarked and stored. Regardless, unit and mission set (i.e. Mechanized Raid, Motorized Raid, etc) integrity must be heavily considered. An initial assignment to shipping should be determined early enough so that embarkation planning can be conducted, finalized and an OEAS messaged submitted to the PHIBRON prior to completion of the last at sea training period.

B. Embarkation Plans and Orders

The MEU will conduct a series of meetings designed to identify, capture and refine the load plan for deployment. The MEU Commanding Officer and Operations Officer provide the primary concept for loading. Once the Commanding Officer's concept is captured, then the MSE Commanders will be briefed on the concept and allowed input as to the supportability of the concept. They will also be allowed to provide requested changes/adjustments IOT better assist that respective MSE. Regardless of who the requesting element is, the MEU Commanding Officer has the final decision with regard to all embarkation issues.

Load Plan Development

Once the MEU Embarkation Officer has received the Commanding Officer's concept for the load plan, he will begin the process of developing a virtual load plan that will provide visual diagrams as well as ensure the equipment requested to be loaded will actually fit aboard each requested ship. The Embarkation Officer will use the following systems to capture and use required embarkation data:

- **MAGTF Deployment Support System II (MDSS II).** MDSS II is the system the Marine Corps uses to maintain and share all required embarkation data. Each MSE is required to continually maintain the accuracy of their MDSS II data. Upon composition each MSE will provide the MEU Embarkation Officer with their MDSS II data (Level IV) IOT merge and refine the overall MEU embarkation requirement.

Navy Embarkation Personnel

There are Navy personnel assigned to either the PHIBRON or ship's staff who have a direct influence on the MEU's ability to successfully conduct embarkation operations. Similar to the MEU's embarkation personnel, they have a responsibility to brief and maintain the situational awareness of all embarkation operations and associated issues. While both the Navy and Marine Corps have separate chains of command, they must work together IOT effectively and efficiently maintain the readiness and capability of the MAGTF.

PHIBRON Combat Cargo Officer (CCO)

The PHBIRON CCO is a counterpart to the MEU Embarkation Officer and functions as a special staff officer to the PHIBRON Commander (a.k.a. Commodore). He works under the cognizance of the Chief of Staff Officer (CSO) as the point of contact in all matters concerning embarkation. The PHIBRON CCO represents the link in the chain of command between the MEU and the ships of the ARG. It is essential that the MEU Embarkation Officer maintain close liaison with him. The CCO will also represent the ships when embarkation matters arise concerning the entire ARG. The PHIBRON CCO should be the central point of contact for collecting, consolidating and forwarding to the MEU Embarkation Officer all embarkation requirements for the Naval Support Element (NSE).

Ship CCO

- On LHD/A, LPD and LSD class ships the CCO functions as a special staff officer to the Commanding Officer of the ship under the direct cognizance of the ship's Executive Officer. The CCO is responsible for the following duties:
- Coordination with Landing Force units and appropriate department heads in the preparation and execution of plans for the embarkation or debarkation of the Landing Force as well as the billeting and messing requirements.
- The CCO is not responsible for handling cargo, operating cargo handling equipment or the cargo safety and security officer

First Lieutenant/Combat Systems Officer

Depending on the class of amphibious ship, either the First Lieutenant or Combat Systems Officer is responsible for ensuring the following:

- All authorized cargo and vehicle loading assemblies are on hand and serviceable
- All vehicles and cargo spaces are ready to accept landing force supplies and equipment
- All MHE, elevators and conveyers are in safe working order
- All cargo is handled properly with cargo handling equipment
- All cargo is properly stowed for sea

Embarkation Duties and Responsibilities

- The MEU Commander will appoint a **Commander of Troops (COT)** in writing (via the MEU Embarkation Officer) for each ship.
- The COT, in turn, will assign a **Team Embarkation Officer (TEO)**. He will also assign a Billeting Officer, Laundry Officer, Mess Officer and any other necessary billets that are required in the troop regulations for the ship.
- The MEU Embarkation Officer will function as a **Group Embarkation Officer** and will have cognizance over MSE Embarkation Officers and Team Embarkation Officers. MSE Embarkation Officers may function as TEOs, but this should be avoided to allow these Embarkation Officers to focus on embarkation/debarkation of their respective MSE and assigned ship.

Commanding Officers

Commanding Officers are directly responsible for the embarkation readiness of their units. The following requirements are essential in the proper management of a unit's embarkation program:

- Assignment and training of personnel in embarkation.
- Knowledge of embarkation techniques and procedures to include the handling, transportation and stowage of various types of cargo.
- Knowledge of procedures in the surface movement of cargo from unit areas to/from Aerial and Sea Ports of Embarkation/Debarkation (APOE/D and SPOE/D).
- Familiarity with facilities at A/SPOE/D's.
- Familiarity of embarkation personnel with the general characteristics and capabilities of Air Mobility Command (AMC) Strategic Cargo Aircraft, commercial passenger/cargo aircraft and amphibious shipping.
- Special training and knowledge of procedures for handling, transportation, and storage of hazardous material/cargo.
- Knowledge of processes and procedures associated with Force Deployment Planning and Execution (FDP&E) in support of Joint Operation Planning and Execution System (JOPES) and development of Time Phased Force Deployment Data (TPFDD).
- Knowledge of processes and procedures associated with Reception, Staging, On-ward Movement and Integration (RSO&I), to include joint operations (JRSO&I), in general support of both tactical and administrative off-load operations as well as Maritime Pre-positioning Force (MPF) operations (assigned as an MPF enabling MAGTF).

Unit Responsibility

Embarkation readiness is not solely the responsibility of those personnel assigned embarkation duties, but it is the responsibility of all members of the unit. All operations conducted by the MEU begin and end with embarkation. Therefore, commanding officers, and especially operations officers, within the MAGTF must be vigilant in understanding and supporting all embarkation requirements. Maintenance and accuracy of embarkation data, proper preparation and marking of supplies and equipment, and accomplishment of necessary individual embarkation matters all require the attention, supervision and tracking of every leader within the MEU.

Embarkation Officer

The MEU Embarkation Officer maintains cognizance over all MSE Embarkation Officers and TEOs as well as provides all supervision of all loading/unloading activities within the MEU. He also advises and assists in the planning and execution of embarkation operations. The MEU Embarkation Officer will execute the following:

- Keep the MEU Commander informed of the state of embarkation readiness within the MEU as well as effect and maintain liaison with higher and adjacent commands. Note: It is the responsibility of the Amphibious Squadron (PHIBRON) Combat Cargo Officer (CCO) to maintain the Commodore's situational awareness with regard to all embarkation operations within the ARG.
- Assist the MEU S-3 in the development of Organization for Embarkation and Assignment to Shipping (OEAS) in support of the Landing Plan.
- Arrange for staging areas in support of embarkation and debarkation operations.
- Consolidate requirements for Material Handling Equipment (MHE), Container Handling Equipment (CHE), Motor Transport, Port Services and any other equipment/services required at POE/D.
- In coordination with the MEU S-4 Chief/Motor Transport Coordinator, identify and consolidate transportation requirements for personnel, supplies and equipment to/from POE/Ds.
- Effect and maintain liaison with appropriate PHIBRON CCO and CCO's onboard assigned Amphibious Ready Group (ARG) ships.
- Supervise all MSE and TEOs in the accomplishment of their duties by hosting coordination meetings and making proper liaison visits to each unit and ship.
- Function as the Unit Embarkation Officer for the MEU Command Element (CE), conduct periodic inspections, and ensure that all equipment is properly prepared for embarkation.
- Consolidate all requirements for the handling, transportation and storage of hazardous materials/cargo.
- In coordination with the PHIBRON CCO, collect, consolidate, review and distribute to each Embarkation Team TEO the embarkation requirements/data (personnel, supplies and equipment) for the Naval Support Element(s) assigned to be embarked onboard their respective ship.

Commander of Troops (COT)

The COT is directly responsible for the proper embarkation of personnel, supplies and equipment on their assigned ship. The COT will be guided in the performance of their duties by the MEU Commander as well as the current regulations for the assigned ship.

Team Embarkation Officer (TEO)

The TEO is the direct representative of the COT for the proper embarkation of personnel, vehicles and equipment assigned to their ship. A close and continuous relationship throughout the work-up, planning and execution phases with the ship either through the CCO or the ship's First Lieutenant is essential to successful embarkation operations. The TEO will execute the following responsibilities:

- Submit embarkation data in a timely manner when requested by HHQ.
- Keep the MEU Embarkation Officer advised of embarkation readiness.
- Act as the direct representative of the COT for the embarkation and debarkation of Landing Force personnel, supplies and equipment.
- Ensure that embarkation personnel are properly informed of their duties and properly trained to accomplish those duties.
- Be further guided in the performance of their duties by the MEU Embarkation Officer and the current troop regulations for their respective ship.
- Ensure that embarkation personnel are guided in the performance of their duties by the MEU Commander, current troop regulations and the Ship Loading Characteristics Pamphlet (SLCP).

- **Integrated Computerized Deployment System (ICODES).** As a ship load planning software tool, ICODES utilizes artificial intelligence (AI) principles to assist embarkation personnel with development of cargo stow plans. This program provides the embarkation specialist with "to scale" images of containers, vehicles, aircraft, etc, along with accurate characteristics of each individual ship IOT allow the most accurate stowage planning.

Formal Load Plans

Once embarkation load planning is complete, final ICODES designs have been established and both the MEU Embarkation Officer and PHIBRON CCO concur with supportability, the formal load plans will be briefed to both the MEU Commander and Ship's Commanding Officer (together if possible). Once both commanders agree on the formal load plans then they will sign the plans and officially approve the plans. Those plans will then act as an agreement between the MEU and ship as to how the ships will be loaded for deployment. Once signed, no changes are authorized without the approval of the ship's Commanding Officer and the Embarkation Team Commander.

The Commodore is not officially part of this process as he is not directly responsible for the safety and care of the individual ship. However, the Commodore may want to be part of the process as well as sign the formal load plans.

C. Execution of Embarkation Operations

Administrative embarkation operations will actually begin prior to the first at sea exercise (PMINT), continue through final deployment loading and complete following the return of the MEU from deployment. IOT properly prepare and execute embarkation operations, the MEU Embarkation Officer will execute the following actions:

Logistics Support Request (LSR)

The Embarkation Officer will coordinate with both the I MEF Embarkation Officer as well as the Navy's Port Services Officer (32nd Street) to establish the MEU's embarkation requirements to include using Lot 4F (staging area), pierside/floating cranes, stern gate ramps, etc. This request is key to ensuring the Navy understands and, more importantly, has time to schedule the areas and services to execute operations.

MEF Movement Control Center (MMCC) Planning Conferences

The Embarkation Officer, along with the MEU S-4 Chief, will coordinate with and establish initial, middle and final planning conferences (IPC/MPC/FPC) IOT identify, refine and solidify all transportation and MHE requirements according to the MEU's loading schedule(s). Embarkation planning conferences provide invaluable opportunities for face-to-face coordination between MEU MSEs and their Navy counterparts. Marine-to-Marine and Marine-to-Navy Initial Planning Conferences (IPCs) for transportation and embarkation will be scheduled no later than E-120, although earlier informal liaison can and should be done. Mid-Planning Conferences (MPCs) should be scheduled on or about E-90. Final Planning Conferences (FPCs) will be scheduled on E-30. During this meeting MEU personnel will meet with MEF G-4 personnel and continuously conduct coordination until completion of all embarkation actions.

Embarkation Letters of Instruction (LOI) for Loading

Prior to each embarkation period, the MEU Embarkation Officer will create and publish the MEU's LOI directing all actions required to load MEU personnel and equipment aboard ARG shipping. While each ship has their own TEO/TEA and Navy embarkation personnel who will load each respective ship according to the formal load plans, they will still receive general guidance from the MEU IOT efficiently execute the actual loading.

Serial Assignment Tables (SAT)

The Landing Force (LF) SAT lists in numerical order the serial numbers (associated to personnel/equipment) of units to be landed from ship-to-shore prior to general offloading of ARG shipping. A serial is a grouping of personnel or equipment that originates from the same ship that will land on a specific beach or helicopter landing zone.

SAT Development

Serial Assignments are developed by the operations sections to assist in the organization of the LF and execution of the overarching landing plan and landing schedule. Serial assignments will be associated to landing craft and aviation assets in accordance within the designated landing plan architecture.

Internal Ship Preparation and Call Away Coordination

Serial assignments will be used by the TACLOG(s) and respective ship's Combat Cargo (CC) agencies to support the preparation of the LF for execution of the landing plan. The TACLOG will coordinate with CC to establish the "Call Away" schedule for units being discharged in order of the landing plan. Therefore, the first elements (pre-boat units) will be called away to stage at debarkation points within the ship(s) according to the landing plan schedule using the established serial assignments.

Serial Assignment Process

Each MSE (CE included) will be allocated (by ship) a block of serial numbers to organize their units with relation to operational requirements. MSEs are highly encouraged to pre-plan their serial assignments within their units to decrease the time associated to this action. By pre-planning their serial assignments they will only need to make minor changes (if required) during the planning phase of operations. Both personnel and equipment to be discharged from each ship will be assigned a serial assignment. Normally, key personnel, who include commanders and primary staff (at all levels), are assigned their own serial assignment for flexibility in moving them ashore. Regular personnel are generally associated into groups of 4 – 6 based on the space limitations of the CH-46 helicopter. Smaller groupings add flexibility to moving serials within the landing plan in case plans are changed or modes of transportation are changed. Vehicle crews (LAV, Tank, HMMWV, etc) are assigned to the same serial as their equipment (flight crews are not assigned serial assignments the same as landing craft crews).

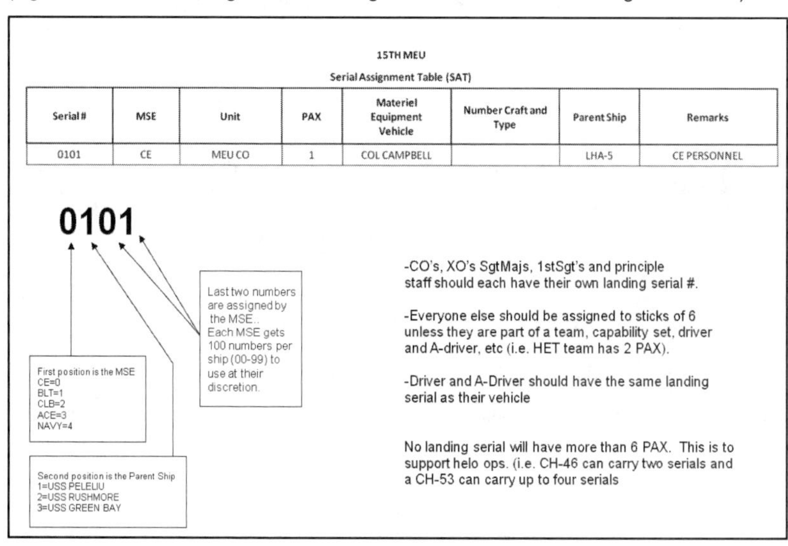

15TH MEU

Serial Assignment Table (SAT)

Serial #	MSE	Unit	PAX	Materiel Equipment Vehicle	Number Craft and Type	Parent Ship	Remarks
0101	CE	MEU CO	1	COL CAMPBELL		LHA-5	CE PERSONNEL

Example Serial Assignment Development Chart

D. Personnel (PAX), Mail & Cargo (PMC)

The PMC process is established to coordinate movement of required personnel and materiel within the ARG as well as from ship-to-shore or shore-to-ship. The PMC process is administrative in nature and not designed to support, or replace, the dedicated planning process associated with real-world or pre-planned exercise while deployed. Normal PMC requirements consist of removing injured PAX from the ARG, cross-decking repair parts/munitions between ships and/or shifting personnel between ships.

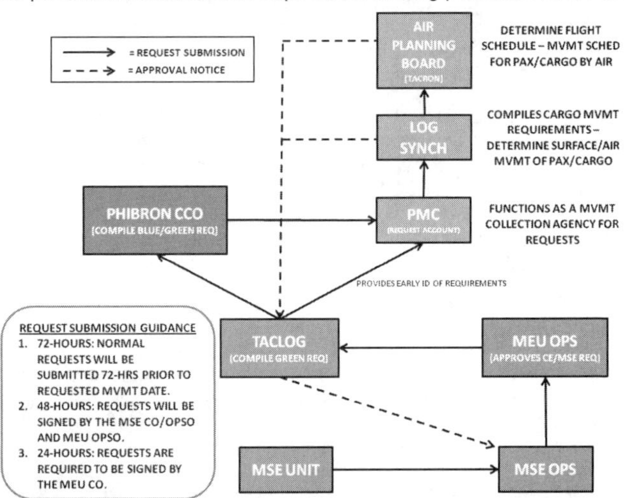

Request Process. Units will initiate their request by filling out and submitting the appropriate ship(s) form (provided by the ship's Combat Cargo agency) to their respective operations section. The MSE operations section will review the request to ensure it supports the commands requirements. Upon MSE approval, the request will be forwarded (via email or hard copy) to the MEU S-3 section (Assistant Air Officer) for review at the Command Element level. If approved, the MEU S-3 will print (if required) the request, authorized the movement by signing the request and forward it to the TACLOG Watch Officer (WatchO). The TACLOG WatchO will scan the request, file the hard copy, and submit the request to both the PMC electronic mail (email) account and the PHIBRON CCO. The PHIBRON CCO will collect all requests from both the Navy and Marine units for review at the Logistics Synchronization (Log Synch) meeting to ensure accuracy of requests and determine the mode of travel required to fulfill the requests (i.e. air or surface).

Log Synch Meeting. The Log Synch meeting is chaired by the PHIBRON CCO and attended by the MEU S-4 (TACLOG) as well as representatives from each of the MSEs. The intent of the meeting is to review the existing requests by date/time (72-hour forecast) along with recently submitted requests to ensure the information submitted within the requests is accurate (i.e. names, cargo information, dates requested, etc). Once the request information is accurate, the meeting will then focus on determining the modes of transportation available to fulfill the requests. Transportation assets include aviation (ACE/Navy), landing craft (LCU/LCAC), small boat (RHIBs/water ferries) and surface support vessels (T-AKE/T-AO/T-AOE) associated to Replenishment-At-Sea (RAS) operations. If the determination is that aviation will support the request(s), then the request(s) will be included on the list of requests that will be presented to the Air Planning Board.

Air Planning Board (APB). During the APB, the PHIBRON CCO/TACLOG representative will brief the existing PMC requests that need to be resolved and scheduled in the air plan. At the conclusion of the APB, the requests will be scheduled within the air plan for the next 72-hours. Each day the air plan and associated requests will be reviewed and adjusted if required. PMC requests are subject to change based on aircraft availability or shifts in the air plan.

Follow-on Actions. Once requests have been associated to transportation (aviation/surface) and scheduled for movement, the TACLOG will be given the staging (date/time/location) guidance by the PHIBRON CCO. That information will be provided to the MSE via the TACLOG to ensure the individuals moving, or coordinating the movement of materiel, have the coordinating instructions to properly prepare for the movement.

Chap 1

VI. Communications (MEU S-6)

Staff Functions

Mission

Plan, install, operate, and maintain information technology/communication systems in order to enable command and control of the Marine Expeditionary Unit.

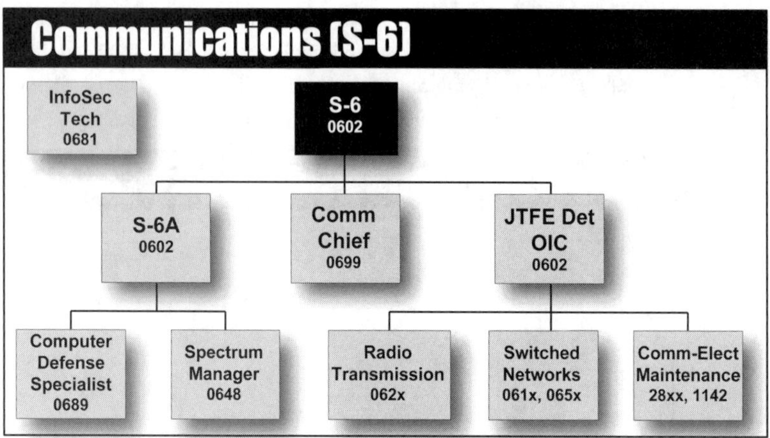

Command Element T/O - 2 × MO, 4 × ME		
Communications Officer	1 × Maj	0602
Assistant Communications Officer	1 × 1stLt	0602
Communications Chief	1 × MSgt	0699
Information Security Technician*	1 × GySgt	0681
Computer Defense Specialist	1 × SSgt	0689
Spectrum Manager	1 × SSgt	0648

Although assigned by TO/E to the S-6 Section, the MEU Information Security Technician is assigned to the MEU XO/Security Manager reporting structure.

Communications Battalion Detachment T/O - 1 × MO, 52 × ME		
JTFE Detachment OIC	1 × 1stLt	0602
Telecommunications Systems Chief	1 × SSgt	0619
Tactical Switching Operator	4 × Sgt-Pvt	0612
Technical Controller	2 × Sgt-Pvt	2821
Radio Chief	1 × GySgt	0629
Field Radio Operator	19 × Sgt-Pvt	0621
Digital Multi-channel Wideband Transmission Equipment Operator	2 × Sgt-Pvt	0622
Satellite Communications Operator	3 × Sgt-Pvt	0627
Communications-Electronics Maintenance Chief	1 × GySgt	2862
Data Chief	1 × GySgt	0659
Data Systems Technician	13 × Sgt-Pvt	0651
Digital Wideband Technician	1 × Sgt-Pvt	2834
Ground Communications Organizational Repairer	2 × Sgt-Pvt	2844
Telephone Systems/Personal Computer Repairer	1 × Sgt-Pvt	2847
Engineer Equipment Electrical Systems Technician	1 × Sgt-Pvt	1142

I. Typical Missions

A. Wideband / Ground Mobile Forces (GMF)

- The MEU S-6 is equipped and manned with a Joint Task Force Enabler (JTFE) Detachment that is capable of supporting a Joint Task Force Headquarters during crisis response operations
- JTFE Detachment provides wideband communications capability to the MEU CE and subordinate elements
- Based around the AN/TSC-156 Phoenix wideband satellite communications terminal
- DISA Standard Tactical Entry Point (STEP) entry for global network interface
- MSE and other MEU elements serviced through SWAN / WPPL connection
- HMMWV mounted, generator powered
- Provides classified/unclassified data network and voice services

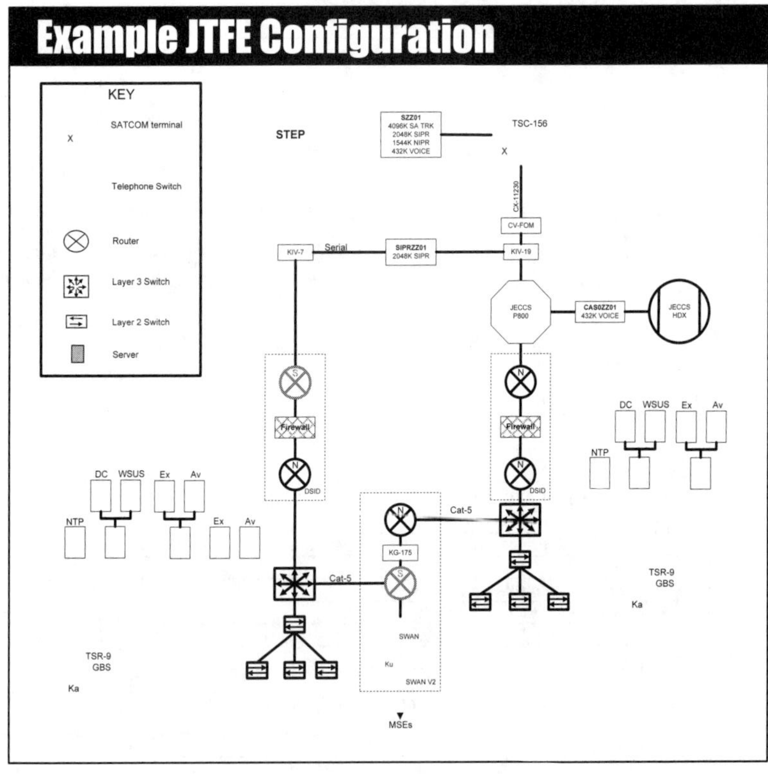

Example JTFE GMF and Data Configuration. *This diagram shows the equipment string employed by the JTFE in order to provide classified/unclassified data network and telephone services.*

Example Wideband Satellite Architechture

STEP
STEP
STZ01 4096K
15th MEU CE
JTFE
TSC-156
X
TSR-9
GBS
Ka
SWAN V2
22
Ku
MRT
YZP01 2048K
YZF01 2048K
GCE
LCE
YZL01 2048K
SWAN V1
19
Ku
YPL01 2048K
YFL01 2048K
SWAN V1
20
Ku
SWAN V1
21
Ku
ACE
YPF01 2048K

Example Wideband Satellite Architecture. *This diagram illustrates the transmissions paths that connect the CE with each MSE using a SWAN network.*

B. Ashore Single Channel Radio Operations

- During operations ashore, MEU elements provide their organic equipment and operators to establish communications links to the MEU CE and their subordinate units
- All single channel radio nets are encrypted with the exception of a required "range safety" net that may be required during exercises

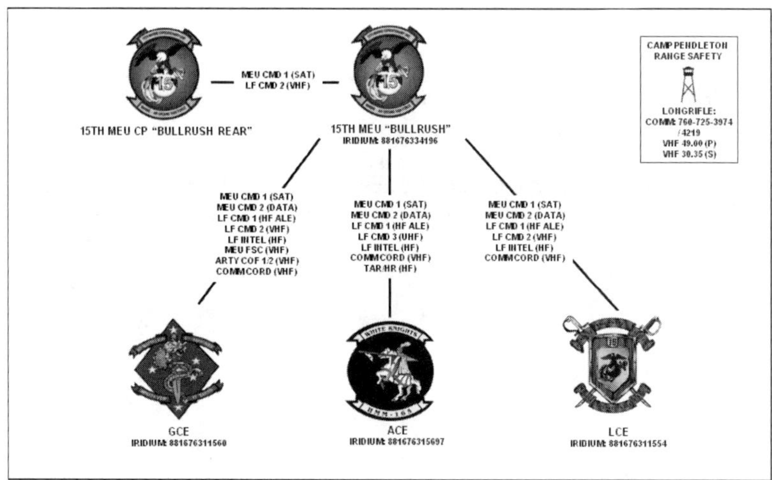

Example Ashore Radio Connectivity Diagram. This diagram provides an example of the different single-channel radio nets established to provide voice communications with each unit.

II. Afloat Operations

Afloat Operations

- While afloat, MEU utilizes ships' wideband and single channel radio assets for command and control
- MEU elements are tasked with supporting communications requirements aboard ships for MEU operations spaces and maintenance of MEU data networks
- MEU CE primarily in LFOC and data helpdesk aboard the LHA/D
- GCE primarily in the TACLOG and data helpdesk aboard the LPD
- LCE primarily in the TACLOG and data helpdesk aboard the LSD
- Regardless of which ship they are embarked aboard, all 0651 Marines will support the data helpdesk of that ship during the requisite continuous operations of the embarked commander

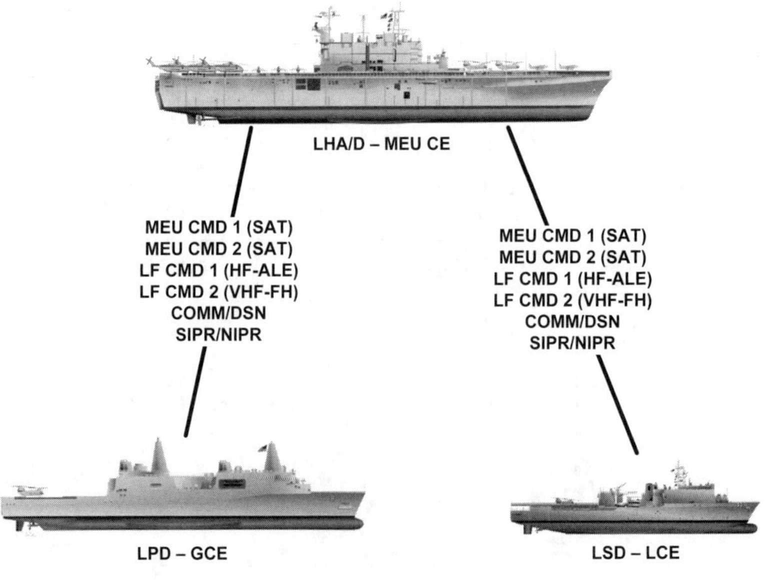

Example Afloat Operations Communications. *This example depicts multiple means of communications typically employed when embarked aboard the Amphibious Ready Group.*

Forward Command Element (FCE)

- Led by an NCO, this team of communications operators and technicians will provide secure voice and data network communications for the MEU FCE:
- 1 × 28XX Comm-Elect Maint Technician
- 1 × 0621 Radio Operator
- 2 × 0651 Data Systems Technician
- Install, operate, maintain redundant HF, VHF, UHF, SATCOM, SIPRNet, NIPRNet links between FCE and MEU CE
- DJC2 Rapid Response Kit (RRK) provides the high bandwidth Global Information Grid (GIG) connection to support SIPRNet, NIPRNet, and commercial telephone access
- Alternate wideband access is provided by the Expeditionary Command and Control System (ECCS) which is routed through I MEF to SIPRNet, NIPRNet and DSN global access
- BGAN (AN/PSC-15) systems provide a tertiary GIG access

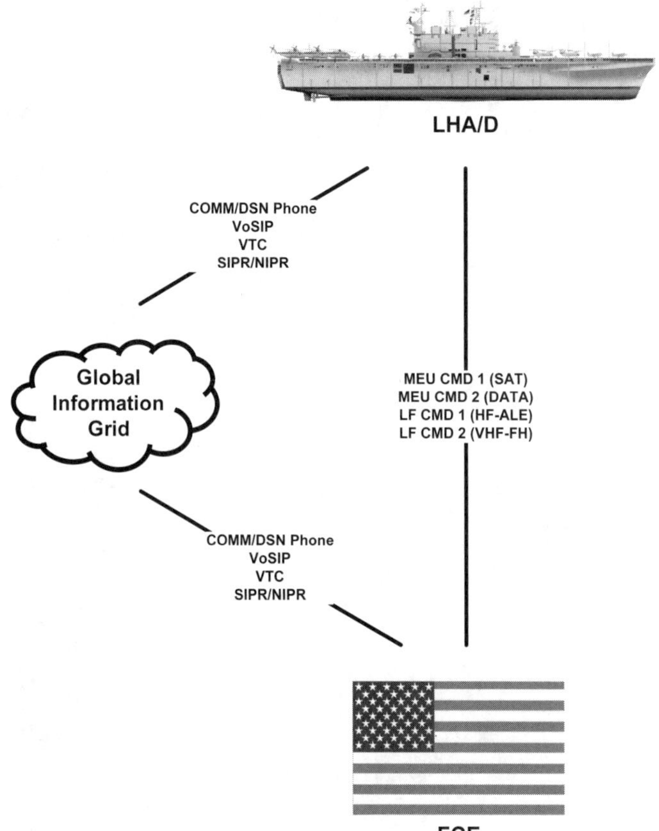

Example FCE Communications Architecture. *This example shows redundant methods (single-channel radio and commercial assets) typically employed with the FCE.*

III. Capabilities/Primary Equipment

Wideband Transmissions

AN/TSC-186 Support Wide Area Network (SWAN) Dv1

1.2m SATCOM terminal provides robust communications services in a rugged, portable suite of equipment

AN/TSC-180A SWAN Dv2, Master Reference Terminal (MRT)

1.8m SATCOM terminal acts as a hub to distribute network connectivity to remote sites

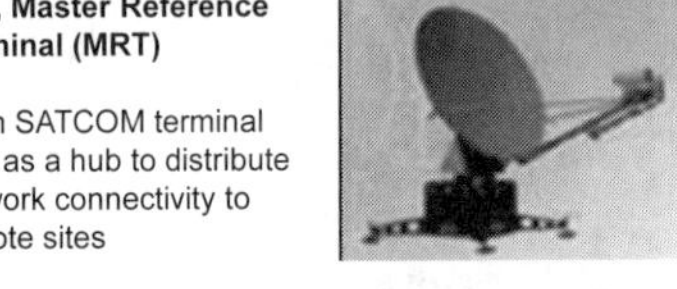

AN/TSC-156 Phoenix

HMMWV-mounted 2.4m quad-band SATCOM terminal provides access to Global Information Grid services

Wireless Point-to-Point Link (WPPL-D)

In lieu of cables, used to extend services to distant sites up to (35) miles away

AN/PSC-15 Broadband Global Area Network (BGAN)

Lightweight, portable, ruggedized suite that provides SIPRNet, NIPRNet, and secure voice services

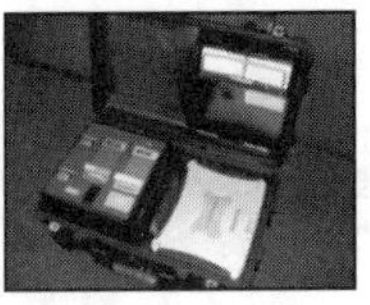

Deployable Joint Command and Control Rapid Response Kit

Scalable, modular suite of SIPRNet, NIPRNet, IP phone

AN/TSR-9 Global Broadcast Service

Receive-only terminals for access to classified and unclassified data, video, and imagery

SWAN Mini

Ultracompact, highly portable terminal that can quickly establish secure voice, video and data communications; can interface with standard SWAN terminals

Single Channel Radio, TACSAT

AN/VRC-110 (VHF, UHF)

Primarily used for VHF supporting convoy operations; can also provide retransmissions to extend effective range up to (80) miles

AN/PRC-117 (VHF, UHF)

Versatile asset employed in all MEU CE missions for voice and limited data applications

AN/PRC-119 (VHF)

Typically employed for short range, tactical ground operations

AN/PRC-148 (VHF, UHF)

Primarily used for terminal control between CAS and JTAC/FAC; used by MRF during WestPac 10-1

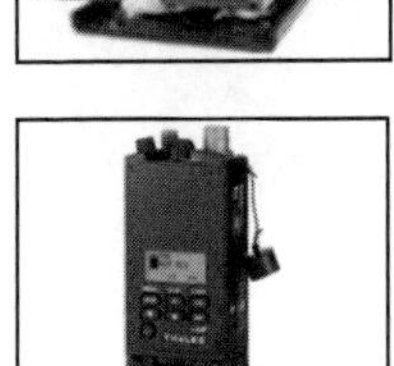

AN/PRC-150 (HF)

Provides reliable, long range voice and limited data communications

AN/PRC-153 (UHF, non-secure)

Mostly used in garrison during non-tactical operations

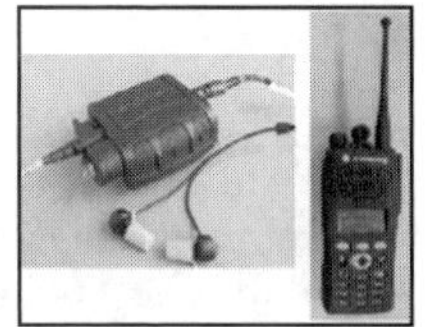

AN/TRC-209 (HF)

Used as our main HF communication asset in all COC configurations; increased power output from 20 to 150 Watts (requires house power 110V-220V)

Iridium Telephone

Used as additional means of communications for beyond LoS requirements; issued to any element operating independent from the CE's AO including MSEs

Tandberg (Cisco) Video Teleconference

Offers real-time video and audio communications over SIPRNet architecture

DSN/commercial phone switchboard

Provides access to voice services over DSN and/or commercial access

Collaboration software

Through the use of Adobe Connect, Microsoft SharePoint, et al; allows users to share/manage information

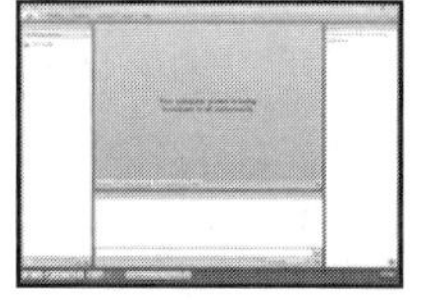

Circuit/Packet Switching

Deployed Security Interdiction Device (DSID)

This hardware-based firewall protects networks (SIPR/NIPR) from unauthorized access

Network Servers

Provides access to essential services for network (SIPR/NIPR) functionality

Voice over Secure Internet Protocol (VoSIP) Unified Communications Manager

Provides telephone services utilizing SIPRNet connections

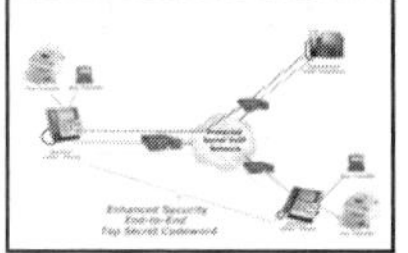

IV. External Interfacing

Defense Information Systems Agency (DISA)

Spectrum Manager

- Frequency request
- UHF Satellite Access
- Wideband Satellite Access
- Gateway Access to Global information Grid (SIPRNet, NIPRNet, DSN)

Information Assurance Manager

- Information Assurance Certification and Accreditation
- System Authority to Operate (ATO)
- Network Authority to Connect (ATC)

Data Chief

- DMS Message routing through MCB Camp Pendleton and afloat communications centers
- EKMS Manager
- Cryptographic Call-out coordination message prior to exercises or operations
- Coordination for Defense Courier Service support

U. S. Navy (USN)

S-6 Officer, Assistant S-6 Officer, Communications Chief

- Coordination across Fleet areas of operation
- Memorandum of Agreement for shipboard operations with each ship of the amphibious ready group
- Daily operations afloat
- Casualty Reports (CASREPS) for "Blue in Support of Green (BISOG)" systems
- Bi-weekly Marine Corps C5I Amphibious Advisory Board (MCAAB) teleconference

Spectrum Manager

- Joint ARG/ MEU Frequency Requests for operations afloat

Data Chief

- Network operations through Navy Regional Network Operations Centers
- Communications Center DMS Message handling afloat

Communications-Electronics Maintenance Chief

- Installation of systems aboard ARG ships

Headquarters, Marine Corps (HQMC)

S-6 Officer, Assistant S-6 Officer, Communications Chief

- Universal Needs Statements and TO&E Change Request

Information Assurance Manager

- Certification and Accreditation of tactical networks

Data Chief

- Routing of network traffic from Marine Corps Enterprise Network to tactical and ships networks
- Information Technology Waiver process for new equipment purchase

Marine Expeditionary Force (MEF)

S-6 Officer, Assistant S-6 Officer, Communications Chief

- Personnel management in coordination with 9th Communications Battalion, MEF Headquarters Group
- Universal Needs Statement requests

Frequency Manager

- Frequency Requests review and routing
- UHF Satellite Access review and routing
- Wideband Satellite Access review and routing
- Gateway Access to the Global Information Grid

Data Chief

- SIPRNet access in garrison (I MEF managed "1MEF" domain)
- NMCI Customer Technical Representative coordination

Major Subordinate Element (MSE)

S-6 Officer, Assistant S-6 Officer, Communications Chief

- Training / integration on MEU operations and equipment
- Coordination of systems afloat

Frequency Manager

- Frequency requests for MSE training and operations

EKMS Manager

- Electronic Key Management Systems key issue and destruction
- Controlled Cryptographic Item accountability and maintenance
- Provide monthly COMSEC training

Data Chief

- Data Network coordination/configuration
- Shipboard operations duty stander assignments

I. Rapid Response Planning Process (R2P2)

The Marine Corps Planning Process (MCPP) is the basis for MEU staff planning. The Rapid Response Planning Process (R2P2) is an accelerated execution of MCPP geared to Crisis Action Planning. The R2P2 process allows the MEU/PHIBRON to anticipate potential missions, create a set of standardized responses through analytical decision-making, and rehearse their responses to achieve full capability within six hours of receipt of a warning or execute order. The planning timeline of 6 hours can be extended based on time available, mission complexity, shaping actions required, and HHQ guidance. The following basic tenants of MCPP will be adhered to:

- Top Down Planning (alignment with Commander's Guidance and Intent)
- Single Battle Concept (Synchronization of all elements across time and space towards a common end-state)
- Integrated Planning (detailed coordination across elements)

R2P2

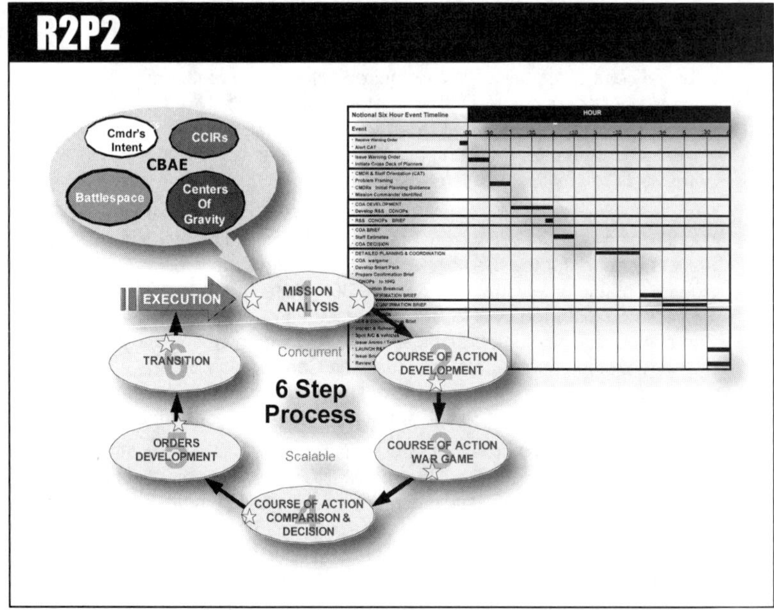

Rapid planning requires extensive training in the techniques and procedures associated with R2P2. R2P2 requires standardized, detailed, parallel, and concurrent command and staff actions using Standard Operating Procedures (SOPs) that are understood by all members of the unit. Established SOPs for potential mission profiles must include such details as standardized task organizations and equipment density lists to facilitate execution in a time sensitive environment.

Mission Planning

R2P2 is a time-constrained, six step process that mirrors the Marine Corps Planning Process of:

- Problem Framing
- COA Development
- COA Wargaming
- COA Comparison and Decision
- Orders Development
- Transition

Upon receipt of a warning, alert, or execute order, a Crisis Action Team (CAT) is assembled to commence initial staff orientation, problem framing, determine information requirements, and identify the commanders guidance for COA development. The CAT meets in the LFOC planning room. The CAT will accomplish its tasks within the first hour.

Once adjourned from the CAT, the Mission Commander---supported by select MAGTF/PHIBRON staff members---develops COAs. COAs include phases, a timeline, a task organization, landing beaches and zones, concept of fires, major end items/equipment, a recommended H/L-hour and advantages and disadvantages for each COA. Typically, the designated Mission Commander takes the lead in developing three COAs. The MAGTF COA planning team has one hour to complete COA development.

At the **two-hour mark**, the Battle Staff convenes in the Wardroom for COA consideration and decision. During this time, the COAs are briefed, operational or intelligence updates provided as required, information requirements and rules of engagement are updated, staff estimates of supportability are conducted and the COA is selected or modified. Once selected, the MEU and PHIBRON Commander's guidance is issued for detailed planning, and a planning order is issued when time permits.

In the following two hours, the MSE staffs in coordination with their PHIBRON counterparts conduct concurrent, parallel, and detailed planning while small unit leaders prepare for the mission. Additionally, immediately following the COA Decision (at approximately the two hour and 30 minute mark), the Reconnaissance and Surveillance (R&S) CONOPS Brief is presented by the R&S Leader to the CAT. Simultaneously, all members of the staff who have any responsibility in the execution or conduct of the mission are preparing the Confirmation Brief. As detailed planning and Confirmation Brief preparation continues, MEU staff members prepare the Concept of Operations message and submit it to higher headquarters.

At the **four hour mark**, the CAT convenes for the R&S Confirmation Brief. Following the R&S Confirmation Brief the respective staffs and essential personnel gather in the Wardroom for the mission confirmation brief. One hour is the goal for the Confirmation Brief; it is not unusual to have over 25 briefers and over 100 slides of information. In order to keep the brief at one hour, known SOPs are critical to allow many items to be briefed by exception.

The **final step** is command and staff supervision. During this hour all energy is focused on the unit preparing to execute the mission. Commanders may meet, if necessary, for final coordination. Final inspections and test firing of weapon are conducted, aircraft are spotted, vehicles are prepared, Marines are staged in the final staging area, manifests are confirmed, and communications checks if possible.

If rapid planning is to be successful, both mission planning and preparation requirements are conducted concurrently. The speed with which a unit can plan an operation varies with the complexity of the mission, the experience of the commander and the staff, and METT-T factors. The R2P2 was developed to enable the MEU to plan and commence execution of certain tasks within six hours.

I. R2P2 Overview

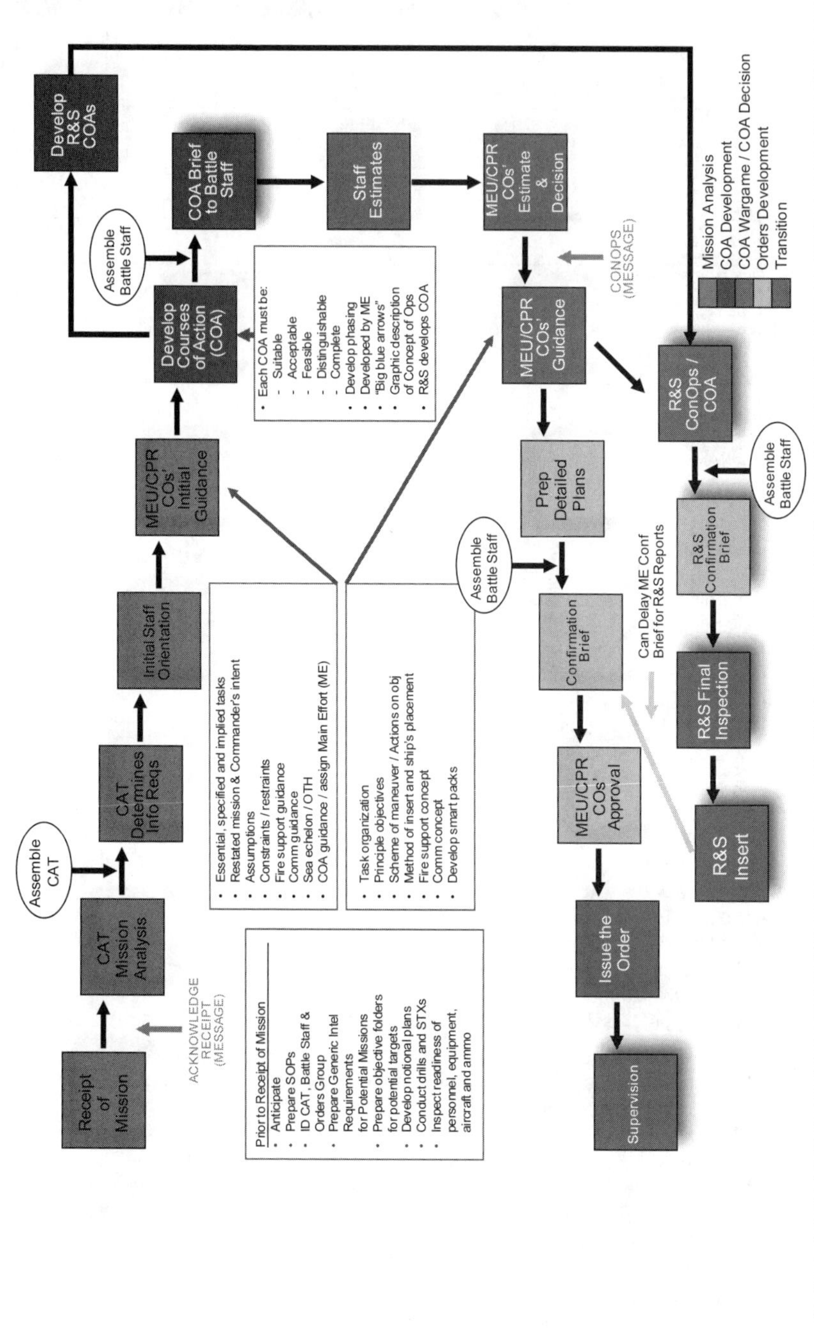

II. R2P2 Sequence/Timeline

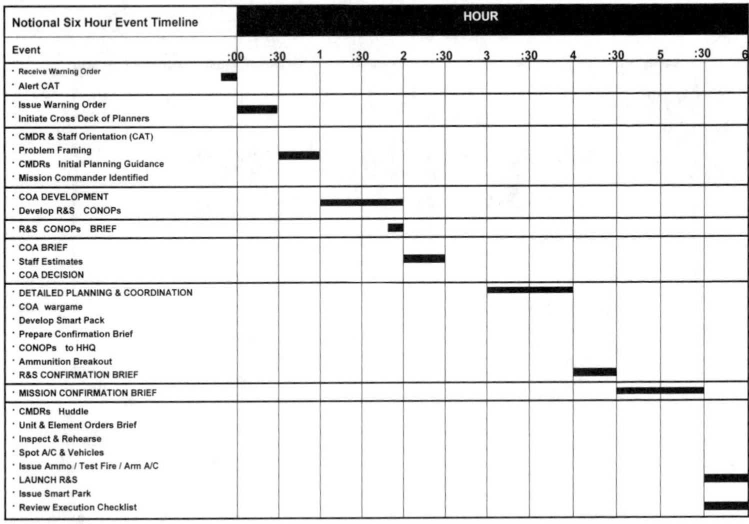

Notional Six Hour Event Timeline	HOUR												
Event	:00	:30	1	:30	2	:30	3	:30	4	:30	5	:30	6
· Receive Warning Order · Alert CAT													
· Issue Warning Order · Initiate Cross Deck of Planners													
· CMDR & Staff Orientation (CAT) · Problem Framing · CMDRs Initial Planning Guidance · Mission Commander Identified													
· COA DEVELOPMENT · Develop R&S CONOPs													
· R&S CONOPs BRIEF													
· COA BRIEF · Staff Estimates · COA DECISION													
· DETAILED PLANNING & COORDINATION · COA wargame · Develop Smart Pack · Prepare Confirmation Brief · CONOPs to HHQ · Ammunition Breakout · R&S CONFIRMATION BRIEF													
· MISSION CONFIRMATION BRIEF													
· CMDRs Huddle · Unit & Element Orders Brief · Inspect & Rehearse · Spot A/C & Vehicles · Issue Ammo / Test Fire / Arm A/C · LAUNCH R&S · Issue Smart Park · Review Execution Checklist													

1. Receipt of Warning Order (00 to 30 min)

- Warning Order received and receipt acknowledged
- Time for CAT call away coordinated with MEU S-3/CPR N-3
- Warning Order reproduced and disseminated to CAT
- Warning Order electronically transmitted with acknowledgement of receipt procedures in place
- Warning Order posted to SIPR home page
- Problem framing brief is constructed
- AirO/TACRON coordinates cross deck requirements
- MEU Ops generates initial CAT slides
- CO and Commodore perform CBAE

2. Problem Framing (+30 min to 1 hr)

- Crisis Action Team (CAT) and battle staff convenes in designated locations
- Roll Call
- Time Hack
- Problem Framing Brief is conducted.
- Intelligence, weather, and operations updates provided
- MEU commanders initial intent/planning guidance and designation of ME
- PHIBRON commanders initial planning guidance
- Warning order disseminated (CAT products posted to SIPR homepage)

3. Course of Action (COA) Development (1 hr to 2 hr)

- Mission Commander leads COA development with mission planning cell reps
- COA graphics, narratives, timeline, fires developed by mission planning
- Standing mission forces reviewed / incorporated into COA
- COAs quickly reviewed by the MEU commander (at 60 min mark)
- Reconnaissance and Surveillance (R&S) planners concurrently develop tentative R&S CONOPs to support potential COAs

4. COA Comparison and Decision (2 hr to 2 hr+30 min)

- COA brief to battle staff
- Staff estimates
- Intel estimate from enemy perspective (S-2)

- MSE commander's estimates of supportability
- ME commander's estimate
- MEU and PHIBRON commanders compare COAs
- COA selected or selected/modified by MEU/PHIBRON commanders
- MEU commander refines intent; issues additional guidance for detailed planning
- PHIBRON commander issues additional guidance for detailed planning
- Concept of the Operation drafted for higher HQ (as required)
- MEU commander refines intent; issues additional guidance for detailed planning
- PHIBRON commander issues additional guidance for detailed planning

4a. R & S CONOPS Development (1hr to 2 hr)

- Mission Commander leads COA development with mission planning cell reps
- COA graphics, narratives, timeline, fires developed by mission planning
- Standing mission forces reviewed / incorporated into COA
- COAs quickly reviewed by the MEU commander (at 60 min mark)
- Reconnaissance and Surveillance (R&S) planners concurrently develop tentative R&S CONOPs to support potential COAs

4b. R & S CONOPS (2 hr + 45 min to 3hr)

- CONOPS brief to MEU and PHIBRON commanders
- MSE commanders and Navy estimates of supportability
- ME Commander's estimate
- MEU and PHIBRON commanders discuss CONOPS
- CONOPS approved and/or modified by MEU/PHIBRON commanders

5. Detailed Planning (2 hr+30 min to 4 hr)

- Mission Planning Cell completes the plan based on MEU/PHIBRO
- Commanders' guidance for detailed planning
- Time permitting Mission Planning Cell wargames critical events with designated red cell
- Standing mission leaders commence planning
- Confirmation brief continues to be prepared
- Review execution checklist with MEU commander

6. R&S Confirmation Brief (3hr +30mins to 4 hr)

- Delivered by R&S Leader to the CAT (MEU and PHIBRON Commanders)
- Supporting efforts brief their parts in the mission
- MEU and PHIBRON commanders approve the plan as confirmed
- R&S conduct final preparations for launch

7. Confirmation Brief (4 hr to 5 hr)

- Delivered by appropriate MSE / USN planners to the MEU & PHIBRON commanders
- Main and multiple supporting efforts brief their parts in the mission
- Standing mission leaders present their plans
- MEU/PHIBRON commanders approve the plan as confirmed
- Smart pack disseminated
- Execution checklist reviewed; pen changes made; version approved

8. Final Mission Preparation and Execution (5 hr to 6 hr)

- Commanders final meeting (if required)
- Rehearsals using Execution Checklist as a Guide
- Ammunition Issue/Test fire weapons
- Unit and aircrew briefings
- Communications checks
- Prepared to launch forces (R&S or raid force) no later than 6 hours from receipt of mission

9. Execute (6 hr mark)

- Launch elements as directed

III. Daily Operations/Intelligence Brief

Gaining and maintaining situational awareness (SA) in anticipation of potential missions is essential to successful rapid planning. Situational awareness encompasses more than the knowledge of what is going on in the present. To be situationally aware, Sailors and Marines must be able to grasp the significance of present events and envision how they might relate to future missions, how the event might apply to a SOP, or how an event might apply to specific billets. Situational awareness, familiarity with SOPs and an ability to share information in a concise and accurate manner are the foundations of successful rapid planning. Rapid planning is the cornerstone of successful MEU operations.

The Operations/Intelligence brief is delivered daily in accordance with the battle rhythm when underway, except for Sunday. It is held in the LFOC planning room and is directed to the CAT members. If missions are in progress, the Ops/Intel update may precede the first meeting/brief of the day in order to set the stage for planning.

Other briefers may present information depending on the circumstances. The intent of this brief is to confine the presentation to those subjects necessary for the audience to maintain and update situational awareness about current, pending or possible missions over the next 24-72 hours. As such, "background" and administrative information is usually omitted. Input to the Ops/Intel meeting is due to the MEU S-3 according to the daily battle rhythm.

Daily Operations/Intelligence Briefing Template

Briefer	Topics
N-3	Operations Comments, Force Lay down, Synch Matrix, Threat Conditions/Status, Warfare Commanders Status, Logistics Summary, PELARG Landing Craft and RIB Status
S-3	Task Organization Overview (PELARG/MEU and Objective/Target) Priorities Missions (Completed, Current, Potential, and Standby) Significant events scheduled for the next 24 - 72 hours Significant events scheduled for the next 30 – 90 days TEEP
N-2	Intelligence updates (Naval focus) PELARG Threat Overview Recommended PIRs
Weather	Weather forecast for next 24-72 hours; impact on operations in progress and on planned operations
S-2	Intelligence updates, R&S updates, and landing sites (MAGTF focus) PELARG collections assets availability PELARG collections sync matrix Theater/National sync matrix
MSE	BLT 3/5, CLB-15, HMM-364 MSE material readiness Priority of work Mission matrix Alert status
TACRON	TACC systems, SAR Helo status, Air plan, Flight Ops, Mode II & IV checks, Navy A/C material readiness, Air space reserved scheduled/adjacent units/deck plan
S-1	Updates on MEU personnel status (If Specifically Required)
S-4	As required logistics/material readiness issues
S-6	Data services, Radio net status, PELARG C5I maintenance, PELARG radio (N-6/S-6) status, PELARG ADP status
PAO	As required
SJA	As required
Medical	Provide updates on current casualties
S-3	Timeline
Ship Commanders	Comments
Command	Comments

The daily Ops/Intel brief will normally be broadcast over the ship's close circuit television system to other planning spaces, such as the LFOC and ready room to allow other staff members to maintain their situational awareness.

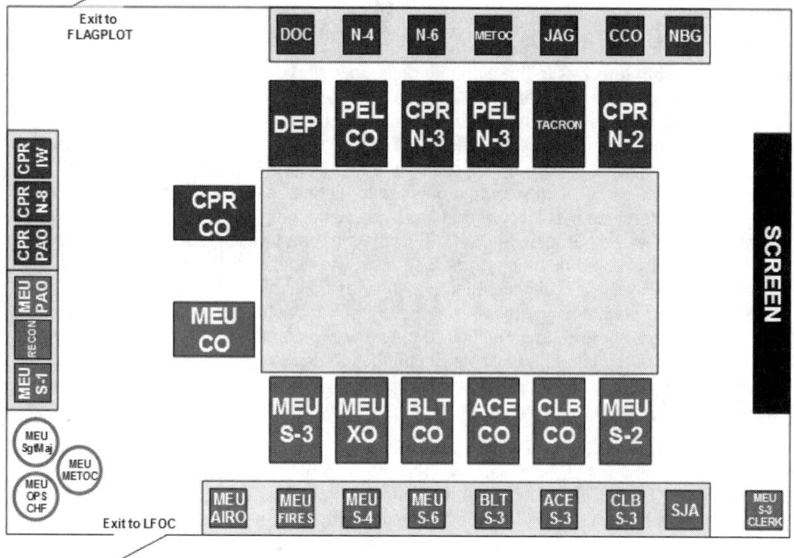

Suggested seating chart for Flagmess and War Room aboard an LHA.

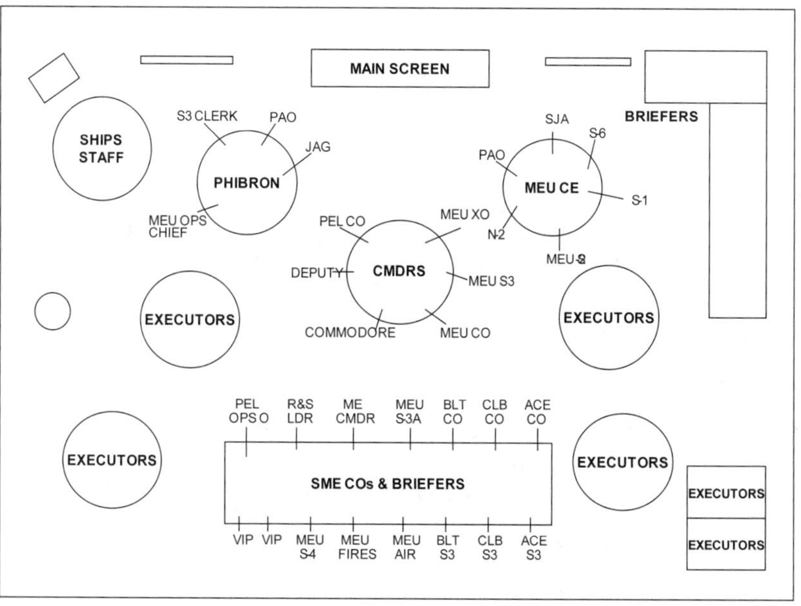

Suggested seating chart for Wardroom aboard an LHA.

IV. Actions Prior to Rapid Planning

To best employ R2P2, a unit must develop capabilities in four areas—integrated planning cells, planning and operations SOPs, intelligence, and information management. If one of these areas is lacking, effective rapid planning may not be achieved.

Integrated Planning Cells

The amount of staff turnover in the planning cells, to include the commander, directly impacts the staff's ability to plan rapidly; therefore, the composition and membership of the various planning cells used in rapid planning should remain constant, especially during the pre-deployment training program and deployment of the MEU and amphibious ready group (ARG). The planning cells employed by the MEU and ARG usually include the CAT, the battle staff, and the mission planning cells. These cells must participate in frequent planning exercises that involve real-world scenarios similar to those the unit might encounter. These exercises ensure the CAT, battle staff, and mission planning cells are thoroughly trained in rapid planning; their members know their commanders and each other; and the planners possess situational awareness of likely contingency missions and areas of operations. Planning cells should understand where they are to meet, what they are to accomplish, and how much time they have to complete their planning efforts. The planning cells also must be capable of conducting concurrent (simultaneous at different echelons of the same command) and parallel (between equivalent echelons of different commands) planning.

Planning and Operations SOPs

SOPs are the cornerstone of rapid planning. The planning SOP should be second nature to all concerned. Operations SOPs are equally important because they allow planners to select proven and practiced tasks that provide solutions to tactical problems. SOPs allow major subordinate elements (MSEs) to carry out familiar tasks effectively and efficiently with minimal or no higher-level guidance or communications. The SOP for each type of mission should include a pre-designated task organization; equipment and ordnance lists; elements of a landing plan; mission execution procedures; and an execution checklist with code words. The SOPs must be studied, rehearsed, executable on a moment's notice, and supported by timesaving factors. For example, standard ordnance packages for likely missions (e.g., tactical recovery of aircraft and personnel [TRAP], platoon-size reinforcements) are pre-staged in readily accessible locations in their magazines in order to reduce the time needed to break out and issue ammunition. In addition, mission smart packs are created for each mission profile. Smart packs contain specific planning information and SOPs based on the mission profile (for example: light, medium, or heavy air assault operation). Smart pack planning and coordination of information are also used as references during mission execution.

Intelligence

The commander and the staff must anticipate possible contingencies based on continual analyses of open-source news and classified intelligence reports. For each situation, the staff should be equipped with the latest intelligence (a MEU usually prepares mission folders), possible targets, area studies, and other relevant information. Periodic reviews of potential contingencies permits situational awareness to be maintained and provides current information. When appropriate, a commander conducts contingency planning and refocuses unit training based on likely scenarios. The intelligence staff must also be familiar with the Generic Intelligence Requirements Handbook (GIRH), which is produced by Marine Corps Intelligence Activity. This handbook contains essential elements of information for various mission types.

Information Management

Due to the time constraints inherent in rapid planning, there is less opportunity for the commander and the staff to analyze information requirements. Also, computer technology is increasing the speed and volume of information flow, so an overabundance of information may obscure vital facts. It is critical that every participant in the planning process realizes the importance of his mission area and take positive steps to appropriately share knowledge. Commanders and staff officers must possess the ability to present clear and concise information. Simple, concise presentations best support rapid planning.

II. Crisis Action Planning (CAP)

The Crisis Action Team

The Crisis Action Team (CAT) is the central planning cell in the MEU/PHIBRON and consists of the MEU Commander and Commodore, their staff principals, Major Subordinate Element (MSE) Commanders, Naval Support Element (NSE) representatives, and other representatives as required. The CAT supports Commanders during all phases of planning. Membership of the CAT is purposely limited due to space considerations and to maximize the efficiency of the time allocated.

A. MEU CAT

The MEU CAT is composed of the following:

- MEU Commander
- ACE Commanding Officer
- MEU Executive Officer
- ACE Operations Officer
- MEU S-1 Adjutant
- GCE Commanding Officer
- MEU S-2 Intelligence Officer
- GCE Operations Officer
- METOC briefer
- LCE Commanding Officer
- MEU S-3 Operations Officer
- LCE Operations Officer
- MEU S-3 Fire Support Officer
- MEU PAO
- MEU S-3 Air Officer
- R&S Leader
- MEU S-4 Logistics Officer
- MEU SgtMaj
- MEU S-6 Communications Officer
- MEU Ops Chief
- MEU SJA

Additional MEU attendees may include:

- Embark Officer
- MEU CBRN Officer
- MEU Medical Planner

The CPR representation in the CAT includes:

- Commodore
- Deputy Commodore
- Ship's CO or N-3
- N-2 Intelligence Officer
- CPR METOC
- N-3 Operations Officer
- CPR CCO
- CPR N-4
- TACRON OIC
- N-6
- CPR PAO
- CPR N-8
- CPR Fleet Surgeon

B. The Battle Staff

The battle staff is a resource a Mission Commander can use to augment and provide inputs to a Mission Planning Cell (MPC). The Battle staff is composed of all staff officers, special staff officers, and their assistants, from the MEU, MSEs, CPR, and NSE staffs. The Battle staff convenes at a designated location when the CAT is called away. Watch officers remain at their posts, but all other staff members assemble at designated locations wherever the ship's closed circuit television can be viewed.

Mission Planning

The Battle Staff is composed of the following:

MEU

- S-3A
- FSO
- TIO
- AirO
- CBRNO
- S-2A
- HET OIC
- RadBn OIC
- S-4A
- EmbarkO
- S-6A
- PAO Chief
- S-1 Chief
- GCE S-3A
- GCE S-2
- GCE FSC
- ACE S-3A
- ACE S-2
- LCE S-3A

PHIBRON

- N-3 rep
- N-2 rep
- CCO
- JAG
- N-6 rep
- NBG rep
- METOC rep
- EOD
- TACRON rep
- IWC rep

LHA

- Ops rep
- CCO
- AirOps
- Handler
- Medical Officer

LPD

- Operations reps and other designated staff

LSD

- Operations reps and other designated staff

C. Mission Commander

Early in the planning process, upon conclusion of problem framing, the MEU Commander will designate a Mission Commander, normally one of the MSE commanders. On some occasions, the COMPHIBRON will be the supported commander and the MEU will support a PHIBRON mission as the Supporting Commander. Mission Commanders develop the mission plans for the tasks they will execute. It is the Mission Commander who will receive planning guidance from the MEU Commander; the Mission Commander is responsible to the MEU Commander for mission execution.

When the MEU is performing multiple, simultaneous missions, the MEU Commander designates the priority mission in order to resolve conflicts and allocate resources.

Central to the rapid planning process is the idea that, "those who execute the mission plan the mission." In a MEU, subordinate forces plan the missions they will execute. The mission and supporting effort (SE) commanders receive planning guidance from the MEU Commander; it is the MEU Commander who has overall responsibility for the mission.

If the situation requires, the MEU Commander can create a MEU zone of operations to better support the mission commander (MC). In the MEU zone of operations, the MEU staff is responsible for shaping operations (kinetic or non-kinetic) in the zone as well as providing adequate representation and assistance to support the planning requirements of the mission commander. The MEU may call on national, theater or organic assets not allocated to the mission commander for shaping operations. This shaping effort is designed to reinforce the single battle focus of the MEU by enabling the mission commander with his allocated resources to focus on the tactical area of responsibility and the accomplishment of the assigned mission.

Tenets of the Marine Corps Planning Process

The tenets of the Marine Corps Planning Process—top-down planning, single-battle concept, and integrated planning—are derived from the doctrine of maneuver warfare. These tenets guide the commander's use of his staff to plan and execute military operations. Top-down planning and the single-battle concept ensure unity of effort, while the commander uses warfighting functions (see app. B) as the building blocks of integrated planning.

Mission Planning

Tenets (Marine Corps Planning Process)

Top-Down Planning

Single-Battle Concept

Integrated Planning

Top-Down Planning

Planning is a fundamental responsibility of command. The commander must not merely participate in planning, he must drive the process. His intent and guidance are key to planning. The commander uses planning to gain knowledge and situational awareness to support his decision making process. His plan, communicated in oral, graphic, or written form, translates his guidance into a concept of operations. His subordinate commanders use his guidance and concept of operations to accomplish the mission.

Single-Battle Concept

Operations or events in one part of the Battlespace may have profound and often unintended effects on other areas and events, therefore a commander must always view the battlespace as an indivisible entity. The single-battle concept allows the commander to effectively focus the efforts of all the elements of the force to accomplish the mission. While the battlespace may be conceptually divided as deep, close, and rear to assist planning and decentralized execution, the commander's intent ensures unity of effort by fighting a single battle.

Integrated Planning

Integrated planning is a disciplined approach to planning that is systematic, coordinated, and thorough. It is based on the warfighting functions of command and control, maneuver, fires, intelligence, logistics, and force protection. Planners use these warfighting functions to integrate the planning effort and supervise execution of the plan. Planners use integrated planning to consider all relevant factors, reduce omissions, and share information across all the war fighting functions.

The key to integrated planning is the assignment of appropriate personnel to represent each warfighting function. This does not mean that a warfighting function representative cannot be a staff representative. A warfighting function representative must be knowledgeable and experienced in his functional area.

Mission Planning

D. Assault Force Commander (AFC)

For most missions involving close combat with an enemy force, the Mission commander designates one of his subordinates as the Assault Force Commander. The raid force commander is responsible for actions on the objective. Assault forces are organized into assault, support and security elements per the applicable SOP for that mission profile. MEU will use "Assault force commander" to refer to subordinate commanders whose missions involve operations characterized by violence of action directed against an enemy target. An Evacuation Control Center (ECC) commander, FARP/RGR Site Commander, or Humanitarian Assistance (HA) Site Commander will be designated for missions requiring those actions.

E. Mission Planning Cell (MPC)

The Mission Planning Cell (MPC) is the Mission commander's planning staff. Each MSE will build Mission Planning Cells from their primary and special staff. The MSE Mission Planning Cell will be augmented, as required, by representatives from the other MSEs, NSE, CPR, and MEU.

Consideration must be given to the feasibility of separate planning cells due to limited staff members; therefore, the mission commander may designate more than one planning cell in order to plan concurrent, contingency, or follow-on missions. Additionally, a separate R&S mission planning cell may be established to plan R&S operations. Each mission planning cell should include appropriate representation from relevant experts. For example, a battalion landing team planning cell might include air and logistic SMEs and Navy representatives. Maintaining the same personnel in the planning cells throughout the work-up and deployment speeds and improves the planning process.

See facing page for further discussion and composition of the MPC.

Briefing File Management

Due to the complexity and volume of information necessary to provide the Commander and Staff during R2P2, the efficient and succinct execution of briefs, from CAT to Confirmation, is of utmost importance. Mastery of briefing is achieved through repetition and just as significant is the data management of each individual briefers portion of each overall brief. To that end, a standardized briefing file management system will be implemented.

Each individual and staff section is responsible for populating the brief in the correct location and ensuring that the briefing material is correct. The overall architecture of the briefs is in the shared files named according to the date which the brief will be conducted, i.e. 15Jan10. Within the subordinate date folders, there will be the folders which hold blank templates for each type of brief, as follows:

- Ops/Intel
- Problem Framing
- COA
- R&S COA
- R&S Confirmation Brief
- Confirmation Brief
- FCE Commander
- TRAP Determination
- TRAP Confirmation
- Standing Missions

The overall brief folders will contain templates for each respective brief. Briefers/staff sections should populate the briefs contained in the folder so that they can be "linked" to the overall brief prior to execution.

E. Mission Planning Cell (MPC)

The Mission Planning Cell (MPC) is the Mission commander's planning staff. Each MSE will build Mission Planning Cells from their primary and special staff. The MSE Mission Planning Cell will be augmented, as required, by representatives from the other MSEs, NSE, CPR, and MEU. MSEs will codify, in mission-specific SOPs, the notional composition of the MPC that will plan each type of mission. MPC members are designated by-name, not by billet or duty. For example, the rotary wing close air support planner for a specific mission profile should be "Captain Smith" each and every time the MPC plans that type of mission. Assigning the same personnel to the MPC each time that mission is planned will assist with developing shared understanding of new circumstances and intuitive decision making skills. MPCs develop COAs, analyze/wargame COAs during development as time permits, and conduct detailed planning.

Note The mission commander once identified will subsequently identify a lead planner for each COA development team. This team could have a variety of SMEs to assist in the development of the COA.*

Example Mission Planning Cells

COA 1

- Mission Planning Cell leader
- MSE planning staff
- MEU S-3 rep
- S-2 rep
- S-4 rep
- CPR N-3 rep
- C2W rep
- TACRON rep
- CCO rep

COA 2

- Mission Planning Cell leader
- MSE planning staff
- MEU S-3 rep
- S-2 rep
- S-4 rep
- CPR N-3 rep
- C2W rep
- TACRON rep
- CCO rep

R&S Mission Planning Cell

- R&S Mission Commander
- FORECON rep
- BLT Recon rep
- RadBn Det rep
- NSWTU Cmdr
- Ship Ops rep
- TACRON rep
- S-2 rep
- MEU S-3 rep
- MEU Fires rep
- MEU S-4 rep
- MEU S-6 rep
- CPR N-3 rep
- ACE rep
- Weather rep

Mission Planning Augments

- Fires
- NGLO
- EOD
- Engineers
- NBC
- RRT
- HET
- CCO
- NAVBEACHGRU
- CSS
- NSW
- FORECON
- Logistics
- LFSP
- SJA
- PAO
- TIO
- IO
- Medical
- Chaplain
- JAG

Marine Corps Planning Process (An Overview)

A commander may begin planning on his own initiative, based on indications and warnings, or in response to specific guidance and direction from HHQ. The planning process is designed to promote understanding among the commander, his staff, and subordinate commanders regarding the nature of a given problem and the options for solving it. The plans which result may be considered hypotheses that will be tested and refined as a result of execution and assessment. The six steps of the planning process are:

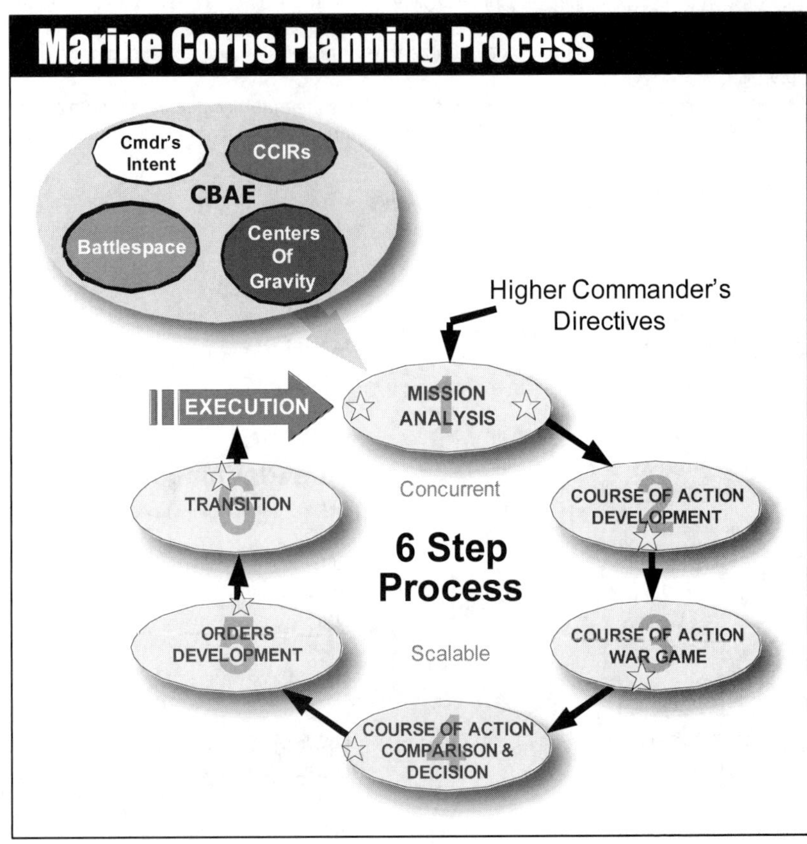

MSTP Pamphlet 5-0.2, fig. 2-1, p. 17.

1. Problem Framing

Problem framing enhances understanding of the environment and the nature of the problem. It identifies what the command must accomplish, when and where it must be done and, most importantly, why—the purpose of the operation. The purpose is articulated in the mission statement (task and purpose).

The purpose of the operation, which is enduring, is restated and amplified as desired in the commander's intent. Since no amount of subsequent planning can solve a problem insufficiently understood, problem framing is the most important step in planning. This understanding allows the commander to visualize and describe how the operation may unfold, which he articulates as his commander's concept— his overall picture of the operation. The commander's concept is also known as the CONOPS, operational concept, or method. As planning continues, the commander's concept becomes more detailed, providing additional clarity and operational context. Design does not end with problem framing, because the situation constantly evolves and requires the commander to continually review and possibly modify his design.

2. Course of Action Development

The COA development step produces options for accomplishing the mission in accordance with commander's intent. It provides options for the commander; refines the design; and promotes understanding of the environment, problem, and the approach to solving the problem.

3. Course of Action Wargaming

The COA war game examines and refines the option(s) in light of adversary capabilities and potential actions/reactions as well as the characteristics peculiar to the operating environment, such as weather, terrain, culture, and non-Department of Defense (DOD) entities or stakeholders. This detailed examination of the operational environment and possible adversary reactions should forge a greater understanding of the environment, the problem, and possible solutions.

4. COA Comparison and Decision

During COA comparison and decision, the commander reviews the pros and cons of the option(s) and decides how he will accomplish the mission, either by approving a COA as formulated or by assimilating what has been learned into a new COA that may need to be further developed and wargamed.

5. Orders Development

The orders development step translates the commander's decision into oral/written/graphic direction sufficient to guide implementation and initiative by subordinates.

6. Transition

The transition step may involve a wide range of briefs, drills, or rehearsals necessary to ensure a successful shift from planning to execution. A number of factors can influence how the transition step is conducted, such as echelon of command, mission complexity, and, most importantly, available time. The Marine Corps doctrinal philosophy of maneuver warfare describes planning as an essential part of the broader field of command and control. The aim of command and control is to enhance the commander's ability to make sound and timely decisions. Effective decision making requires both the situational understanding to recognize the essence of a given problem and the creative ability to devise a practical solution. Hence, an essential function of planning is to promote understanding of the problem—the difference between existing and desired conditions— and to devise ways to solve it. Planning involves elements of both art and science, combining analysis and calculation with intuition, inspiration, and creativity.

- Direct and coordinate actions
- Develop a shared situational awareness
- Generate expectations about how actions will evolve and how they will affect the desired outcome
- Support the exercise of initiative
- Shape the thinking of planners

I. MEU Commander's Initial Orientation (CIO)

The commander's initial orientation allows key staff to gain an understanding of the battlespace, define the problem(s) trying to be solved, and to create an initial vision for success. It answers the fundamental questions of:

- Where are we?
- Where do we need to go?
- How are we going to get there?

CIO is conducted by the MEU and PHIBRON commanders with the assistance of their key staff (MEU XO/S2/S3, PHIBRON CO/N2/N3). The specific method and output are time and mission dependent, but CBAE should always provide at least an initial framework from which to initiate mission planning using the R2P2 process.

The primary CIO elements are as follows:

A. Understanding of Battlespace (Where are we?)

- Friendly, enemy, and other actors in the battlespace and how they interact
- Variables in the environment (physical environment, nature of the state, sociological factors, culture, regional/global relationships, military capabilities, technology applications, informational battlespace, external organizations in play, national will, time, economics, other factors as applicable)
- Centers of Gravity and Critical Vulnerabilities if apparent
- Tools for understanding battlespace: orientation planning products, Area of Interest/Operations map with appropriate overlays, leader's recon
- Expressed as "Commander's Orientation"

B. Definition of Problem (Where do we need to go?)

- Why are we here?
- What military problem are we trying to solve?
- What's the message?
- Tools for definition of problem: HHQ tasking and/or interaction, quality THINKING drawing on experience, education and training, and sound military judgment
- Expressed as restated mission (if able) or more broadly as "purpose" with goals, objectives, key tasks, and message being sent

C. Initial Vision for Success (How are we going to get there?)

- Concept of Employment (battlespace framework, asset allocation and acquisition/external help, priorities)
- Risk Management Framework
- Expressed as "Commander's Intent"

Commander's Battlespace Area Evaluation (CBAE)

Normally the Commanders will express their CBAE orally during Problem framing. However, time permitting and based on direction of the commanders, the staff can provide input to assist the Commanders' develop their CIO.

See facing page for a list the staff should be ready to address during a CBAE analysis, mostly led by the intelligence sections.

Commander's Battlespace Area Evaluation (CBAE)

Normally the Commanders will express their CBAE orally during problem framing. However, time permitting and based on direction of the commanders, the staff can provide input to assist the Commanders' develop their CIO. The following list are areas that the staff should be ready to address during a CBAE analysis, mostly led by the intelligence sections.

S-2

General Situation

Special Situation

Terrain

Area of Interest Map

Area of Influence Map

Area of Operations Map

Climate

(3 Month):

Light Planner

Temp

Precipitation

Winds

Seas

Population

Enemy SITTEMP Slide:

- Enemy Strategic CC/CR/COG/MDCOA/MLCOA

Friendly/Adjacent Force lay down

Host Nation Security Force SITTEMP

HN Civilian pop density map in AO

Political divisions nationally

Political divisions in AO

Tribal lay down and disposition in AO

Economy in AO: (AO Map showing key economic infrastructure):

- Major Hospitals
- Power plants
- Pipelines
- High tension lines
- Ports
- Airfields
- Railroads
- Freeways

II. Receipt of Mission

Upon receipt of an alert or warning order, the LFOC Watch Officer notifies the MEU Operations Officer, Executive Officer and Commanding Officer by telephone; the alternate method is messenger. The LFOC Watch Officer acknowledges receipt of the order to the originator per instructions contained in the order. The LFOC Watch Officer notifies the PHIBRON watch officer via telephone and chat. The LFOC watch then e-mails copies of the order to the recipients list (distribution list) specified in the LFOC desktop procedures and post the warning order to the MEU SIPR homepage (share point).

The LFOC watch officer supervises the production and distribution of the order according to the below matrix. The CPR duty, located in the JOC, will distribute to CPR/Ship personnel.

Alert / Warning / Execution Orders Distribution Plan

Billet	Alert/Warning	Execution
MEU CO	*1	*1
Commodore	#*1	*1
LHA CO	#1	1
MEU XO	1	1
CPR CSO	#1	1
MEU S-3	*1	*1
CPR N-3	#1	1
MEU S-3A	1	1
LHA OpsO	#1	1
TACRON	#1	1
LFOC WO	1	1
METOC	#1	1
MEU S-2	1	1
IWC	#1	1
MEU S-4	1	1
MEU SJA	1	0
MEU S-6	1	1
MEU AirO	1	0
MEU FSO	1	0
MEU PAO	1	1
GCE	2	0
ACE	2	0
LCE	2	0
R&S Coordinator	1	1

* = Deliver hard copy immediately
# = Delivered by CPR Watch Officer
Alert, Warning, Execution Orders are posted to SIPRNET Website and auto emailed to all listed above.

Following the review of the order, the MEU Commander/Operations Officer decides when to call away the CAT. When the decision is made to call away the CAT, the LFOC watch officer will request that the bridge announce over the 1MC "Assemble the Crisis Action Team in LFOC planning room at (time).

Copies of the (mission type, warning/alert/execute order) are available for pickup in the LFOC." This announcement over the 1MC is the trigger for the staff and MSE staffs to assemble in their designated spaces to view the CAT via CCTV, or if applicable VTC.

Once the CAT announcement is made, the LFOC watch officer will notify MEU forces on the other ships that the CAT is being convened. When the CAT announcement is made ships are prepared to accommodate cross-decking of key personnel. The nature of the mission will determine who is cross-decked; mission specific SOPs will identify individuals required for the Mission Planning Cells.

Watch Clerk in the LFOC watch section produces copies of the order for the CAT per the distribution matrix. The MEU Operations Chief ensures that LFOC planning room is prepared for the CAT and networked in via CCTV or VTC.

The MEU S-2, in coordination with the S-3, will determine the map chip used for planning, briefing, and mission execution. Prior to the receipt of a warning order the MEU S-2/S-3 should already have an Area of Operations map; upon receipt S-2 will create mission maps. Maps are defined as listed below.

- **Area of Interest Map**: Regional map displaying areas that could impact MEU or Enemy Ops
- **Area of Influence Map**: Generally about 250mi radius around ARG/MEU location; the area that the ARG/MEU can exert combat power
- **Area of Operations Map**: Identified MEU AOR
  - Normally 1:50,000 scale
  - Terrain elevation
  - Roads, Ports, Airfields
  - High tension wires
  - Major towns named and populated areas marked
- **Mission Map:** Created after receipt of warning order as the one common map for all elements for this mission; can use the AO map if scale is appropriate
  - Appropriate scale to include area around all of this Mission's Objectives or key nodes
  - Confirmed HLZs marked
  - Confirmed BLSs marked
- **Objective Map**: Used to plan air/ground/fires actions on a single objective; can use as mission map if 1:50 scale supports.
  - ALWAYS 1:50,000 or 1:100,000
  - Approximately 10km around single Objective
- **GRG**: Used for air ground coordination; hang for all mission briefs.
  - CIB1 is standard
  - CIB5 or other if required; should be oriented North and directly overhead
  - Buildings numbered
  - Roads named
  - Alphanumeric grid overlay

III. Conduct Problem Framing

Problem framing enhances understanding of the environment and the nature of the problem. It identifies what the command must accomplish, when and where it must be done and, most importantly, why—the purpose of the operation. The purpose is articulated in the mission statement (task and purpose).

The purpose of the operation, which is enduring, is restated and amplified as desired in the commander's intent. Since no amount of subsequent planning can solve a problem insufficiently understood, problem framing is the most important step in planning. This understanding allows the commander to visualize and describe how the operation may unfold, which he articulates as his commander's concept— his overall picture of the operation. The commander's concept is also known as the CONOPS, operational concept, or method. As planning continues, the commander's concept becomes more detailed, providing additional clarity and operational context. Design does not end with problem framing, because the situation constantly evolves and requires the commander to continually review and possibly modify his design.

Problem framing begins with an update to the situation since the last operations and intelligence summary. In most cases, these updates are succinct, as most of the CAT possesses current information from the daily operations/intelligence summaries. In the case of a rapidly developing situation, or an unanticipated mission, these updates may take significantly longer.

Synopsis of the CAT Problem Framing

1. The MEU Operations Officer presents the **higher commander's mission and intent** as it is explained in the order. If the higher mission and intent is unclear, or if the higher commander has failed to provide the purpose of the operation to the MEU/PHIBRON in the warning or alert order, the MEU and PHIBRON commanders will initiate action to get the purpose clarified. While awaiting clarification, planning will proceed based on assumptions regarding the purpose of the operation.

2. The CAT members identify the **specified tasks** contained in the higher order and determine what implied tasks can be derived from the higher order. **Essential tasks** are highlighted. The CAT members conduct a review of limitations contained in the higher order.

3. At this stage, the CAT members may make **assumptions** to allow planning to proceed. Assumptions are normally made about the enemy, the terrain and weather and friendly force capabilities/availability. Assumptions may become basis for Commanders Critical Information Requirements (CCIRs), Priority Intelligence Requirements (PIRs), Requests for Information (RFIs) or left invalidated. Assumptions made to allow planning to continue will be validated before the confirmation brief. Invalidated assumptions will be briefed as such during the confirmation brief and the associated risk identified.

4. The CAT may identify **additional issues** for mission clarification---items that relate to what actions the issuing HHQ regards as essential to mission accomplishment. The MEU S-3 will seek answers to the issues that require clarification and update them during subsequent briefs.

5. Additional **information requirements** are recorded and projected for the CAT members to review. Priority Intelligence Requirements (PIRs) become the basis of the collections plan. Essential Elements of Friendly Information (EEFIs) become the basis for deception and force protection planning. Friendly Force Information Requirements (FFIRs) get answered through RFIs to other friendly forces. The Intelligence Officers will take the PIRs for action. The Operations Officer will act on the RFIs during COA development and detailed planning. Before the confirmation brief, the information requirements are reviewed. Unfulfilled critical information requirements may be briefed as part of the "No Go" criteria for mission launch during the confirmation brief. Answers to RFIs will be collected by the MEU RFI Manager who is resident in the MEU S-3 and made available to mission planners on the MEU SIPR webpage. Standing information requirements for each mission are contained in the Generic Intelligence Requirements Handbook.

6. The MEU Staff Judge Advocate reviews the **Rules of Engagement (ROE)** provided in the higher order. The MEU SJA will also identify any broad operational law issues which will affect COA development. At this time, the CAT members will ask for clarification on any ROE that are unclear and will recommend supplemental ROE that may aid mission accomplishment. As supplemental ROE are approved, the SJA will ensure they are recorded into the SJA section of the Confirmation Brief. Supplemental ROE requested but not approved by the point of the confirmation brief will be considered "denied" and not briefed. Standing ROE can be found in Enclosure (3).

CAT I / Problem Framing Brief Guide

CAT/Problem Framing Brief Guide

Briefer	Topic
MEU Ops Chief	Roll Call Time Hack
Commanders	Commanders' Orientation Commanders' Battlespace Area Evaluation Initial Guidance
MEU S-3	MEU Wire Diagram PHIB/MEU Task Organization S-3 Orientation -MEU location, Friendly Forces -Objective location, Friendly Forces Missions -Current -Projected Assets Available
PHIBRON N-3	Naval situation orientation
MEU Meteorologist	Current/Future Weather (at Obj area and along routes) Impacts to mission (if known)
MEU S-2	Terrain/Environment Analysis Intelligence Update COG & CV Target Information Analysis -SALUTE -DRAW-D -MPCOA/MDCOA Priority Intelligence Requirements (PIR) Collection Assets status
PHIBRON N-2	Maritime/littoral Intelligence Update Threats to ARG or Craft in transit to shore
MEU S-3	HHQ Mission HHQ Purpose, Method, and Endstate Standing & Mission Specific CCIRs Specified/Implied Tasks, Essential Tasks Constraints and Restraints ROE Mission Clarification Assumptions External Support Requirements Restated Mission RFIs Cross Deck Refined Commanders Intent COA Guidance
Commanders	Comments, intent, and guidance
MEU S-3	Planning Cell Timeline

Before departing the CAT, the MEU S-3 enumerates the **augmentation** required to support the mission planning cell. CAT members will assign, by-name, these augmentees and ensure they report to the planning cell location. A review of the planning timeline is the final event of the CAT. The CAT "outputs" will be posted to the shared files and posted to the MEU SIPR webpage for ARG wide viewing.

While the CAT meeting is underway, the MEU and MSE remaining staff assembles in the designated space under the cognizance of the MEU S-3A to concurrently build their **situational awareness**. By the time the CAT brief concludes, the staff should be reasonably up to date on the higher order and the current situation. In some cases an additional staff orientation brief may be given, however, this should be considered the exception rather than the rule.

7. The mission may require the activation of **standing mission forces (TRAP, Sparrowhawk, etc.)** to respond to potential contingencies or to enable mission accomplishment. The CAT reviews potential requirements for standing mission forces. The MEU Operations Officer recommends, and the MEU Commander approves, what standing mission forces will prepare plans to support the Main or Supporting Efforts. Forces activated will brief, as necessary, their plans at the confirmation brief.

8. At this point, the MEU and PHIBRON Commanders should have a clear idea of what is required to satisfy the purpose of the task contained in the higher order. The draft **restated mission** is prepared which will include the essential tasks identified during the analysis. The approved restated mission statement becomes the basis for the warning order that goes out at the conclusion of the CAT.

9. Once the mission for the MEU and PHIBRON is approved, the PHIBRON commander issues **planning guidance** to the Navy elements supporting the mission.

10. The MEU commander will either appoint a R&S leader or assign that mission planning to the BLT Commander who may delegate that task within his organization. The MEU commander will then issue planning guidance regarding R&S employment or a review of the available assets the R&S Mission leader may use for planning. Upon conclusion of the **R&S guidance**, the MEU commander will provide guidance to the Main and Supporting Effort Commanders regarding acceptable ways to accomplish the assigned mission. Planning guidance will be recorded on the initial CAT slides and posted to the MEU SIPR webpage for all to review. The Mission commander will identify the space used to lead **COA development**.

11. At the conclusion of the CAT brief, the MEU Operations Officer issues the **first warning order** for the mission to follow. Contents of the warning order will include, as a minimum:

- The mission statement for the MAGTF
- The Main and Supporting Efforts and the R&S leader
- A planning timeline in local time; and specific actions that may commence upon receipt of the order that are not normally included as part of the MEU's SOP for the mission

IV. Course of Action (COA Development)

The Mission commander assembles the mission planning cell (MPC) at the designated place and time.

The Mission commander's operations officer calls roll for membership in the Mission Planning Cell per the applicable SOP concurrently the lead for each COA will be identified. Functional area representatives stand and identify themselves by-name to the Mission commander. The Mission commander will pass his planning guidance once he is satisfied that all MPC members are present. In some cases, the Mission Planning Cell might include experts who will be required for COA development but not for detailed planning (for instance, if the COA selected does not include LCAC use, the ACU detachment rep to the MPC may no longer be required for detailed planning, despite being required for COA development).

The Mission commander passes understanding of the MEU commander's intent, the problem framing and the CAT meeting proceedings to the Mission Planning Cell. MPC members, at this time, begin developing their list of information requirements and recommended CCIRs for the Mission commander. Members should begin mentally wargaming potential friendly and enemy actions that might impact on COA.

See following pages for further discussion of COA Development.

Staff Preferences

Once the COAs have been presented, the MEU S-3 summarizes the presentation and calls for staff preferences.

Staff Estimate Recording Sheet

Staff Member	COA A	COA B	COA C	Remarks
MEU S-1				
MEU METOC				
PHIBRON METOC				
MEU S-2				
PHIBRON N-2				
MEU IO				
PHIBRON IWC				
MEU SJA				
PHIBRON JAG				
MEU PAO				
PHIBRON PAO				
MEU Air Operations				
SHIP Air Operations				
TACRON				
MEU Fires				
MEU S-4				
PHIBRON N-4				
PHIBRON CCO				
MEU Medical				
PHIBRON Surgeon				
MEU S-6				
PHIBRON N-6				
Naval Beach Group				
PHIBRON N-31				
PEL Ship Operations				
DUB Ship Operations				
PHB Ship Operations				
Force RECON				
MEU S-3				
PHIBRON N-3				
MEU XO				
Deputy				
CLB Commander				
ACE Commander				
GCE Commander				
Tally				

Guidelines for voting criteria are established by the MEU XO prior to conducting the meeting. For example, staff members understand 1 is better than 2, therefore if COA 1 receives a lower score it will be designated as the more desirable COA.

The MEU S-2 will present an estimate of supportability from the intelligence perspective. After the staff preferences conclude, the MSE Commanders provide their estimates of supportability. An estimate of supportability informs the MEU Commander which COA the MSE Commander would recommend adopting and why. Normally, estimates of supportability revolve around efficient use of assets, ease of support, assets left available for other missions if a specific COA is adopted and so forth. MSE Commanders use their estimates to inform the MEU Commander as to which COA makes best use of the MSEs' assets. The designated Mission commander will give his recommendation last.

The MEU Operations Chief records the numerical value for each COA using the spreadsheet in this section. The lower score the better, COA with the lowest score indicates to the MEU Commander which COA is favored as a whole by the MEU/CPR staffs.

The MEU and PHIBRON commanders will discuss and compare the COAs and the MEU Commander will announce his decision if he is the supported commander and vice versa if the Commodore is the supported commander.

Mission Planning

Staff Estimates/Considerations

Effects of each of these should be considered for COA 1, COA 2 and COA 3

Weather
Area to be Analyzed
Effect on Flight Ops
Effect on LCAC Ops
Sea State Requirements
Density Altitude Impacts
Thermal Crossover Impact
Shadow Effects
Personnel Survivability
Effect on Radio Transmission
Impact on Sensors
Wx at FARP site (if req'd)
Conclusions

MEU S-2
Estimate/Considerations
Area to be Analyzed
Number of Teams Required
Ease of Insert/Recovery
Threat of Compromise
Coverage of Objective
Mutual Support
Duplicate Coverage of Vital Areas
Requirement for ITG
Time Available for R&S
Conclusions
PHIBRON N-2
Estimate/Considerations
Area to be Analyzed
Collections can support targeting/objective
JIC/EXPLOT able to provide I&W
Analysts adequate
Linguist availability
Intel "pull" supportable in EMCON posture/INFOSEC condition
Conclusions

Information Warfare
Area to be Analyzed
INFOSEC requirements
OPSEC requirements
EW requirements
MILDEC requirements
PSYOPS effectiveness
Impact of River City
Conclusions

Staff Judge Advocate
Area to be Analyzed
Supplemental ROE
Likelihood of Civilian Casualties
Proportionality
Proximity to Protected Sites/Persons
Likelihood of Claims
Numbers of EPWs that will result
Neutral Over flight
Difficulty of Interpreting "Hostile Intent"
Sovereignty – Land/Sea (internal & territorial/ Over flight
Requires supplemental ROE – Likelihood of approval/weapon release authority
Coalition and HN ROE compatible?
International treaty obligations (HR/Mines/Conventional Weapons/Chemical)
Proportionality/proximity to protected sites/persons
Likelihood of civilian casualties
Self-defense and interpreting "Hotile Act/Intent"
Detainees and EPW: Legal basis/ apabilities to process, evacuate, medical/asylum, refugee & IDP
Likelihood of claims/claims authority (single service)
HN Law, SOFA criminal jurisdiction
Information operations issues
Fiscal/Contracting issues
Contractor and civilian support
Conclusions

Public Affairs Officer
Area to be Analyzed
Easily Explained to Media
Ability to Document
Likelihood of Media Interest
Media Accessibility
Political Sensitivity
Conclusions

MEU Air Operations
Area to be Analyzed
Requirement for external support
Requirement for crossdecks to support planning or execution
Number of assets required
Number of lillypads reqd
AR required
FARP required
Conclusions

TACRON
Area to be Analyzed
Airspace Deconfliction
Air Traffic Density
Complexity
SAR requirements
CSG asset requirements
Conclusions

Flagship Air Operations
Area to be Analyzed
Ease of Deck Cycle
Number of Refuelings
Time Required to Spot Deck
Conclusions

Ship's Operations Officer
Area to be Analyzed
Overlap of 3A and flight operations
Crew day
Material readiness
Ship's schedule
Time-Space factor
Conclusions

MEU Fire Support Officer
Area to be Analyzed
Observation
Fire Support Coordination Measures
Assets Committed
Geometry
Reliance on External Assets

Duration of Support Required
Maximum Engagement Range
Conclusions

MEU S-4 Logistics

Area to be Analyzed
Duration of operation
Ease of recovery
Requirement for reconfiguration
Requirement for resupply
Requirement for Host Nation Support
Transportation required
Monetary cost
Health services impact
Conclusions

PHIBRON Combat Cargo

Area to be Analyzed
Duration of ship to shore movement
Offload complexity
Requirement for simultaneous boat/craft and helo operations
Requirement for reconfiguration of existing loads
Requirement for ammunition cross-decks
Number of personnel to move / test fire/ issue ammo
Conclusions

CATF Surgeon Medical

Area to be Analyzed
Meets "golden hour"
Ease of CASEVAC
Duration/degree of exposure to threats ashore
Environmental concerns
Conclusions

MEU Communications

Area to be Analyzed
Terrain effects on comm
Distance
Complexity of comm plan
Reliance on relay
Comm assets committed
Redundancy
Conclusions

PHIBRON N-6

Area to be Analyzed
Systems status
Ranges between ARG ships
SATCOM takeoff angle
Redundancy
Complexity
Deck mounting required?
Conclusions

Naval Beach Group

Area to be Analyzed
Requirements for crew day
SUROBS available
Transit distance
Sea state impact on craft
Duration of operation
Conclusions

"Red Cell"---Enemy Perspective

Area to be Analyzed
Ease of Countering Insert
Ease of Detecting the Raid Force prior to Actions on the Objective
Ease of Isolating Raid Force
Enemy Ability to Reinforce
Easiest to Down A/C
Enemy Advantage in Force Ratio on Objective
Conclusions

PHIBRON N-3 Operations Officer

Area to be Analyzed
Surface movement ship-to-shore
Hazards to navigation
Defense of the ATF
Ability to achieve geometry
Time available to maneuver ships to position
Conclusions

MEU S-3 Operations Officer's

Area to be Analyzed
Supports Cmdr's Intent
Supports Higher Intent
Effect on Enemy Critical Vulnerability
Mass
Objective
Offensive
Speed
Surprise
Economy of Force
Maneuver
Ease of Cmd and Control
Security
Simplicity
Mutual Support
Maximizes Combined Arms
Risk
Facilitates Future Ops
External Coordination required
Conclusions

Ground Combat Element

Area to be Analyzed
Organic fires available
Surface fires available
Simplicity
C2 ashore
Mutual support
Flexibility
Reserve available
Mass
Combat power overmatch
Duration
Self-reliance
Minimizes casualties
Conclusions

Aviation Combat Element

Area to be Analyzed
Aircraft available vs. number used
Aircrew available
Circadian rhythms/crew day
Weather
Time on station
LZ suitability
A/C survivability and detection
Ordnance utilization
Deconfliction
Time-space analysis
KC-130 use
MACG considerations
LAAD coverage
Number of waves required
Conclusions

CAT II / COA Brief Guide

COA Brief Guide

Briefer	Topic
MEU S-3	Orientation -MEU location, Friendly Forces -Objective location, Friendly Forces Missions -Current -Projected Mission CCIRs Restated Mission Mission Clarification/RFIs/Assumptions
PHIBRON N-3	Current Location/orientation Time and space to launch points Location of FSA's (if applicable) NSFS available
MEU Meteorologist	Weather (Tailored to specific mission and time METOC impacts on the mission)
MEU S-2	Intel Update Updated Collection Effort (PIRs, etc.) Target graphics-big to small Time/distance considerations Proposed HLZ/BLS photos and characteristics Line of sight diagrams/shadow studies Topography effects
PHIBRON N-2	Orientation Map Collections Synch Matrix
MEU S-6	Data Services Status Radio Net Status
PHIBRON N-6	CPR-3 Radio Status CPR-3 ADP Status PELARG C5I Status
Courses of Action	
Mission commander (MSE S-3)	Courses of Action Slide -Summary of forces involved -Major CPR/MEU assets required -Describe actions within COA -Phasing -Actions on the objective -Main Effort -Supporting efforts -Reserve / Stand-by forces -Priority of fires -Timeline -Advantages / Disadvantages
Red Cell	Wargame
MEU S-3	Summarize COAs Staff Estimates
Commanders Decision and Planning Guidance	
Commanders	Confer/select a COA/issue additional guidance
MEU S-3	Planning Cell Timeline

Course of Action Criteria

Normally, the MPC tries to develop two or three courses of action; each of which should meet the following criteria:

- **Suitable**. Does the COA accomplish the purpose and tasks? Does it comply with the commander's planning guidance?
- **Feasible**. Does the COA accomplish the mission within the available time, space, and resources?
- **Acceptable**. Does the COA achieve an advantage that justifies the cost in resources?
- **Distinguishable**. Does the COA differ significantly from other COAs?
- **Complete**. Does the COA include all tasks to be accomplished? Does it describe a complete mission?

Simply varying the insertion means does not guarantee that a COA "differs." In a MEU construct, COAs vary in which way they influence the enemy at the objective, rather than by the means of insertion. A frontal attack that gets to the objective by helicopters is not significantly different from the same frontal attack inserted by AAVs.

Normally, COAs are built from pre-existing mission-specific SOPs, where the task organization of the force to be employed is pre-designated. Mission-specific SOPs contain generic forces that require a minimum of tailoring to be appropriate to the task being undertaken. Central to rapid planning, SOPs provide potential generic solutions and serve as the "tools in a tool bag" that prevent planners from having to invent potential solutions from scratch each mission.

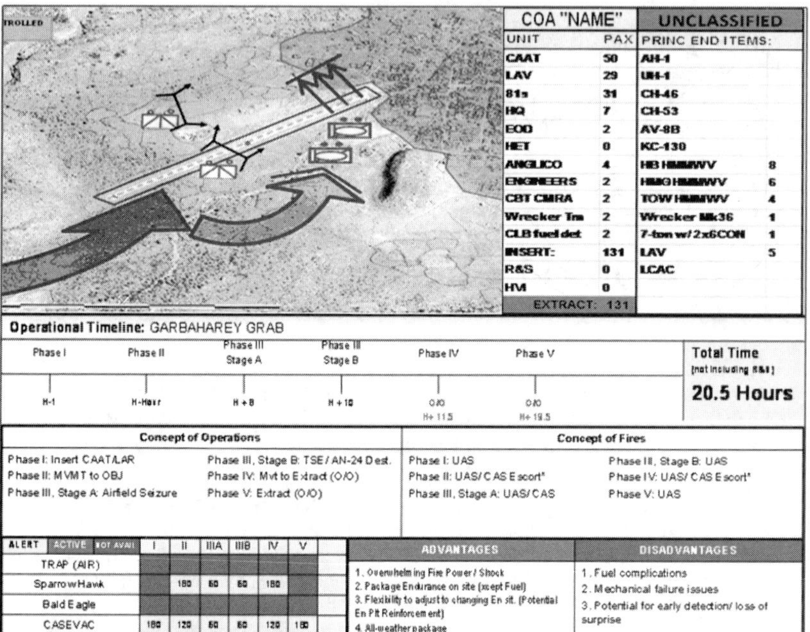

Example COA Brief Slide

COAs get depicted with on computer-generated graphics large enough to be seen across the wardroom. A narrative that describes the COA will accompany the graphics. The COA will cover the following standard phases: 1) Insertion, 2) Movement to the Objective Area, 3) Actions on the Objective, 4) Movement to the Extraction Point(s) and 5) Extraction to ARG Shipping.

The COA includes an overview statement, a proposed task organization, a timeline for the mission; major MEU/CPR end items required, description of the main effort's actions, a description of the supporting efforts actions, fire support plan and any other information needed to explain how the COA accomplishes the mission.

Standard Mission Phases:

1) Shaping
2) Insertion
3) Actions on the Objective
4) Extraction
5) Reconstitution

V. Commander's Decision

For most standard missions the MEU Commander announces his decision after conferring with the PHIBRON Commander. The MEU Commander may select one of the COAs presented, modify one of the COAs, combine the COAs, or reject all COAs for one of his own design.

Upon deciding on the COA, the MEU Commander provides guidance for detailed planning to the MSE. In some cases, planning guidance may include direction to continue planning. This provides flexibility and provides an alternate plan to be readily enacted. Once selected, the COA becomes the Concept of Operations (CONOPS) for the MEU. Detailed planning will be fill out the concept of the operation that can be presented in a confirmation brief and understood by all hands involved in the mission.

The MEU Operations Officer posts selected portions of the approved COA brief to the MEU SIPR webpage, and e-mails portions to Commanders of Troops on the other ships and to the Forward Command Element (if required). If higher HQ requires the MEU to inform them of the MEU Concept of the Operation, the MEU Operations Officer will provide a CONOPS message based on the selected COA.

Before departing the CAT II brief, the Mission commander identifies the augments he requires for detailed planning. Detailed planning commences once the planning cell augments are identified by-name and the location for planning known. The MEU S-3 reviews the planning timeline and detailed planning commences.

VI. Reconnaissance and Surveillance (R&S) Planning

R&S Leader

During the CAT I brief, the MEU commander will designate an R&S leader. They may specify the number of teams the R&S leader may use for planning. If the MEU commander has withheld teams for MEU/PHIBRON level requirements there may be fewer teams available to support the Mission commander than would normally be the case.

For MEU missions, the Force Reconnaissance or BLT Reconnaissance Platoon Commander is the R&S Leader. Other R&S leaders (Radio Battalion Det OIC, Scout Sniper Plt Cmdr) serve as subject matter experts on their unit capabilities and limitations. R&S planning cell augmentees are identified, by name, at the CAT. R&S planning cell augmentees may be "dual-hatted" and may have to be assigned to support the Mission commander in the planning as well. Their first duty is to assist the R&S leader until the R&S Concept of Operations is approved. The R&S leader will designate the Reconnaissance Operations Center (ROC).

See following pages for further discussion to include R&S CONOPS/COA Brief Guide (p. 2-29) and R&S Confirmation Brief Guide (pp. 2-30 to 2-31).

Reconnaissance Operations Center (ROC)

The ROC is located in the LFOC and receives all R&S team information. As the information arrives, it is evaluated and entered into the ROC watch log. Urgent information is immediately relayed to the LFOC Watch Officer, R&S Leader and the S-2. Non-urgent information is sent via e-mail to the Joint Intelligence Center (JIC) for processing before it is disseminated further. Each R&S element is responsible for providing augmentation to the ROC during R&S operations.

If R&S forces operate in the objective area before the Mission commander commences operations, they may provide information that causes the confirmed plan to change. If information obtained from R&S forces invalidates the confirmed plan or fulfills a "NO GO" criterion, the CAT may reconvene to consider the changed information. The MEU Commander may abort a mission already in progress, decide against a mission not yet launched ("NO GO" criteria met), or put the mission on hold and reconvene the CAT to consider the impact of the new information.

R&S CONOPS/COA Brief Guide

Normally conducted in LFOC planning room. Only update information since COA Brief.

R&S CONOPS/COA Brief Guide

Briefer	Topic
MEU S-3	Orientation Missions in progress (including R&S) Mission CCIRs Mission statement Mission Clarification/Answered RFIs
PHIBRON N-3	Current Location/orientation Time and space to launch points Location of FSA's (if applicable) NSFS available
MEU Meteorologist	Weather(Tailored to specific mission and time METOC impacts on the mission)
MEU S-2/N-2	Intel Update Updated Collection Effort (PIRs, etc.) Target graphics-big to small, distances shown Proposed HLZ/BLS photos and characteristics Line of sight diagrams, shadow studies, etc. Topography effects on insert and transit to Obj
Courses of Action	
R&S Leader	Courses of Actions Mission, purpose, tasks IRs to be fulfilled T/O and EDL Brief by phase/team Insert means, actions on objective, exfil Timeline
Staff Estimates	Staff Estimates (same process as with COA Brief)
Commanders Decision and Planning Guidance	
Commanders	Confer/decide/additional guidance
MEU S-3	Identify augments for detailed planning Timeline

The R&S Leader develops and briefs a CONOPS to the Staff and Commanders that accomplishes coverage of the target area and fulfills MEU intelligence requirements as directed by the MEU S-2. There may be cases in which the R&S CONOPS must be selected prior to the Mission COA being selected. The R&S Leader may present multiple R&S COAs that accomplish coverage of the target area, however the distinguishing feature may only be insertions methods. The R&S Leader provides representation to the key planner to ensure situational awareness is maintained.

R&S COA

The R&S COA contains details as to the number of teams used, insertion means, teams committed elsewhere, PIRs that can be answered by the teams and PIRs that may go unfilled. The MSEs present estimates of supportability of the R&S CONOPS. Based on inputs from the staff, the MSEs and the Mission commander, the MEU commander may approve or modify the R&S CONOPS.

The R&S Leader confirms the R&S plan as a stand-alone confirmation brief to the CAT. This brief will ensure that all team members understand the intelligence collection requirements and how they support the Commander's intent.

After plan confirmation and team insertion, the R&S Leader continues to coordinate with the Mission commander to ensure that changes in the plan are supportable by the deployed R&S teams. Any changes in the overall plan are relayed to and ensured fully understood by the deployed teams. Special care should be paid to link up instructions between the raid force and R&S teams on the objective.

R&S Confirmation Brief Guide

Normally conducted in Wardroom Lounge. **Bold** *indicates what will be briefed during each Confirmation Brief. All others brief changes only.*

R&S Confirmation Brief Guide

Briefer	Topic
MEU Ops Chief	Roll Call **Time Hack (GPS)**
MEU S-3	**Orientation (Ground)** Friendly Force locations Missions Current and Projected **Review Mission CCIRs/RFIs** **Restate Mission**
PHIBRON N-3	**Naval Orientation**
MEU Meteorologist	Weather METOC impacts on the mission
MEU S-2	**Intel Update** Objective IPB **MLCOA/MDCOA** Current PIRs
PHIBRON N-2	Naval Intelligence Update Hydrography
R &S Ldr	**Mission** **Commander's Intent** **Task Organization** **Concept of Ops** **Phase I- Insertion (ship to shore/LZ)** **Phase II- Movement to Objective Area** **Phase III- Actions on the Objective** **Phase IV- Movement to Extraction Point** **Phase V- Extraction (shore/LZ to ship)** **Mission Timeline** **Load Plan** **Bump Plan** **Coordinating Instructions** **Comm Windows** **No Comm Plan** **WIA/KIA/CASEVAC Plan** **Emergencey Extract** **Detainee Plan**
FSC/MEU FSO	**Essential Fire Support Tasks** **Priority of Fires** **Allocation of Fires** **Fire Support Coordination Measures** **Fire Support Execution Matrix** **Target Precendence** Priority of Fires Attack Guidance Matrix
PHIBRON CCO	Debarkation Timeline/Serial Call Away LCAVAT/Craft Loads
TACRON	Air Space Considerations AOA Altitudes Entry & Exit Points (ATC) Helo Lanes Comm/IFF Return to Forces Procedures Diverts SAR plan
Ship's Air Ops	Air Plan Sorting Plan

Air Mission Commander (AMC)	**Mission Assets**
	Timeline
	Scheme of maneuver
	Launch/Rendezvous
	Primary Route
	Alternate Route
	Control measures
	Routing diagram(s)
	Objective area arrival
	    Comm
	    Clearance
	    Holding
	    IP
	    Flow
	    Landing plan
	Obj area diagram(s)
	LZ diagram(s)
	Bump Plan
	Contingencies Plan
	FARP/RGR/AR Plan

E&R Plan (ACE S-2)	Evasion and Recovery Plan **(SAFE's only)** E&R points and time of service Theater Designated Areas for Recovery (DAR)
ME S-4	Concept of Logistics Pre-staged/Pre-planned Support Maintenance Recovery External/Host Nation support available/coordinated
MEU S-6 / PHIBRON N-6	Comm Plan (Net diagram) Challenge & Password Anticipated impact on Comm due to urban/rural terrain and atmospheric effects during the mission Cryptographic changes that affect mission Naval Comm Plan (Net Diagram)
Medical (PHIBRON)	Assets Ashore CASEVAC procedures Chain of Evacuation Time/distance from point of injury to ARG Primary and alternate means of CASEVAC Medical Regulating PCRTS: Beds, ORS, Blood SCRTS: Beds, ORS, Blood
MEU SJA PHIBRON JAG	Review Standing ROE Supplemental ROE granted Detainee Handling Civilian Handling Mission specific legal issues
ORM / Safety	Navy ACE GCE LCE (as required)
Standby Mission (as required)	CASEVAC MASCAS Air TRAP Surface TRAP Sparrowhawk Bald Eagle
MEU S-3	**Review Master Execution Checklist** **Review Master Timeline** **Manifest due to TACLOG NLT 2 hours post brief** **Summary**
Commanders	Comments, Approval
MEU S-3	Timeline

VII. Detailed Planning

By 2 hours 30 minutes after receipt of mission, the MPC commences detailed planning using the selected COA and MEU/CPR Commander's guidance. Detailed planning is a participatory and collective activity. Planners who plan the mission come from the forces executing the mission.

Personnel assigned to planning cells execute known roles, so planning proceeds in an organized manner with a minimum of duplication of effort.

The execution checklist needs to be confirmed by the MEU S3 prior to the confirmation brief.

When rehearsing the mission, the execution checklist is "walked" to ensure that the events are well understood, particular trigger events. During the rehearsal, conducting "what if" exercises identifies potential "branches" to the base plan. In addition a review of the specified and implied tasks from the problem framing is conducted to ensure all tasks have been accounted for in the plan.

VIII. Confirmation Brief

The Confirmation Brief is an oral issuance the plan delivered to the MEU and PHIBRON commanders and mission participants.

The Confirmation Brief is the de facto operations order, therefore, it must explain the plan in sufficient detail so that those involved in executing, and supporting and supervising the execution of the mission can understand how the parts are synchronized.

The Confirmation Brief will normally follow the format contained in the SOP for that mission profile in order to prevent duplication or omissions. Individual briefers prepare their slides for the Confirmation Brief, which will be compiled from the shared files folders for the mission by the MEU S-3 section. Confirmation Briefs are presented in PowerPoint. Briefers will ensure they have prepared paper copies of their slides should there be a computer malfunction during the brief.

Standing missions not already confirmed will be briefed during the Confirmation Brief.

The Confirmation Brief is normally limited to one hour. Because so much information is compressed into such a short time, SOPs must be well understood and thoroughly rehearsed. SOP items are not normally reviewed during a Confirmation Brief; mission-specific details make up the bulk of the brief. Mission profile SOPs will contain the templates of the slides normally presented in a confirmation brief for that type of mission. Confirmation Brief attendees should be able to follow the brief and "fill in the blanks" of the mission-specific details by following along in their copies of the planning handbook.

Towards the end of the Confirmation Brief, the MEU S-3 will highlight specific items of the Execution Checklist and call attention to trigger events. This review will provide an opportunity for mission participants to match execution checklist items to specific events in the mission. This final review provides all hands a "mental map" of the mission from launch to recovery. The MEU S-3 will review the execution timeline at the conclusion of the Confirmation Brief.

Once the Confirmation Brief concludes, no changes to the plan are authorized without the MEU Comds approval. If changes become necessary after the confirmation brief, the plan may need to be re-confirmed. Delays caused by weather or other unforeseen circumstances may cause mission participants to change.

Flight, aircrew and raid force briefs follow the confirmation brief. Normally, a raid force representative attends the ACE mission brief.

See confirmation brief guide on following pages (2-34 to 2-37).

Confirmation Brief Attendees

The primary location for Confirmation Briefs is the wardroom of the USS Peleliu. The following chart depicts the notional organization for the MEU/PHIBRON Confirmation Brief briefers/attendees. Not all individuals listed will be required to participate in all Confirmation Briefs. It is the responsibility of the MEU S-3 to control the size and composition of the Confirmation Brief based on guidance received from the Commodore and MEU Commander. This list of attendees is flexible.

MEU Attendees

CE
CO, XO, S-2, S-2A, S-3, S-3A, S-3 Chief, S-4, S-4A, AirO, AAirO, SJA, FSO, TIO, S-6, S-6A, SgtMaj, EmbarkO, CBRNO, RadBn Det OIC, HET OIC, PAO, Medical, ATFPO, S-1, LFOC Watch Officers and radio supervisors planned to be on duty during mission execution
GCE
CO, XO, S-2, S-3, S-3A, Gunner, S-4, AirO, S-6, Raid Force Element Commanders, FSC, Sparrowhawk Cmdr, Bald Eagle Cmdr, TRAP Plt Cmdr, and other key leaders as required
ACE
CO or XO, Air Mission Commander, Escort Flight Leader, Assault Flight Leader, MACG Det OIC/Rep, Strike Flt LDR, other key leaders as required and available
LCE
CO, XO, S-2, S-3, S-4, S-6, Mass Casualty Cmdr, and other key leaders/individuals as required

PHIBRON and Ship's Attendees

PHIBRON
Commodore, Deputy, N-2, N-3, N-31, N-6, Judge Advocate, Combat Cargo Officer, CATF Surgeon, IWC, Naval Beach Group OIC, TACRON Det OIC, PAO, and SAC OIC
Ships
Ship COs and/or OpsOs, Flagship Air Boss/mini-Boss or handler, ships' CCO, Air Ops, First Lieutenant, PCS Ops, Medical Officer, other key leaders/individuals as directed by CPR

Mission Planning

Confirmation Brief Guide

**The MEU Commander, MEU Operations Officer, Mission Commander, Raid Force Commander, Air Mission Commander, and other designated mission participants will conduct a leader's rehearsal using the Execution Checklist post the Confirmation Brief.*

***Bold** indicates what will be briefed during each Confirmation Brief. All others brief changes only.*

Confirmation Brief Guide

Briefer	Topic
MEU Ops Chief	Roll Call **Time Hack (GPS)**
	SITUATION
MEU S-3	Friendly Force Update Mission Updates HHQ Mission/Intent/updates Assumptions validated and remaining **Review Mission CCIRs/RFIs/PIRs**
PHIBRON N-3	Naval Orientation ARG Position/Geometry/Timeline Assets available and locations Force Protection Posture Weapons postures and Readiness conditions
METOC	Weather METOC impacts on the mission from ship to objective (tides, sea state, currents, winds)
PHIBRON N-2	Naval Intelligence Update Naval Order of Battle (NOB)/Coastal Asymmetric Threat Hydrograph
Main Effort S-2	**Terrain/Environment Analysis** **Enemy Analysis** **MLCOA/MDCOA** **Collection Plan status** Center of Gravity, Critical Vulnerability) Analysis of Enemy Capabilities (DRAWD,
ACE S-2	Air Threat/Air Order of Battle (AOB) Missile Order of Battle (MOB)
	MISSION/EXECUTION
MEU S3	**Mission** **Task Organization** **Overall Concept of Operations by phase**
	Standing Missions (as required by phase) CASEVAC MASCAS Air TRAP Surface TRAP Sparrowhawk Bald Eagle
N3 MEU FSO ME Commander AMC	**PHASE 1 SHAPING** **Naval Geometries** **Fires** **Maneuver** **Air**
N3 MEU FSO ME Commander AMC	**PHASE 2 INSERTION** **Naval Geometries** **Fires** **Maneuver** **Air**

N3 MEU FSO ME Commander Raid Force Commander Designated Element Leaders (NEO/HADR)	**PHASE 3 ACTIONS ON OBJECTIVE** **Naval Geometries** **Fires** **Maneuver** Task Organization (# of Marines/Sailors in force) EDL (Emphasis on mission related items) Insert load plan Bump Plan Concept of Operations **Stage 1 (Insertion; ship to shore/LZ)** Landing plan Beach Landing Site actions LZ actions / Emergency Extract **Stage 2 (Movement to objective)** R&S Link-Up (if applicable) **Stage 3 (Actions on the objective)** Security Element (T/O, Tasks, Scheme of Maneuver) Support Element (T/O, Tasks, Scheme of Maneuver) Assault Element (T/O, Tasks, Scheme of Maneuver) Mission Specific briefs Beach Landing Site actions Steep Earth Climb/Cliff Assault Evacuation Control Center operations Humanitarian Assistance operations HUMINT exploitation team actions Site exploitation plan (SSE) Demolition plan Sniper engagement plan Combat Camera **Stage 4 (Extract; shore/LZ to ship)** MACO Procedures/Accountability R&S Link-Up (if applicable) EPW/Civilian Detainee Plan Casualty Handling/CASEVAC Vehicle Recovery Plan Linkup Plan if reinforced by SPARROWHAWK Missing Marine Plan Timeline/Rehearsal Plan Raid Force Contingencies
FSC/MEU FSO	**Essential Fire Support Tasks** **Assets Available/Location (incl NSFS if available)** **Fire Support Coordination Measures** **Fire Support Execution Matrix** **Attack Guidance Matrix** Priority of Fires Target Precedence
Air Mission Commander (AMC)	**Mission Assets** **Mission Timeline** **Scheme of maneuver** **Launch/Rendezvous sequence** **Primary Route** **Alternate Route** **Control measures** **Routing diagram(s)** **Objective area arrival** **Comm** **Clearance** **Holding** **IP** **Flow** **Landing plan** **Obj area diagram(s)** **LZ diagram(s)** **Bump Plan** **Contingencies Plan** **FARP/RGR/AR Plan** **FARP Diagram**

Continued on next page

Continued on next page

Confirmation Brief Guide (cont.)

PELELIU Air Ops	Air Plan Spotting/Priority
C-130 Planner	Mission (If required) Tanking Radio Relay Aerial Delivery PAX / Cargo Movement Asset Capabilities F/W Tanking R/W Tanking Radio Status PSC-5 SatCom Antennas ARC-210 KY-58/58 Location (Base) Routing TOS Crew Day
TACRON	Air Space Considerations AOA Altitudes Entry & Exit Points (ATC) Helo Lanes Comm/IFF Air Space Control Areas Return to Forces Procedures Divert Field SAR plan
E&R Plan (ACE S-2)	Evasion and Recovery Plan **(SAFE's only)** E&R points and time of service Theater Designated Areas for Recovery (DAR)
PHIBRON CCO Ship's CCO	Debarkation Timeline/Serial Call Away LCAVAT/Craft Loads Test Fire Plan Cross-deck Requirements Class I/V issue Reconfiguration Fueling Bump Plan PCS Briefer Waterborne Ship-to-Shore movement (as required) Timeline
N3 MEU FSO ME Commander AMC	**PHASE 4 IEXTRACTION** **Naval Geometries** **Fires** **Maneuver** **Air**
N3 MEU FSO ME Commander AMC	**PHASE 5 RECONSTITUTION** **Naval Geometries** **Fires** **Maneuver** **Air**
ADMIN & LOGISTICS	
ME S-4	Concept of Logistics Pre-staged/Pre-planned Support Maintenance Recovery External/Host Nation support available/coordinated

Continued from previous page

Continued from previous page

Medical (PHIBRON)	Assets Ashore CASEVAC procedures Chain of Evacuation Time/distance from point of injury to ARG Primary and alternate means of CASEVAC Medical Regulating PCRTS: Beds, ORS, Blood SCRTS: Beds, ORS, Blood
IO	IO considerations/message IO Pillars
MEU PAO	Public Affairs Plan Media in place or expected Active or Passive posture Command message
COMMAND AND SIGNAL	
MEU S-6	**Comm Plan (Net diagram)** **Challenge & Password** **Anticipated impact on Comm due to urban/rural terrain and atmospheric effects during the mission** **Cryptographic changes that affect mission**
PHIBRON N-6	Naval Comm Plan (Net Diagram)
IWC	IWC Considerations Operational Security Plan/INFOCON and EMCON River City Considerations
MEU SJA PHIBRON JAG	Review Standing ROE Supplemental ROE granted Detainee Handling Civilian Handling Mission specific legal issues
ORM / Safety	Navy N3 ACE S3 GCE S3 LCE S3
MEU S-3	**Proposed Go/No Go (criteria and authority)** **Proposed Abort Authority (criteria and authority)** **Proposed Delegation of Authority** **Review Master Execution Checklist** **Review Master Timeline** **Manifest due to TACLOG NLT 2 hours post brief** **Summary** **Timeline until execution**
Commanders	Comments, Approval

**The MEU Commander, MEU Operations Officer, Mission Commander, Raid Force Commander, Air Mission Commander, and other designated mission participants will conduct a leader's rehearsal using the Execution Checklist post the Confirmation Brief.*

***Bold** indicates what will be briefed during each Confirmation Brief. All others brief changes only.*

IX. SMARTPACK

The MEU S-3 prepares a SMARTPACK for each mission; however, content is provided by main effort commander. The SMARTPACK contains mission-specific information in an easy-to-use, single-sheet reference. This information can be directly extracted from the slides in the confirmation brief, but would not normally be available to mission participants in written form unless it was provided. SMARTPACK prevent transcription errors with frequencies, call signs and other detailed information. SMARTPACK will be distributed at the confirmation brief; they will be version controlled in the event it is necessary to collect and re-issue.

The input files for the SMARTPACK will be contained in File SMARTPACK within that missions specific confirmation brief file. The input for the mission SMARTPACK will be dropped in the shared files as listed below:

Smartpack Guide

Author	**Product**
MEU S-3	Overall Mission Timeline
MEU S-2	Grid Reference Graphic (GRG) E&R Safe Points – If Applicable HVI List – If Applicable
MEU S-6	Comm Diagram and Guard Chart (include frequencies, net ID's, button colors and call signs)
MEU SJA	Rules of Engagement (Update as required)
Mission Commander	Concept of Operations Graphics (include Obj Area Diagram with maneuver graphics) Fire Support Overlay Execution Checklist

Chap 2

III. Operational Risk Management (ORM)

Mission Planning

Operational Risk Management (ORM) is a process that assists the commander in enhancing hazard identification in the operational environment in order to mitigate risks by reducing them to acceptable levels. 15TH MEU integrates risk assessment into our planning and decision making process by considering risk to the force and the risk to the mission. The 15TH MEU/CPR-3 will consider both Risk to Force and Risk to Mission. Each MSE will supply their own ORM.

Operational Risk Management (ORM)

1. Identify hazards associated with tasks
2. Assess hazards
3. Develop controls and make decisions
4. Implement controls
5. Supervise

OPERATIONAL RISK MANAGEMENT

Hazard Severity

I – Catastrophic: death, permanent disability, major property damage
II – Critical: Permanent partial disability, major system or minor property damage
III – Marginal: Minor injury, minor system or property damage
IV – Negligible: First aid, minor system repair

Mishap Probability

A Frequent
B Likely
C Occasional
D Unlikely

Risk Assessment Code (RAC)

1Critical (RED)
2Serious (ORANGE)
3Moderate (DARK YELLOW)
4Minor (YELLOW)
5Negligible (GREEN)

RAC ASSESSMENT CODE MATRIX

		MISHAP PROBABILITY			
SEVERITY		A	B	C	D
CATASTROPHIC	I	1	1	2	3
CRITICAL	II	1	2	3	4
MARGINAL	III	2	3	4	5
NEGLIGIBLE	IV	3	4	5	5

ME Commander ORM

For each mission, the 15TH MEU/CPR-3 ORM worksheets for Risk to Force and Risk to Mission will be the reporting tools used to document identified risks to the MEU Commander/Commodore with proposed mitigating actions.

The MEU Safety Officer will consolidate the Risk to Force worksheets from each MSE for presentation during the Confirmation Brief. This consolidated matrix provides an easy to understand picture of medium and high risk factors identified, controls proposed to mitigate those risks, and adjusted risk factors resulting from the implementation of those controls. When ORM is being presented during the Confirmation Brief, each MSE will have the opportunity to highlight any concerns associated with the mission being confirmed.

The MEU Fires section will prepare in coordination with the Mission Commander and MSEs the Risk to Mission slide focused on actions landward and/or Green Side that could lead to mission failure.

The CPR staff will prepare the Blue Side Risk to Force and Risk to Mission slides and present them during the confirmation brief.

Commander ORM

Phase	Hazard	RAC	Controls Implemented	RES RAC
Phase I: Ship to BLS	Man overboard, hazards on the LCAC deck, accountability, LCAC collision	I/D=3	MACO designated by company, facilitating accountability, specific control measures established to control time and movement of troops as they load the LCAC, all Marines maintain current swim and HEAT qualifications, LCAC pilots have current training requirements, coord between GCE and LCAC personnel.	II/D=4
Phase II: BLS to Objective	Accountability, fratricide, fragmentation, enemy direct fire, dismounted personnel injuries, lost Marine	I/C=2	MACO confirms accountability, Marines maintain proper eye wear and PPE, Marines are guided to LCAC to avoid vehicle collisions and personnel injuries, security estab outside threat ring of LCAC, proper weapons conditions/safety rules, multiple units will provide complementary and cover fires to support insertion of troops	I/D=3
Phase III: Actions on the Objective **Stage A: Isolate Obj** **Stage B: Pre-planned Fires** **Stage C: Clear/TSE**	Fratricide, fragmentation, enemy direct fire, dismounted personnel injuries, lost Marine	I/B=1	Use of NVGs, positive control of fires, deconflicted geometry of fires, TRPs, safe distances from traffic during movement, proper PPE worn, accountability maintained at all times through small unit leaders, RW platforms will provide on scene CASEVAC	II/C=3
Phase IV: Objective to BLS	Lost Marine, fratricide, fragmentation, enemy direct fire	I/D=3	PPE worn, reconfirmed accountability, security maintained at LZ site, positive control of fires, deconflicted geometry of fires, TRPs, overwatch established while assault force extracts, safe distances from traffic during movement, EOF SOP identified and rehearsed if civilians are encountered	II/D=4
Phase V: Extract	Accountability, man overboard, hazards on the LCAC deck, accountability, LCAC collision	I/C=2	MACO designated by company, facilitating accountability, specific control measures established to control time and movement of troops as they load the LCAC, all Marines maintain current swim and HEAT qualifications, prior coordination with LCAC personnel ensuring weight requirements are maintained for insert/extract	I/D=3
Risk Assessment Code 1-Critical 2-Serious 3-Moderate 4-Minor 5-Negligible				

Confirmation Brief

During the confirmation brief ORM will consist of 4 slides: MEU Risk to Force, MEU Risk to Mission, CPR Risk to Force, CPR Risk to Mission.

Chap 3

Mission Essential Tasks

Mission Matrix

Mission Matrix			
Mission	**Primary**	**Alternate**	**Tertiary**
Raid (Helo)	L Co	K Co	
Raid (Motorized)	K Co	CAAT/LAR	
Raid (Mech)	I Co		
Airfield Seizure	L Co	I Co	K Co
Sparrow Hawk (Helo)	L Co	I Co	Battery
Sparrow Hawk (Surf)	LAR/CAAT	I Co	K Co
Bald Eagle (Helo)	L Co	I Co	Battery
Bald Eagle (Surf)	CAAT/LAR	I Co	Battery
TRAP (Helo)	81's Section	I Co	
TRAP (Surf)	LAR/CAAT	ALPHA	K Co
NEO Sec (Helo)	L Co	L Co	Battery
NEO Sec (Surf)	Battery	K Co	CAAT/LAR
NEO ECC *	CLB-15	L Co	
HAO Sec (Helo)	L Co	I Co	Battery
HAO Sec (Surf)	Battery	K Co	CAAT/LAR
HAO	CLB-15		
MRF	1st Force Plt		
VBSS	MRF		
CBRN Security	K Co		
FCE	MEU CE		
MAGTF CM CBRN	MEU CE/BTRY		
HAST	CLB-15		
MCRT	CLB-15		

Purposes of Operations

Ref: MSTP Pamphlet 5-0.2, Operational Planning Team Leader's Guide (Jul '09).

In special circumstances, tactical tasks may be modified to meet the requirements of METT-T. The commander must clearly state he is departing from the standard meaning of these tasks. One way this can be done is by prefacing the modified task with the statement, "What I mean by [modified task] is…"

Understanding of the task to be accomplished is important, but the purpose or "in order to" of the mission is enduring and quite possibly even more important to get correct. The purpose of the operation will be included in both the commander's intent and the higher commander's intent. A clear understanding of your and higher's purpose is essential for maintaining tempo in both planning and execution. A purpose should do one of two things as articulated in the mission statement – allow the main effort to do something or prevent the enemy from doing something to the main effort.

The following are commonly used purposes of operations in which you may receive from higher headquarters. While not doctrinally defined it is important, as with tasks, to receive clear guidance from the commander, or ask for clarification.

Allow
To permit something to happen or exist.

Create
To cause to happen; bring about; arrange, as by intention or design.

Enable
To make able; give power, means, competence, or ability to; authorize.

Influence
The action or process of producing effects on the actions, behavior, opinions, etc., of another or others.

Protect
To defend or guard from attack, invasion, loss, annoyance, insult, etc.; cover or shield from injury or danger.

Cause
A person or thing that acts, happens, or exists in such a way that some specific thing happens as a result; the producer of an effect.

Deceive
To mislead or falsely persuade others.

Facilitate
To assist the progress of.

Prevent
To keep from occurring.

Support
A person or thing that gives aid or assistance.

Chap 3

I. (NEO) Noncombatant Evacuation Operations

Intent

Deliberately process all evacuees to _________ airfield/landing zone for further transportation to the ISB __________ unless situation dictates changing to hasty processing to ARG shipping. Take full advantage of transportation available--no empty vehicles / aircraft / craft leave from shore. Allow local authorities to handle dissidents and crowds where prudent. Make maximum use of DOS / Embassy Officials to designate authorized evacuees.

Preconditions

- Weather
- Collection point identified / established
- Warden plan in effect

Guidance

- MEU S-3 develop insertion distraction plan
- BPT transport evacuees from remote sites
- Force protection throughout
- Protection of evacuees during processing and Evac
- "When in doubt, take 'em out"
- No pets, unless directed by Ambassador
- Cursory search of Ambassador designated personnel
- Fire support to cover avenues of approach / withdrawal
- Include ship reception plan
- Plan for 3 x the number of projected evacuees
- Plan for crowd / riot control
- Expect transition to hostile environment
- Primary / alternate plans for withdrawal
- Identify additional equip / support requirements ASAP

Desired End State

- Evacuate all AMCITS and designated TCNs desiring to leave
- Strict accountability of evacuees
- NEO force with all equipment safely withdrawn to ARG

Mission Essential Tasks

NEO Considerations

1. Uncertain Environment

- HN assets / pers ISO NEO will be minimal
- Airfields may not be usable
- MANPADS will not preclude air ops
- Road networks may not support overland Evac plans
- Warden plan is in effect
- AMCITS will be extracted from EAP designated assembly areas
- EAP is current
- Evacuation points have no electricity / comms available
- U.S. Consulate has provided limited info to AMCITS
- Suitable BLS / HLZ in vicinity of evacuation points
- Air defense threat will not preclude air operations
- Assume three times the number stated in the F77 report
- ISB is available
- DOS has designated suitable intermediate safe haven

2. Information Requirements (IRs)

- How many potential evacuees are there?
- Which designated third country nationals (TCN) will require evacuation
- How many TCNs will require evacuation?
- Determine immediate and potential threat to mission, U.S. forces, or Embassy
- Identify disposition of hostile forces / closest reinforcements
- Identify / verify point of entry, ECC, evacuation routes, ISB
- Identify / locate all evacuees (F-77 & TCN)
- Have the screening and processing areas been verified?
- Where is the HN military and police forces?
- What are the alternate Evac sites?
- Who are the potential troublemakers?
- What local cultural nuances should Evac forces be aware of?

3. Planning Considerations

- Are any wardens/evacuees available to assist with processing and screening?
- Will HN be providing / augmenting security?
- Will interpreter support be available?
- Will medical support be available from HN?
- Will food be required?
- What action should be taken in the event a mission official refuses evacuation?
- Will comm support be available from the Embassy?
- Will any US officials be remaining behind?
- Any sensitive equipment requires Evac?
- What actions should the ECC take for those not on the list of evacuees?
- Policy for seriously wounded evacuees?
- What action should be taken for those seeking asylum?

Mission Essential Tasks

- Who will be available to help search female evacuees?
- What proof of U.S. citizenship is acceptable?
- What should be done about pets?
- What is the media plan?
  - Will troops be sent after missing evacuees?
  - Any changes to standard Evac priorities?

NEO Dilemmas

Because each NEO is unique, situation may arise that require special consideration. ARG/MEU (SOC) personnel should be briefed and prepared to deal with the following:

- Questions concerning use of deadly force or a given weapon system in a given situation. When deadly force is authorized?
- Interpretation of the ROE
- Hostile detainees who present themselves
- Civil disturbances, from passive resistance or civil disobedience to violence
- Terrorism
- Bomb Threats
- Snipers
- Non-ambulatory evacuees
- Language problems
- Religious problems
- Potential evacuee's name not on list provided by the Embassy but appearing to be a bona fide evacuee
- Death of evacuees and evacuation of remains
- Listed evacuees or unlisted potential evacuee with unknown identifications
- Evacuee carrying contraband and disposition of the contraband

- Overwhelming numbers of civilians coming to assembly areas or at the evacuation sites to request evacuation
- Listed evacuee refusing evacuation
- Evacuee attempting to give bribes to gain favor
- Inaccurate evacuation list
- Large numbers of international journalists converging on the area

NEO Planning Guidance

This page provides questions that may be used to provide a common framework for evacuation planning and operations. These questions may serve as focus for the detailed planning and operational dialog between diplomats and military forces that must precede any successful evacuation operation.

- Will this be a permissive, uncertain, or hostile NEO? If the evacuation is permissive, are unarmed hostilities expected? If the evacuation is uncertain or hostile, will pursuit forces be necessary? What is the likelihood of terrorist activities?
- What multinational forces will be operating in the area?
- Are multinational forces integrated into the JTF plan?
- How are plans being de-conflicted if the evacuations are separate?
- What is the current situation in the country? In the Embassy? Near the US citizens?
- Who is the senior US official in charge of the evacuation operation?
- Who will give the JTF permission to complete the evacuation and to leave the evacuation site?
- What is the chain of command for US military forces?
- What is the relationship between the CJTF and the Ambassador?
- Will all US missions and/or embassy officials be leaving? If not, who will remain? What action should be taken in the event an Embassy official refuses evacuation?
- Who will screen the evacuees?
- Are there Embassy personnel assigned to screen?
- Are there any evacuees (e.g., wardens) who will be able to help with processing and screening?
- What are the JTF requirements for screening?
- Who makes the final determination of evacuee accounting prior to final evacuation departure?
- Is the Embassy's EAP available? Is it up to date?
- Who is the primary point of contact within the Embassy to work with the JTF on details of the operation?
- What steps are being taken by the Embassy to get the evacuees ready for evacuation?
- Are there any members of the JTF, or anyone reasonably available, who have been in the host nation recently.
- Is there any intelligence needed immediately from the evacuees?
- Have the primary and alternate assembly areas, evacuation sites, and routes been verified and surveyed?
- Have the screening and processing areas been verified?
- What is the total number of US personnel to be evacuated?
- What action should be taken concerning individuals not on the list of evacuees (e.g., TCNs)? What is the total number of TCNs to be evacuated?
- Number per priority/category
- Identification
- What will be the composition of the evacuees? Will there be a crossed section of those listed in the EAP?
- What discipline problems are expected from the evacuees? Who are the potential troublemakers?
- What action should be taken if there is an outbreak of violence among evacuees?
- What action should be taken if someone asks for political asylum?
- Will it be necessary to search the baggage and personal property of all evacuees for weapons or explosives?
- Who will be available to physically search female evacuees?
- What proof of US citizenship is acceptable?
- Are there any changes in the standard priorities for evacuation?
- Will the US Embassy be able to assign evacuation priorities before it schedules evacuation?
- What are the arrangements for evacuee housing, security, and transfer? Will clothing be required? Will food be required?
  - Type
  - Quantity
  - Location
- Are any animals (pets) prohibited from traveling on the designated transportation? Have restrictions concerning animals been identified at the safe haven location?
- Will JTF search teams be sent after missing evacuees?
- Is there any sensitive equipment or material that will be evacuated or destroyed? Will personnel with requisite clearances be required to assist in the evacuating or destroying sensitive equipment or material?
- Are their procedures to handle claims against US civilians?
- If required, who will provide an emergency resupply of ammunition for the advance party?
- What cultural nuances and customs should be known by the JTF evacuation force to avoid confrontation.
- Who are the key host country personnel and what are their attitudes toward the evacuation?

- Will medical support be available from the Embassy or host country? Have MEDEVAC procedures been coordinated with the host country? Where are the host country health services?
- Location
- Availability
- Capacity
- What is the policy concerning seriously wounded evacuees? Should they be given precedence over all other evacuees? What is the physical condition of all evacuees? Are assets required? If so, is there a need to pre-stage those assets nearby, and what are the medical evacuation procedures?
- Where are the host nation police forces?
  - Location
  - Availability
  - Capacity
  - Loyalty to the host government
  - Hostility to the United States
  - Factional infighting present
- Where are the country fire services?
  - Location
  - Availability
  - Capacity
- Where are the host nation military forces?
  - Location
  - Availability
  - Capability
  - Loyalty to the host government
  - Hostility to the United States
  - Factional infighting present
- Will the host government be providing any security for the assembly areas of evacuation sites?
  - Location
  - Unit
  - Size of security force
- What is the potential threat?
  - Strength
  - Composition
  - Disposition
  - Probable tactics
  - Weapons available
- Will interpreter support be available from Embassy or the host nation?
- What communications support will be available from the Embassy and how will the communication architecture be set up to support the operations (i.e., networks, frequencies, secure equipment availability, need for relays)?
- Can portable communications equipment be sent to the Embassy to facilitate improved and secured communications?
- Will transportation support be available for the Embassy or the host country?
  - Type
  - Location
  - Capacity
  - Condition
- Who will prepare the PA plan? How often will it be updated? Who is the lead PA director? Will media representatives be activated?
- Are there areas from which the media are restricted access? IS there a media support plan?
- What are the ROE for the JTF?
- What is the guidance on the use of PSYOP?
- What coordination has been made with the HN media to support the NEO and/or the NEO PSYOP plan?
- Will the HN media provide support for the NEO and/or the NEO PSYOP plan?
- What is the role of Civil Affairs in NEO?
- Does the JTF have permission to drop sensors and insert special operation forces?
- Who provides country studies for JTF with information such as LZs, concentration of US citizens, port facilities, landing beaches? How will this information be transmitted to JTF?
- Have all requirements for strategic transportation systems been directed to the USTRANSCOM command center and/or crisis action team?
- What is the best means of transportation to evacuate personnel?
- Can commercial airlift provide more timely evacuation than deploying U.S. military assets?
- Have air requirements for units and equipment been identified in the Joint Operation Planning Execution System?
- Are US naval assets readily available to stage off the coast?
- What are the appropriate command and control arrangements if the NEO is conducted as a combined operation?
- Who will provide climate, meteorological, and oceanographic information?
- What support is available from other US sources?
- What support is required by other US agencies?
- What support is available from other participating nations?
- What support is required by other participating nations?
- Are trained EOD personnel available through the HN?
- Are map products of the JOA and Embassy compound available? What are the sources?
- Who controls and ensures familiarity with NEO-PACKS's and other geographic information?
- Which evacuees have special medical needs such as pregnancy, infectious disease, exceptional family member, or pediatric health care problems?
- What are the ROE?
- Is an ISB available? Where? How extensive are facilities and support capabilities?
- Will the Ambassador allow the FCE to deploy?

NEO Rules of Engagement

Nothing in these rules limits the inherent right and obligation to self defense and defense of the unit.

Standing ROE

DO NOT CHANGE - MEMORIZE THEM

Supplemental ROE

SUPP ROE ARE SUBJECT TO CHANGE

Forces Declared Hostile

May be engaged without observing hostile act/intent are declared hostile.

Civilians

You may stop, search and detain all individuals who attempt to interfere with the mission or whose presence is an interference. Use the minimum force necessary. Handle detainees as EPWs. Release as soon as the situation permits. Use of minimum force necessary to protect AMCITS and XXX (designated TCNs) is authorized.

Evacuees

All evacuees (except for the U.S. Ambassador and anyone he designates) will be searched for weapons or other dangerous material before loading on any USMC or USN platform.

Property

Use of deadly force authorized to protect following property: XXX.

Force Escalation Posture

- If confronted by unarmed mobs, demonstrators or rioters, attempt to control the situation by the following means:
- Verbal or other warnings to demonstrators
- Show of force to include riot control formations
- Use of riot control agents (as/if authorized)
- Other reasonable uses of force necessary under the circumstances and proportional to the threat
- RCAs (not) authorized

Asylum

Requests for political asylum will not be granted by MEU/ARG personnel. All requests will be referred to the Ambassador or NCA via chain of command for action. Temporary refuge may be granted only when the requester's life is in actual jeopardy. Only SECNAV may authorize release once granted.

II. Humanitarian Assistance/ Disaster Relief (HA/DR)

Guidance

HA/DR is about helping people. Initially transport equipment and people ashore in order to provide a quick, visible relief to the suffering. Build capability to provide basic life support services as rapidly as possible using both surface and air. When prudent, allow local authorities to handle lawbreakers and crowds, but continually assess the security and protection of own forces.

- Plan to support displaced persons __x amount_
- BPT move to remote/isolated sites to provide aid
- Initially an uncertain environment, BPT deal w/hostile
- Force protection throughout
- Protection of displaced persons while in our control
- Plan for turnover to Embassy designated NGO / host nation
- BPT conduct convoy operations
- PAO plan
- Plan for crowd control
- Plan for gradual reduction of services provided and forces ashore
- Primary / alternate plans for withdrawal
- Identify additional equip / support requirements ASAP
- Interview selected displaced persons for Intel / force protection

Desired End State

- Forces ashore safely, camp set up and services/support being provided as required/feasible
- Upon turnover of mission, all forces and equipment safely withdrawn to ARG

Assumptions

- HN has requested U.S. assistance
- Airfields in ______________ not usable
- Road networks not usable
- Bridges are not damaged / destroyed
- Roads / bridges repairable
- AMCITS isolated in areas of ________
- Water/food availability--suitable for consumption
- Medical facilities damaged / overcrowded
- Mass looting / rioting / banditry
- Looters interspersed with insurgents
- Insurgent / popular uprising
- Sewage systems damaged / inoperable
- Disease(s) are not epidemic
- Air defense threat will not preclude air operations
- Electricity is not available / repairable
- NGO / PVO presence
- LOCs are available
- Three times the estimated number of people requiring assistance
- Basic life support must be provided
- Looters / Bandits
- Hazmat present

Humanitarian Assistance (HA) Operations Planning Guidance

Preconditions

- Weather
- Identified HA/DR site with trafficable routes to / from BLS / HLZ suitable for movement of displaced persons to / from the site
- Area suitable for making water and conducive to distribution

Refugees

- What is the number of refugees requiring support?
- Where are the refugees located?
- Are the refugees located in an established camp?
- Does shelter for the refugees have to be provided?
- Have the leaders amongst the refugees been identified? If so, who are they and where are they located.
- What is the attitude and disposition of the refugees? (Hostile/Calm)
- Is it necessary to process the refugees?
- Do the refugees need to be relocated?
- What unique cultural customs exists that will impact on the operation? (Do's/Don'ts)
- What unique tribal/family unit considerations must be made?
- Are there any refugee conflict areas?
- What types of food can/cannot be provided due to cultural reasons?

Host Nation Support Available

- What Host Nation Security forces exist that can be relied upon?
- Are there Host Nation water production facilities?
- What water sources exist in the vicinity of the refugees?
- What Host Nation transportation is available for transporting personnel, water, fuel supplies? (vehicle/boat/plane)
- Is translator support required and available?
- What is the condition of the Host Nation phone system?
- What Host Nation fuel resources exist? (location/type/capacity)
- What Host Nation construction material is available?

Ports

- What security features exist around the port? (limiting access/crowd control)
- Feasibility of conducting LCU/LCAC operations in the port? (location/type of landing sites)
- What staging areas exist in the vicinity of the port? (location/size/security)

Airfields/Landing Zones

- What is the condition/capacity of the airfields in the vicinity of the refugees and which is preferred considering access and security?
- What security is available at the airport?
- What HLZs are in the vicinity of the refugees and which is preferred considering access and security?
- Location/capacity/security of staging areas in the vicinity of the airfield/HLZ?
- What hangers are available for use (SIZE)?

Routes From/To Likely Points of Entry

- What routes exist from likely points of entry to refugee areas? (Ports/HLZ/Beaches/Air Field)
- What security threats exist along the routes? (man made or natural obstacles/choke points)
- Number of bridges along each route? What are their condition, capacity and what repairs are necessary if any?
- What tunnels exist along the routes? (Height/width)

Aid Organizations (NGO/PVO)

- What Aid organizations (NGO/PVO) are working in country?
- Where are they located?
- Who are the points of contact at each organization?
- What services do they provide?
- What supplies do they have and where are they located?
- What organic transportation do they have for transporting supplies?
- What organic security do the Aid organizations (NGO/PVO) have at storage, transportation and distribution of supplies?
- What sort of identification do the organization members and Host Nation employees of these organizations have?

Military Organizations

- What Host Nation organizations are operational and where are they located?
- What third country military organizations are operational and where are they located?
- What is the loyalty and reliability of the forces?
- What equipments do these forces posses?
- Location of controlling authority for Host Nation/Third Country forces?
- What is the anticipated interference/support from these forces?
- What are the roles and missions of these forces?
- What other U.S. Military units are in country/location?
- What are their roles/missions?

Medical

- What medical organizations exist in country/location?
- Who are the points of contact?
- What is the most significant problem from a medical perspective?
- What medical support is expected of the MEU/ARG?
- What mortuary capability/problems exist in country?
- What sanitation requirements exist or need to be emplaced?

Media

- What media organizations are present? (U.S./Foreign)
- Has a U.S. media pool been established?
- Is the U.S. Embassy capable of providing PAO support?
- Will the U.S. Embassy coordinate media coverage?

Information Requirements (IRs)

- What is the number of refugees requiring support?
- Where are the refugees located?
- What is the threat? Who? How many? How are they armed?
- Are there any special medical considerations?
- Are the refugees located in an established camp?
- Does shelter for the refugees have to be provided?
- Have the leaders amongst the refugees been identified? If so, who are they and where are they located?
- What is the attitude and disposition of the refugees? (Hostile/Calm)
- Is it necessary to process the refugees?
- Do the refugees need to be relocated?
- What unique cultural customs exists that will impact on the operation? How will female Marines be perceived?
- What unique tribal/family unit considerations must be made?
- Are there any refugee conflict areas?
- What types of food can/cannot be provided due to cultural reasons?
- Where is nearest potable water source?

Rules of Engagement (ROE)

Nothing in these rules limits the inherent right and obligation to self defense and defense of the unit.

- Avoid provocative measures and take no action that might be interpreted as initiating hostilities. Use minimal force to accomplish mission and exercise self defense. Discontinue force when no longer necessary to accomplish immediate purpose.
- Minimal force may be used to protect XXX from imminent threats to their life or serious bodily harm.
- Civilians - you may stop, search and detain all individuals who attempt to interfere with the mission or whose presence is an interference. Use minimum force necessary. Handle detainees as EPWs. Turn over to local authorities or release as soon as situation permits.
- Force Escalation Posture - If confronted by unarmed mobs, demonstrators or rioters, attempt to control the situation by the following means:
  - Verbal or other warnings to demonstrators.
  - Show of force to include riot control formations
  - Use of riot control agents (as/if authorized)
  - Other reasonable uses of force necessary under the circumstances and proportional to the threat
  - RCAs (not) authorized
- Asylum – Requests for political asylum will not be granted by ARG/MEU (SOC) personnel. All requests will be referred to xxx Ambassador or NCA via chain of command for action. Temporary refuge may be granted only when the requester's life is in actual jeopardy. Only SECNAV may authorize release once granted.

Specified or Implied Tasks

- Provide medical/dental care
- Provide security for HA/DR site
- Conduct convoy ops
- Conduct crowd control
- Insert IRT
- Coordinate with HN officials/AMEMB/NGO/PVOs

III. Reconnaissance & Surveillance (R&S)

Intent

Insert R&S quickly to maximize observation of target and satisfy intelligence Requirements. Insertion means must ensure force is not compromised. Full coverage of the target is the goal. Identify routes for national forces or MSOC from BLS/HLZ/link-up point to ORP/LCC/objective. R&S leader is on-scene commander until turnover to Raid Force Commander. R&S must not be compromised!

Preconditions

- Weather/sea state
- Time! Reverse plan from Op/Obj area
- Night/reduced visibility

Guidance

- Insert means to be coordinated with (ship/boat CO/ACE/SBU/HET)
- Plan for clandestine insertion
- Plan for sufficient ops to accomplish mission
- Plan for foot / vehicular observation
- Place snipers / designated marksmen as required
- Coordinate with HET
- Branch plan in case of target relocation
- Plan to provide ITG for assault force / MSOC strike
- Plan for link-up and status brief to MSOC Cmdr
- Plan to chop control to MARSOC commander
- Determine any unique equipment requirements
- Plan for multiple days of reconnaissance effort

Desired End State

- Safe insertion of R&S
- Reliable & continuous comms with MEU within 4 hours
- Strict personnel accountability within R&S
- Continuous eyes on target
- Fulfillment of SIRs
- Uncompromised operation throughout

Assumptions

- Sufficient time to receive useful reporting after insert
- Potential reporting gains outweigh risk of compromise
- Terrain will support collection requirements for ground reconnaissance
- Time / space to move to op is sufficient
- Suitable BLS / HLZ reasonably distanced from target loc
- Insert point will not compromise mission
- Enemy has observation / early warning network capabilities
- Air defense threat will not preclude air insert / extract

Rules of Engagement

Nothing in these rules limits the inherent right and obligation to self defense and defense of the unit.

- Forces Declared Hostile - may be engaged without observing hostile act/intent.

Reconnaissance Fundamentals

Ref: Adapted from MCI 7501B, Tactical Fundamentals.

Reconnaissance is a mission undertaken to obtain, by visual observation or other detection methods, information about the activities and resources of an enemy or potential enemy; or to secure date concerning the meteorological, hydrographic, or geographic characteristics of a particular area.

All reconnaissance operations vary in accordance with the situation and conditions in the area in which they are conducted, and with the size, type, composition, and assigned missions of the employed units. However, all such operations are guided by the following fundamentals:

1. Orient on the Objective

In order to stay with the enemy, reconnaissance elements must orient their operations on the enemy, not his parent unit. The only way to remain oriented on the enemy is to move with him if he moves; consequently, free maneuver is required on the part of reconnaissance elements. In this respect, it is preferable that the patrol have superior mobility to that of the enemy, particularly if a single patrol is employed to determine the actual size or area occupied by an enemy force. In practice, however, it is seldom that one patrol would be used to locate both flanks -- or even an extensive portion of the enemy's front. Rather, several probes or combat patrols would probably be employed to determine the enemy's dispositions.

2. Report All Information Accurately and Promptly

The individual members of a reconnaissance patrol do not posses the background to determine whether a piece of information is significant or not. However, the commander and his S-2 will be able to judge the relative importance of information. Therefore, it is essential that all information be passed immediately to the S-2, who can best utilize it. As a matter of SOP, patrols reports such things as progress, initial contact, and items of obvious importance. However, it takes a debriefer to dig out the less obvious information. Negative information (or absence of activity) can at times be more important than positive information.

3. Avoid Decisive Engagement

We are interested in acquiring as much information as possible without tipping off the enemy of our interest. However, patrols are provided the means to collect information or perform screening missions by close combat, if necessary; in fact, the so-called "reconnaissance in force" is actually a raid or limited objective attack to test the enemy's disposition and strength. Normally reconnaissance patrols resort to combat only if it is absolutely necessary to accomplish the assigned mission, or to prevent destruction or capture. In general, it is preferable to conduct a reconnaissance by stealth and surveillance without the enemy being aware.

4. Maintain Enemy Contact

"Physical contact" is not intended, but rather reconnaissance-type contact. It is essential that patrols, whether mounted or foot, strive to gain contact as rapidly as possible and maintain it continuously. The purpose of such activity is obvious: the only way to find out anything about the enemy is to locate him early and stay with him. In this respect, the reconnaissance activity is usually much heavier prior to initial contact than after contact has been made.

5. Develop the Situation

This is our final principle. Once contact is made, the reconnaissance force immediately takes action to determine the enemy's strength, composition, disposition, and, perhaps, intentions with a special effort made to determine the flanks of his position. At this point, a decision to engage, avoid, or bypass is normally made.

IV. Information Operations (IO)

Basic Considerations

- Coordinate IO plans with higher headquarters to ensure an integrated focus of effort exists
- Utilize organic and non-organic assets to maximize IO capabilities
- The MEU IO Cell is chaired by the CPR IWC and consists of the following personnel: N2, S2, CRC, Radio Bn Det OIC, MEU IO Rep, MEU PAO, N6, S6 rep, SJA, and as necessary an N3 rep, ACE rep, GCE rep, CLB rep, TACRON, and ship's OPS.
- IO acts as a force multiplier, allowing for improved mission success

Information Operations (IO) Capabilities

Core IO Capabilities

- Pyschological Operations (PSYOP)
- Military Deception (MILDEC)
- Operations Security (OPSEC)
- Electronic Warfare (EW)
- Computer Network Operations (CNO)

IO Supporting Capabilities

- Information Assurance (IA)
- Physical Security
- Physical Attack
- Counterintelligence
- Combat Camera

IO Related Capabilities

- Public Affairs (PA)
- Civil-Military Operations (CMO)
- Defense Support to Public Diplomacy (DSPD)

MEU IO Considerations

Deception

When planning deception operations always include a target, an objective, the deception story, the deception means, and means for feedback/measures of effectiveness. Does the plan need to be Limited Distribution (LIMDIS)/close-hold? Is the deception feasible and does the target have the ability to detect, assess, and react to the deception story? Use the following or any variation: FEINT – diversionary force makes physical contact with the enemy, RUSE – an elaborate scheme involving false information, DEMONSTRATION – positioning/activity of forces away from the focus of main effort, DISPLAY – static presentation of fake forces.

PSYOPS

The greatest weapon is TRUTH. Resist use of PSYOPS to deceive, this reduces the credibility of future perception campaigns. Design PSYOPS themes based on sound cultural intelligence. Many cultures respond very differently to a PSYOP product than U.S. personnel would. The Geographic Combatant Commander retains approval authority for all PSYOP themes. Consider leaflets, posters, loudspeakers, radio, and television for delivery methods. Collaborate with theater-level PSYOPS assets to obtain access to more resources and products.

Electronic Warfare (EW)

Has adequate intelligence analysis been conducted on adversarial capabilities? Have we taken adequate measures to protect our use of the electromagnetic spectrum from enemy interference or eavesdropping? Have we identified the critical adversary communication links and the appropriate means to attack them? Ensure a risk vs. gain assessment is made in regards to intelligence loss when targets of electronic attack are selected. Coordinate with non-organic assets as early as possible for support. Evaluate the impact of all aspects of EW on friendly capabilities and mission success.

Operational Security (OPSEC)

Identify Essential Elements of Friendly Information (EEFI) and the adversary's capability to collect each EEFI then develop a plan to aggressively protect them. Use the following measures as much as possible: stealth, cover of darkness, careful route selection to avoid populations, multiple ingress routes to hide force size, use routes that hide the final objective, hide our aural signature, EMCON, encrypted comms, comms other than HF, ZIPLIP, civilian clothes, cover stories. Many OPSEC measures support deception operations, use them together. Do not use cell phones, enforce basic security measures, and be aware of classification levels.

Physical Destruction

Base IW target selection on in depth nodal analysis of critical adversarial links and nodes. Present targets to the Targeting Board/MEU (SOC) fires rep as soon as possible for incorporation into the plan for fires. Ensure a risk vs. gain assessment is made in regards to intelligence loss and infrastructure impact when targets are selected.

Information Assurance

Identify critical vulnerabilities to our information systems. Always maintain the most current virus protection software. Do not open e-mail attachments that end in ".exe". Use non-dictionary passwords. Be prepared to implement INFOCON measures in response to threats. Minimize volume/size of e-mail and web-browsing. Utilize Rivercity conditions when necessary.

Civil Affairs

Use Civil Affairs efforts to promote positive attitudes in local populations for support of our presence and missions.

Public Affairs

Coordinate all PSYOP and Public Affairs messages to prevent contradictions.

V. Consequence Management Operations

Intent

Reduce the effects of a deliberate or accidental release of chemical war gasses, Toxic Industrial Materials (TIM), or Toxic Industrial Chemicals (TIC), that produce effects on American citizens, American allies, or third world/host nation citizens. Be prepared to provide level I and II medical treatment and to safely evacuate immediate triage casualties to level III facilities either aboard ARG shipping or ashore.

Preconditions

- Weather
- Personal Protective Equipment is sufficient
- Chemical does not need to be known

Guidance

- MEU S-3 develop insertion distraction plan
- BPT transport evacuees from remote sites
- Force protection throughout
- Protection of evacuees during processing and Evac
- "When in doubt, take them out"
- Fire support to cover avenues of approach/withdrawal
- Include ship reception plan
- Plan for 3 x the number of projected evacuees
- Plan for crowd/riot control
- Expect transition to hostile environment
- Primary/alternate plans for withdrawal
- Identify additional equip/support requirements ASAP
- Decon plan necessary for personnel and or equipment

Desired End State

- Mitigate effects against all AMCITS and designated TCN
- Strict accountability of force and victims
- CM force with all equipment safely withdrawn to ARG

Consequence Management Assumptions

FCE Insert

- Consulate/embassy will be able to contact AMCITS
- Formal request from DOS to DOD for support
- Size of FCE permitted
- Consulate/Embassy will have communications
- Consulate/Embassy will have electricity / food / water
- Consulate/Embassy will not be able to provide initial security
- Transportation will be provided
- Weapons are authorized

CMO (uncertain environment)

- HN assets/pers ISO CMO will be minimal
- MANPADS will not preclude air ops
- Road networks may not support overland plans
- AMCITS will be extracted from EAP designated assembly areas
- EAP may not be current
- Evacuation points have no electricity/comms available
- U.S. Consulate has provided limited info to Amcits
- Suitable BLS/HLZ in vicinity of evacuation points
- ISB is available

Information Requirements (IRs)

- Determine immediate and potential threat to mission, U.S. forces, or Embassy
- Identify disposition of hostile forces/closest reinforcements
- Identify/verify point of entry, ECC, evacuation routes, ISB
- Identify/locate all evacuees
- Where are the HN military and police forces?
- What are the alternate Evac sites?
- Any sensitive equipment/intelligence requiring Evac?
- Who are the potential troublemakers?
- What local cultural nuances should forces be aware of?

Planning Considerations

- Will HN be providing/augmenting security?
- Will HN be providing HAZMAT Teams/First Responders?
- Will interpreter support be available?
- Will medical support be available from HN?
- Will food be required?
- Will comm support be available?
- Will any US officials be available?
- Policy for seriously wounded evacuees?
- Who will be available to help female evacuees?
- What proof of citizenship is acceptable?
- What is the media plan?
- Will troops be sent after missing evacuees?
- Any changes to standard Evac priorities?
- CM Initial Response Force insert:
  - Time sensitive due to nature of volatility and effects of agents
  - IRF insert via air or surface (air preferred due to time)
  - Normally executed on request/order of American Ambassador or Combatant Cdr
  - Possibly called on for HAO/NEO like scenarios under small-scale chemical attack or industrial chemical accident
  - Can occur in an uncertain or permissive environment
  - May require aircraft or vehicle decontamination
  - May require on-site medical evacuation and/or mass casualty support
  - May require augmentation with Engineer and/or Medical subject matter experts
  - May require sustainment on scene 6 hours to 15 days

VI. Amphibious Raid Planning

Preconditions

- Weather/sea state
- BLS/HLZ/CLZ identified
- Aircraft/LCAC/CRRCs available

Guidance

- Develop deception plan
- Fire support plan ISO actions on objective/withdrawal
- Detailed plan for demolition/destruction
- Navy plan to isolate objective area
- Electronic attack plan to support scheme of maneuver
- Plan TPOD mission for AV-8B (Harrier)
- Alternate plan for destruction
- Offset LZs by 10 KM, BLS by 5 KM from objective
- LZ/BLS away from populated areas
- No Comm plan
- Collect all intelligence at crisis site, use IC
- Alternate plans for rapid withdrawal/use of ALT BLS/LZ
- Identify additional equip/support requirements ASAP
- Plan timeline to support _____ assault on objective
- PAO Plan for media control/support
- Plan for refinement (Sparrow Hawk/Bull Eagle)

Desired End State

- Successful accomplishment of mission's task and purpose
- Continuous Comm between raid force and MEU
- Documentation of mission success
- Safe return of all raid force personnel & equipment
- Collect of INTEL, numbers, one of each WPN FWD to HHQ

Raid Assumptions

- Permissive/uncertain/hostile environment
- Weather will permit
- Favorable force ratio exists
- Country team/DOS handles Coord with HN government officials (FCE)
- Expect light/medium/heavy resistance
- Target location confirmed prior to execution
- Use of a specific BLS/airfield/LZ
- Overflight rights granted

- Operation can be completed in _______days/hrs
- Limited/no external organization assets available
- No other tasking at the same time
- Media interest/presence

Information Requirements (IRs)

- Identify suitable HLZ/BLS
    - Include composition, slope, length, width, gradient, obstructions, backshore conditions, beach exits, hinterland features, tides, riptide present, surf conditions, currents
- Confirm/describe target site (layout, security, defenses, early warning capability), location of critical facilities/Cache on site
- Enemy reinforcement potential
- Civilian population density, activity, affiliation
- Enemy communications capability
- What are the avenues of approach?
- Key target components?
- What is the enemy's current security posture at the target?
- What is the enemy's vulnerability to deception ops?
- Ability to detect landing, beach defenses, enemy camo techniques
- Enemy air defense capabilities?

Common Go/No-Go Criteria

- Sea state greater than 3
- Significant change in enemy strength/situation
- Planned and required fire support not available
- Required raid forces exceed capacity of operable transportation assets
- Impassable sea state
- Air Defense threat greater than that which would allow mission success
- More than an acceptable number of helos become inoperative before launch

Rules of Engagement (ROE)

Nothing in these rules limit the inherent right and obligation to self defense and defense of the unit.

- Forces Declared Hostile: may be engaged without observing hostile act/intent. XXX are declared hostile.
- Civilians: you may stop, search and detain all individuals who attempt to interfere with the mission or whose presence interferes with the mission. Use the minimum force necessary. Handle detainees as EPWs. Release as soon as the situation permits.
- Property - Use of deadly force authorized to protect following property: XXX.

Amphibious Operations Primary Decisions

1. Amphibious Force Mission: (Mutual Decision)

Amphibious Force commanders may decide on a coordinated mission statement or develop separate but supporting mission statements. The determination of a coordinated amphibious force mission statement is a mutual decision.

2. Amphibious Force Objective(s): (Mutual Decision)

Amphibious force objectives are physical objectives, either terrain, infrastructure, or forces, that must be seized, secured, or destroyed in order to accomplish the mission. Amphibious force objectives are designated in alphabetical order. (e.g. Amphibious Force Objective A).

3. Course of Action (Determine/Select): (Mutual Decision)

Amphibious force planners develop COAs based on guidance from Amphibious Force Commanders. Normally, LF Planners will provide an LF COA for ATF Planners to develop a supporting COA.

4. Landing Areas: (Mutual Decision)

The landing area is that part of the operational area within which the landing operations of an amphibious force are conducted. It includes the beach, the approaches to the beach, the transport areas, the fire support areas, the airspace occupied by close supporting aircraft, and the land included in the advance inland to accomplish the initial objectives.

5. Landing Beaches: (Mutual Decision)

Portion of the shoreline usually required for the landing of a BLT may also be that portion of a shoreline constituting a tactical locality over which a force may be landed. Landing beaches are selected from within the selected landing areas.

6. Sea Echelon Plan: (CPR-3 Determines)

The sea echelon plan is the distribution plan for amphibious shipping in the transport area to minimize losses due to threat attacks and to reduce the area swept by mines.

7. Landing Force Objective(s): (CO MEU Determines)

LF Objectives facilitate the attainment of amphibious force objectives and/or ensure continuous landing of forces and material designated by LF and a number. (e.g. LF OBJ 1)

8. Landing Zones/Drop zones: (CO MEU Determines)

9. Date and hour of Landing: (Mutual Decision)

The date and hour of the landing are selected unless they are specified in the order initiating the amphibious operation. H-Hour and L-Hour are confirmed prior to commencement of the landing based on weather, enemy, situation and other factors

Amphibious Raid Considerations

Ref: JP 3-02, Amphibious Operations (Aug '09) and MCRP 3-11.1A, Commander's Tactical Handbook (Nov '98).

An amphibious raid is an operation involving a swift incursion into or the temporary occupation of an objective to accomplish an assigned mission followed by a planned withdrawal. Amphibious raids are conducted as independent operations or in support of other operations. Generally, amphibious raids are conducted to:

- Destroy certain targets, particularly those that do not lend themselves to destruction by other means
- Harass the enemy by attacks on isolated posts, patrols, or headquarters
- Capture or kill key personnel
- Support forces engaged with the enemy by attacking the enemy rear or flank positions on a seacoast
- Obtain information on hydrography, terrain, enemy dispositions, strength, movements, and weapons
- Create a diversion in connection with strategic deception operations
- Evacuate individuals or materiel
- Establish, support, or coordinate unconventional warfare activities

Amphibious Helicopterborne Assault

The following coordinating instructions are common to two or more elements:

- Assembly area for loading
- Heliteam wave and serial assignment table submitted by (time) and (location)
- Heliteams formed by (time) and (location)
- Tactical spread loading and bump plan
- Manifest submitted by (time) and (location)
- Zone inspection, planning, preparing and operation (ZIPPO) brief at (time) and (location) given by (who) for (whom)
- Heliteam organization
- Landing plan
- Landing zone organization (flying out)
- Landing zone organization (flying in)
- L-hour
- Portion of landing zone reported as secure
- 12 o' clock is ______
- Tentative extraction plan

Amphibious Surface Assault

The following coordinating instructions are common to all elements:

- H-hour and L-hour
- Staging areas/boat stations
- Boat team organization, ensuring tactical spread loading and bump plan
- Serial assignment tables submitted by (time) and (location)
- Manifest submitted by (time) and (location)
- Assault stage by (time) and (location)
- Boat teams formed by (time) and (location)
- Ship-to-shore movement
- Landing plan
- GO/NO GO criteria

VII. Airfield Seizure Planning

Planning Considerations

- Usually have minimal terrain masking
- Associated with built up areas
- Usually near road networks
- High probability of civilian air traffic
- Civilians likely to be within small arms range of the airfield
- Follow on requirements for runway improvement

Potential Go/No-Go Criteria

- Significant enemy armor vicinity of the airfield
- Enemy defends airfield with significant force
- Air defense threat greater than SA-7
- Lack of U.S. air superiority

Rules of Engagement

Nothing in these rules limits the inherent right and obligation to self defense and defense of the unit

- Forces Declared Hostile = may be engaged without observing hostile act/intent. XXX are declared hostile.
- Civilians You may stop, search and detain all individuals who attempt to interfere with the mission or whose presence is an interference. Use minimum force necessary. Handle detainees as EPWs. Release as soon as safety permits.
- Use of minimum force necessary to protect AMCITS and designated TCNs is (not) authorized
- Indirect fires (not) authorized
- Use of deadly force authorized to protect following property: XXX
- RCAs (not) authorized
- Electronic warfare (not) authorized
- Minimize Collateral Damage to airfield and its buildings
- Possible key targets:
  - Air defense sites
  - Control tower
  - C2 facilities
  - Aircraft
  - Hangar and repair facilities
  - React forces
  - Navigation aids
  - Road network / runway intersections

Assumptions

- Runway is not fouled
- A/F is not capable of supporting ________ aircraft
- A/F fuel is not contaminated
- A/F is repairable and suitable for future operations
- Local air control is / is not operating
- Commercial air traffic will / will not interfere
- Airfield infrastructure is intact / usable

Information Requirements (IRs)

- What is the enemy disposition and size?
  - What is the enemy's air defense capability? Where located?
  - (Reaction time)
  - Where are the nearest reinforcements and how long to reinforce? (Which direction)
- Are there any runway obstructions?
  - What is the condition of the runway?
- What type of field is it?
  - What is its principal use?
  - What is the airfield category?
  - What are the normal operating hours of the field?
  - Any obstacles to flight within 5-10 km of the airfield?
  - Is the airfield tied into regional / national IADS? (Tie into a Go or No-Go plan)
  - What is the 8 digit grid of control tower and ends of runway?
  - How many runways are there?
  - Where are the taxiways?
  - Where are the hard stands?
  - Are there any navaids? What type? And when do they operate?
  - Are there any lighting aids? What type?
  - Are there any comm facilities? Frequency, range, power output?
  - Are there any POL storage areas?
  - Are there maintenance facilities?
  - GSE equipment available?
  - Covered storage available?
  - Where are the hangars?
  - Are there any administrative buildings?
  - What are the characteristics of the adjacent terrain?

Critical Tasks

- Insert R&S, scout sniper teams
- Identify enemy strength and location
- Identify requirements for runway clearance
- Establish observation of ingress routes
- Isolate the airfield physically and electronically
- Clear runway of obstacles (if required)
- Vector in assault force
- Isolate and capture/destroy security and defense forces IAW established

Chap 3

VIII. Limited Duration Small Scale Raid

A raid is an operation, usually small scale, involving a swift penetration of hostile territory to secure information, confuse the enemy, or to destroy his installations. It ends with a planned withdrawal upon completion of the assigned mission. Raids may be conducted as separate operations or in support of other operations. Examples of separate operations include raids for psychological purposes, destroying enemy assets not susceptible to other action, harassment, to gain combat information, a spoiling attacks to keep enemy forces off balance, and to recover or rescue friendly personnel and equipment.

Mission Essential Tasks

Raid Planning

Raid planning is characterized by coordinated, thorough, and detailed planning by the raid force, supporting, and supported organizations. Parallel planning for the raid is conducted concurrently by Navy, MAGTF, and raid force staffs, as appropriate. Each staff has special concerns, but all work to the common mission of the raid force and production of the raid plan. The raid force is the supported organization and should include aviation, ground combat, and combat service support staff representation.

For further discussion, see MCWP 3-43.1, Raid Operations. Raid operations are planned and executed in accordance with procedures delineated in Joint Pub 3-02, Joint Doctrine for Amphibious Operations, and Joint Pub 3-02.1, Joint Doctrine for Landing Force Operations.

Assumptions

- Uncertain/hostile environment
- Suitable fast rope points will be available near target site
- Adequate entry points will be available
- Threat force will use improvised explosive devices.
- Suitable extract HLZ/BLS will be available vic crisis site and not fouled
- Site turnover will/will not be conducted
- Cargo/personnel can be handled/transported by organic assets
- Negotiations/demands have started
- Air defense threat will not preclude air assault
- Site has external security lighting

Information Requirements (IRs)

- Confirm location of crisis site/target
  - Confirm presence of hostages within the crisis site
  - Determine/locate number, description of terrorists and weapons on site
  - Identify Potential HLZ/BLS
  - Determine time/distance/capability of nearest reinforcements
  - Determine the location and description of potential breach points into the target building (special attention to breach site door or window material and hinge construction, avenues of approach, obstacles, and possible last covered and concealed sites)

- Determine high traffic areas, entrances, and exits
  - Detail target site to include security routine, defenses, obstacles
  - Determine communications procedures and equipment
  - Identify ORPs/LCCs
  - Availability of safe houses/Recon urban hide sites
  - Identify suitable FSB/ISBs & identify threat
  - Terrorists' photos/nationality/language
  - Terrorist early warning/security patterns
  - Local government: permissive/uncertain/hostile
  - Civil/military maritime and aviation activity
  - Local population: permissive/uncertain/hostile

Specified or Implied Tasks

- Confirm location of target
- Recover the designated item/material or personnel
- Minimize collateral damage
- Transfer hostages/cargo to ARG or second site
- Coordinate with Amemb or U.S. officials/ HN officials
- Submit DA CONOPS NLT-------
- Submit R&S CONOPS NLT--------
- Execute net ------- and/or NLT ----------
- Safe extract of all U.S. forces
- Insert R&S net------- and/or NLT --------
- Isolate the objective
- Recover intelligence/evidence
- Conduct EOD ops
- Conduct counterintelligence
- Insert FCE
- Combat photography: video/still
- Monitor terrorist communications
- Recover/destroy weapons and equipment
- Minimize footprint (physical/electronic)
- Conduct turnover of site to US or HN official
- Contingencies: CASEVAC and TRAP

IX. Visit, Board, Search, Seizure (VBSS)

Intent

Use surprise and violence of action to overwhelm non-compliant crew. Objective is to ensure that the assault preserves the capability to neutralize the crew while taking control of the ship.

Preconditions

- Ship is pier side/known location
- Cargo is still aboard
- Vessel is in international waters
- Host nation cooperation
- Weather permits at sea take down
- Unarmed vessel

Guidance

- Cobra/Harrier support
- Put ashore using PMC as deception
- Isolate the ship/pier
- Minimize injuries to innocent crew/damage to ship
- If SEALS, detailed coordination--control measures?
- Positive communications throughout takedown
- Use ship's radios as backup
- Detainee handling
- Plan for turnover of ship to ________ (ship boarding team)
- Plan for rehearsals -- schedule . . . .
- Withdrawal plan
- Look at plan for sniper(s) as force protection
- Document cargo / TGT seizure, turnover, and condition of ship

Desired End State

- Ship seized, crew under positive control, ship turned over to designated authority
- Collect relevant info and seize all weapons?
- Weapons turnover to -- (host nation?) -- ??
- Force withdrawn safely to ARG

Planning Assumptions

- Ship can be located
- ARG closure rate will support operations
- Ship's crew is permissive / uncertain / hostile
- Weather will permit
- Ship is not burning
- US forces will need to pilot the ship / follow on forces required
- SAR aircraft is available
- Suitable climbing points
- No AA / SAM capability
- Functional surface radar
- Chemical / halon / POL / HAZMAT cargo
- Suitable landing points / fouled flight deck
- Ship is in international waters or HN approved
- USN hailing attempts will fail

Information Requirements (IRs)

- Determine location, direction and speed of target ship
  - Location / numbers/ weapons of security force on ship
- Configuration of the ship (special attention to HLZ and fast rope points to include bridge wings, weather decks, weapons, surface access points to bridge, and superstructure or obstructions blocking flight operations, the bridge, radio room, engine room, and aft steering)
  - Determine ships draft, freeboard and estimated rate of speed
  - Determine ships navigation equipment capabilities
  - Determine distance from waterline to closest potential surface embark/debark point
  - Identify shipboard weapon systems, EW, radar, and comm capabilities
  - Determine location of illegal cargo on board
  - Identify ship's master, captain, crew nationalities, language and likely affiliation
  - Where is hazmat/POL on-board? Quantity?

Follow-on Missions/Tasks

- Forward evidence/materials up the chain
  - Provide after action reports
  - Repair or recover aircraft, ship, and equipment
  - ITT
  - Care for detainees
  - Reinforce security aboard vessel
  - Provide ship boarding team
  - Tow ship
  - Respond/treat mass casualties
  - Assume floating reserve/QRF mission
  - Security reinforcement (Sparrow Hawk)

R&S Planning Considerations

- Use ships radar/electronics/RADBN/air RECCE/CVBG assets
- How to get RFC real-time info on EEIS, enemy ability to withdraw or reinforce
- Plan for visual and electronic surveillance of target ship and known enemy capable of interfering with recovery

Rules of engagement

Nothing in these rules limits the inherent right and obligation to self defense and defense of the unit.

- Forces Declared Hostile - may be engaged without observing hostile act/intent.
  - XXX are declared hostile. (belligerent ships within 2500m)
  - The crew of XXX are/not declared hostile
- Crew-Members - Any crew-members or individuals that may compromise the mission may be searched or detained. Handle detainees as EPWs. Release as soon as the situation allows.
- Use of Force
  - Minimum force necessary to cause XXX to stop & submit to inspection is permittec
- Warning shots may be fired ahead of the XXX (not) permitted
- You may illuminate the XXX by any means
- Training your weapon systems or energizing fire control radar in the direction of the ship (not) permitted
- Electronic warfare (not) authorized
- Flying directly toward or overhead the XXX (not) permitted
- Asylum – Requests for political asylum will not be granted by ARG/MEU (SOC) personnel. All requests will be referred to XXX Ambassador or NCA via chain of command for action. Temporary refuge may be granted only when the requester's life is in actual jeopardy. Only SECNAV may authorize release once granted.

Chap 4

Standing Missions

Standing missions are on-call supporting efforts established by the Mission Commander to assist the Raid Force Commander in accomplishing his mission:

- **Bald Eagle.** Company-size reinforcement
- **Sparrowhawk.** Platoon-size reinforcement
- **Tactical Recovery of Aircraft and Personnel (TRAP).** Air and surface *(see pp. 4-3 to 4-8 for further discussion)*
- **Mass Casualty Response Team (MCRT).** Triage and stabilization *(see pp. 4-9 to 4-10 for further discussion)*

I. Alert Status for Standing Missions

When a standing mission is placed on alert 60 or less, the leader for that standing mission is locate in the LFOC. He will receive a brief from the MEU LFOC Watch Officer, MEU JIC Watch Officer on intelligence, and from the METOC rep (applicable to possible area for their employment). Alert status and standing missions also need to be briefed to the LFOC watch standers during the staff stand-up. For Alert 120, the standing mission commander is required to regularly contact the LFOC for updates.

Alert Status will be set for standing missions during the Confirmation Brief. The MEU Commander may specify an alert status prior to the Confirmation Brief.

Alert Status Matrix

ALERT POSTURE	ALERT 120 (INDEFINITE)	ALERT 60 (MAX 10 HRS)	ALERT 30 (MAX 10 HRS)	ALERT 15 (MAX 6.5 HOURS AV-8B 4 HOURS	ALERT 5 (MAX 2 HRS)
AH-1Z UH-1Y	-A/C designated, slashed, preflighted -Minor maintenance may be performed at HAC discretion -Ordnance loads pre-built and stored in RSL	A/C designated, slashed, preflighted -Minor maintenance may be performed at HACdiscretion -Ordnance loaded or stored in RSL if A/C slashed	-Spotted for launch -Preflighted -Ordnance uploaded -No maintenance performed -Mission fuel loaded -Comm and Systems checks complete	-Spotted for immediate launch -Ordnance uploaded -System checks completed -Mission fuel loaded -APU running -Refuel as required	-Turning on spot for immediate launch or airborne -Ordnance uploaded -System checks completed -Mission fuel loaded
CH-46E CH-53E	-A/C designated, slashed, preflighted -Minor maintenance may be performed at HAC discretion -Ordnance loads pre-built and stored in RSL	A/C designated, slashed, preflighted -Minor maintenance may be performed at HAC discretion -Ordnance loaded -Mission fuel loaded	-CH-53 spotted -CH-46 may be slashed w/direct access to spot -Preflighted -No maintenance performed -Ordnance loaded -Mission fuel loaded -Comm and Systems checks complete	-Spotted for immediate launch -Ordnance loaded -System checks complete -Mission fuel loaded -APU running -Refuel as required	-Turning on spot for immediate launch or airborne -Ordnance uploaded -System checks completed -Mission fuel loaded
AV-8B	-A/C designated, slashed, preflighted -Minor maintenance may be performed -Ordnance loads pre-built and stored in RSL	-Slashed -Preflighted -Minor maintenance may be performed -Ordnance uploaded	-Slashed -A/C preflighted/ground turned, FMC -Ordnance uploaded	-Engine start and final checks completed, may shut down to APU if status is not upgraded -Ordnance/systems checks complete -Pilot IVO A/C	-A/C started, T/O checks complete -On spot for immediate launch -Ordnance armed -Systems check complete
AIRCREW	-Identified -Standing mission brief complete -Check in/out w/ODO -Crew rest authorized	-Briefed and readily available -Check in/out w/ODO -Flight gear accessible -Crew chiefs/plane captains to A/C or at flight line	-Aircrew located in ready room, briefed, flight gear on hand -Crew chiefs/plane captains at A/C or at flight line -Standby crews preflight A/C, start and spin R/W A/C	-Aircrew/pilots on A/C -AV-8B plane captain in seat w/APU online -AV-8B pilot IVO A/C	-Aircrew strapped in -Troops loaded
STANDING MISSION FORCE	-Alert force CMDR reports to LFOC for updates (OPS/INTEL/WX) -Marines in berthing, gear, and equipment staged -Ammo in RSL	-Alert force CMDR in LFOC -Force staged on hangar deck -Ammo, COMM, and essential gear staged on hangar deck	-Alert force CMDR in LFOC -Force staged on flight deck ramp ready to move to A/C -Ammo issued -Test fire complete -Coord w/LFOC	-Alert force CMDR in LFOC -Force staged on flight deck ramp ready to move to A/C -Ammo issued -Test fire complete -Coord w/LFOC	-Force loaded on A/C
FLIGHT DECK	-As required to meet Green deck time	-Flight deck crew prepared to accomplish re-spots and Green deck time -Flight quarters may be set	-A/C directors, flight deck linemen, launch officers, and aviation ordnance personnel standing by in island -Flight quarters set	-A/C directors, flight deck linemen, launch officers, and aviation ordnance personnel standing by for launch -LSO w/watchdog in tower	-A/C directors, flight deck linemen, launch officers, and aviation ordnance personnel standing by for launch -LSO w/watchdog in tower

Standing mission briefs are normally conducted when the MEU departs a port. The MEU CO will adjust the alert levels of the standing mission based upon the current situation and ongoing missions. When the need to employ a standing mission arises, the CAT will convene to provide the requisite information to the MEU CO prior to his decision. This Standing Mission Determination Board will normally convene in LFOC planning room. Depending on the complexity of a TRAP mission, the MEU CO will decide whether a TRAP Confirmation Brief is required. If so, the TRAP Confirmation Brief will be conducted in the Wardroom.

II. Standing Mission Briefs

Bald Eagle (Company-sized reinforcement)

Bald Eagle Commander
- Task and Purpose
- T/O & EDL
- Alert Status
- Concept of Operations (generic)
- Load/Bump plan
- Go/No-Go plan
- Linkup/MACO/ITG/Signals plan
- Contingencies
- Simultaneous Mission (MCRT)
- ORM
- Comm plan w/connectivity diagram
- Execution Checklist

Sparrowhawk (Platoon-sized reinforcement)

Sparrowhawk Commander
- Task and Purpose
- T/O & EDL
- Alert Status
- Concept of Operations
- Load/Bump plan
- Go/No-Go plan
- Linkup/MACO/ITG/Signals plan
- Contingencies
- Simultaneous Mission (MCRT)
- ORM
- Comm plan with connectivity diagram
- Execution Checklist

Assault Support

Bald Eagle/Sparrowhawk Commander
- Task and Purpose

Air Mission Commander
- Fire Support Plan (EFL)
- Assets
- Key personnel & A/C procedures
- Potential Insert LZ's that support mission
- HWSAT
- Go/No-Go criteria

Mass Casualty Response Team (MCRT)

MCRT Commander
- Mission
- T/O & EDL
- Location aboard ship
- Capabilities
- Load Plan
- Bump plan
- Concept of Operations (generic)
- Insert Landing plan
- Organization on the ground
- Movement to objective
- Actions on the Objective
- Triage Plan
- Withdrawal plan
- Go/No-Go plan
- Comm plan w/connectivity diagram
- Timeline
- ORM
- Execution Checklist

SJA
- LOAC issues
- Protected status
- Loss of protected status

Air Mission Commander
- Assets available
- E&R Plan

MCRT
- Task and Purpose
- T/O & T/E
- Special Equipment
- Concept of Operations
- Contingencies
- ORM

Medical Officer
- Shipboard reception plan for MCRT

Tactical Recovery of Aircraft and Personnel (TRAP)

Surface TRAP Commander
- Task and Purpose
- T/O & EDL
- Special Equipment
- Concept of Operations
- CCIRs
- Brief by Phase
- Execution Checklists
- Coordinating Instructions
- ROE considerations
- Public affairs guidance
- Detainee plan
- MACO Plan
- Bump Plan
- Signal Plan
- Casualty Plan
- Missing Marine Plan
- Comm Plan
- ORM
- Succession of Command

Helicopter borne TRAP Commander
- Overview
- Packages
- Task and Purpose
- T/O & EDL
- Special Equipment
- Concept of Operations
- CCIRs
- Execution Checklists
- Coordinating Instructions
- MACO Plan
- Signal Plan
- Casualty Plan
- Missing Marine Plan
- Comm Plan
- Succession of Command

Air Mission Commander (AMC)
- Mission Assets
- Special Equipment
- Concept of Operations
- Load plan
- Authentication Procedure
- TRAP Packages
- Zones/Levels
- Bump Plan (aircraft)
- Contingencies
- Fire Support Plan (EFL)

Evasion and Recovery (E&R)

ACE S-2
- Definitions
- Objective
- Requirements
- Conditions to initiate Evasion
- Recovery assets available
- Navigation plan
- Comm procedures
- CSAR Information (SARNEG, Pro-Word)
- SafeNavPlan

Commanders
- Comments (as desired)

MEU S-3
- Timeline

Chap 4

I. Tactical Recovery of Aircraft & Personnel (TRAP)

I. TRAP Zones

Trap Zones are based upon ground threat.

Zone I - No threat

Security element not required. Recovery by any asset available.

Zone II - Minimal Threat

Up to squad-size hostile force. Security element required. Actions on objective not manpower or time intensive.

Zone III – Moderate Threat

Squad to platoon hostile force or near urban unknown sentiment terrain. May require Sparrowhawk or Bald Eagle reinforcement. Anticipate manpower and time intensive actions on the objective.

Zone IV - Significant Threat

Platoon (-) and/or near urban hostile terrain. TRAP ground force requires Sparrowhawk/Bald Eagle reinforcement.

Zone V - High Threat

Platoon or larger and/or near populated hostile terrain. TRAP (rein) not feasible, requires amphibious raid or Special Operations aircraft and personnel.

II. TRAP Levels

TRAP Levels are based upon enemy air defense capabilities. These standard levels can be mitigated through various TTPs to include conducting operations during periods of darkness, Terrain Following (TERF) routing, etc.

Level I - No Threat

Safe over water or overland. No threat to survivor(s) or recovery aircraft and forces. Recovery can be initiated immediately without undue hazard to participating personnel.

Level II - Minimal Threat

Over land possible small arms threat. Survivor(s) location can be effected by enemy small arms within 2-3 hours. The TRAP should be executed immediately before the threat level increases. Escort aircraft are highly recommended.

Level III – Moderate Threat

Small arms threat. The threat level has increased, but the downed aircrew or isolated personnel can safely move to the designated area for rescue if needed. The air defense threat can be mitigated by aircraft routing and successful recovery is possible. Location of isolated personnel must be known more precisely than 1 nautical mile (NM), and communications with isolated personnel is recommended. A well planned recovery is required. Rotary wing and fixed wing escort recommended.

Level IV - Significant Threat

Low density anti-aircraft artillery (AAA)/ infrared (IR) missile threat. Detailed rehearsed recovery plan is required. Threat requires non-organic assets to execute. Additionally, isolated personnel's location must be precisely known (six or eight digit grid or lat/long), and communications with isolated personnel is required.

Level V - High Threat

Medium to high density integrated air defense system (IADS). Airborne recovery is not possible without further loss of personnel and assets. The threat must be significantly reduced or the isolated personnel must move to a less hostile environment for airborne TRAP execution.

III. TRAP Zones & Levels

	ZONES *Zones based on ground threat*				
LEVELS *Levels are based on enemy air defense capabilities*	**1**	**2**	**3**	**4**	**5**
1	A	A,B	C,D	C,D,E	SOF
2	A	A,B	C,D	C,D,E	SOF
3	A	A,B	C,D	C,D,E	SOF
4	A	A,B	C,D	C,D,E	SOF
5	SOF	SOF	SOF	SOF	SOF

TRAP Packages are indicated in within table.

Package	Distance	Conditions	Aircraft	Lift (as required)
A	<90 NM	Over water	2xCH-46E 2xMV-22B 2xUH-1Y(1)	Corpsman 1 SAR Swimmer
B	>90 NM	Over water (KC-130 may be required for HAAR/TRAAR distances beyond 250 NM)	2xCH-53D/E 2xMV-22B	Corpsman 1 SAR Swimmer
C	<90 NM	Day / Night over land	2xCH-46E 2xMV-22B 2xCH-53D/E 2xAH-1W 2xUH-1Y(1) 2xAV-8B 2xFA-18	24-48 Man TRAP Corpsman
D	>90 NM	Day / Night over land (long range FARP or TBFDS required for AH-1W)	2xCH-53D/E 2xMV-22B 2xAH-1W 2xUH-1Y(1) 2xAV-8B 2xFA-18	24-48 Man TRAP Corpsman
E	>90 NM	Day / Night over land (KC-130 may be required for HAAR/TRAAR distances beyond 250 NM)	2xCH-53E 2xMV-22B 2xAV-8B 2xFA-18	24-48 Man TRAP Corpsman

* AO, METT-TSL will drive mission planning considerations of the actual TRAP package composition.

NOTE:
(1) Planning consideration should be given to the role of the UH-1Y as either RESCORT or Recovery Vehicle depending on lift requirements. However, in a given element, the UH-1Y shall only fill one of the two roles, not both.

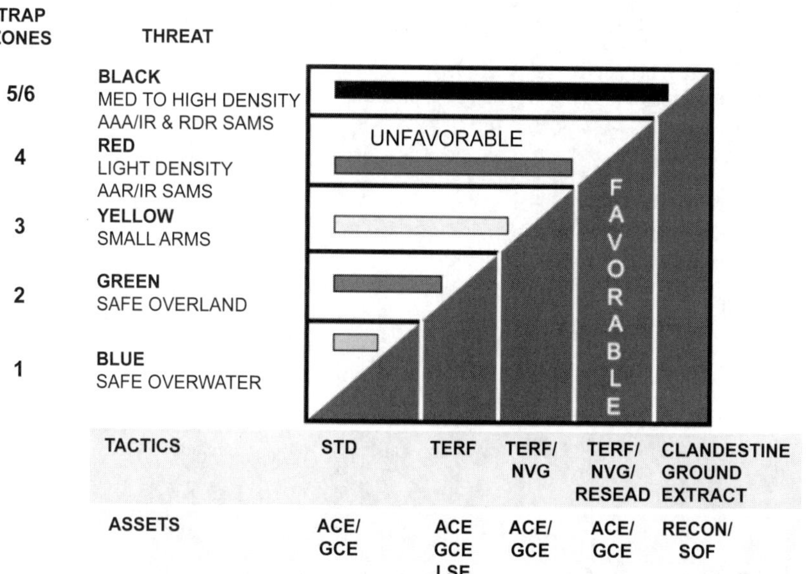

Embedded (built-in) TRAP

- TRAP embedded within force conducting mission.
- Planned and briefed concurrently with primary mission.

On-call TRAP (Airborne or Deck Alert)

- Airborne or strip alert
- Dedicated GCE and ACE assets
- Planned and briefed concurrently with primary mission

Deliberate TRAP

- TRAP developed, planned and briefed on receipt of TRAP mission

TRAP mission profile types

Aircraft

1. Repair
2. Recovery
3. Destruction

- Recover pilot & destroy aircraft in place

Personnel

1. Rescue downed pilot
2. Walking wounded or non-ambulatory
   - Recover downed crews
3. Walking wounded or non-ambulatory
   - Recover isolated MEU personnel
   - Support recovery of R&S forces that initiated E&R contingency plan

IV. TRAP Determination

TRAP Launch Criteria (CCIRs)

- Indications of a survivor(s) and their status. (FFIR)
- Survivor location known. (FFIR)
- Authentication information available. (FFIR)
- Isolated personnel not in danger of immediate capture. (PIR)
- Required assets available. (FFIR)
- TRAP elements properly briefed.
- Equipment to recover or destroy

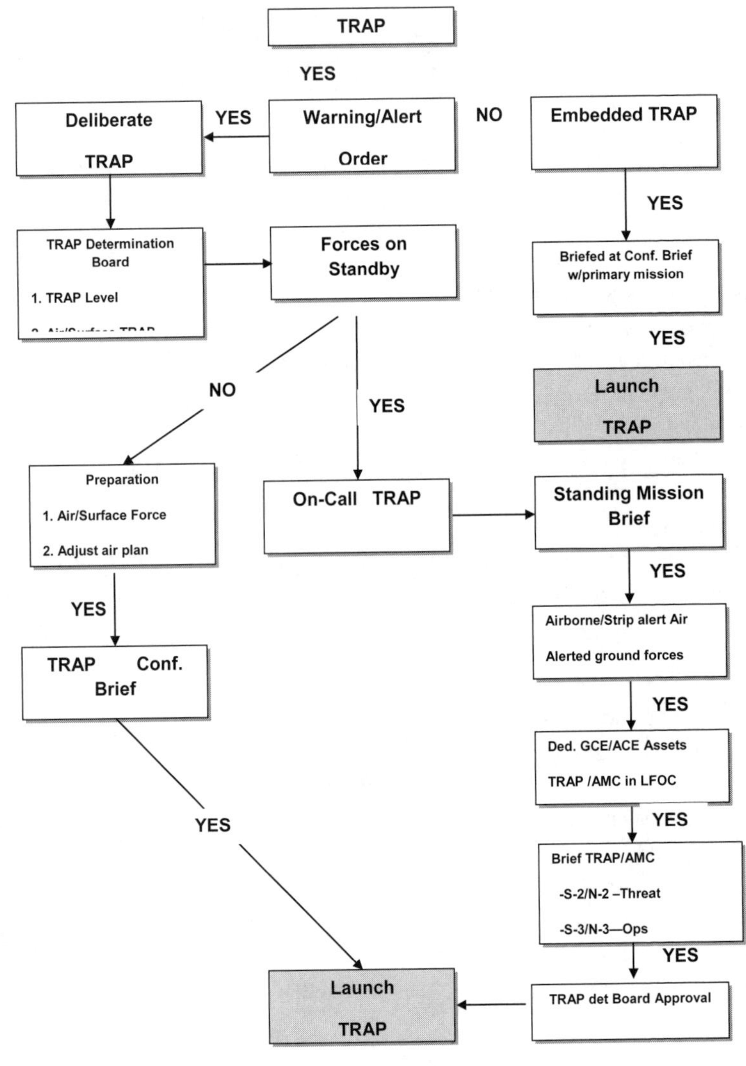

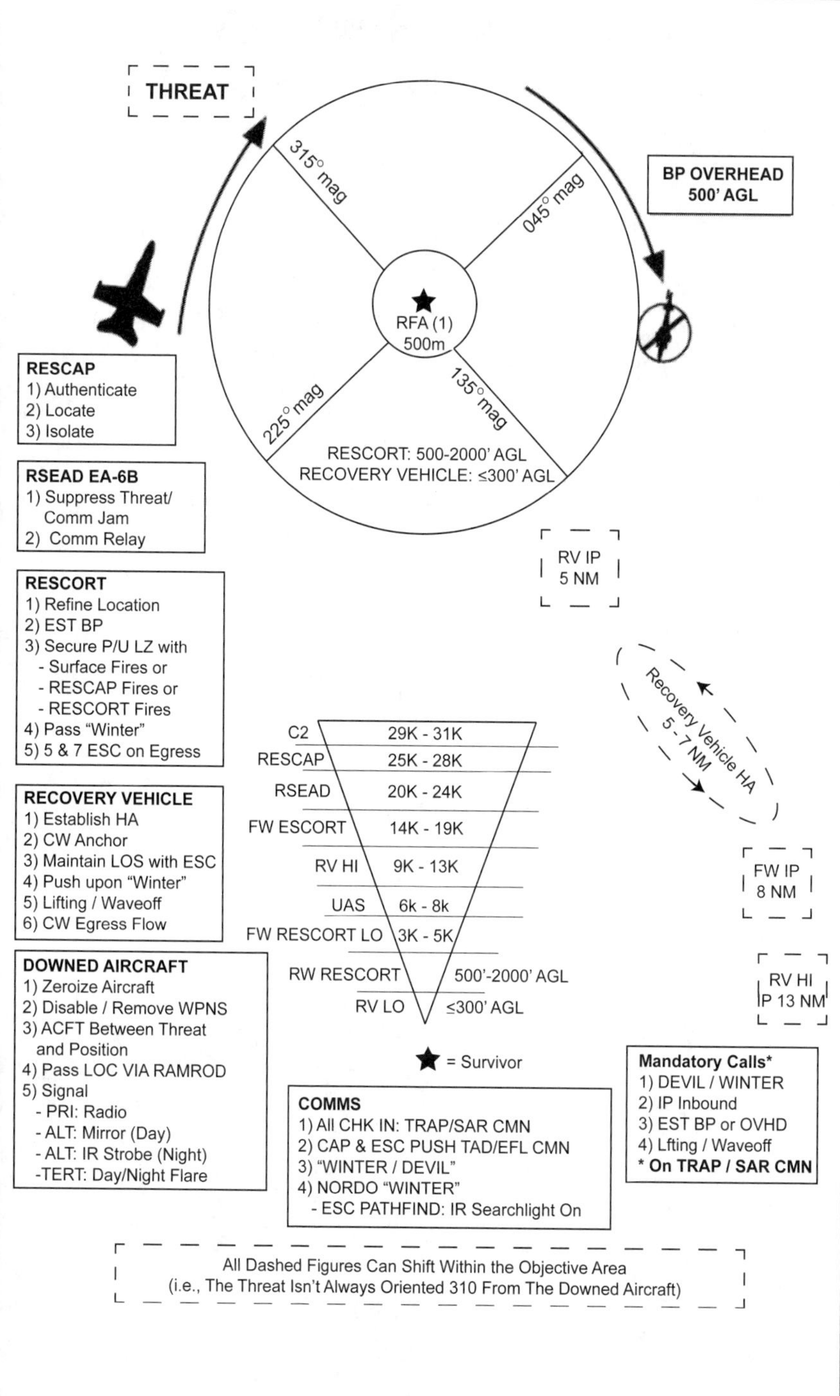
THREAT
315° mag
045° mag
BP OVERHEAD
500' AGL
RFA (1)
500m
225° mag
135° mag
RESCORT: 500-2000' AGL
RECOVERY VEHICLE: ≤300' AGL
RESCAP
1) Authenticate
2) Locate
3) Isolate
RSEAD EA-6B
1) Suppress Threat/ Comm Jam
2) Comm Relay
RESCORT
1) Refine Location
2) EST BP
3) Secure P/U LZ with
- Surface Fires or
- RESCAP Fires or
- RESCORT Fires
4) Pass "Winter"
5) 5 & 7 ESC on Egress
RV IP
5 NM
Recovery Vehicle HA
5 - 7 NM
C2
29K - 31K
RESCAP
25K - 28K
RSEAD
20K - 24K
FW ESCORT
14K - 19K
RV HI
9K - 13K
UAS
6k - 8k
FW RESCORT LO
3K - 5K
RW RESCORT
500'-2000' AGL
RV LO
≤300' AGL
FW IP
8 NM
RV HI
IP 13 NM
RECOVERY VEHICLE
1) Establish HA
2) CW Anchor
3) Maintain LOS with ESC
4) Push upon "Winter"
5) Lifting / Waveoff
6) CW Egress Flow
DOWNED AIRCRAFT
1) Zeroize Aircraft
2) Disable / Remove WPNS
3) ACFT Between Threat and Position
4) Pass LOC VIA RAMROD
5) Signal
- PRI: Radio
- ALT: Mirror (Day)
- ALT: IR Strobe (Night)
-TERT: Day/Night Flare
★ = Survivor
COMMS
1) All CHK IN: TRAP/SAR CMN
2) CAP & ESC PUSH TAD/EFL CMN
3) "WINTER / DEVIL"
4) NORDO "WINTER"
- ESC PATHFIND: IR Searchlight On
Mandatory Calls*
1) DEVIL / WINTER
2) IP Inbound
3) EST BP or OVHD
4) Lfting / Waveoff
* On TRAP / SAR CMN
All Dashed Figures Can Shift Within the Objective Area
(i.e., The Threat Isn't Always Oriented 310 From The Downed Aircraft)

V. TRAP Determination Brief Guide

MEU S-3
- Orientation (Ground)
- Friendly Force locations
- Missions Current and Projected
- TRAP Determination

PHIBRON N-3
- Orientation (Naval)
- ARG Position/Geometry/Timeline
- Friendly Force locations

MEU Meteorologist
- Weather
- METOC impacts on the mission from ship to objective

MEU S-2/PHIBRON N-2
- Provide Intel Update
- Naval Orientation (by exception)
- Ground Orientation
- Threat (Air/Ground) points of entry
- Other threats
- E&R Plan of personnel/Equip to be recovered

MEU SJA/PHIBRON JAG
- Rules of Engagement

MEU S-3
- TRAP Zones and Levels
- TRAP Packages
- TRAP Determination Matrix
- Assets Available
- HHQ Mission
- HHQ Commander's Intent
- CCIRs
- Specified/Implied Tasks
- Essential Tasks
- Constraints and Restraints
- Launch Criteria
- Assumptions
- External Support Requirements
- Mission Clarification
- RFIs/PIRs/EEFIs/FFIRs/CCIRs
- Restated Mission
- Refined Commanders Intent
- Cross Deck

MEU S-3
- Launch Criteria
- Mission CCIRs

Commanders
- Comments/Guidance

MEU S-3
- Planning Cell
- Timeline

Air TRAP (AMC)

AMC
- Mission
- General Overview
- TRAP Level Matrix
- Mission Assets
- Mission Asset Takeaways
- Key Players
- Mission Timeline
- Launch
- Concept of Operations

Flight Escort Lead
- Fire Support Assets Available
- Orientation Map
- Control of Fires

AMC
- FARP Considerations
- Contingencies
- Command and Signal
- Coordinating Instructions
- TRAP Command and Signal
- Flight Lead Degradation
- Proposed Delegation of Authority
- Execution Checklist Review
- Aviation ORM

Commanders
- Comments/Approval

MEU S-3
- Timeline

CAAT/LAR TRAP

BLT S-2
- WX
- Aircraft / Personnel Information
- SPINS
- Enemy Overview

MEU S-3
- MEU Location
- Mission
- Commander's Intent
- Phasing Ashore
- Task Organization
- Detailed LCAC Load Plan
- Mission Essential Equipment
- Orientation
- Fire Support Assets Available
- Concept of Fires
- Aircraft Timeline
- Key Players
- Air C.I.
- Phase I & IV Targets
- Target List Worksheet
- Concept Of Operations
- Phases I through IV
- Air Details
  - Orientation Maps
  - Coordinating Instructions
  - ITG BLS Day
  - Criteria to Launch
  - Enabler Tasks
  - Recovery COAs
  - BUMP/NO-GO
- Communications Diagram
- Frequencies
- MACO Procedures
- Marking Plan
- Signal Plan
- CASEVAC Plan
- LZ Locations
- Casualty Plan
- EPW Handling Plan
- Challenge & Pass
- Succession of Command
- Contingencies
- IED Actions upon Contact
- Reinforcement Plan
- Link-Up Plan
- Missing Marine Plan (Unit)
- Missing Marine Plan (Individual)
- Missing Vehicle Plan
- HMMWV Vehicle Recovery
- LAR Vehicle Recovery / Bump Plan
- No Communications Plan
- Destruction Plan
- In stride Breach Plan
- CAAT/LAR ORM
- Execution Checklist
- Timeline

Commanders
- Comments/Approval

MEU S-3
- Timeline

II. Mass Casualty Recovery Team (MCRT)

Casualty producing situations are often confusing in the initial moments. The true magnitude of such a situation might not be fully known for an intermediate period of time. Therefore, to prepare to receive casualties in an optimal state of readiness, mass casualty preparations are activated when it is known that the number of casualties will exceed the capabilities of the medical department alone, or if the magnitude of casualties is unknown.

I. Definition

A MCRT situation is one in which the number of casualties has overwhelmed the medical capabilities of the supported unit. It differs from an emergency MEDEVAC because the number of casualties is large enough that triage and stabilization is necessary prior to evacuation.

II. Mission

The 15TH MEU prepares to conduct hellebore and/or surface MCRT missions on short notice, over long range, at day or night, during limited visibility, in a hostile or non-hostile environment. The MCRT conducts immediate triage, stabilization, and evacuation of casualties. The ARG prepares to receive, treat, and/or process the casualties based on the type and level of injury.

III. Responsibilities

The USS Peleliu Senior Medical Officer (SMO) is responsible for planning, organizing, and directing the Mass Casualty Bill aboard ARG shipping. The CO, 15TH MEU is responsible for deploying MASSCAS Teams ashore to assist units whose medical capabilities have been overwhelmed.

MEU Commander/LFOC Watch Officer

The MEU can launch up to two twenty-four man MASSCAS Teams via ground or air. Based upon METT-T, one of these four options will be utilized. If time permits, a determination team is assembled to assess the best method of execution.

CLB-15 MCRT Teams

When the MEU has personnel ashore, CLB-15 maintains the capability of employing at least one MASSCAS Team. Alert conditions vary depending on mission requirements.

CATF Surgeon

The CATF Surgeon activates the ship's Mass Casualty Bill when he/she is aware of incoming casualties which exceed the capabilities of the Medical Department alone. The CATF Surgeon is also responsible for patient transfer and evacuation.

Medical Regulating Officer

The Medical Regulating Officer is responsible for tracking patient transfers and evacuation. He/she can activate the ship's Mass Casualty Bill when aware of incoming casualties which exceed the capabilities of the Medical Department alone.

Triage Officer

The Triage Officer is responsible for sorting patients for transportation and treatment as outlined above.

IV. Casualty Routing & Triage

Casualty Routing

Casualties transported to the ship are initially triaged and treated in the Flight Deck Triage area or the Main Battle Dressing Station (BDS). They are then routed to the Main Medical spaces. Internal casualties are routed to an initial triage and treatment area (usually the Flight Deck Triage, Main Medical BDS or other BDS) by the Air Officer or DCA. After initial treatment, the patients are then routed to the Main Medical spaces.

Triage (Sorting)

Triage is the evaluation and classification of injured personnel to establish priorities for treatment and evacuation. Triage is further broken down into four broad categories. MASSCAS Teams ashore use classification color codes consistent with the ship to ensure the efficient triage and treatment.

Immediate Treatment (Group I) Color Code Red

Includes casualties requiring emergency life saving procedures. These procedures should not be time consuming and must concern only those patients with a high chance for survival.

Delayed Treatment (Group II) Color Code Yellow

Includes casualties in need of time consuming procedures but whose general condition permits delay in surgical treatment without unduly endangering life or limb.

Expectant (Group III) Color Code Black

Includes casualties with life threatening injuries and are unlikely to respond to medical treatment.

Minimal Treatment (Group III) Color Code Green

Includes casualties with relatively minor injuries who can effectively care for themselves or who can be helped by non-medical personnel.

Chap 5

I. Forward Command Element (FCE)

The Forward Command Element deploys to an area of operations in advance of the main force when deemed necessary by the Commanders of the MEU and CPR and authorized by HHQ/U.S. Embassy/Host Nation. The FCE mission has three parts:

- Coordinate ARG/MEU activities with U.S. Embassy and host nation authorities as authorized by the directing headquarters
- Establish a communication link between the MEU and Embassy
- Prepare to assume other missions as directed

Intent

Insert designated personnel to inform and advise the Ambassador and country team of the ARG/MEU capabilities and limitations, and to act as a means by which they may communicate their concerns and requirements to the ARG/MEU.

Pre-conditions

- DIRLAUTH with Embassy authorized by appropriate HHQ and Combatant Commander
- Permission from Ambassador to insert FCE ashore
- Necessary clearances (air, country) obtained from HN, DOS and Regional Combatant Commander
- ARG in position to effect insert of element

Guidance

- Task organize team IAW mission
- Communicate with embassy staff and describe plan/request permission to insert
- Determine clothing and equipment requirements
- Brief country team on ARG/MEU capabilities
- Determine political-military constraints
- Identify American Embassy support requirements
- Establish and maintain communications with the MEU
- Review Emergency Action Plan (EAP) with country team
- Determine terrorist threat/potential
- Seek embassy ideas to assist mission accomplishment
- Work with embassy personnel to answer Commander's information requirements
- Determine host nation support available
- Validate F-77 Report

Desired End State

- Safe insertion of FCE
- Reliable communications established between Embassy and MEU
- American Embassy advised on ARG/MEU capabilities

FCE Task Organization

The FCE is task-organized based upon the assigned mission. Personnel and equipment requirements are built around a core element and increase or decrease in size based upon mission taskings. Because the number allowed into the country may be limited, the actual FCE may have to be reduced in size. Careful considerations must be made when determining the required personnel to ensure basic capabilities are maintained. The "core" FCE is comprised of the following:

MEU XO

The MEU XO acts as the Officer-In- Charge (OIC) of the FCE. He provides direct liaison with the senior Embassy representative to ensure the synchronization of landing force missions and DOS political issues. Additionally, he directs and coordinates all efforts of the FCE personnel in order to establish and maintain liaison between the landing force and the Ambassador.

Logistics Planner

The CLB XO normally acts as the Logistics Planner, although based on the mission, the S-4A from the MEU Command Element may be used instead. The Logistics Planner is also the Assistant OIC of the FCE. He is prepared to discuss, coordinate and personally assist designated country team personnel on logistical matters in support of landing force operations. In the event that Embassy officials request immediate assistance in the expeditious processing of American Citizens (AMCITS), Third Country Nationals (TCNs), or other designated evacuees, he provides direction and coordination for the conduct of a hasty Evacuation Control Center (ECC). Additionally, while the MEU is still aboard ARG shipping, he works closely with landing force planners to ensure the flow of operational information between the FCE and the Landing Force Operations Center (LFOC) is accomplished in a timely manner.

FCE Intelligence Section

This section is led by the HET OIC and provides a conduit for all-source intelligence directly from the embassy, evacuation site(s) and crisis site(s). Additionally, it coordinates required site surveys and force protection assessments with the country team. Employment of an SST may also be considered based on mission requirements and Embassy approval.

FCE Operations Section

This section is made up by an Officer or SNCO who establishes and operates the FCE COC. He is responsible for maintaining all mission binders, requests for information (RFIs) listings, and daily update briefs to the Embassy.

FCE Communications Section

This section is led by a SNCO, and a number of data/radio Marines to be determined by the communications assets required. The Communications detachment will provide secure voice and data communications to the FCE. It will maintain and monitor redundant HF, VHF, UHF, SIPRNET, NIPRNET, and SATCOM communication nets in order to establish the necessary communications links and facilitate information flow between the FCE and ARG/MEU.

FCE Public Affairs Section

This section is comprised of the PAO Chief and works in coordination with the embassy's Public Diplomacy Officer to coordinate media affairs.

Forward Control Element

BILLET	REQ	GRADE	UNIT	WEAPON	CORE	CORE PLUS	DET
OIC	1	LtCol	CE	9mm	X		
Com Chief/Data	1	SSgt	CE	9mm	X		
Radio Operator	1	Cpl/LCpl	CE	M-16	X		
Radio Operator	1	Cpl/LCpl	CE	M-16	X		
Data Systems	1	Cpl	CE	M-16	X		
AOIC (Air)	1	Maj	CE	9mm		X	
NCOIC (OPS)	1	GySgt	CE	9mm		X	
HET/Intel Officer	1	CWO/Capt	CE	9mm		X	
COMCAM	1	Cpl	CE	M-16		X	
BLT Planner	1	Lt/Capt	BLT	9mm		X	
ACE Planner	1	Capt	ACE	9mm		X	
CLB Planner	1	Lt/Capt	CE	9mm		X	
Log Planner	1	Capt	CE	9mm		X	
ATFP	1	Lt/Capt	CE	9mm		X	
NCIS Agent	1	Civ	CPR	9mm		X	
PAO	1	SNCO	CE	9mm		X	
Corpsman	1	ENL	CE	9mm		X	
Intel Chief (FAS)	1	SNCO	CE	9mm		X	
Navy Planner	1	LT	CPR	9mm		X	
Radio Operator	1	LCpl	CE	M-16		X	
Data Systems	1	LCpl	CE	M-16		X	
Medical Planner	1	LT	CLB	9mm		X	
Contracting	1	Off/SNCO	CE	9mm		X	
SST	4	TBD	CE	9mm			X
HET	2	SNCO	CE	9mm			X
EOD	2	TBD	CLB	9mm			X
R&S Team	4	NCO	BLT	T/O			X
Sniper Team	6	NCO	BLT	T/O			X
Security Det	13	TBD	BLT	T/O			X
Others	TBD	TBD	TBD	TBD		X	X
Total					5	18 +/-	31 +/-

MEU Liaison & Survey

FCE Brief

FCE Brief	
Briefer	**Topic**
MEU S-3	Orientation Missions in progress Restate mission/intent RFIs
PHIBRON N-3	Naval Force Disposition
MEU Meteorologist	Weather
MEU S-2	Intel Update
PHIBRON N-2	Naval Intel Update
FCE Cmdr	Mission Task Organization EDL Preconditions Priority of Work Specific Intelligence Requirements Collections priorities Brief by Phase Phase I – Insert Phase II- Movement to Objective Phase III – Actions on the Objective Phase IV – Link Up/Withdrawal Phase V- Extraction to ARG shipping Load Plan/Bump Plan Go/No-Go Abort Authority & Criteria Coordinating Instructions Admin & Logistics Command & Signal
FSC/MEU FSO	Essential Fire Support Tasks Assets Available/Location (incl NSFS if available) Fire Support Coordination Measures
MEU S-1	Status of Country Clearances
PHIBRON **MEU** **NCIS** **ATFPO**	ATFP assessment
PHIBRON/MEU PAO	Public Affairs Posture
PHIBRON JAG **MEU SJA**	Review ROE Mission specific legal issues
TACRON	Airspace
Air Mission Cmdr	AMC/AFL/EFL Considerations Routing Control Measures LZ Diagrams
PHIBRON CCO	Embark Plan manifests serial assignments
SHIP AIR OPS	Aircraft spotting
Medical	Assets Ashore CASEVAC procedures Chain of Evacuation Time/distance from point of injury to ARG Primary and alternate means of CASEVAC Medical Regulating PCRTS: Beds, ORS, Blood SCRTS: Beds, ORS, Blood
MEU S-6	Communications Plan
ORM-Safety	Navy ACE GCE LCE (as required)
MEU S-3	Review Execution Checklist Review Mission CCIRs Review Master Timeline
Commanders	Decision/Comments
MEU S-3	Timeline

II. Humanitarian Assistance Survey Team (HAST)

The Humanitarian Assistance Survey Team serves as the tactical level reconnaissance of a Humanitarian Assistance Operation by conducting an initial ground truth assessment of the conditions that exist in an area and providing requirements to the PHIBRON and MEU Commander prior to the arrival of the humanitarian assistance force. Additionally, the HAST coordinates with Department of State personnel and/or HN/NGO/PVOs, as well as local leadership in order to identify potential assets available in the AOR that are required for the MEU to perform it's mission. The establishment of a cordial and professional relationship with individuals in the HN/NGO/PVOs and local populace is essential to the conduct of the HAO.

Upon the arrival of the humanitarian assistance force, the HAST must be prepared to establish either a Humanitarian Assistance Coordination Center (HACC) or a Civil-Military Operations Center (CMOC) as both serve as the interface to coordinate the requirements of the HN/NGO/PVOs without compromising military operational security. The HAST must be task organized for each specific mission to not only determine the needs of the afflicted populace, but also to assess the environment that the HAO forces will be operating in. This may include but is not limited to an assessment of Force Protection/Security Posture, Potential Water Production sites, Terrain and Weather, Local Equipment available, and Medical Facilities available.

Intent

Insert designated personnel to make liaison with HN/NGO/PVOs in order to quickly assess the current situation and provide feedback to higher headquarters. Collect information that will ultimately be incorporated into the planning process in order to plan and conduct a successful Humanitarian Assistance operation. HAST should also be prepared to educate HN/NGO/PVOs and Embassy country team on ARG/MEU capabilities and limitations.

Preconditions

- Permission from Ambassador (if one exists) to insert HAST
- Necessary clearances (air, country) obtained from HN, DoS, and Combatant Commander
- ARG in position to insert HAST
- Secure environment for HAST to operate within

Guidance

- Spend a minimal amount of time on the ground
- Execute the mission tactically, but unthreatening
- Develop rough estimate to develop courses of action
- Task organize the team; right kind of assistance in the right place
- Speed of execution sends the message that we are responsive, furthers IO efforts
- Utilize intelligence sources to support the operation (demographics, culture, language)
- Force protection is constant from start to finish (Guardian Overwatch, NLW, etc.)

- Public affairs opportunity; manage the press and place key assets into the mission up front (CMO, PAO, HET, etc.)
- Establish priority of work first
- Assess the local environment immediately (permissive, uncertain, hostile)
- Determine if there are any political constraints on our objectives

Desired End State

- Safe insertion of HAST
- Reliable communication established between HAST and ARG/MEU
- HN/NGO/PVO knowledgeable as to ARG/MEU capabilities
- Sufficient information to assist Mission/MEU commander during COA development and mission planning

Questions MEU staff may ask of Ambassador/Host Nation regarding HAST insertion

(If time and comm are available)

- Size/composition of HAST allowed in country
- Method of insert
- Location of insert
- Weapons authorized (Y/N)
- Civilian clothes
- Equipment
- Level of self-sustainment required
- Anticipated duration
- Embassy assessment of AT/FP and anticipated threat

HAST Task Organization

Similar to the FCE, the HAST is task-organized based upon the assigned mission. Personnel and equipment requirements are built around a core element and increase or decrease in size based upon mission taskings. Because the number allowed into the country may be limited, the actual HAST may have to be reduced in size. Careful considerations must be made when determining the required personnel to ensure basic capabilities are maintained. The "core" HAST is comprised of the following:

HAST

Billet	Req	Grade	Unit	Weapon
HAST OIC	1	Maj	CLB	9mm
A/HAST OIC	1	CWO	CLB	9mm
HAST SNCOIC	1	SSgt	CLB	9mm
Health Services	1	LT	CLB	M-4
PMT	1	HM1	CLB	M-4
Military Police	1	SSgt	CLB	M-4
Comm RTO	2	Sgt/Cpl	CLB	M-16
HET or intel rep	1	SNCO	CLB	9mm
Engineering	1	Sgt	CLB	M-16
Drivers	2	Cpl	CLB	M-16
Total	**12**			

Notes: (1) Usually filled by the CLB XO; also on the FCE T/O

**Most officers and SNCO are issued a M-4 carbine in addition to the M9 pistol and depending on clearance and situation can bring both or either weapon.

HAST Augments (As Required)

Billet	Req	Grade	Unit	Weapon
CPR/Ship Reps	TBD	TBD	CPR	9mm
ACE Planner	1	Capt	ACE	9mm
IO Rep	1	Off	CE	9mm
CMO	1	Maj	CE	9mm
PAO	1	Capt	CE	9mm
Contracting	1	Off	CE	9mm
Linguist	1	Any	Any	9mm
Security	TBD	TBD	BLT	M-16
CEB OIC	1	1stLt	BLT	TBD
RMT	2	TBD	CE	9mm

Notes : (1) Security Element could include NLW capability

HAST Assessment Questions

General Situation

- What is the type of disaster and what are its causes - both short term and from a historical perspective?
- When did it occur and is it still occurring?
- What area has been affected?
- Within that area, how extensive was the damage to the infrastructure?
- How many people have died and how many have been injured?
- How many people are in need of assistance from the government and or other agencies?
- Who's in charge? NGO/PVO/local government?
- Why can't the needs be met by the above agencies?
- What will be the MOE's used to allow for our exit strategy?
- How do we transfer responsibility and to whom?

Water

- What are the water needs of the population that only the military has the capability to meet?
- How many people lack a sufficient quantity of appropriately potable water?
- What is preventing people from obtaining water from traditional sources?
- Do people have sufficient water collection equipment?
- Why is water contaminated?
- Why are traditional means of making water potable not sufficient?

Sanitation

- What are the sanitation needs of the population that can only be met by the military?
- How many people are in need of improved assistance in the area of sanitation?
- What are people using for excreta disposal?
- Are excreta disposal and isolation methods sufficient to prevent contamination of water and food sources?
- Are sanitation facilities (toilets, defecation fields) adequate in size, location, and cleanliness to convince people to utilize them?

Food

- What are the nutrition needs of the population that can only be met by the military?
- How many people are in need of food?
- Are there signs of malnutrition among the population?
- Is the total amount of food being delivered equal to total needs in terms of calories per day?
- What is obstructing the delivery of food?
- Are the most vulnerable people obtaining adequate food?
- Is the food culturally appropriate?
- Do people have the appropriate utensils, cooking fuels, etc., to prepare foods?
- What actions are being taken to ensure that people have sufficient food and equipment?

Shelter

- Are shelters sufficient in quantity and quality?
- Approximately how many people are without adequate shelter?
- Do people need supplies to rebuild their homes?
- How urgent is the need for shelter given the environment?
- What actions are being taken to ensure that people have sufficient shelter?

Health

- What are the health needs of the population that can only be met by the military?
- Approximately how many people are in need of health care?
- What types of assistance do people need to be able to properly bury deceased relatives?
- What are the immediate health care risks?
- What type of health care system exists to meet those needs?
- What health care needs are not being met?
- What problems are preventing those health care needs from being met?
- What actions are being taken to ensure that people have sufficient health care?
- What can the military do to assist in addressing unmet health care needs?

Facilities and Infrastructure

- What problems with infrastructure and facilities are impeding relief efforts?
- What is causing insufficient throughput rates at ports and airfields - damage to facilities, lack of equipment, intermittent electricity, or problems in management?
- Where are the bottlenecks that prevent delivery of relief supplies?
- Are there sufficient transportation assets for delivery of relief aid?
- Where is additional aid needed most critically - and how much is needed?
- What actions are being taken to ensure that facilities and infrastructure are in sufficient working order to facilitate the relief effort?

Coordination

- What are the key agencies with whom the military must coordinate?
- What are the key coordination issues that are not being addressed - either due to lack of personnel or lack of subject matter expertise?
- What actions are being taken to improve coordination efforts?
- What support is available in regards to local guides and translators?

Preparations for Exit

- Who will take over the humanitarian function?
- How long will it take them to do so?
- How will the transfer of responsibility and authority occur between the outgoing and incoming parties?
- Have efforts been coordinated in such a way as to ensure that everyone involved has a clear understanding of who is in charge at all times?
- When will temporary functions no longer be necessary - and how will we measure it?
- What are the agreed upon MOE that indicate when the desired endstate is achieved?
- What are the activities that should not be conducted by US forces?

HAST Brief (Ward Room)

HAST Brief (Ward Room)	
Briefer	**Topic**
MEU S-3	Orientation Missions Current and Projected Restated mission RFIs
PHIBRON N-3	Naval Force Disposition
MEU Meteorologist	Weather
MEU S-2	Intel Update
PHIBRON N-2	Naval Intel Update
HAST Cmdr	Mission Task Organization EDL Preconditions Priority of Work Specific Intelligence Requirements Collections priorities Brief by Phase Phase I – Insert Phase II- Movement to Objective Phase III – Actions on the Objective Phase IV – Link Up/Withdrawal Phase V- Extraction to ARG shipping Load Plan/Bump Plan Go/No-Go Abort Authority & Criteria Coordinating Instructions Admin & Logistics Command & Signal
IO/IWC	As required
MEU S-1	Status of Country Clearances (if required)
PHIBRON NCIS **MEU AT/FPO**	ATFP assessment (if required)
PHIBRON/MEU PAO	Public Affairs Posture
MEU SJA	Review ROE Mission specific legal issues
TACRON	Airspace
AMC	AMC/AFL/EFL Considerations Routing ACMs LZ Diagrams
PHIBRON CCO	Embark Plan/manifests/serial assignments
SHIP AIR OPS	Aircraft spotting
Medical	Assets Ashore CASEVAC procedures Chain of Evacuation Time/distance from point of injury to ARG Primary and alternate means of CASEVAC Medical Regulating PCRTS: Beds, ORS, Blood SCRTS: Beds, ORS, Blood
MEU S-6/CPR N-6	Communications Plan
ORM-Safety	Navy ACE GCE LCE (as required)
HAST Commander	Execution Checklist
MEU S-3	Review Exec. Checklist Review Master Timeline Review Mission CCIRs
Commanders	Decision/Comments
MEU S-3	Timeline

III. MAGTF Consequence Management (CBRN)

The MAGTF Consequence Management CBRN Equipment Set

The MAGTF Consequence Management CBRN Equipment Set provides the MEU Commander a Toxic Industrial Material (TIM) assessment, detection, identification, and sample collection capability in environments too hazardous for organic Individual Protective Equipment (IPE). The MAGTF Consequence Management CBRN Equipment Set is employed as directed by the MEU Commander. Generally, these situations will fall into one of these categories:

A. Site Exploitation

The unit discovers a possible Weapons of Mass Destruction (WMD) or TIM source requiring investigation to update the Commander's operational environment and Force Protection needs.

B. Maritime Raid Force formerly known as: Visit, Board, Search and Seizure (VBSS)

The unit is directed to board or seize a ship and uses the set to ascertain the presence of, or lack of, WMD/TIM.

C. Non-combatant Evacuation Operations (NEO)

Identify WMD/TIM hazards in the process of, or to facilitate, NEO operations.

AMEMB/Host Nation Support

Provide assessments of the presence of WMD/TIM at the request of AMEMB or Host Nations. Capabilities of the MAGTF Consequence Management CBRN Equipment Set include:

- Conduct initial assessments to determine the presence of, or lack of, WMD/TIM
- Conduct limited, presumptive gas identification
- Conduct Chemical/Biological sampling for confirmatory analysis
- Initiate chain-of-custody procedures for samples

Limitations of the MAGTF Consequence Management CBRN Equipment Set include:

- Identify all WMD/TIM. Current capabilities give the team the ability to identify many chemical warfare agents, limited biological agents, and several known TIM. Unidentified agents/TIM can be collected through sampling and turned over to other departmental agencies for identification.
- Conduct Mass Casualty decontamination.(decontamination limited to MAGTF Consequence Management CBRN team members)
- Mitigate the situation beyond that needed for self protection (putting the lid back on, closing the door, turning of the valve)
- Site must be secure before employment of MAGTF Consequence Management CBRN team

Team Organization & Equipment

Team Table of Organization (TO)

The MAGTF Consequence Management CBRN team can be tasked organized to respond to specific threats or situations based on METT-T. Twenty-two personnel throughout the MEU are trained on the operation of equipment and procedures required to employ the set. Those personnel include:

Team Table of Organization (TO)

Unit	Billet
CE	MEU CBRN Officer
CE	MEU CBRN Chief
CE	MEU CBRN Specialist
BLT	BLT CBRN Officer
	BLT
BLT	BLT CBRN Specialist
BLT (x 2)	RADIO Operator
BLT (x 2)	Corpsman
BLT (x 12)	Various MOS Trained in ID and Assessment
CLB	CLB CBRN Specialist
ACE	ACE CBRN Specialist

* For planning purposes, all personnel are located aboard the LHD with the exception of the CLB CBRN specialist. All MAGTF CM CBRN equipment is embarked on the LHD.
** EOD from CLB is equipped to augment.

Team Table of Equipment (TE)

METT-TSL will determine the equipment required for MAGTF CM CBRN team operations. The site commander will determine necessary equipment based on size of team employed. The equipment listed below is a sampling of equipment contained in the set.

Team Table of Equipment (TE)
Level B Protective suits
IPE (SARATOGA OR JSLIST) (M40A1)
Self Contained Breathing Apparatus
Voice Communication Adaptors
MultiRAE (TIC/TIM detectors)
Biological Assay Tickets
Draeger (TIC/TIM detector) Kits
Chemical Agent Monitors
Automatic Chemical Agent Detectors
AN/VDR-2 (radiological detector)
Stretchers
Collapsible basins
Weed sprayers
Skeds
Trash cans
Pelican rescue lights
Bauer (bottle refill)
5 gallon water jugs
Decontaminants

Load Plan

Two CH-53 or equivalent will be required to employ all MAGTF CM CBRN personnel and required equipment ashore. The mission will dictate number of team members required and amount of equipment needed to support operations.

A. Marshalling Area Control Officer (MACO)

Pre-Event Requirements

- MACO Team to support LZ Operations is identified and tasked
- LZ Marking kit is prepared
- Communications established
- Medical team established
- LZ control team identified
- LZ brief cards produced
- Aviation call signs and frequencies identified
- ITG team identified and tasked
- Marking procedures identified

MACO Procedures in the Pickup Zone

- Stick Leaders coordinate with MACO
- MACO Gate been identified/marked in the Pickup Zone
- Ensure Sticks pass thru the MACO Gate
- MACO accounts for every Marine passing through the MACO Gate
- MACO reports counts to PZCO
- MACO maintains positive communication with the Stick Leaders
- MACO establishes and maintains positive communication with the aircraft
- Stick Leader knows which aircraft he is taking his stick once he passes thru the MACO Gate
- Stick Leader has a means of identifying his serial number for the Crew Chiefs
- Crew Chief locates the correct stick
- Crew Chiefs and Stick Leaders communicate before entering the aircraft
- Crew Chiefs lead the Stick Leaders and Sticks onto the aircraft

MACO Procedures in the Landing Zone

- MACO positioned with the assault force support element for insert and extract
- MACO sends reconnaissance team to sweep the landing zone
- ITG team positioned for near and far ITG
- Obstacles in zone marked
- Landing zone and landing points marked (consideration for both day and night operations)
- Localized security established
- MACO gate marked and established
- MACO conducts serial call-away
- Stick leaders provide stick manifests to MACO
- LZ Control net operational and LZ brief conducted
- MACO marshals all forces onto assault support aircraft as they land in zone

- MACO conducts final accountability off of the flight manifest
- MACO is the last individual on the last aircraft in zone
- MACO is up on ICS and reports numbers of extracted force to pilot via ICS

Additional Comments

- During the serial call-away, the MACO needs to ensure they is time separation to minimize serials stacking up at the MACO gate and creating additional congestion.
- The MACO should be the last individual out of the extract LZ

B. Reception Plan Checklist

When conducting Amphibious Operations or Marine Expeditionary Unit (MEU) operations, constraints of amphibious shipping will be a consideration for both embark and debark of assault support aircraft. There are multiple benefits of conducting air assault operations from amphibious shipping:

- Shared familiarity with the ACE composite squadron and GCE
- Multiple planning and execution enablers organic to amphibious shipping
- Dedicated Combat Cargo personnel
- Dedicated staging and loading procedures developed and organized

Below is a step by step procedure on a proposed reception plan when the assault force returns to amphibious shipping after completion of the mission. It begins when the assault force returns to amphibious shipping and ends when all personnel and equipment accounted for and all ammunition, intelligence and equipment and weapons turned in.

Reception / Re-embarkation procedures: Marines will move through the stations in single file to prevent anyone from being missed. Marines will not be allowed to leave the Reception Area until the entire force has been processed.

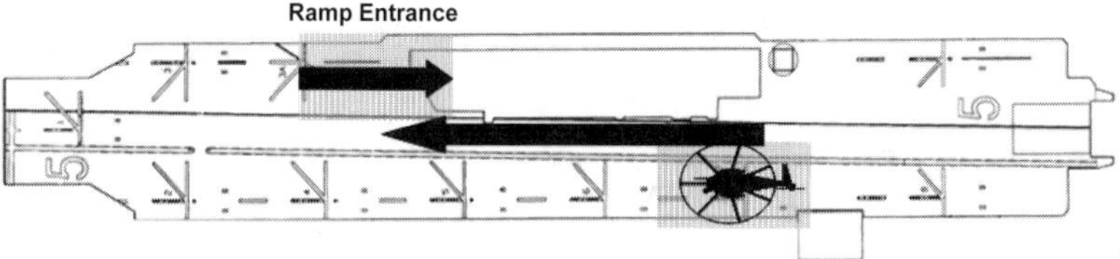

Once aircraft return, combat cargo will physically escort and guide sticks from aircraft to the reception ramp for processing.

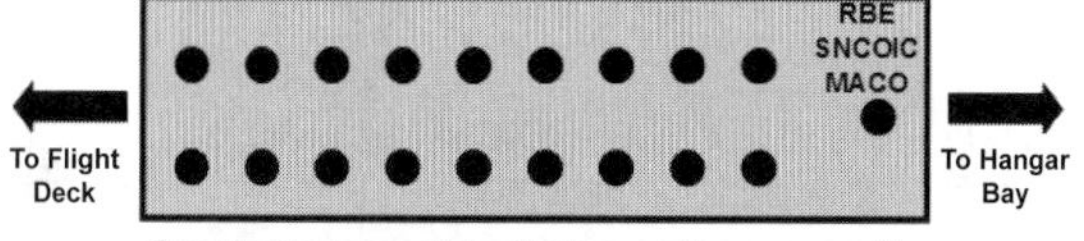

Once inside ramp, stick will stage and be processed in by RBE SNCOIC MACO for accountability.

KEY Players

- Remain Behind Element (RBE) OIC/SNCOIC. (The senior Marine and reception team from the assault force who do not take part in the mission.)
- BLT command representatives
- S-4 representatives
- Intelligence representatives
- Medical personnel
- Combat Cargo personnel

Reception Stations

Reception Plan

Internal View of Hangar Bay and Reception Station Plan

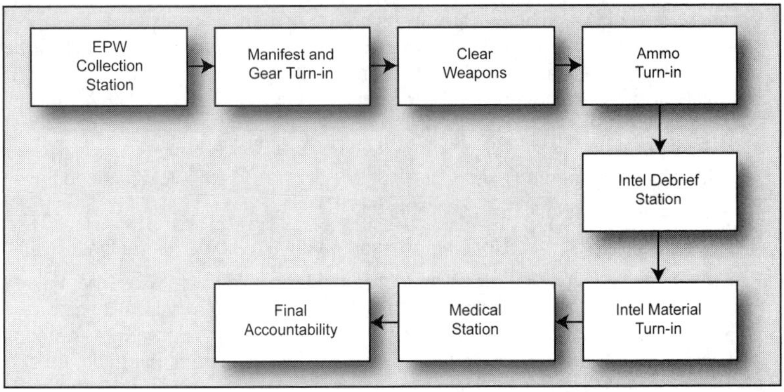

Once the assault force has been processed through all applicable stations, accomodations should be made to address human factors (chow, hot beverages, water, and a gear and weapons cleaning area).

When the RBE OIC/SNCOIC is notified from the COC/LFOC that the force is inbound, he coordinates with higher HQ S-4 who establishes reception stations as follows:

1. The RBE/SNCOIC - establish a MACO gate. On ship establish at the top of the ramp from the flight deck down to the hanger bay. At a FOB establish a control point at the LZ.

2. Detainee/EPW reception- Military police or Ships Master at Arms should be prepared to take custody of any EPW/Detainees. (Remember chain of custody)

3. Manifest Check – RBE SNCOIC (and Combat Cargo if on ship) checks every Marine's name off the mission manifest roster as they pass through the MACO gate. RBE SNCOIC will account for any members of the assault force not returning with the force (CASEVAC). On ship return LPU to Combat Cargo.

4. Weapons Clearing – dedicated stations for Marines to clear weapons. Remember to account for all the weapons systems on the assault force Equipment Density List (EDL).

5. Ammo Turn In – The RBE OIC/SNCOIC will establish a series of containers where Marines will turn in their unused ammunition, pyrotechnics, and ordnance.

6. Intelligence Debriefing – the S-2 will establish a debriefing station to interview Marines about the mission, a standardized, short-form should be constructed and used.

7. Intel Turn in – The S-2 will establish collections stations for any intelligence materials removed from the objective area. (Maintain chain of custody)

8. Medical will establish a station to treat any injured personnel.

9. Final Accountability. A final shakedown will be conduct by senior leadership of the assault force. The Senior SNCO will conduct an all hands formation of personnel, weapons and equipment and release the assault force from the reception area to berthing.

C. Checklist for Phasing Control (Ashore/Afloat)

I. Phasing Control Ashore

Checklist user may place a check when each item is completed, action, or DTG.

Line	Completed	Requirement
1		**BLT NGLO** established communication with the NSFS observers on Ground Spot, Air Spot (if necessary) and SFCP nets. BLT NGLO establishes communications with NSFS ships on Ground Spot and NSFS Control/Support nets.
2		**BLT Air Officer** established communication with FAC's on TACP local and with the TACC on TAR/HR. If the ASE is established with the BLT then they should have communication on TAR/HR, TATC, HD and TAD nets.
3		**BLT Arty LNO** established communication with Artillery FOs and the Artillery Battery on COF nets.
4		**BLT 81mm rep** established communication with observers and 81mm mortar sections on 81mm COF nets.
5		The FSC contacts the SAC on LF FSC net with the following message: "**(BLT Callsign) is prepared to take control of Fire Support coordination. I have communication on all required fire support nets."**
6		SAC passes tactical updates to the FSC over the LF FSC net in the following sequence:
NOTE: *This information (lines 6a-6l) is passed by exception from the last time when the BLT FSC was present in the SACC.*		
6a		**Naval Surface Fire Support Ships:** Ship Name: ________________ FSA: ________________________ Mission: ________________ Grid Location: ________________ Ship Name: ________________ FSA: ________________________ Mission: ________________ Grid Location: ________________
6b		**Artillery Battery:** Unit ___________ Grid Location ________________ AOF ________ # Guns up _______ Current Missions ___________________________
6c		**Mortar Platoon:** Unit ___________ Grid Location ________________ AOF ________ # Guns up _______ Current Missions ___________________________ Unit ___________ Grid Location ________________ AOF ________ # Guns up _______ Current Missions ___________________________

		<u>Ammunition Status:</u> **NSFS**: **Ship**: ____________ HE-CVT: ____________ Illum: ____________ HE-PD: ____________ Spec Mun: ____________ **Ship**: ____________ HE-CVT: ____________ Illum: ____________ HE-PD: ____________ Spec Mun: ____________ **Arty**: HE: ____________ Illum: ____________ WP: ____________ M825: ____________ DPICM: ____________ Spec Mun: ____________ **Mortars**: Platoon: ____________ Illum: ____________ HE: ____________ WP: ____________ RP: ____________ Platoon: ____________ Illum: ____________ HE: ____________ WP: ____________ RP: ____________
6e		**<u>Airborne aircraft:</u>** <u>Fixed Wing:</u> Section Composition: ____________ Mission: ____________ Ordnance: ____________ Section Composition: ____________ Mission: ____________ Ordinance: ____________ <u>Rotor Wing</u> Section Composition: ____________ Mission: ____________ Ordinance: ____________ Section Composition: ____________ Mission: ____________ Ordinance: ____________
6f		**Aircraft alert status**: ____________
6g		**Air Defense condition**: ____________
6h		**<u>Current and on order FSCM in effect:</u>** FSCL: ____________ ____________ ____________ CFL: ____________ ____________ ____________ ACA: ____________ ____________ ____________

		NFA: ________________ ________________ ________________ RFA: ________________ ________________ ________________ ________________ ________________ ________________ ________________ ________________ ________________ FFA: ________________ ________________ ________________
6i		**Missions in progress:** Tgt # ________________ Agency: ______________________ TOT: ________________ Grid Position: ________________ Tgt # ________________ Agency: ______________________ TOT: ________________ Grid Position: ________________ Tgt # ________________ Agency: ______________________ TOT: ________________ Grid Position: ________________ Tgt # ________________ Agency: ______________________ TOT: ________________ Grid Position: ________________
6j		**All Target Bulletins (TARBULS)**: ____
6k		**Friendly unit locations:** Unit: ________________ Grid Location: ________________ Unit: ________________ Grid Location: ________________ Unit: ________________ Grid Location: ________________ Unit: ________________ Grid Location: ________________ Unit: ________________ Grid Location: ________________ Unit: ________________ Grid Location: ________________ Unit: ________________ Grid Location: ________________ Unit: ________________

		Grid Location: ______________ Unit: ______________ Grid Location: ______________ Unit: ______________ Grid Location: ______________ Unit: ______________ Grid Location: ______________
6l		**OP locations:** OP: ______________ Grid Location: ______________ OP: ______________ Grid Location: ______________ OP: ______________ Grid Location: ______________ OP: ______________ Grid Location: ______________ OP: ______________ Grid Location: ______________
7		The LF FSO informs the CLF that the BLT FSCC is prepared to take control of Fire Support coordination.
8		The SAC informs the CATF that the BLT FSCC is prepared to take control of Fire Support coordination.
9		Upon approval from both commanders, the SAC contacts the FSC and passes over the LF FSC net"**You now have control of all Fire Support coordination within the BLT zone of action."**
10		The FSC responds with "**Roger, I now have control of all Fire Support coordination within the BLT zone of action**."
NOTE Upon completion of this "handshake" with the BLT FSC, SACC no longer has control or coordination of Fire Support Operations. The SACC will monitor all nets. All fire support agencies will receive their approval or denial for their call for fires from the BLT.		
11		SAC announces in SACC that (BLT Call Sign) now has control of Fire Support coordination.
12		The NGLO contacts all stations on the ground spot nets and states **"(BLT Call Sign) now has control of Fire Support coordination. Approval for all fires within the BLT zone of action will come from (BLT Call Sign)."**
13		The Air Officer contacts all stations on the TAR and TACP nets and states **"(BLT Call Sign) now has control of Fire Support coordination. Approval for all fires within the BLT zone of action will come from (BLT Call Sign)."**
14		The Arty LNO and 81mm rep do the same as above for their observers and firing agencies.

Appendices & Reference

II. Phasing Control Afloat

Checklist user may place a check when each item is completed, action, or DTG.

Line	Completed	Requirement
1		NSFS CO establishes communication with the NSFS observers on Ground Spot and Air Spot (if necessary). NSFS CO establishes communications with NSFS ships on Ground Spot and NSFS Control nets.
2		ASC / TACC established communication with FAC's on TACP, TAR/HR, TAD and HD nets.
3		Arty RT operators establishes communication with Artillery FOs and the Artillery Battery on COF nets (if Arty is established).
4		81mm RT operators establishes communication with observers and 81mm mortar sections on 81mm COF nets (if Mortars are established).
5		The SAC contacts the BLT FSC on LF FSC net with the following message: **"(SACC Call Sign) is prepared to take control of Fire Support coordination. I have communication on all required fire support nets."**
6		BLT FSCC passes tactical updates to the SACC over the LF FSC net in the following sequence:
***** **NOTE:** ***This information (lines 6a-6l) is passed by in its entirety to the SACC in order to ensure complete receipt of information.***		
6a		**Naval Surface Fire Support Ships:** Ship Name: ________________ FSA: ________________________ Mission: ________________ Grid Location: ________________ Ship Name: ________________ FSA: ________________________ Mission: ________________ Grid Location: ________________
6b		**Artillery Battery:** Grid Location: ________________ Mission: ________________ Grid Location: ________________ Mission: ________________
6c		**Mortar Platoon:** Grid Location: ________________ Mission: ________________ Grid Location: ________________ Mission: ________________
6d		**Ammunition Status:** **NSFS**: Ship: ________________ HE-CVT: ________________ Illum:________________ HE-PD: ________________ Spec Mun: ______________ Ship: ________________ HE-CVT: ________________ Illum: ________________ HE-PD: ________________ Spec Mun: ______________

Appendices & Reference

		Arty: HE: ______ Illum: ______ WP: ______ M825: ______ DPICM: ______ Spec Mun: ______ **Mortars**: Platoon: ______ Illum: ______ HE: ______ WP: ______ RP: ______ Platoon: ______ Illum: ______ HE: ______ WP: ______ RP: ______
6e		**Airborne aircraft:** Fixed Wing: Section Composition: ______ Mission: ______ Ordnance: ______ Section Composition: ______ Mission: ______ Ordnance: ______ Rotor Wing Section Composition: ______ Mission: ______ Ordnance: ______ Section Composition: ______ Mission: ______ Ordnance: ______
6f		**Aircraft alert status**: ______
6g		**Air Defense condition**: ______
6h		**Current and on order FSCM in effect:** FSCL: ______ CFL: ______ ACA: ______ NFA: ______ ______ ______ RFA: ______ ______ ______ FFA: ______

Appendices & Reference

6i		**Missions in progress:** Tgt # ________________ Agency: _____________________ TOT: ________________ Grid Position: ________________ Tgt # ________________ Agency: _____________________ TOT: ________________ Grid Position: ________________ Tgt # ________________ Agency: _____________________ TOT: ________________ Grid Position: ________________ Tgt # ________________ Agency: _____________________ TOT: ________________ Grid Position: ________________
6j		**All TarBuls**: ____ ____
6k		**Friendly unit locations:** Unit: ________________ Grid Location: ________________ Unit: ________________ Grid Location: ________________ Unit: ________________ Grid Location: ________________ Unit: ________________ Grid Location: ________________ Unit: ________________ Grid Location: ________________
6l		**OP locations:** OP: ________________ Grid Location: ________________ OP: ________________ Grid Location: ________________ OP: ________________ Grid Location: ________________ OP: ________________ Grid Location: ________________
7		The LF FSO informs the CLF that the SACC is prepared to take control of Fire Support coordination (if time permits).
8		The SAC informs the CATF that the SACC is prepared to take control of Fire Support coordination (if time permits).
9		Upon approval from both commanders (if time permits) the SACC responds to the FSCC on the LF FSC net "**I now have control of all Fire Support coordination within the AOA.**"

10		The FSCC responds with "**Roger, you now have control of all Fire Support coordination within the AOA."**
***** **NOTE** ***Upon completion of this "handshake" with the BLT FSC, SACC now has control and coordination of Fire Support within the AOA. All fire support agencies will receive approval or denial of their call for fires from the SACC.***		
11		SAC announces in SACC that SACC now has control of Fire Support Coordination.
12		The NSFS CO contacts all stations on the ground/air spot nets and states **"(SACC Call Sign) now has control of Fire Support coordination. Approval for all fires will come from (SACC Call Sign)."**
13		The ASC contacts all stations on the TAR/HAR and TACP nets and states **"(SACC Call Sign) now has control of Fire Support coordination. Approval for all fires will come from (SACC Call Sign)."**
14		The Arty LNO and 81mm rep do the same as above for their observers and respected firing agencies

D. Aircraft Reference & Specifications

Basic Capabilities of ACE Aircraft

These numbers are for bare-bones planning purposes only and vary greatly based upon ambient conditions, fuel load, configuration, flight regulations, and mission requirements, to name a few. Consult Subject Matter Experts (SME) in the ACE or the publications listed below for more specific and refined capabilities.

Basic Aircraft Capabilities (ACE)

AIRCRAFT	MAX AIRSPEED (KIAS)	BEST RANGE AIRSPEED	ENDURANCE	MAX PAYLOAD (LBS)
CH-46E	145	110-130	3+00	4500
MV-22	280	215	3+00	12,500
CH-53E	150	130	4+00	36,000 (external)
UH-1N	130	105	1+30	VARIES
UH-1Y	170	130	2+30	VARIES
AH-1W	170	125	2+15	N/A
AH-1Z	200	140	2+30	N/A
AV-8B	585	380	1+00	N/A
KC-130J	315	290	13+00	60,000

See also III(b). Air Operations (S-3 Staff Functions), pp. 1-51 to 1-56 and Air Operations Quick Reference, pp. 6-29 to 6-40.

References

NAVAIRINST 00-80T-106

LHA/LHD NATOPS Manual

OPNAVINST 3710.7U

NATOPS General Flight and Operating Instructions

MARFORPACO 3501.2A

SOP for HRST

I MEFO 3501.1

SOP for MEU (SOC)

WgO P3710.39D Chg 1-5

SOP for Air Operations

GruO P3710.29H

SOP for RW Air Operations

CH-46E Sea Knight

CH-46E Sea Knight	
Dimensions	
Height	16 feet 8 inches
Weight (empty)	16,500 pounds
Maximum gross weight	24,300 pounds
Rotor diameter	51 feet
Length	84 feet 4 inches
Airspeed	
Max endurance	70 KIAS
Planning Airspeed	100 KIAS
Maximum airspeed	145 KIAS
Fuel Capacity	
Pounds/Gallons	4488 / 660
Endurance	
Payloads	4300 pounds 18 PAX
Endurance	3 + 15 hours
Weapons Systems	
Guns	2 x .50 Caliber XM-218, 1 x M240D 7.62mm
Other Systems	
GPS Navigation	Miniature Airborne GPS Receiver (MAGR) System
Blue Force Tracker	Spiral 3 EDM
Communications Equipment	
VHF/UHF	2 x AN/ARC-210 w/KY-58 Encryption Device
Aircraft Survivability Equipment (ASE)	
RWR	AN/APR-39(V)1 Radar Warning Receiver
IRCM	AN/ALQ-157(V)1 Infrared Jammer
DIRCM	AN/AAQ-24(V)25 IR Missile Laser Jammer
Countermeasure Dispensing	AN/ALE-47 Countermeasures Dispenser
Missile Warning	AN/AAR-47 Missile Warning System

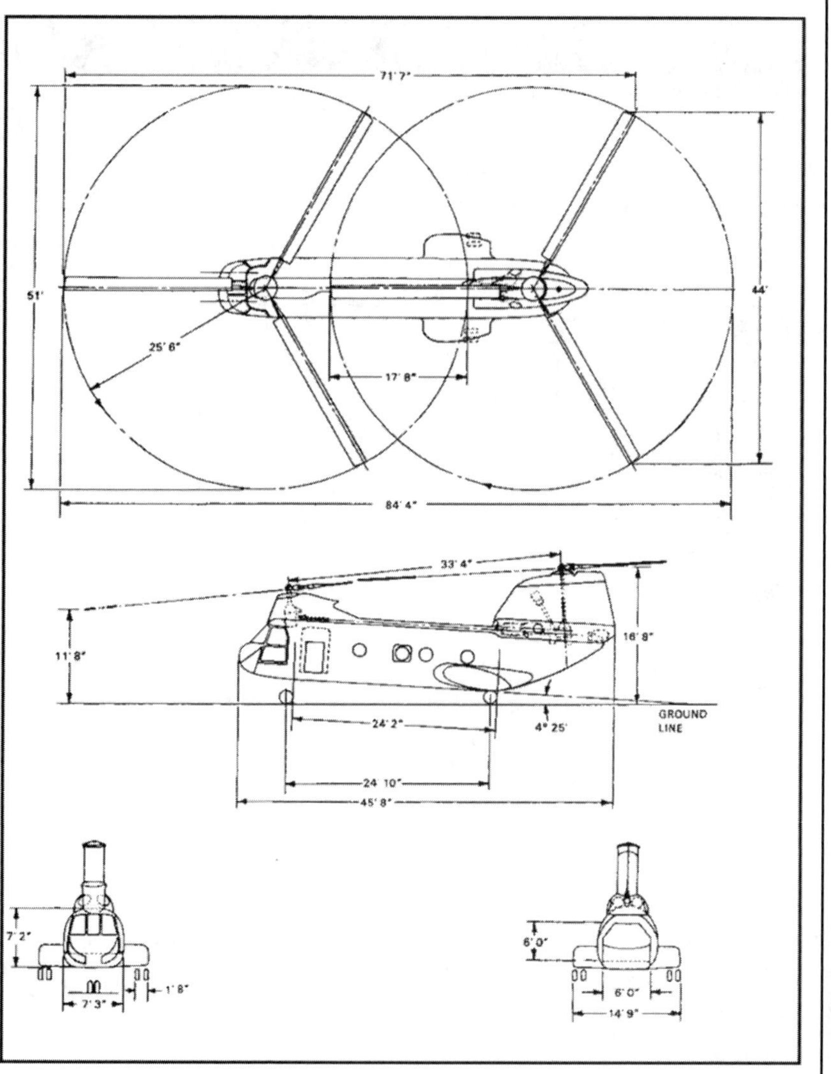

Appendices
& Reference

CH-53E Super Stallion

CH-53E Super Stallion	
Dimensions	
Height	28 feet 4 inches
Weight (empty)	36,000 pounds
Maximum gross weight	73,500 pounds
Rotor diameter	79 feet
Length	99 feet 1/2 inches
Airspeed	
Max endurance	75 KIAS
Planning Airspeed	120 KIAS
Maximum airspeed	150 KIAS
Fuel Capacity	
Pounds/Gallons	15,000 / 2277
Endurance	
Payloads	20,000 pounds Internal Cargo 24 to 55 pax
Endurance	4 +00 hours (typical) Indefinite (best case w/ Aerial Refueling)
Weapons Systems	
Guns	2 x .50 Caliber XM 218 / 1 x GAU 21 .50 Caliber (RMWS)
Other Systems	
FLIR	AN/AAQ29B
GPS Navigation	Miniature Airborne GPS Receiver (MAGR) System
Communications Equipment	
HF	1 x AN/ARC-94 or AN/ARC-174
UHF / VHF / SINCGARS / HQ	2 x AN/ARC 210 w/KY-58 Encryption Devices
Aircraft Survivability Equipment (ASE)	
RWR	AN/APR-39(V)1 Radar Warning Receiver
DIRCM	AN/AAQ-24 Directional Countermeasure
Expendables	AN/ALE-47 Countermeasures Dispenser
Missile Warning	AN/AAR-47(v)2 Missile Warning System

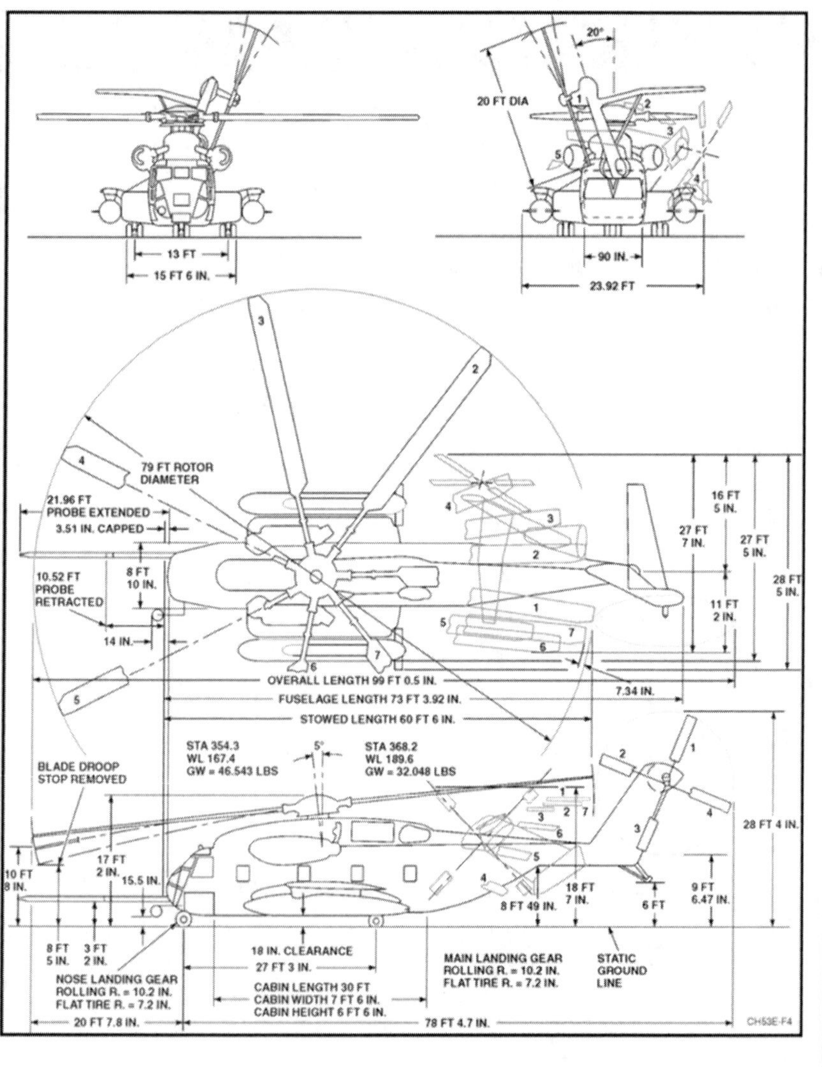

Appendices & Reference

UH-1Y

UH-1Y	
Dimensions	
Height	14 feet 7 inches
Weight (empty)	18,500 pounds (maximum gross weight)
Maximum gross weight	8 feet 6 inches
Rotor diameter	48 feet
Length	58 feet 4 inches
Airspeed	
Max endurance	120 KIAS
Maximum airspeed	150 KIAS
Fuel Capacity	
Pounds/Gallons	2,600 / 386
Endurance	
Payloads	2,000 pounds (in addition to full internal fuel)
Endurance	2 +15 hours (typical)
Weapons Systems	
Guns	M240D/GAU-16/17/21
Ordnance	2.57 inch rockets
Typical Ordnance Mix	
Command and Control	400x.50cal/3000x7.62mm/7-14x2.75-inch rocket
OAS	Hellfire / TOW II Air / 5-inch and 2.75-inch rocket / 20mm
Escort	AIM-9 Sidewinder / 2.75-inch rocket / 20mm / (TOW II / Hellfire)
Other Systems	
Target Sight System	Star SAFIRE/ BRITE Star Block I & II
GPS Navigation	Miniature Airborne GPS Receiver (MAGR) System
Laser Range Finder	Eye Safe
Laser Designator	Pulsed Repetition Selectable (PRF) 1111-1788
Communications Equipment	
UHF / VHF	3 x AN/ARC 210 w/KY-58 Encryption Devices
Aircraft Survivability Equipment (ASE)	
RWR	AN/APR-39 B(v)2 Radar Warning Receiver
Expendables	AN/ALE-47 Countermeasures Dispenser
Missile Warning	AN/AAR-47(v)2 Missile Warning System

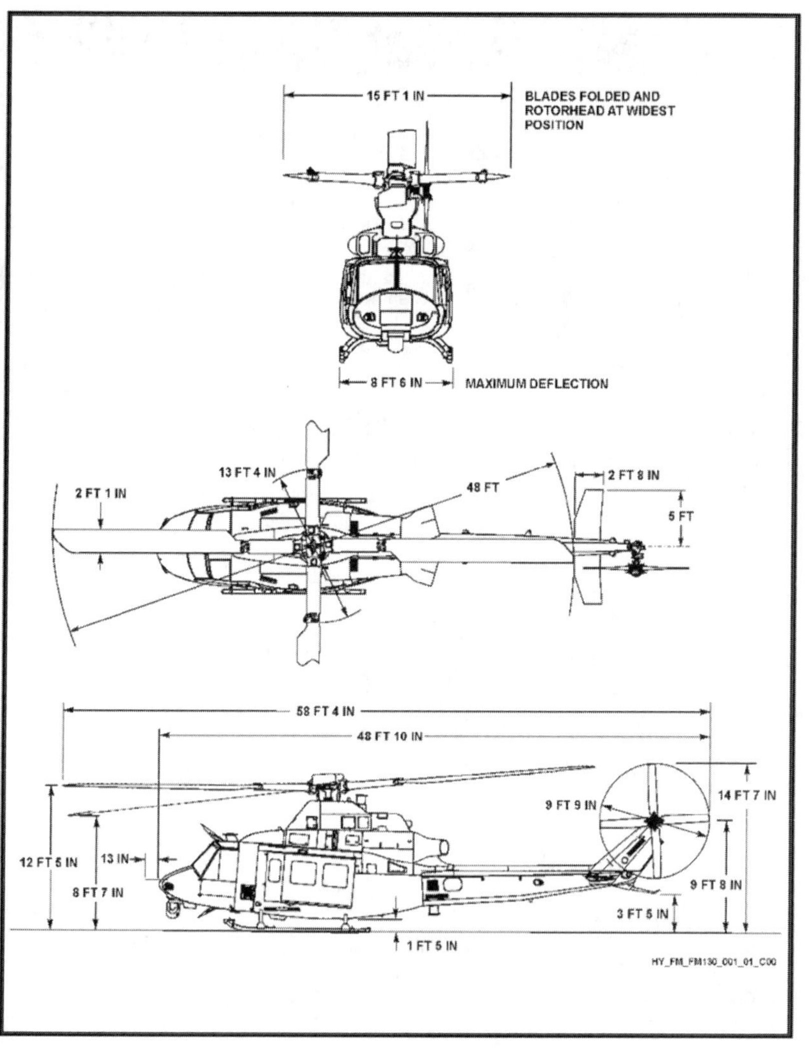

Appendices & Reference

AH-1Z Viper

AH-1Z Viper	
Dimensions	
Height	14 feet 4 inches
Weight	18,500 pounds (maximum gross weight)
Fuselage width	14 feet 6 inches (includes wing stubs)
Rotor diameter	48 feet
Length	58 feet 3 inches
Airspeed	
Max endurance	70-80 KIAS (TOS speed)
Maximum airspeed	200 KIAS
Fuel Capacity	
Pounds/Gallons	2,800 / 412.5
Endurance	
Payloads	2,000 pounds (in addition to full internal fuel)
Endurance	2 +00 to 2 +30 hours depending on configuration
Weapons Systems	
Guns	20mm Cannon
Missiles	AGM-114 Hellfire
Ordnance	AIM-9 Sidewinder / LAU-61/68 (2.75-inch)
Typical Ordnance Mix	
AAW	2 x AIM-9 / 2.75-inch flechette rocket / Hellfire / 20mm
OAS	Hellfire / 2.75-inch RP/HE / Illumination / Rocket / 20mm
Escort	AIM-9 Sidewinder / Hellfire / 2.75-inch RP/HE rocket / 20mm
Other Systems	
Target Sight System	AN/AAQ-30 (TSS) / DVR / FLIR / TV
GPS Navigation	Miniature Airborne GPS Receiver (MAGR) System
Laser Range Finder	Pulsed / 1064 nm
Laser Designator	Pulsed Repetition Selectable (PRF) 1111-1788
IR Pointer	Laser Diode Pointer (imbedded in TSS)
Communications Equipment	
UHF / VHF	2 x AN/ARC 210 w/KY-58 Encryption Devices
Aircraft Survivability Equipment (ASE)	
RWR	AN/APR-39 B(v) 1/2 Radar Warning Receiver
Expendables	AN/ALE-47 Countermeasures Dispenser (120 capable load)
Missile Warning	AN/AAR-47(v)2 Missile Warning System

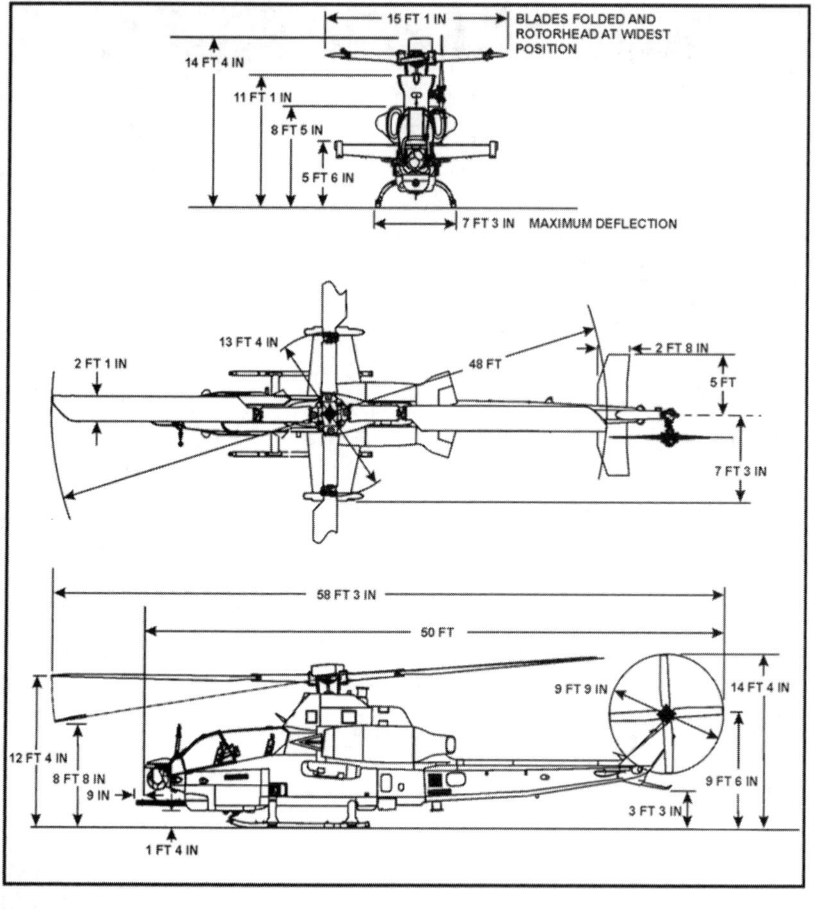
15 FT 1 IN
BLADES FOLDED AND ROTORHEAD AT WIDEST POSITION
14 FT 4 IN
11 FT 1 IN
8 FT 5 IN
5 FT 6 IN
7 FT 3 IN MAXIMUM DEFLECTION
13 FT 4 IN
2 FT 1 IN
48 FT
2 FT 8 IN
5 FT
7 FT 3 IN
58 FT 3 IN
50 FT
9 FT 9 IN
14 FT 4 IN
12 FT 4 IN
8 FT 8 IN
9 IN
9 FT 6 IN
3 FT 3 IN
1 FT 4 IN

Appendices & Reference

AV-8B

AV-8B	
Dimensions	
Height	11 feet 8 inches
Weight	14,600 pounds (empty) 32,000 pounds (max gross weight)
Wingspan	30 feet 3 inches
Airspeed	
Max endurance	230 KIAS
Maximum airspeed	585 KIAS/ 1.0 IMN
Fuel Capacity	
Pounds	11,500 pounds (7,000 internal)
Gallons	1,720 gallons (1.141 gallons internal, 600 gallons external)
Endurance	
Payload	Varies significantly with ordnance load and mission profile
HI LO HI profile	6 MK 82s, DECM and full gun (1.2 hours)
HILOHI profile	6 MK 82s, DECM and full gun with full external tank (1.5 hours)
HI HI HI profile	TPOD, 2 x GBU-38, 1 x GBU-12, DECM and full gun (1.4 hours)
HIHIHI profile	TPOD, 2 x GBU-38, 1 x GBU-12, DECM and full gun with external tank (1.4 hours)
Weapons Systems	
Bombs	MK 82-83, MK 20 ROCKEYE, MK 77 FIREBOMB, GBU-12, GBU-16 (LGB), GBU-32, GBU-38
Missiles	AGM-65E laser maverick AIM-9 sidewinder, AIM-120 AMRAAM
Guns	GAU-12 25mm gun
Rockets	LAU-10 (5-inch rockets), LAU-61 (2.75-inch rockets)
Miscellaneous	
	LUU-2B/B parachute flares
	LUU-19 parachute flares
Other Systems	
FLIR	Navigation FLIR
Laser	Dual mode tracker (TV / laser spot tracker)
Camera	VTR HUD / dual-mode tracker
Radar	APG-65
	Listening II targeting pod FLIR, IR marker, laser and CCD TV
Communications Equipment	
UHF / VHF	2 x AN/ARC 210 w/KY-58 Encryption Devices
Aircraft Survivability Equipment (ASE)	
RWR	AN/ALR-67 Radar Warning Receiver
DECM	AN/ALQ-164 (pod-mounted DECM system)
Expendables	AN/ALE-39 Countermeasures Dispenser

McDonnell Douglas AV-8B Harrier II

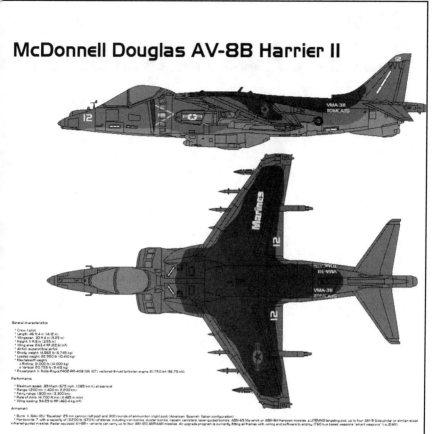

General characteristics

* Crew: 1 pilot
* Length: 46 ft 4 in (14.12 m)
* Wingspan: 30 ft 4 in (9.25 m)
* Height: 11 ft 8 in (3.55 m)
* Wing area: 243.4 ft² (22.6 m²)
* Airfoil: supercritical airfoil
* Empty weight: 14,865 lb (6,745 kg)
* Loaded weight: 22,950 lb (10,410 kg)
* Max takeoff weight:
  * Rolling: 31,000 lb (14,000 kg)
  * Vertical: 20,755 lb (9,415 kg)
* Powerplant: 1x Rolls-Royce F402-RR-408 (Mk 107) vectored-thrust turbofan engine, 21,750 lbf (96.75 kN)

Performance

* Maximum speed: .89 Mach (675 mph, 1,085 km/h) at sea level
* Range: 1,200 nm (1,400 mi, 2,200 km)
* Ferry range: 1,800 nm (3,300 km)
* Rate of climb: 14,700 ft/min (4,485 m/min)
* Wing loading: 94.29 lb/ft² (460.4 kg/m²)

Armament

* Guns: 1x GAU-12U "Equalizer" 25 mm cannon (left pod) and 300 rounds of ammunition (right pod) (American, Spanish, Italian configuration)
* Hardpoints: 7 with a capacity of 13,200 lb (STOVL) of stores, including iron bombs, cluster bombs, napalm canisters, laser-guided bombs, AGM-65 Maverick or AGM-84 Harpoon missiles, a LITENING targeting pod, up to four AIM-9 Sidewinder or similar-sized infrared-guided missiles. Radar equipped AV-8B+ variants can carry up to four AIM-120 AMRAAM missiles. An upgrade program is currently fitting airframes with wiring and software to employ 1760 bus based weapons "smart weapons" (i.e. JDAM).

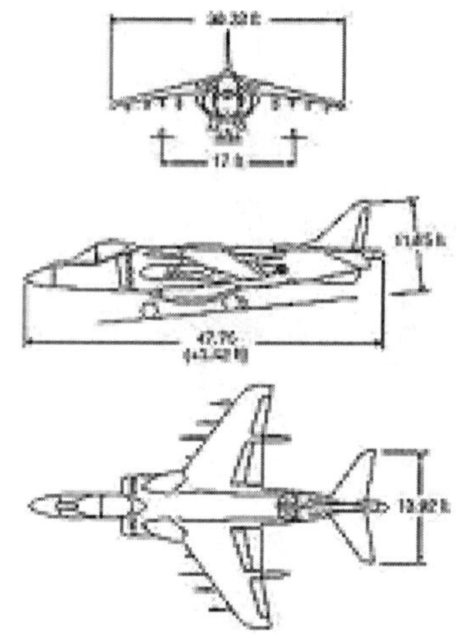

Appendices & Reference

KC-130J

KC-130J	
Dimensions	
Height	38 feet 3 inches
Weight	91,000 pounds (cargo empty) / 93,000 pounds (tanker empty) / 130,000 pounds (normal op weight) / 165,000 (max takeoff) / 175,000 pounds (max overload)
Wingspan	132 feet 7 inches
Length	97 feet 9 inches
Airspeed	
Long Range Cruise	290 KTAS
Max Airspeed	315 KIAS
Min Airspeed	105 KIAS
Refueling low-speed drogue	110-120 KIAS
Refueling high-speed drogue	185-250 KIAS
Fuel Capacity	
Tanker configuration	64,000 pounds (normal) / 81,000 pounds (overload)
Cargo configuration	57,500 pounds
Endurance	
	Determined by fuel offload requirements at max endurance, approximately 13 hours
Weapons Systems	
	None
Miscellaneous	
	LUU-2 parachute flares
	LUU-19 parachute flares
Other Systems	
	HUD, moving map
Communications Equipment	
UHF	2 x AN/ARC-164 w/KY-58 Encryption Devices
VHF	2 x AN/ARC-222 w/KY-58 Encryption Devices
HF	2 x AN/ARC-190 w/KY-58 Encryption Devices (unusable during AAR)
SATCOM	1 x AN/ARC-210
Aircraft Survivability Equipment (ASE)	
RWR	AN/ALR-56M Radar Warning Receiver
IRCM	AN/ALQ-157V2 Infrared Jammer
Expendables	AN/ALE-47 Countermeasures Dispenser
Missile Warning	An/AAR-47V2 Missile Warning System

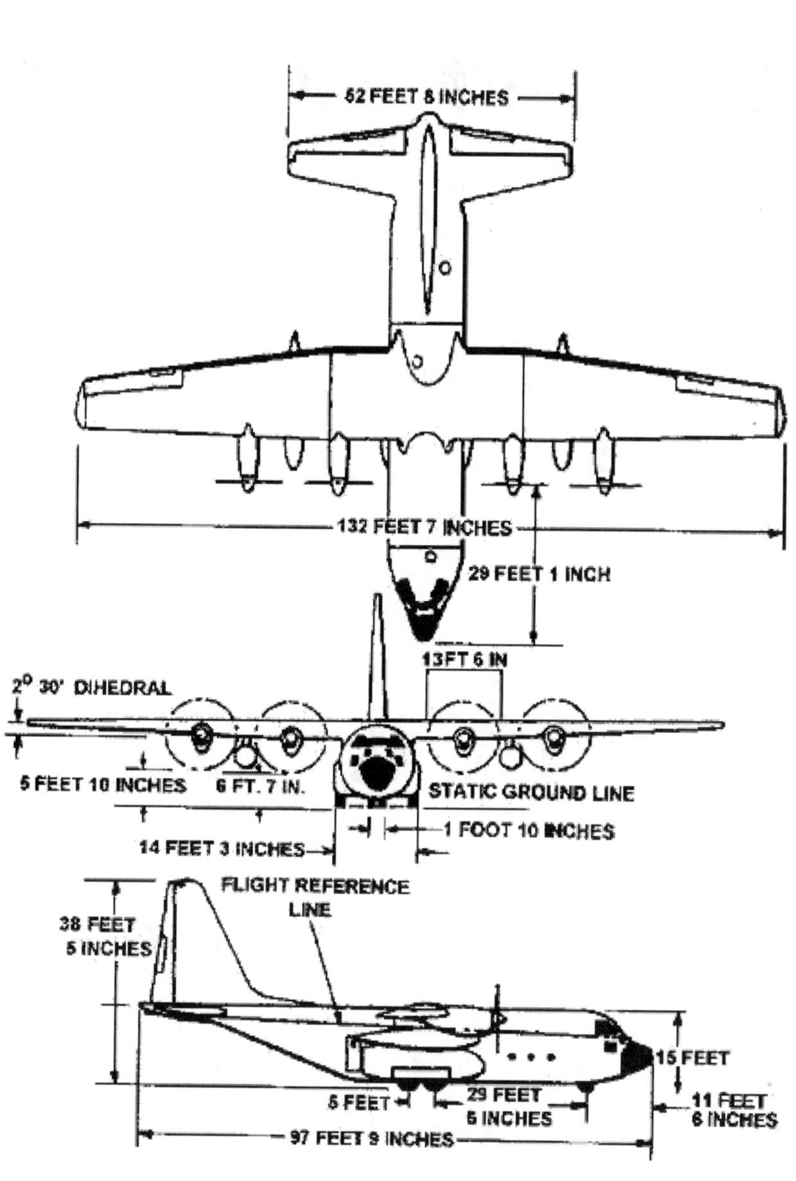

Airplane dimensions

Appendices & Reference

MV-22B Osprey

MV-22B Osprey	
Dimensions	
Height	28 feet 4 inches
Weight (empty)	36,000 pounds
Maximum gross weight	73,500 pounds
Rotor diameter	79 feet
Length	99 feet 1/2 inches
Airspeed	
Max endurance	75 KIAS
Maximum airspeed	150 KIAS
Fuel Capacity	
Pounds/Gallons	15,000 / 2277
Endurance	
Payloads	20,000 pounds Internal Cargo 24 to 55 pax
Endurance	4 +00 hours (typical) Indefinite (best case w/ Aerial Refueling)
Weapons Systems	
Guns	2 x .50 Caliber XM 218 / 1 x M-3M .50 Caliber (RMWS)
Other Systems	
FLIR	AN/AAQ16B
GPS Navigation	Miniature Airborne GPS Receiver (MAGR) System
Communications Equipment	
HF	1 x AN/ARC-94 or AN/ARC-174
UHF / VHF	2 X AN/ARC-182 / 2 x AN/ARC 210 w/KY-58 Encryption Devices
Aircraft Survivability Equipment (ASE)	
RWR	AN/APR-39(V)1 Radar Warning Receiver
IRCWM	None
Expendables	AN/ALE-47 Countermeasures Dispenser
Missile Warning	AN/AAR-47(v)2 Missile Warning System

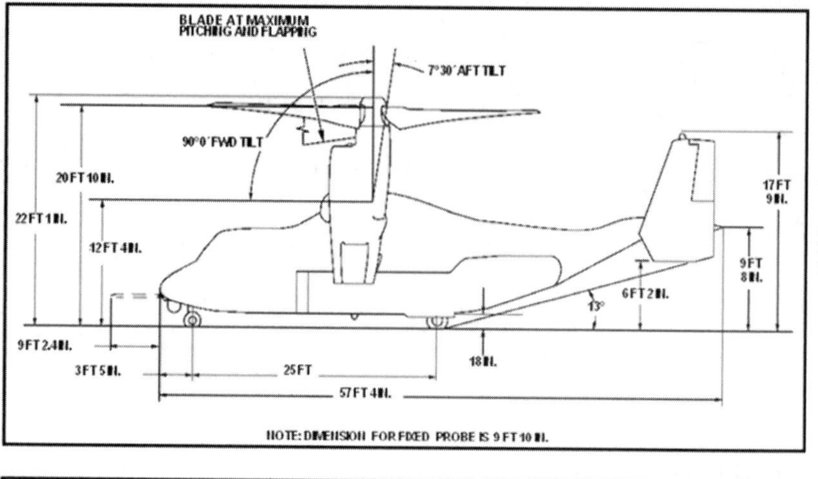

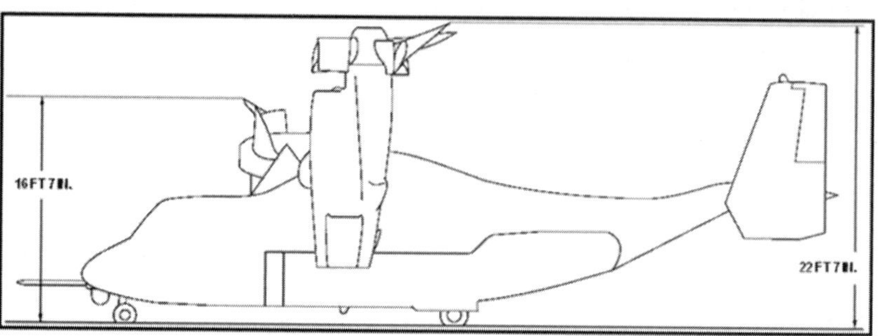

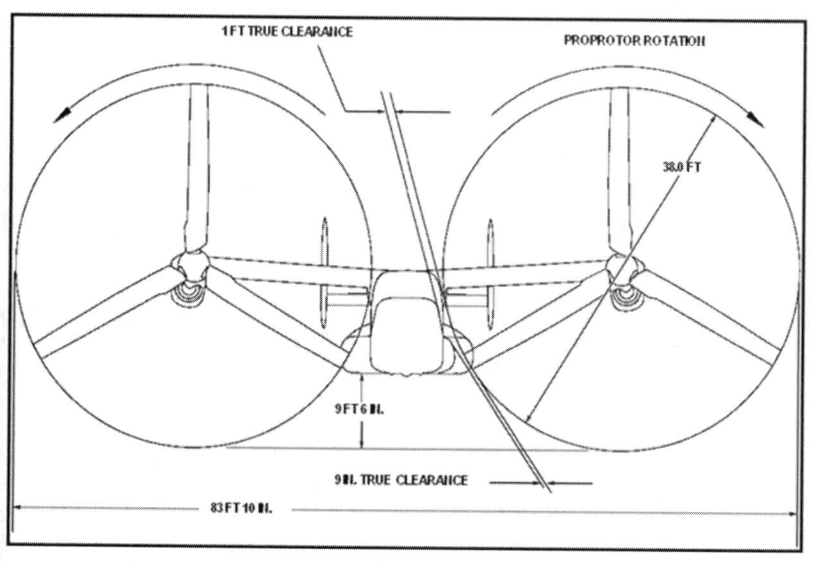

Continued on next page

Continued on next page

Appendices & Reference

MV-22B Osprey (Continued)

Continued from previous page

84FT 7 IN.
19FT
BLADE AT MAXIMUM PITCHING
AND FLAPPING (10°30')
4FT 8 IN.
TRUE CLEARANCE
CONVERSION AXIS
14°24'
4FT 4 IN.
13FT
15FT 5 IN.
50FT 11 IN.

VIEW LOOKING AFT

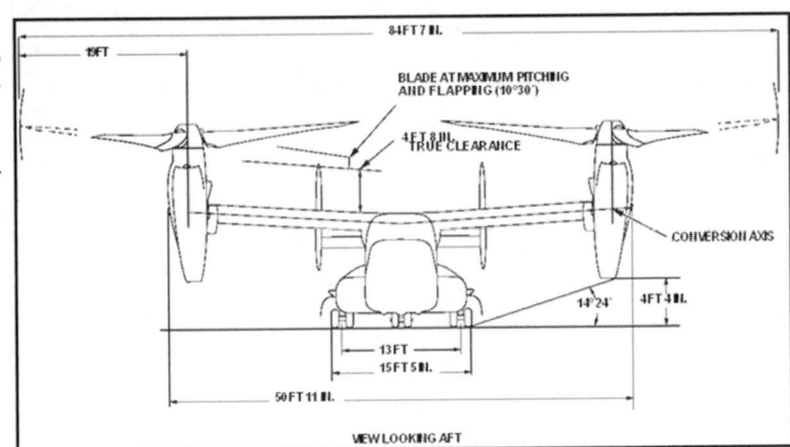

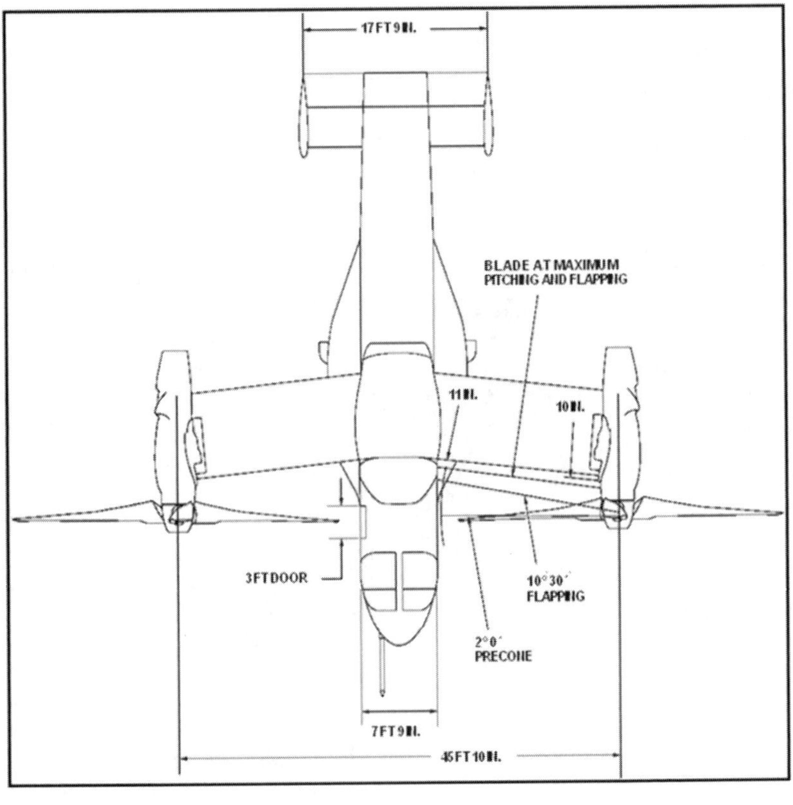

17FT 9 IN.
BLADE AT MAXIMUM
PITCHING AND FLAPPING
11 IN.
10 IN.
3FT DOOR
10°30'
FLAPPING
2°0'
PRECONE
7FT 9 IN.
45FT 10 IN.

Continued from previous page

Appendices & Reference

E. Air Operations Quick Reference

See also III(b). Air Operations (S-3 Staff Functions), pp. 1-51 to 1-56 and D. Aircraft Reference & Specifications, pp. 6-13 to 6-28.

I. Aircraft Embark Procedures

Staging

Embarking begins when the raid force is staged on the starboard side of the ramp leading from the hanger deck to the flight deck.

- Serials will be lined up in serial order from the first to be loaded at the top of the ramp, to the last at the bottom.
- Serials will be a sufficient length apart to avoid confusing Marines from one serial with Marines of another.
- Within each serial, Marines will face aft, down the ramp, with their gear on. Individuals in each serial will be positioned
- The Company 1stSgt will conduct a final accountability and inspection of the entire raid force at this time.

LPU (Life Preserving Unit) Issue

Inflatable life preservers & HABD bottles will be issued to the raid force by Combat Cargo in the Hanger Bay

- Marines will don LPU's, wearing them over their cammies
- Marines will then conduct an LPU / HABD inspection
- Inflation tube: present, functional, screw is closed
- Salt water battery: present, plugs in place, stow in bag
- CO2 canister: present, screwed in, pull toggle accessible
- Lanyard w/ toggle: present, stowed in poncho
- If LPU items are missing, Marines will report the deficiency to their serial leader who will insure their LPU is replaced.
- HABD bottles will be inspected by aircrew prior to issue. Inspection will include, at a minimum, structural integrity of bottle and components (cracks in bottle / no major leaks), bottle air level is at a minimum of 2700 PSI and the bottle is turned on ready for issue
- HABD bottles will be issued upon boarding aircraft by the crew chief or aerial gunner / observer to the embarked personnel
- HABD holster, when available, will be used to stow the HABD bottle on each embarked person. In the interim period, HABD bottles will be stowed in the individual's blouse
- Once the aircraft is within auto-rotational distance to the land the LPUs and HABD bottles will be collected by the crew chief or aerial gunner / observer

Required Equipment

- Helmet or Cranial (cranial with goggles can be provided by the crew chief or aerial gunner / observer)
- Eye Protection
- Ear Protection
- Gloves
- Marines will carry their flak jacket, pack and weapons in hand

Loading

Crew chiefs report that they are ready for loading, Combat Cargo Marines will guide each serial to their respective aircraft. The RBE SNCOIC will ensure that each serial is placed on the correct aircraft. Marines will carry their flak jacket and all mission essential gear.

Assistant Serial Leader

Stops at aircraft with the crew chief approximately 2 meters from the CH-53 tail rotor or 5 meters from the CH-46 ramp. Confirms that the serial is boarding the correct aircraft by the Serial sign held at the tail ramp by the crew chief. Counts serial on board then signals to the serial leader "All Accounted For".

Individual Actions

Marines move into the aircraft with weapons inverted (muzzle down) and take seats left and right successively from the front of the aircraft to the rear. Upon loading, all large packs and hand-carry items will be stowed in the vicinity of the last three-man seat in the CH-46E and strapped to the deck. In the CH-53E and UH-1Y all gear stowage will be directed by the crew chief or aerial gunner / observer and strapped to the deck. Marines will find their respective seat, place their vests and assault packs under their legs, fasten their seatbelt, and place their hands in the "thumbs up" signal when they are completely ready for lift off. Once acknowledged by the heliteam leader, they put their hands down. Weapons will not be dummy corded when flying over water with the exception of the M9 service pistol.

Reference Points

Marines will then find their emergency ditching reference point, close their eyes and ingrain its position in their memory. This is an important safety measure. Do not skip it.

Serial Leader

Takes the first seat port side forward, puts on Inter-Comm System (ICS) cranial and conducts a comm check with the pilot. He cannot hear the radios on the CH-46. Do not interrupt the pilot until it is necessary. He will be able to hear the radios on a CH-53E. He will ensure a gunner's belt is available for himself should he need to move with the aircraft in flight.

II. Aircraft Disembark Procedures

Serial Leader

Once airborne and w/ the permission from the pilot and crew chief, the Serial Leader moves to jump seat of CH-53E where he can view aircraft instrumentation beneficial to navigation and situational awareness. On the CH-46, the Serial Leader can look out of the bubble window or move to a kneeling position between the pilot and the co-pilot. When moving forward to the cockpit ensure you have permission from the crew chief or aerial gunner / observer and use the utmost care in movement forward for the safety of all personnel.

Communications and Information Updates

Pilots will pass intelligence updates or other information from the mission commander to the Serial Leader via the ICS. This is a critical information link for last minute situation updates. This relay is the only communication link the Serial Leader has since no ground radios can be used inside the aircraft. All Marines will remain alert during the flight in case the Serial Leader passes any information via the white board.

The Serial Leader will use his In-Flight Serial Leader Info Board to pass information to Marines in the raid force that is on his helicopter. The Serial Leader will write information on the board and pass it down his side of the helicopter. Once it reaches the last man on that side of the helicopter it will be passed to Marines on the other side of the helo until it reaches the Marine across from the Serial Leader. The Serial leader will use a blue chemlight at night so Marines on his helo can read the information. A recommended technique is to tear only a portion of the sleeve / packaging which the chemlight comes in to minimize interference with night vision devices being utilized by the aircrew.

Remove LPU's

On the command "Feet Dry" from the crew chief, the Serial leader gives the "Remove LPU" signal. The Marines will remove the LPU & HABD bottle and pass it to the crew chief. The Marines will then put on their flak jacket.

Load Weapons

Weapon conditions will be specified before the operation. On the command "Conduct Penetration Checks" from the pilot, the Serial Leader gives the command "Load," Marines go to condition 3 for rifles and automatic weapons. On the command "IP inbound" from the pilot, the Serial Leader gives the command "Make Ready," Marine with rifles go Condition 1 and automatic weapons remain in Condition 3

Condition 1

- M16A4/M4-magazine inserted, round in chamber, weapon on SAFE
- SAW/M240G- open feed tray cover, insert belt into feed tray, close feed tray cover, lock bolt to the rear, weapons on SAFE

Condition 3

- M16A4/M4- magazine inserted, chamber empty, bolt home, weapon on SAFE
- SAW/M240G - ammunition on the feed tray, feed tray cover closed, bolt home on an empty chamber, weapon on FIRE

III. Aircraft Marking Plan

The aircraft marking plan is designed to be marked by aircraft crew with chemlite configuration in both port and starboard windows so that serials may see which aircraft they are to board during nighttime operations. Aircraft marking is an important task in order to ensure Marines are properly embarked and accounted for during initial embark and extract after action on the objective are complete. Chemlites will be placed as roman numerals to determine aircraft numbers.

Aircraft Number	Marking	
1	1 Vertical Chemlight	I
2	2 Vertical Chemlights	II
3	1 Vertical Chemlight 1 Horizontal Chemlight	I–
4	2 Horizontal Chemlights	=
5	2 Chemlights in a V	V
6	2 Chemlights inverted V	Λ
7	3 Horizontal Chemlights	≡
8	4 Horizontal Chemlights	–≡

Appendices & Reference

IV. Air Operations Requirements

TERF (with PAX embarked) IOT TERF with PAX during training:

1. Minimum crew is Pilot, Copilot, Crew Chief, AO/Gunner
2. All crew must be qualified, proficient and current per NAVMC DIR 3500.14; 401.1.i and respective T/M/S T&R Manual.
3. Utilize only approved TERF routes or on tactical missions
4. Event has been approved by MEU commander
5. Waiver authority is MEF CG

NVG Operations (with PAX) IOT conduct NVG training with troops:

1. Min crew: pilot, co-pilot, crew chief and AO/G
2. Pilot, co-pilot, crew chief and AO/G must be NSQ (for appropriate light level) and flown 1 hour NVG time in last 15 days (WgO P3710.39D; 4109.2; GruO P3710.29H)

- All HACs must have flown at night in last 30 days to carry PAX at night

General

- Seatbelts will be worn from takeoff until landing. IBLE Packs will not be worn onto the aircraft, they will be hand carried.
- During Tactical assaults only day packs are authorized to be hand carried. IBLE packs must be flown in as part of logistical sustainment or re-supply.

Shipboard Operations

- If wind gust spread is more than 10 kts, max winds for engage/disengage shall be reduced by 10 kts in all quadrants (NATOPS)
- LPU-34 will be worn on all over water flights
- To conduct night shipboard ops with PAX (GrO P3710.29H; 6007.1):
  1. Pilot and co-pilot CQ and 2 night shipboard flights in last 15 days, crew chief and AO/G CQ and 1 night shipboard flight in last 15 days*
  2. One night shipboard flight, 30 min in duration within 15 days for pilot and co-pilot*

  * Most restrictive requirement for crew chief & AO/G
- No PAX transport over water at night unless emergency or authorized by CO, MEU
- No guns in the windows for CH-46 and CH-53 during over water training with PAX

Crew Day

- 12 hour crew day for all aircrew, 10 hours for NVG/night flights.
- Aircrew should limit crew day to 10 hours unless 12 hours is needed for mission planning for night flights.
- Crew rest should allow for 8 hours uninterrupted rest, crews should not be scheduled for more than 18 hours continuous alert (OPNAV 3710.7U)
- Accumulated individual flight time should not exceed the number of hours indicated below:

Accumulated Flight Time

PERIOD (DAYS)	Single Piloted Aircraft (AV-8B/AH-1W/UH-1N)	Multi-Piloted Aircraft (MV-22B/CH-46E/CH-53E)
1	6.5	12
7	30	50
30	65	100
90	165	265
365	595	960

REF: OPNAVINST 3710.7U; FIG 8.8

V. Bump Plan (& Passenger Load Limits)

The Bump Plan is a crucial document that should be attached as the last page of the ASSAT. Serials should be listed in order of priority from least critical for mission success. It is not necessary to list every serial for the entire lift; only a percentage of the total serials need to be listed based off of the total number of aircraft available for the mission.

For example, if there are a total of 24 serials and 6 CH-53E or MV-22 aircraft flying the mission you will be able to put 4 serials of 6 Marines per aircraft. In the event that more than 3 aircraft go down for mechanical or other reasons you are safe to assume that this will meet the no-go criteria (mission dependant). Therefore, you would likely only need to list a total of 12 (or less) of the 24 serials on the bump plan.

ASSAULT SUPPORT SERIAL ASSIGNMENT TABLE BUMP PLAN			
WAVE	BUMP PLAN IN ORDER OF PRIORITY	DESCRIPTION	
			NOTES:

Passenger Load Limits

Passenger Load Limits					
T/M/S	MAX ALLOWABLE PASSENGERS	AVAILABLE SEATING NON-COMBAT	AVAILABLE SEATING COMBAT	NOTE	REFERENCES
CH-53E	24	37	32	1,2,3	(WgO P3710.39D; 4101.6)(GruO P3710.29H; 4019.7)
CH-46E	12	12	12	2,3	Same as above
UH-1Y	8			2,3,4	Same as above

(1) Per CMC guidance maximum allowable passenger for the CH-53E is 24.

(2) HACs shall limit number of PAX to the number for which there are adequate seats, safety belts, and water survival equipment.

(3) The MEU Cmdr has been delegated the authority to waive restrictions as required for training/contingency operations/extraordinary mission requirements.

(4) UH-1Y seating is restricted to space available based on configuration.

VI. Air Launch/Recovery Requirements

*For routine training flights, AV-8B shall use training pitch/roll limits as noted in the table above. Ship pitch/roll motion in excess of normal limits (3/5) requires an advanced LSO for flight operations – Use extreme caution while taxiing. All aircraft shall be chocked and chained whenever the ship is in a turn. Ship pitch/roll greater than 5/10 during the day and 4/8 at night or with a wet deck should be considered the operational limit. If the maximum allowable pitch/roll limit has been reached, operations should be terminated and all aircraft chocked and chained in place.

1. Recovery Cases:

   Case I---visibility 1000'/3nm and above

   Case II---visibility between 1000'/3nm and 500'/1nm

   Case III---visibility below 500'/1nm

Whenever weather conditions at the ship are Case II mins, Case III rules and instrument approach mins apply.

2. These are max values. Exceeding these values will normally abort a launch.

3. Winds are defined as relative winds across the deck.

4. Winds for launch are maximum values with relative wind on the ships bow. The values decrease significantly as relative winds change from the bow (IAW T/M/S NATOPS).

5. Ship pitch and roll limitations are left to the judgment of the ship's CO and embarked squadron commander. NAVAIR 00-80T-106

Assumptions

1. Case II – Visual Descent/Approach Procedures.
2. Pilots are Deck Landing Qualified (day and night).
3. Pilots are NVG qualified and current.
4. Pilots are current for mission type per the applicable T&R.
5. Pilots have met crew rests minimums.

Air Matrix Launch/Recovery Requirements

ACFT TYPE	DAY/ NIGHT	LHD P/R	LHA P/R	LSD P/R	LPD P/R	CG P/R	DDG P/R	FFG P/R
AH-1W	DAY	2/5 spot 1-7 2/4 spot 9	2/5 spot 1-7 2/4 spot 8	3/6	3/6 spot 1-2 2/6 spot 3-6	2/4	2/4	2/4
	NIGHT	2/5 spot 1-7 2/4 spot 9	2/5 spot 1-7 2/4 spot 8	3/6	3/6 spot 1-2 2/6 spot 3-6	2/4	2/4	2/4
UH-1N	DAY	2/4	2/4	3/6	3/6 spot 1-2 2/6 spot 3-6	2/4	2/4	2/4
	NIGHT	2/4	2/4	3/6	3/6 spot 1-2 2/6 spot 3-6	2/4	2/4	2/4
CH-46E	DAY	2/4 3/3 spot 9	2/4 3/3 spot 8	2/6	2/8	2/4	2/4	2/4
	NIGHT	2/4 3/3 spot 9	2/4 3/3 spot 8	2/6	2/4	2/4	2/4	2/4
CH-53E	DAY	2/4	2/4	2/6	2/6	N/A	N/A	N/A
	NIGHT	2/4	2/4	2/6	2/6	N/A	N/A	N/A
AV-8B	DAY	2/4 Training 3/5* 5/10 Max	2/4 Training 3/5* 5/10 Max	N/A	3/5	N/A	N/A	N/A
	NIGHT	2/4 Training 3/5* 4/8 Max	2/4 Training 3/5* 4/8 Max	N/A	3/5	N/A	N/A	N/A

CAUTION The data for AH-1W and UH-1N is to be used as a baseline planning factor. The planning data is for the AH-1Z and UH-1Y is yet to be determined.*

Pitch and Roll Limit
P=Pitch R=Roll

VII. Weather Minimum Mission Planning Chart

Weather Mins Mission Planning Chart			
MISSION	**WEATHER (DAY) Ceiling/Visibility**	**WEATHER (NIGHT) Ceiling/Visibility**	**REFERENCE**
TACTICAL TROOP LIFT	500/3	1000/3	WgO P3710.39D; 4107
VBSS (SHIP-SHIP)	500/3	-	WgO P3710.39D; 4107
HRST OPS	500/3	1000/3	WgO P3710.39D; 4107
ADMIN PAX LIFT (VMC)	500/3	1000/3	WgO P3710.39D; 4107
OVERWATER ADMIN PAX LIFT	500/3	PROHIBITED	WgO P3710.39D; 4211.4
TRAINING	500/1	1000/3	WgO P3710.39D; 4107

VIII. Rotary-Wing Over Water Flight Matrix

The over water flight matrix below should be used as a guide for mission planning and execution while embarked and operating in a shipboard environment. The matrix is not capable of covering every contingency which may arise. The combination of weather, aircraft capability, pilot proficiency, supporting facilities and mission precedence gives every situation its own character and should be taken into consideration when planning over water flights.

The distances shown in the matrix reflect only over water flight (ship to ship, ship to shore, shore to ship, and shore to shore) between the aircraft and suitable landing areas, not necessarily the distance between point of departure and destination. The aircraft or flight must maintain the ability to reach a suitable landing area within a radius of length specified in the table below.

Over Water Flight Matrix				
DISTANCE	**UP TO 25 NM**	**26-50 NM**	**51-100 NM**	**OVER 100 NM**
Single Aircraft	Yes	No	No	No
Multiple Aircraft	Yes	Yes	Yes **(Note 1)**	Yes
VFR Weather Ceiling/Visibility	Day 500 / 1 NVG 1000 / 1 PAX 500 / 3	1000 / 3	3000 / 3	3000 / 3
Positive COMM or TACAN Lock with Departure/Destination	Yes	Yes	Yes **(Note 2)**	Yes **(Note 2)**
Approval Authority	ACE/SQDN CO	ACE/SQDN CO	ACE/SQDN CO	MEU/Group CO

Appendices & Reference

IX. Over Water Flight

Pre-Event Requirements

- Air movement plan is in support of the landing plan tied to the ground tactical plan
- Fire support plan should be coordinated and integrated to support the air movement plan
- Air movement plan is prepared predominantly by the ACE with GCE inputs

Air Movement Plan Execution

- Stick Leader maintains positive communication with the Pilot/Crew Chief on ICS
- Pilot/Crew Chief passes updates to the Stick Leader
- Stick Leader informs the Marines of updates from the Pilot/Crew Chief
- Stick Leader is allowed access to jump seat to get an orientation of objective by the pilot
- Marines follow all directions and instructions from the Crew Chief
- Marines maintain positive control of their weapons and gear throughout the flight
- Pilot/Crew passes 5 min, 2 min, 1 min warnings to the Stick Leader prior to the aircraft entering the landing zone in addition to intelligence updates
- For nighttime operations, assault forces break IR chemlites for self-marking (per unit SOP)
- Stick leader passes inbound landing information to embarked Marines
- Marines acknowledge receiving this information with hand/arm signal ("Thumbs Up")
- Stick Leader keeps the Marines informed of in-flight changes
- Stick Leader orients the Marines on the location/direction of the objective
- Marines remove all of their gear from the aircraft

Command and Control

- AFC and AMC establish and maintain communication
- AFC and FAC establish and maintain communication

Additional Remarks

- Stick leaders must have a way to communicate information to embarked troops during flight, either through well-rehearsed hand and arm signals, or a small dry-erase board or sketch pad to make sure all information is passed to all members during the flight. Oral communication is very limited due to noise restriction in-flight on most T/M/S
- Gear and weapons must be streamlined on each individual to ensure accountability and also to ease the transition from Air Movement Plan to the Landing Plan
- Crews must ensure that all flight gear and ammunition onboard are streamlined and organized to facilitate rapid actions once assaults are in the landing zone

X. AV-8B Currency

AV-8B Day Currency

Days Since Last Ship Landing	FCLP Requirement	Weather	Deck	Divert Field	Currency Requirement
1 to 14 Days	FCLP Not Required	Ship's Minimum s	All Condition s	Not Required	One Landing
15 to 29 Days	FCLP Refresh at Discretion of the CO	TACAN Minimum s	Steady Deck Or (1)	Divert Available	One Landing
30 to 59 Days	FCLP Refresh (2)	TACAN Minimum s	Steady Deck Or (1)	Divert Available	One Landing
60 Days to 6 Months	FCLP Refresh (2)	800/3 (3)	Steady Deck Or (1)	Divert Available	One Landing
6 to 12 Months	FCLP Refresh (2)	1000/3 (4)	Steady Deck Or (1)	Divert Available	One Landing
Greater than 12 Months	Refer to Initial Carrier Qualification	- - -	- - -	- - -	Refer to Initial Carrier Qualification

Notes:

1. Steady Deck is defined as roll equal to or less than +/- 5 degrees and/or pitch equal to or less than +/- 1 degree.
2. See pilot performance in paragraph 3.4 of the V/STOL Shipboard & LSO NATOPS Manual, NAVAIR 00-80T-111.
3. May be waived to TACAN minimums by the Commanding Officer or his appointed direct representative.
4. May be waived to 800/3 by the Commanding Officer or his appointed direct representative.
5. All initial qualifications should have a steady deck, divert available and the same weather requirements as to 12 months.

AV-8B Night Currency

Days Since Last Night Ship Landing	Requirement prior to a Night ship landing or takeoff	Requirement prior to a Night ship landing or takeoff	Weather	Deck	Divert Field	Currency Require ment
1 to 14 Days	Not Required	None	Ship's Minimu ms	All Conditi ons	Not Required	One Landing
15 to 29 Days	CO Discretion (2)	1 day landing/ takeoff same day or 2 day landings/ takeoffs w/in 48 hrs	TACAN Minimu ms	Steady Deck (1) Or	Divert Available	One Landing
30 to 59 Days	FCLP Refresher (2), (8)	2 day landings/ takeoffs w/in 36 hrs & no less than 1 hr flight time (day or night)	800/3 (3)	Steady Deck (1) Or	Divert Available	One Landing
60 Days to 6 Months	FCLP Refresher (2), (8)	Same as 30 to 59 Day	1000/3 (4)	Steady Deck (1) Or	Divert Available	One Landing
6 to 12 Months	FCLP Refresh (2)	Same as 30 to 59 Day	1500/5	Steady Deck (1) Or	Divert Available	Four Landings
Greater than 12 Months	Refer to Initial Qual (2)	Refer to Initial Qual	Note 7	Note 7	Divert Available	Refer to Initial Carrier Qual

Notes:

1. Steady Deck is defined as roll equal to or less than +/- 5 degrees and/or pitch equal to or less than +/- 1 degree

2. See pilot performance in paragraph 3.4 of the V/STOL Shipboard & LSO NATOPS Manual, NAVAIR 00-80T-111.

3. May be waived to TACAN minimums by the Commanding Officer or his appointed direct representative.

4. May be waived to 800/3 by the Commanding Officer or his appointed direct representative.

5. For initial CQ, a minimum of four landings must be completed one-half hour after sunset.

6. When a day ship takeoff/landing is required, a practice Case 3 approach utilizing OLS & HPI (or its equivalent) to complete the landing should be utilized.

7. All initial qualifications should have a steady deck, divert available & same weather requirement as 6 to 12 months.

8. When FCLPs are required, but an appropriate field facility (as defined in 3.3.1 of the V/STOL Shipboard & LSO NATOPS Manual, NAVAIR 00-80T-111) is not available, Day Case 3 recoveries may be substituted. Day landings should be followed by dusk approaches/landings.

9. NVD qualified pilots shall conduct one unaided Case 3 approach and landing every 30 days. If outside this 30-day window, the pilot's next approach & landing shall be unaided, unless waived by the Commanding Officer or his appointed direct representative.

XI. Helicopter Currency (T/M/S)

Type/Model/Series (T/M/S) Helicopter Currency

DAY (Carry PAX)			
Days Since Last Ship Landing	**FCLP Requirement**	**Weather**	**Currency Requirements**
1 to 30 Days	FCLP Not Required	500/3	None
31 Days to 12 Months	FCLP Not Required	500/3	2 Landings AH: see Note 1
Greater than 12 Months	5 FCLP Landings	500/3	5 Landings AH: see Note 1

NIGHT (Carry PAX*)			
Days Since Last NVG Ship Landing	**FCLP Requirement**	**Weather**	**Currency Requirements**
1 to 15 Days	FCLP Not Required	1000/3	None
16 Days to 12 Months	FCLP Not Required	1000/3	2 NVG Landings AH: see Note 3
Greater than 12 Months	5 NVG FCLP Landings	1000/3	5 NVG Landings AH: see Note 3

Notes:

Note 1: AH-1 pilots need 5 landings per year to maintain currency. If 12 months is exceeded since last ship landing, 2 FCLP landings must be completed prior to any ship landings.

* Administrative transport of PAX to/from amphibious aviation and air capable ships at night is prohibited except under emergency situations or when authorized by the MAGTF Commander.

* T&R Program Manual currency requirements for carrying PAX still apply.

**All Helicopter Aircraft Commanders (HACs) must have flown within 15 days IOT sign for an aircraft (day or night).

***: AH-1 pilots need 5 landings per year. If 12 months is exceeded since last night ship landing, 2 NVG FCLP landings must be completed prior to any night ship landings.

Appendices & Reference

F. Authorization to Fly Civilians/Foreign Nationals

The Commandant of the Marine Corps controls whether or not civilians can fly on USMC aircraft. In order to fly any civilians or foreign nationals aboard USMC aircraft a request needs to be submitted to the designated authority. The following message from MARFORPAC delineates who is the approving authority for what type of person:

R 052155Z MAR 03 DMS COMMARFORPAC G3

TO CG I MEF FWD

UNCLAS

MSGID/GENADMIN/COMMARFORPAC G3/AIR//

SUBJ/MARFORPAC POLICY ON TRANSPORTATION OF FOREIGN NATIONALS AND /US CIVILIANS ABOARD DOD ACFT// REF/A/DOC/OPNAVINST 3710.7S/ YMD:20011115// REF/B/DOC/DOD 4515.13R CHG3/YMD:19980409// REF/C/DOC/ DOD DIRECTIVE 4500.56/YMD:19970307// REF/D/MSG/CMC/220020ZMAY2001// REF/E/MSG/COMMARFORPAC/190301ZJUN2001// REF/F/MSG/ CMC/241618ZJAN2003//

REF/G/DOC/CMC/MCO 4631.10A/YMD:19970429//

NARR/REF A IS NATOPS GENERAL FLT AND OPERATING INSTRUCTION. REF B IS DOD AIR TRANS ELIGIBILITY ORDER. REF C IS DOD POLICY ON USE OF GOVT ACFT AND AIR TRAVEL. REF D DELEGATES AUTH TO MARFORPAC (MFP) TO APPROVE DOD CIVILIAN (CIV) EMPLOYEES, DOD CIV CONTRACTORS, LOCAL US CIV NEWS MEDIA, AND FOREIGN NATIONALS (FORNATS) TRANSPORTATION ABOARD DOD ACFT. REF E IS MFP PROCEDURES FOR TRANS OF FORNATS AND US CIV ABD DOD ACFT. REF F PERMITS MFP TO DELEGATE AUTH GRANTED IN REF D NO LOWER THAN THE MEB LEVEL. REF G IS MCO ON OPERATIONAL

SUPPORT AIRLIFT MANAGEMENT.// POC/W.T. AKANA/LTCOL/MARFORPAC G3 AIR/-/TEL:477-8619/-//

RMKS/1. PURPOSE. TO PROMULGATE THE MARFORPAC POLICY AND DELEGATION OF AUTH TO APPROVE FORNATS AND US CIV ABOARD DOD ACFT. THIS MESSAGE SUPERCEDES REF E; PORTIONS OF REF E NOT COVERED IN THIS POLICY ARE COVERED BY OTHER INSTRUCTIONS./

2. OVERVIEW OF APPROVAL AUTHORITIES.

A. THE TABLE BELOW OUTLINES RELEVANT APPROVAL AUTHORITIES CONTAINED IN THE REFS.

		MARCENT CMFC			
	I MEF	III MEF	MFP	CMC	NOTES
FORNAT DIGNITARY				X	1
FORNAT MIL (O7 ABOVE)			X	X	
FORNAT CIV (O7 ABOVE EQUIV)			X	X	
FORNAT MIL (O6 BELOW)		X	X	X	2
FORNAT CIV (O6 BELOW EQUIV)		X	X	X	2
DOD CIV	X	X		X	2

	MARCENT CMFC				
	I MEF	III MEF	MFP	CMC	NOTES
DOD CONTRACTOR EMPLOYEE	X	X	X	X	2
US AMBASSADOR/SENIOR DEP			X	X	3
US MIL FAMILY MEMBER			X	X	5
US NEWS MEDIA (LOCAL)			X	X	
US NEWS MEDIA (NATL/INTL)			X		1
FOREIGN NEWS MEDIA			X		1
FED EMPLOYEE/CONGRESS			X		1
US CIV (NOT COVERED ELSEWHERE)			X		
US CIV/FORNAT FLT IN TACTICAL ACFT			X		4

B. TABLE NOTES:

(1) CONSIDERED HIGH INTEREST ACTIVITY AND REQUIRES CMC APPROVAL.

(2) IRT REF F, AUTH TO APPROVE DOD CIVILIANS IS DELGATED TO MEF COMMANDERS. MEF COMMANDERS MAY FURTHER DELEGATE THIS AUTH TO THE MEB. REF B GRANTS SPECIAL APPROVAL TO OVERSEAS COMMANDER, E.G. CG III MEF, TO APPROVE FORNATS. WHEN I MEF IS DEPLOYED OVERSEAS, THEY CAN ALSO APPROVE FORNATS (06 AND BELOW).

(3) IAW REF B MFP CAN APPROVE WHEN INVITED TO TRAVEL BY CG MARFORPAC. OTHERWISE APPROVAL AUTH IS CMC.

(4) DOES NOT INCL PAX CAPABLE ACFT, E.G. CH46, CH53, UH1, KC130.

(5) IAW REF B, PARA C2.2.3.3.1. SPACE REQUIRED STATUS (GUARANTEED SEAT) IS NORMALLY LIMITED TO SPOUSES OF 3 AND 4 STAR GENERAL OFFICERS. REQUIRES INVITATIONAL TRAVEL ORDERS PERSONALLY SIGNED BY CG MARFORPAC. SPACE AVAIL TRAVEL IS ALWAYS PERMITTED.

C. GENERAL NOTES:

- WHEN COMUSMARCENT IS DESIGNATED OR COMMARFORPAC DECLARES COMMANDER COMBINED MARINE FORCES COMMAND (CMFC) ESTABLISHED, MARCENT/CMFC HAS SAME AUTH AS MFP.

- FOREIGN EXCHANGE OFFICERS AND FORNAT MIL PARTICIPATING IN COMBINED OPERATIONS OR TRAINING/EXERCISES SPONSORED BY JCS, COMBATANT COMMANDERS, OR COMPONENT COMMANDERS ARE AUTOMATICALLY AUTHORIZED TO FLY IAW REF B. SEE REF B FOR FURTHER DETAILS.

- ALL APPROVALS UNDER THIS POLICY ARE VALIDATION OF THE MIL AIR REQUIREMENT ONLY AND NOT AN AUTHORIZATION TO SCHEDULE AIRCRAFT OR JUSTIFY SCHEDULING A MISSION. USE NORMAL AIRLIFT REQUEST PROCEDURES.

- MARFORPAC, MARFORLANT, AND MARFORRES AVIATION UNITS ASSIGNED OPCON TO MFP, MARCENT, OR CMFC ARE SUBJECT TO THIS POLICY IN ADDITION TO THOSE IMPOSED BY THE COMBATANT COMMANDER. WHERE CONFLICTS OCCUR, THE COMBATANT COMMANDER POLICY HAS PRECEDENCE.

- FOR CASES NOT COVERED BY THE TABLE, CONSULT APPROPRIATE REF AND SUBMIT REQUEST TO MARFORPAC OR OTHER APPROPRIATE AGENCY. /

3. EMERGENCY SITUATIONS. IAW REF B LOCAL COMMANDERS MAY AUTH TRANSPORTATION ABOARD DOD ACFT FOR THE FOLLOWING WHEN DANGER TO PUBLIC HEALTH OR SAFETY IS OF SUCH IMMINENT SERIOUSNESS AS TO PRECLUDE OBTAINING PRIOR APPROVAL.

A. INDIVIDUALS ENGAGED IN SEARCH AND RESCUE.

B. INDIVIDUALS WHO ARE IN IMMEDIATE DANGER OF LOSS OF LIFE, LIMB, OR SIGHT TO PLACES WHERE ADEQUATE SAFETY OR MEDICAL CARE IS AVAILABLE./

4. POLICY FOR MARINE EXPEDITIONARY UNITS AND TASK FORCES AFLOAT.

A. WHEN OPCON TO A NAVY FLEET, REQUESTS SHOULD BE FORWARDED THRU THE OPERATIONAL CHAIN OF COMMAND FOR APPROVAL BY THE NAVAL COMPONENT OF THE COMBATANT COMMANDER, INFO COMMARFORPAC AND CMC.

B. LONG TERM APPROVALS GRANTED FOR DOD CIV/CONTRACTORS BY MEF OR MFP, PRIOR TO CHOP, REMAIN IN EFFECT UNTIL EXPIRATION OF THE ORIGINAL APPROVAL, EVEN WHEN OPCON CHANGES BTWN NUMBERED FLEETS OR TO SHORE BASED COMMANDS./

5. SUBMITTING REQUEST FOR AUTH TO FLY.

A. ALL COMMANDS REQUESTING APPROVAL OF AUTH TO FLY SHALL BE FAMILIAR WITH THE REFS PRIOR TO SUBMITTING A REQUEST.

B. ALL REQUESTS AND APPROVAL MESSAGES, EVEN THOSE APPROVED AT THE MEB LEVEL, SHALL INFO MARFORPAC AND CMC (CODE ASM). THIS HQ REQUIRES THE INFO IN ORDER TO SUBMIT SEMI-ANNUAL FEDERAL TRAVELER REPORTS IAW REF C.

C. REQUESTS SHALL BE VIA NAVAL MESSAGE THRU THE CHAIN OF COMMAND. DIRLAUTH FOR COORDINATION WITH CMC IS GRANTED TO MEF COMMANDERS FOR ANY REQUEST, KEEP MFP G3 AIR INFORMED. DIRLAUTH MAY BE DELEGATED TO THE MEB LEVEL.

D. ALL REQUESTS TO CMC(ASM) REQUIRE 5 WORKING DAYS ADV NOTICE.

E. BLANKET/LONG TERM AUTH ARE NORMALLY DISCOURAGED. BUT IF REQUIRED, INCLUDE DETAILED JUSTIFICATION IN ORDER TO PERMIT PROPER CONSIDERATION BY THE APPROVAL AUTHORITY.

F. FORMAT OF REQUEST MUST CONTAIN THE FOL INFO:

(1) NAME

(2) SSN (IF APPLICABLE)

(3) RANK, MILITARY OR CIVILIAN (IF APPLICABLE)

(4) POSITION (IDENTIFY DOD OR GOVT EMPLOYEES/LIST OF US NEWS MEDIA REPS AS LOCAL OR NATIONAL.)

(5) DATE/TIME OF LIFT

(6) TYPE ACFT

(7) POINT OF DEPARTURE AND PLACE OF INTENDED LANDING

(8) JUSTIFICATION FOR LIFT

(9) REMARKS (E.G., WHETHER THE FLIGHT IS OVER WATER, IF SPECIAL REQUIREMENTS EXIST, ETC.)

6. THIS POLICY MESSAGE REMAINS IN EFFECT UNTIL CANCELLED OR SUPERCEDED.//

Extended Civilian Flight Clearance

When submitting for a DOD civilian who is going to be with the MEU for an extended period of time, or is going to come and go throughout the deployment or workups, it is best to submit them to MFP for the duration of the expected deployment, plus 30 days. Of particular note WRT these requests are the DGSIT personnel who will come out for one of the work up periods to verify ships technical equipment. The Navy will need an assist in moving them, so ensure the DGSIT coordinator at MEF gets their authorization to fly taken care of. Utilize the below message format:

PTTUZYUW RHOVLHA001 1110330-UUUU--RHMCSUU

ZNRUUUUU

P 070818Z NOV 07

FM XX MEU

TO CG X MEF G-3(uc)

UNCLAS

MSGID/GENADMIN/CG I MEF FOPS/AIR//

SUBJ/REQUEST TO EMBARK AND TRANSPORT DOD CONTRACT CIVILIANS ABOARD

USMC AIRCRAFT// REF/A/RMG/CMC (ASM)/051323Z JAN 07/-/NOTAL// REF/B/

DOC/OPNAVISNT3710 .7T/950501// REF/C/DOC/MCO P5720.73/960806//

NARR/REF A IS CMC DELEGATION OF APPROVAL AUTHORITY FOR THE TRANSPORT OF FOREIGN NATIONALS AND CIVILIANS ABOARD USMC AIRCRAFT. REF B IS NATOPS GENERAL FLIGHT AND OPERATING INSTRUCTIONS. REF C IS MARINE CORPS AVIATION SUPPORT OF THE COMMUNITY RELATIONS PROGRAM MANUAL. //

POC/BROWN D.T./CAPT/15MEU ASST AIRO/-/TEL: 619-545-0539 DANIEL.T.BROWN@USMC.MIL

RMKS/1. PER REFS A THRU C, CO MEU REQUESTS APPROVAL TO EMBARK AND TRANSPORT DOD CONTRACT CIVILIANS ABOARD USMC AIRCRAFT TO AND FROM ESG SHIPPING BETWEEN XX NOVEMBER XX AND XX DECEMBER XX.

2. THE FOLLOWING IS THE LIST OF CONTRACT CIVILIANS TO BE TRANSPORTED VIA USMC ACFT:

NAME	RATING	LAST FOUR SSN	BLOOD TYPE
WILLIS, MATT	N/A	XXXX	X
SELBY, LENNY L	N/A	XXXX	X

3. JUSTIFICATION: MR WILLIS IS CONTRACTED BY MARCORSYSCOM TO PROVIDE A MOBILE TRAINING TEAM FOR XX MEU S-2. MR WILLIS NEEDS TO FLY OFF VIC OF HAWAII FOR RTB. MR SELBY AND MS BRICENO ARE MARCORSYSCOM CONTRATOCTORS PROVIDING TRAINING TO XX MEU LOGISTICS FOR VARIOUS SYSTEMS. MS BRICENO WILL FLY OFF VIC HAWAII, MR SELBY WILL DEPART PRIOR TO INCHOP INTO FIFTH FLEET.//

4. ALL SAFETY REQUIREMENTS AND PRE-REQUISITES WILL BE MET BEFORE FLIGHT IN ACCORDANCE WITH THE REFERENCES.//

BT

#0001

Chap 6

G. Diplomatic Clearances

DIP clearances are not the direct responsibility of the Air Shop although they affect all movement. The TACRON det will submit DIP clearances for aircraft while the S-1 will submit DIP clearances for personnel. The reference for all clearances is the Foreign Clearance Guide found on the NIPR and the SIPR at the following addresses:

NIPR: https://www.fcg.pentagon.mil

SIPR: https://www.fcg.pentagon.smil.mil

Example Dip Clearance

PAAUZYUW 3141741-UUUU--.

ZNR UUUUU

P ddhhmmZ NOV 2007

FM COMTARESG

TO USDAO SINGAPORE SN

XX MEU

BT

UNCLAS

MSGID/GENADMIN/TARESG/-/NOV//

SUBJ/AIRCRAFT CLEARANCE REQUEST ISO TARESG//

REF/A/DOC/FOREIGN CLEARANCE GUIDE/27SEP2007//

AMPN/REF A IS ELECTRONIC FOREIGN CLEARANCE GUIDE.//

POC/NICHOLS/CDR/TARESG AIR OFFICER/LOC:EMBARKED TARAWA /EMAIL:NICHOLST(AT)CPR1.NAVY.SMIL.MIL//

RMKS/1. IAW REF A, REQUEST DIPLOMATIC CLEARANCE TO ENTER SINGAPORE IN SUPPORT OF TARESG OPERATIONS.

2. AIRCRAFT INFORMATION:

A. TYPE OF AIRCRAFT, TAIL NUMBER, CALL SIGN.

CH-46E	00	LUCKY 00
	01	LUCKY 01
CH-53E	24	LUCKY 24
	25	LUCKY 25
SH-60B	60	SIDEFLARE 60
	66	SIDEFLARE 66

B. ALTERNATE AIRCRAFT:

CH-46E	02	LUCKY 02
	03	LUCKY 03
CH-53E	26	LUCKY 26
	27	LUCKY 27

C. MISSION NUMBERS: TO BE DETERMINED.

D. PURPOSE OF FLIGHT: LOGISTICS ISO TARESG OPERATIONS 30NOV-2 DEC 2007. ALL FLIGHTS WILL ORIGINATE AND TERMINATE ABOARD USS TARAWA. DO NOT ANTICIPATE AIRCRAFT BASING OR REMAINING ASHORE OVER NIGHT.

3. ITINERARY: TBD

A. POINT OF DEPARTURE: USS TARAWA (LHA1) 30 NOV DEC 2007.

B. LOCATIONS IN ROUTE: PAYA LEBAR (WSAP), SINGAPORE CHANGI (WSSS) AND SEMBAWANG (WSAG) WILL BE USED AS AN EMERGENCY DIVERT ONLY.

C. FINAL DESTINATION: USS TARAWA (LHA1) 30 NOV 2007.
4. CREW INFORMATION:
A. NUMBER OF CREW:
CH-46E/2 PILOTS AND 2 CREWMEN PER AIRCRAFT/8 TOTAL.
CH-53E/2 PILOTS AND 2 CREWMEN PER AIRCRAFT/8 TOTAL.
SH-60B/2 PILOTS AND 2 CREWMEN PER AIRCRAFT/8 TOTAL.
24 TOTAL AIRCREW.
B. ALL PILOTS AND CREWMEN ARE US CITIZENS.
5. CARGO AND PASSENGERS:
A. NUMBER OF PASSENGERS ANTICIPATED TO BE LESS THAN 20.
B. NO DISTINGUISHED VISITORS ANTICIPATED.
C. CARGO WILL BE PERSONNEL AND EQUIPMENT ISO TARESG OPERATIONS.
6. OTHER SUPPORT:
A. FUEL SERVICES REQUIRED AT EACH LOCATION: UP TO 8000LBS FOR A FLIGHT OF 2 AIRCRAFT.
B. AIRCRAFT SERVICES REQUIRED AT EACH LOCATION:N/A
C. FUND CITE FOR AIRCRAFT SERVICES:N/A
D. OTHER LOGISTICAL SUPPORT REQUIRED:N/A
E. FUND CITE FOR OTHER LOGISTICAL SUPPORT:AA 17 8 1106.27A0 000 68450 0
067443 2D M20177 CTBH8SU010020 M2017708SU00020
F. POC:NICHOLS, T.M./CDR-OIC/TACRON ELEVEN DET TWO/
EMAIL:NICHOLST(AT)CPR1.NAVY(.SMIL).MIL/COMM:619-545-0189/
7. COUNTRY SPECIFIC INFORMATION:
A. ROUTE OF FLIGHT:
1. FIR ENTRY POINT: N/A. USS TARAWA WILL BE INSIDE THE FIR.
2. ROUTE OF FLIGHT: USS TARAWA, PAYA LEBAR, USS TARAWA.
3. FIR EXIT POINT: N/A. USS TARAWA WILL BE INSIDE THE FIR.//
BT
#
NNNN

Block Dip Clearance for Exercises

RTTSZYUW RHOVLHA0003 0321804z-SSSSRHMCSUU.
ZNY UUUUU
R 010530Z FEB 08
FM ELEVENTH MEU
TO USLO DJIBOUTI DJ
HQ USCENTCOM MACDILL AFB FL//THEATER TRAVEL CELL//
INFO
AMEMBASSY DJIBOUTI
DIA WASHINGTON DC
COMUSCENTAF SHAW AFB SC
MARCENT FWD
MARCENT COORDINATION ELEMENT HOA
COMUSMARCENT
COMUSMARCENT//G5//
XX MEU
CPR-1
COMUSNAVCENT
COMEXSTRGRU THREE
CTF 51

BT
UNCLAS //N03000//
MSGID/GENADMIN/COMTARESG/-/JAN//
SUBJ/AIRCRAFT CLEARANCE REQUEST ISO TARESG//
REF/A/DOC/FOREIGN CLEARANCE GUIDE/27NOV2007//
NARR/REF A IS ELECTRONIC FOREIGN CLEARANCE GUIDE.//
POC/NICHOLS/CDR/TARESG AIR OFFICER/LOC:EMBARKED TARAWA
/EMAIL:NICHOLST(AT)CPR1.NAVY.SMIL.MIL//
RMKS/1. IAW REF A, REQUEST DIPLOMATIC CLEARANCE TO ENTER DJIBOU-TIAN
AIRSPACE IN SUPPORT OF THEATER SECURITY COOPERATION MISSION IN DJIBOUTI.//
2. AIRCRAFT INFORMATION://
2.A. TYPE OF AIRCRAFT, TAIL NUMBER, CALL SIGN.//

CH-46E	01	MOOSE HEAD 01//
CH-46E	02	MOOSE HEAD 02//
CH-46E	03	MOOSE HEAD 03//
CH-46E	04	MOOSE HEAD 04//
CH-46E	05	MOOSE HEAD 05//
CH-46E	06	MOOSE HEAD 06//
CH-53E	24	MOOSE HEAD 24//
CH-53E	25	MOOSE HEAD 25//
UH-1N	31	MOOSE HEAD 31//
UH-1N	32	MOOSE HEAD 32//
AH-1W	41	MOOSE HEAD 41//
AH-1W	42	MOOSE HEAD 42//
AH-1W	43	MOOSE HEAD 43//
AV-8B	51	MOOSE HEAD 51//
AV-8B	52	MOOSE HEAD 52//
AV-8B	53	MOOSE HEAD 53//
AV-8B	54	MOOSE HEAD 54//
MH-60S	61	PILE DRIVER 61//

2.B. ALTERNATE AIRCRAFT://

CH-46E	07	MOOSE HEAD 07//
CH-46E	10	MOOSE HEAD 10//
CH-53E	26	MOOSE HEAD 26//
CH-53E	27	MOOSE HEAD 27//
AH-1W	44	MOOSE HEAD 44//
AV-8B	55	MOOSE HEAD 55//
AV-8B	56	MOOSE HEAD 56//

2.C. MISSION NUMBERS: TO BE DETERMINED.//
2.D. PURPOSE OF FLIGHTS: FOR UNILATERAL AND BILATERAL AVIATION AND GROUND TRAINING WITHIN THE AIRSPACE AND RANGES OF DJIBOUTI.
2.E. FLIGHTS WILL ORIGINATE FROM USS TARAWA (LHA1) 29MAR2008.
2.F. FINAL FLIGHT WILL TERMINATE ABOARD USS TARAWA NLT 04APR2008.//
3. ITINERARY:
3.A. TO BE DETERMINED. ALL FLIGHTS WILL BE COORDINATED WITH FRENCH
CCOA AND BE INCLUDED ON THEIR FLIGHT SCHEDULE TRACKER.
3.A.1. POINT OF DEPARTURE: FLIGHTS WILL ORIGINATE FROM USS TARAWA
3.A.2. FINAL DESTINATION: FLIGHTS WILL TERMINATE ABOARD USS TARAWA

3.B. EXCEPTIONS
3.B.1. IN ORDER TO SUPPORT CASEVAC REQUIREMENTS AT GODORIA RANGE, (2)
CH-46E WILL BE POSTED AT GODORIA RANGE EACH NIGHT FROM 30MAR08 TO
02APR08 WITH THE FOLLOWING SCHEDULE.
3.B.1. POINT OF DEPARTURE: (2) CH-46E, 1400Z, USS TARAWA (LHA1)
3.B.2. INTERMEDIATE STOP: (2) CH-46E, 1445Z, GODORIA RANGE
3.B.3. INTERMEDIATE DEPARTURE: (2) CH-46E, 0800Z, GODORIA RANGE
3.B.4. FINAL DESTINATION: (2) CH-46E, 1000Z, USS TARAWA (LHA1)//
4. CREW INFORMATION:
4.A. NUMBER OF CREW:
CH-46E/2 PILOTS AND 2 CREWMEN PER AIRCRAFT/4 TOTAL
CH-53E/2 PILOTS AND 2 CREWMEN PER AIRCRAFT/4 TOTAL
UH-1N /2 PILOTS AND 2 CREWMEN PER AIRCRAFT/4 TOTAL
AH-1W /2 PILOTS AND 0 CREWMEN PER AIRCRAFT/2 TOTAL
AV-8B /1 PILOTS AND 0 CREWMEN PER AIRCRAFT/1 TOTAL
MH-60S/2 PILOTS AND 2 CREWMEN PER AIRCRAFT/4 TOTAL
4.B. ALL PILOTS AND CREWMEN ARE U.S. OR U.K. CITIZENS.//
5. CARGO AND PASSENGERS:
5.A. CARGO: TO BE DETERMINED.
5.B. NUMBER OF PASSENGERS:
5.B.1. CH-46E MAXIMUM 12 PAX PER AIRCRAFT/MAXIMUM 72 TOTAL.
5.B.2. CH-53E MAXIMUM 24 PAX PER AIRCRAFT/MAXIMUM 48 TOTAL.
5.B.3. UH-1N MAXIMUM 4 PAX PER AIRCRAFT/MAXIMUM 8 TOTAL.
5.B.4. MH-60S MAXIMUM 8 PAX PER AIRCRAFT/MAXIMUM 8 TOTAL.
5.C. NO DISTINGUISHED VISITORS ANTICIPATED.
5.D. CARGO WILL BE PERSONNEL AND EQUIPMENT TRAINING OPERATIONS.//
6. OTHER SUPPORT:
6.A. FUEL SERVICES REQUIRED AT EACH LOCATION: TBD
6.B. AIRCRAFT SERVICES REQUIRED AT EACH LOCATION: TBD
6.C. FUND CITE FOR AIRCRAFT SERVICES: R53973 S/N 0102-LF-068-1901
6.D. OTHER LOGISTICAL SUPPORT REQUIRED: TBD
6.E. FUND CITE FOR OTHER LOGISTICAL SUPPORT: AA 17 8 1106.27A0 000 68450 0
067443 2D M20177 CTBH8SU010020 M2017708SU00020
6.F. POC:NICHOLS, T.M./CDR-OIC/TACRON ELEVEN DET TWO/
EMAIL:NICHOLST(AT)CPR1.NAVY(.SMIL).MIL/COMM:619-545-0189//
7. COUNTRY SPECIFIC INFORMATION:
7.A. ROUTE OF FLIGHT:
7.A.1. FIR ENTRY POINT: ALL FLIGHTS ORIGINATE WITHIN DJIBOUTI FIR
7.A.2. ROUTE OF FLIGHT: USS TARAWA (LHA1) - TRAINING AREAS - USS TARAWA (LHA1)
7.A.3. FIR EXIT POINT: ALL FLIGHTS TERMINATE WITHIN DJIBOUTI FIR
DECL/ORIG:COMTARESG/15A/DATE:31JAN2009/X4//
BT
#0003
NNNNNN

H. Signal Plan & Communications

I. Suggested Signal Plan

(Will be mission dependent.)

Signal Plan

Event	Day	Day No Comm	Night Low Vis	Night Low Vis No Comm
HLZ ITG	Radio	Signal Mirror Smoke	Radio NATO Y or NATO T	Ir Or Red Chemlight In NATO Y or NATO T IR Buzzsaw
HLZ ID Landing Points	Radio W/ Air Panel	Smoke Air Panel	Radio NATO Y NATO T	IR/Red Chemlight NATO Y or NATO T
L/U Far	Radio	Moving Unit: Hand On Top Of Cover/ Stationary Unit: Iron Cross	Radio	NVG IR or Red Lens: 3 Stationary 2 Moving 1 Stationary
L/U Near	Challenge and Password	Challenge and Password	Challenge and Password	Challenge and Password
Reinforce Assault Element	Radio	Yellow Smoke	Radio	White Chemlight Buzzsaw
OBJ Secure	Radio	Green Smoke	Radio	Green Chemlight Buzzsaw
CASEVAC	Radio	Air Panel	Radio	Blue Chemlight Buzzsaw
Emergency Extract	Radio	Air Panel	Radio	Red Chemlight Buzzsaw
Immediate Reembark	Radio	Air Panel	Radio	Green Star Cluster
Shift Fire	Radio	White Star Parachute	Radio	White Star Parachute
Cease Fire	Radio	2 White Star Parachutes	Radio	2 White Star Parachutes

II. Waterborne Signals

Waterborne Signals

Event	Signal	Action to Be Taken
Raid force unable to locate launch platform	(D) Red Flare (N) Red Flare	Ship lights up its yard arm blinkers
Raid force in trouble requires emergency recovery	(D) RSP (N) RSC	Ship takes appropriate action to render assistance
AAV inoperable	(D) NOV flag (N) WSC	
AAV sinking	(D) Wave NOV flag (N) RSC	
CRRC Down	(D) NOV flag, 1 arm over head waving (N) 1 WSC, 1 orange chemlight	RF will tow to ship/or BLS

III. R&S No Communication Plan

R&S No Communication Plan

	Miss 1 Comm Window or loss of comm during planned comm window	Miss 2 Comm Window	Miss 3 Comm Window	Miss 4 Comm Window
R&S Team	- Set up alt antenna - Relay through alt unit - Set up alt comm	- Continue to attempt to establish comm.	- Comm becomes ME	- Abort mission - Execute E&R plan
MEU LFOC/COC	- SARC informs LFO WO - LFOC WO informs MEU CO/ME CMDR	- Reposition ARG shipping, if feasible - Establish retrans	- Launch vehicle and/or air patrol to establish comm. or obtain visual	- Execute E&R plan

Appendices & Reference

Chap 6

I. Missing Marine/ Sailor Plan

I. Missing Marine / Sailor Plan (Individual Actions)

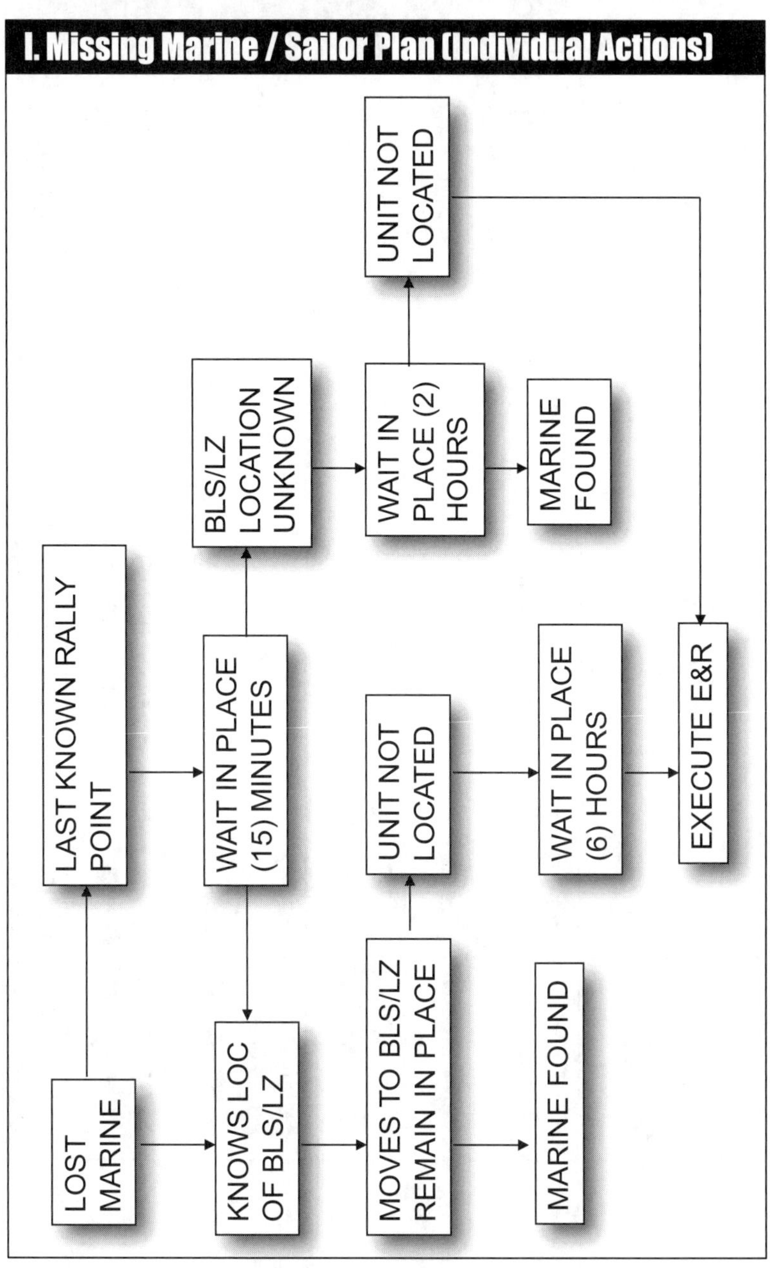

Appendices & Reference

II. Missing Marine / Sailor Plan (Unit Actions)

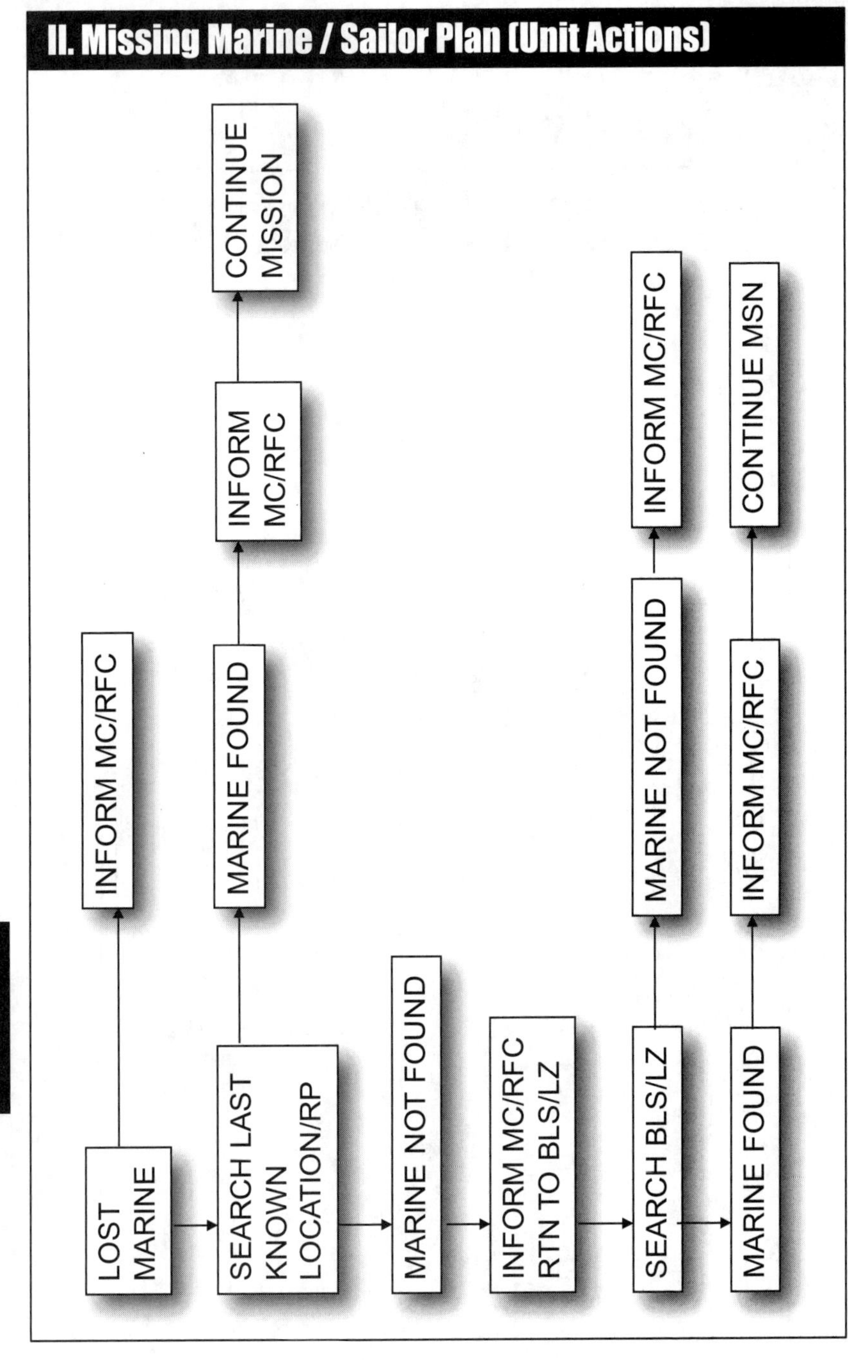

J. Critical Thresholds & Sea State Chart

Critical Thresholds

Critical Thresholds

Unit	No-Go	Initiator	Executor	Action
AAV	VIS <2000m SS >3 (2-4 ft) MSI >6 Safety Boats: 1 for 1-5 AAVs 2 for 6+ AAVs	-METOC -Landing craft -PCS ship -R&S ashore	- LFOC watch officer in conjunction with the CPR/MEU Commander	-Postpone landing craft movement.
LCU Well Deck Ops	VIS < 1nm SWH > 10 ft MSI > 6 (Trng) > 12(Ops) Wind> 35 kt SS sill >+/- 2 ft at the sill	-Well deck officer -LCU craft-master	- Flagplot watch officer, in conjunction with the CPR/MEU Commander	- Postpone loading and movement of LCU into well deck
LCAC -Dry Well Ops -Surf Zone	VIS <1nm SS >= 4 (5-8 ft) Wind >35 kt (Temp/load dependent) SS>=4 Breakers > 4-8 ft	-METOC -LCS	- CPR Commander	- LCAC cease movement ashore/to ship
LCAC (**Heavy**) -Surf Zone	VIS <1nm SWH >1-3ft Temp/Load dependent Breakers > 0-4 ft	-METOC -LCS	- CPR Commander	- LCAC cease movement ashore/to ship -Shift load plan
LARC	MSI >6 (Trng) >9 (Oper) Current > 4 kt Wind > 25 kt Swell > 6 ft Chop >4 ft	-METOC -PCS -LCU Craftmaster	- PCS recommends to CPR /MEU Commander for decision	- Postpone
CRRC -Surf	6 ft seas or Small Craft Warning in effect Breaker Ht vs. Period Table (Surf Zone) (example Threshold: 6 ft brkr w/12sec period)	- METOC - CRRC Cmdr - R&S ashore	- Flagplot Watch Officer in Conjunction with CPR/MEU Commanders	- Postpone
Swimmers	Current: >2kt	- METOC - Unit Cmdr - R&S ashore	- LFOC watch officer in conjunction with the CPR/MEU Commander	- Postpone
RHIB Launch/ Recovery	>6 ft seas SS >3	- METOC - NSWTU OIC	- CPR Commander	- Postpone

Based upon BMUONE INST 3500.1B

Sea State Chart

Sea State	Description	Wind Force (Beaufort)	Wind Description	Wind Range (kt)	Wind Velocity (kt)	Average Wave Height (ft)	Significant Wave Height
0	The sea is like a mirror.	0	Calm	< 1	0	0	0
	Ripples with the appearance of scales are formed but without foam crests.	1	Light air	1-3	2	0.05	0.08
1	Small wavelets, still short but more pronounced form, crests have a glassy appearance but do not break	2	Light breeze	4-6	5	0.18	0.29
2	Large wavelets form; crests begin to break. Foam of glassy appearance forms; there may be scattered whitecaps.	3	Gentle breeze	7-10	8.5 10	0.6 0.88	1.0 1.4
3	Small waves form; becoming longer; whitecaps are fairly frequent.	4	Moderate breeze	11-16	12 13.5 14 16	1.4 1.8 2.0 2.9	2.2 2.9 3.3 4.6
4	Moderate waves appear, taking a more pronounced form; there are many whitecaps and chance of some spray.	5	Fresh breeze	17-21	18 19 20	3.8 4.3 5.0	6.1 6.9 8.0
5	Large waves begin to form; white foam crests are more extensive everywhere. There is some spray.	6	Strong breeze	22-27	22 24 24.5 26	6.4 7.9 8.2 9.6	10 12 13 15
6	The sea heaps up and white foam from breaking waves begins to be blown in streaks along the direction of the wind. Spindrift begins.	7	Moderate gale	28-33	28 30 30.5 32	11 14 14 15	18 22 23 26
7	Moderately high waves of greater length form; edges of crests break into spindrift. The foam is blown in well-marked streaks along the direction of the wind. Spray affects visibility.	8	Fresh gale	34-40	34 36 37 38 40	19 21 23 25 28	30 35 37 40 45
8	High waves form. Dense streaks of foam appear along the direction of the wind. The sea begins to roll. Visibility is affected.	9	Strong gale	41-47	42 44 46	31 36 40	50 58 64

K. MEU Daily Read Board & Rapid Request Form

MEU Daily Read Board

MEU Daily Read Board

TAMCN	PARENT UNIT	NOMENCLATURE	SERIAL #	DOWN DTG	MCT/RECOVERY MSN #	STATUS/REMARKS

MEU Rapid Request Form

RAPID REQUEST FORM			
RAPID REQUEST #		INTERNAL REQUEST	EXTERNAL REQUEST

A	REQUESTING UNIT	
B	POINT OF CONTACT	
C	SUPPORT MISSION	
D	LOCATION	
E	TYPE/AMOUNT OF CLASS I (MRE, UGR, H20, subsistence)	
F	TYPE/AMOUNT OF CLASS II (clothing, individual equipment, tools, admin, supplies)	
G	TYPE/AMOUNT OF CLASS III (petroleum, oils, lubricants)	
H	TYPE/AMOUNT OF CLASS IV (construction materials)	
I	TYPE/AMOUNT OF CLASS V(W) (ground ammunition)	
J	TYPE/AMOUNT OF CLASS VII (major end items, pylons)	
K	TYPE/AMOUNT OF CLASS VIII (medical)	
L	TYPE/AMOUNT OF CLASS IX (repair parts, consumables, SECREPS)	
M	TYPE/AMOUNT OF CLASS X (nonmilitary program materials)	
N	MOTOR TRANSPORT SUPPORT REQUIRED	
O	ENGINEER SUPPORT REQUIRED	
P	MATERIAL HANDLING EQUIPMENT REQUIRED	
Q	EQUIPMENT REQUIRING EVACREPAIR BY TAMCN	
R	CLARIFYING INSTRUCTIONS	

FOR USE BY MEU			
RECEIVED BY			
TIME / DATE RCVD			
PRIORITY ASSIGNED	ROUTINE	IMMEDIATE	URGENT
VALIDATED BY			

Appendices & Reference

Chap 6

L. Naming Conventions

Naming Conventions

Air	
Air Routes and Control Measures	States and cities w/in those states
Landing Zones (LZs)	Birds
Holding Areas (HA)	Female names
Battle Positions (BP)	Snakes
Initial Point (IP)	Car makes
Forward Arming and Refueling Point (FARP)	Fast Food restaurants
Mission Control Area (MCA)	Sodas
Ground	
Beaches	Colors
Ground Routes	Beer Names
Phase Lines	Tools or Metals
Emergency Rally Point (ERP)	Single Digit Numbers

All others will be referred to according to proper nomenclature. For example, BLT release point will be referred to as "Release Point"

Common naming of geometries and fire plans is important to assure no unit's naming will conflict with another's when data has the potential to be electronically distributed force wide. (For example, two phase lines named green will result in confusion and in some systems, will overwrite each other.) This enclosure provides conventions for the naming of geometry and fire plans. All names are limited to six characters to allow for reception at the least capable systems (TACFIRE systems such as BCS).

Appendices & Reference

Naming Procedure

The procedure dictated here is an extension of that formulated in the FMFM 6-18-1. Names are composed of **six characters** divided into **three parts**.

1. **Fire Plan or Geometry Type.** This is a two character abbreviation of the type of fire plan or measure. Geometry types are defined in table 2, fire plan names are defined in table 3.
2. **Sequential Number.** Sequential number is a value form 1-9 that allows the creation of more than one measure of the given type by a given unit. This allows a single unit to create on-call and planned geometries such as an on-call CFL or multiple geometries such as multiple phase lines.
3. **Unit Tag Name.** Unit tag name is a three character unique name for a unit. The method for creating unit tags is based on FMFM 6-18-1 and is provided in table 1.

Table 1. Unit Tag Names

Table 1. Unit Tag Names

UNIT	TAG
MEF	The arabic numeral followed by MF: III MEF = 3MF
MEB	The arabic numeral followed by MB: 1st MEB = 1MB
MEU	The arabic numeral followed by U: 15TH MEU = 15U
MAW	The arabic numeral followed by MW: 1 MAW = 1MW
MAG	The MAG number followed by G: MAG 39 = 39G
DASC	The arabic numeral representing the wing, followed by DA: DASC 3 MAW = 3DA
TACC	The arabic numeral representing the wing, followed by TA: TACC 2 MAW = 2TA
DIVISION	The arabic numeral followed by MD: 1ST MARDIV = 1MD
REGIMENT	The arabic numeral followed by MR: 7TH MARINES = 7MR; If two digit regiment number: 25th MARINES = 25M
BATTALIONS	The battalion number followed by the letter "A" and the regiment: 2st BN 4th MARINES = 2A4; If two digit regiment number: 3rd BN 11th MARINES = 311
COMPANY/ BATTERY	The company/battery letter followed by the regiment number and the letter "M": A 1st BN 8th MARINES = A8M If two digit regiment number: A 1st BN 25th MARINES = A25
SEPARATE BATTALIONS:	Battalion number followed these letters: AAV BN = AA CAB = CA LAAD BN = AD LAR BN = LA TANK BN = TK

Exceptions

Some specialized geometry requires specific naming. These fall into three categories.

- **Radar zones.** Radar zones are named based on the type of zone (ATI, CFFZ, etc.) followed by a single number 1-9. This is required since the receiving Firefinder radar stores the zone by the single digit number and not by alpha-numeric name. AFATDS units that plan for radar employment but do not communicate with the radar directly are responsible for naming the sensor zones and transmitting these geometries of the controlling station for dissemination to the radar.
- **Battle areas and support areas.** Battle areas (deep, close and rear) and support areas (division support area, etc) are named using three letter identifiers and the tag name of the responsible or supported unit. For example, a division support area for 1st MARDIV is DSA1MD and the deep battle area for I MEF is DBA1MF.
- **AFATDS generated measures.** AFATDS creates safety measures as required to support the employment of special munitions. These include platoon area hazards, targets area hazards, missile flight paths and FASCAM safety zones. These are automatically named using the target number that caused the geometry to be created. AFATDS operators will not edit these names. The names must remain as generated because most of these measures are automatically deleted when missions are completed. Changing the name will cause the measure to remain after it should have been deleted.

Table 2. Geometry Names

The following matrix applies to standard MEU Fire Support Operations. For measures whose naming includes number designators, the next sequential number will apply when more than one of the same geometry is created. For example Air Corridor number 1 in the MEU Zone/AO will be designated AC115U followed by AC215U.

Table 2. Naming of Geometry

MEASURE	SHORT NAME EXAMPLE (_: sequential number)
ATI ZONE	ATI-must be followed by a sequential number
AIR CORRIDOR	AC_15U
AIRSPACE COORDINATION AREA	AC_15U
AMMUNITION HOLDING AREA	AH_15U
AMPHIBIOUS OBJECTIVE AREA	OA_15U
ASSAULT OBJECTIVE	OB_15U
ASSAULT POSITION	AP_15U
ASSEMBLY AREA	AA_15U
ATTACK POSITION	AP"SNAKE NAME"15U
Battle Position	BP_15U
Beach Support Area	BSA followed by supported brigade tag.
Biological Contaminated Area	BC_15U
Brigade Support Area	SU_15U
Call For Fire Zone	CFFZ_15U
Censor Zone	CZ_15U
Chemical Contaminated Area	CC_15U
Close Battle Area	CBA_15U
Combat Service Support Area	CS_15U
Critical Friendly Zone	CFZ_15U
Dead Space Area	DS_15U
Deep Battle Area	DBA followed by the establishing unit tag.
Division Support Area	DSA – followed by the establishing unit tag.
Drop Zone	DZ_15U
Engagement Area	EA"ANIMAL NAME"15U
Fascam Safety Zone	AFATDS names based on target number.
Fire Support Area	SA_15U
Forward Arming And Refueling Point	FAR – followed by the establishing unit tag.
Free Fire Area	FF_15U
Helicopter Lane	HL_15U
Landing Zone	LZ_15U
Landing Zone Support Area	LZS_15U
Limited Access Position Area	LA_15U
Mine Field	MF_15U
No Fire Area	NF_15U
Obstacle Area	OO_15U
Pickup Zone	PZ_15U
Platoon Area Hazard	AFATDS names based on target number.
Position Area	PA_15U
Radioactive Area	RAD_15U
Rear Battle Area	RBA_15U
Restrictive Fire Area	RF_15U
Shorad Zone	SZ_15U
Strong Point Area	SP_15U
Target Area Hazard	TA_15U
Target Build Up Area	TB_15U
Target Geometry	TG_15U
Target Value Area	TV_15U
Vulnerable Area	VA_15U
Zone Of Responsibility	ZO_15U
Air Head Line	AL_15U
Axis Of Advance	AX_15U
Boundary Line	Named using the tag name of unit on left then right.
Bridgehead Line	BL_15U
Coordinated Fire Line	CF_15U
Crossover Line	CO_15U
Direction Of Attack	DA_15U
Feint	FT_15U
Final Coordaintion Line	FL_15U
Force Beachhead Line	FB_15U
Ford Crossing	FC_15U
Fortified Line	FL_15U
Forward Edge Of Battle Area	FE_15U
Forward Line Of Own Troops	FL_15U
Holding Line	HD_15U

Appendices & Reference

MEASURE	SHORT NAME EXAMPLE (_: sequential number)
Lane Crossing	CR_15U
Light Line	LL_15U
Limit Of Advance	LA_15U
Line Of Contact	LC_15U
Line Of Departure	LD_15U
Line Of Departure/Contact	LC_15U
Main Attack	MA_15U
Main Supply Route	MSR"BEER NAME"15U
Mine Field Line	ML_15U
Obstacle Line	OL_15U
Phase Line	PL"COLOR NAME"15U
Probable Line Of Deployment	PD_15U
Restricted Fire Line	RL_15U
Supporting Attack	SP_15U
Air Control Point	AC"U.S. CITY NAME"15U
Ambush Point	AP_15U
Bridge Site	BR_15U
Bypass Difficulty	BD_15U
Checkpoint	CP_15U
Communcations Checkpoint	CM_15U
Contact Point	CN_15U
Coordination Point	CR_15U
Decon Point	DP_15U
Departure Point	DE_15U
Fire Support Station	SS_15U
Firing Point	FP_15U
Ford Crossing	FC_15U
Hide Point	HP_15U
Initial Point	IP"CAR NAME"15U
Launch Point	LP_15U
Linkup Point	LN_15U
Obstacle	OO_15U
Overhead Point	OV_15U
Passage Point	PP_15U
Penetration Control Point	PC_15U
Point Of Departure	PD_15U
Pop Up Point	PU_15U
Rally Point	RP_15U
Reduced Width Point	RW_15U
Rendezvous Point	RZ_15U
Reload Point	RE_15U
Traffic Control Point	TC_15U

Table 3. Fire Plan and Future Plan Names

Fire plans created in the current or planned situation can be transmitted through the force to IFSAS, BCS or FDS units for execution. As such, these must be named in a fashion that will allow the fire plan and schedule of fires to be received. In addition to fire plans, future plans are assigned a PLAN ALIAS to allow these to be transmitted to IFSAS. Fire plans and future plans are named as dictated in para. 2 above. Table 3 provides the first two characters for the plan name.

Table 3. Fire Plan and Future Plan Naming

PLAN TYPE	SHORT NAME
Future Plan PLAN ALIAS	PN "PLAN ALIAS"15U
Counter Prep	CP_15U
Group	GP_15U
Prep	PP_15U
Programs: Anti-Air Anti-Mech SEAD	 AP MP SD, ETC
Quick Fire Plan	QP_15U
Series	SE_15U

Chap 6

M. Watch Information

Watch Officer Responsibilities

1. In the absence of the SWO or the S3, the watch officer will make critical decisions as to the allocation of MEU assets/resources.

2. Manage the CAT slides for the S3 upon receipt of any WARNOs

3. Manage the LFOC watch chief and clerk

4. Control the LFOC floor including the flow of information between the LNOs, PHIBRON and Ships Watch Officer

5. Update the COP/S3 power point slides overnight for the O&I brief

6. Draft or task the drafting of CONOPs/Storyboards

7. Provide briefs and situational awareness for senior officers/MEU decision makers

8. Conduct a thorough handover with oncoming watch officer to include but not limited to

- Current Situation Update to include all LNOs and watch standers.
- Ongoing missions brief.
- Location of key individuals.
- Projected operations/tasks that are ongoing ie.CAT II or Confirmation briefs.
- Standing Missions and alert status
- Who is the SWO on duty.

Watch Officer Actions

1. On receipt of a warning order inform the OPSO/AOPSO immediately. Either calling the OPSOs brick or sending a runner to wake him up. Make 5 copies of the warning order (CO/XO/OPSO and two for the PSOs to read in the LFOC). Email the warning order to watch officers, post it on the share drive and drop the details in the chat window where it is saved. Ensure that it is acknowledged to higher that the WARNO has been received.

2. Whenever a CNSE is triggered inform the OPSO/AOPSO. This is to be done via phone and then written down so the OPSO can brief higher as required.

3. When told to "call away the CAT" you are to ring the bridge and BWC and inform them to announce over the 1MC that the CAT will assemble at time X – guidance received from OPSO/AOPSO

4. During a confirmation brief, the watch officer that will be on duty is to attend and is responsible for drafting the CONOPs to send to higher – this is to be in conjunction with the AOPSO (this can be started after the CAT II brief and finalized after the CAT I brief.

5. The night watch officer is responsible for cleaning the day up – this includes finishing briefs, powerpoints and most importantly the night watch officer is responsible for compiling the S3 and orientation component of O&I for 0800h.

Default Watch Computer Requirements

Watch Clerk

- C2PC
- Chat
- Data Log Spreadsheet
- Google Earth with Blue Force Tracker Overlay

Watch Chief

- Chat
- Exec Check Power Point
- Quadchart Timeline
- Email

Watch Officer

- Chat (LFOC chat room, Ship chat room, as a minimum)
- C2PC
- Watch Officer Report for last 24 hours
- Email

Chap 6

N. Daily Meetings

Daily Meetings

BUBBAS- 0900 daily

a. Purpose-Synchronize, plan and create operations plan for the next 72 hours based on Commander's guidance.

b. Attendees-MEU OpsO, N3, TACRON, MEU S-4, N-4, MSE rep, Ships reps (some via VTC), MEU air rep, Fires rep, MEU Medical rep

Log Sync-0900 daily

a. Purpose-synchronize internal and external logistic requirements to included ship to shore movement and personnel movement (PMCS)

b. Attendees-S4A, CCO, Embark, TACRON, MEU transportation coordinator, Ammunition chief, MSE S-4 reps,

APB (Air Planning Board) 1000 daily

a. Purpose-Identify air requirements, allocate air assets and create air plan for up to 72 hours.

b. Attendees-TACRON, ships air ops, ACE rep, MEU air rep, deck handler, MEU S-4, CCO, PHIBRON N-3 rep

See pp. 2-6 to 2-7 for further discussion and briefing template for a daily operations/ intelligence brief.

Appendices & Reference

O. Major Marine Corps Ground Equipment

Ref: http://www.marines.com/operating-forces/equipment/vehicles

LAV

Marine Light Armored Vehicles combine speed, maneuverability and firepower to perform a variety of functions, including security, command and control, reconnaissance and assault.

AAV-7

The AAV-7A1 is used to land the surface assault elements of the landing force to inland objectives and to conduct mechanized operations and related combat support in subsequent mechanized operations ashore.

M1A1 Abrams Tank

The principal battle tank of the Marine Corps, the M1A1 provides armor-protected firepower in support of Marine ground forces.

HMMWV

Marine HMMWVs are multipurpose vehicles, serving such functions as command and control, troop transport, shelter carrier, towed weapons mover, armament carrier, TOW missile system carrier and ambulance.

MRAP

With V-shaped hulls, raised chassis and armored plating, the Mine Resistant Ambush Protected Vehicle (MRAP) has proven to be the single most effective counter to Improvised Explosive Devices (IEDs).

MATV

Smaller, lighter and faster than the Mine Resistant Ambush Protected (MRAP) vehicle, the MATV has become the Marine Corps' off-road vehicle of choice, ideally suited for operating in mountainous terrain.

Assault Breacher Vehicle (ABV)

Built on the chassis of a M1A1 Abrams Tank, the tracked ABV is equipped with a mine-clearing plow, a .50 cal machine gun and a device that fires a rocket-propelled line of C4 explosives up to 150 yards.

HIMARS

Transportable by the KC-130, the High Mobility Artillery Rocket System (HIMARS) is the Marine Corps' most advanced artillery system, accurately engaging targets over great distances and under all weather conditions.

MTVR

With a highly survivable armor package, off-road mission profile and large cargo and crew compartment, the MTVR brings Marines and supplies to the fight fast, even in the most austere environments.

Chap 7

Execution Checklists

The Execution Checklist is a written description of the major events associated with the mission, listed in the sequence in which the ME Commander expects them to occur.

Execution Checklists are both "Situational Awareness (SA)" tools and a means through which commanders may execute command and control of the mission.

By no means does the execution checklist substitute for timely combat reporting IAW standard NATO/MEU formats; however the brevity codes on the execution checklist are tools for Communications Security (COMSEC), reducing the incidences and duration of broadcasts.

Events on the execution checklist may indicate that preconditions for mission execution have been met ("Line 1: Host nation vehicles awaiting R&S at insert LZ", for example, might have to occur before the MEU would insert forces) or they might serve as triggers for other events. An example trigger event might be "Line 7: Raid force departing ORP," which may trigger the launch of on-call extract aircraft that held on deck awaiting a code word to launch.

Execution Checklist formulation is an integral part of planning and briefing a mission. While designing the concept of the operation, commanders must identify the key events that best explain the flow of the mission and need to be known by mission participants and those mission representatives on watch in the LFOC.

Prior to confirming the plan, the execution checklist should be reviewed with the MEU commander and the major mission participants to ensure that the events are well-understood. Trigger events, in particular must be understood to mean the same thing by all mission participants.

When executing the mission, radio operators will be careful to use the "line number" rather than the code-word itself to talk over events that have not yet occurred. "Requesting status of Line 7" is appropriate---while "What time do you think you'll have 'Jaguars'?" risks causing confusion if the word is heard on the net before the event happens.

Generic execution checklists describe what might occur in a typical sequence for a given mission profile. Execution checklists should be customized to ensure they reflect the details of the specific mission they describe. Commanders may remove lines that do not apply to the mission and add lines that better describe the specifics of the mission being executed. Commanders will complete the checklist with the mission specifics of the nets over which the events will be reported, the station from and to whom the report will be made, to whom the item should be passed and the expected time of the event if the mission proceeds as planned. The execution checklist is incomplete if these entries are not made.

Naming Conventions for Execution Checklists

	Event	Words	Remarks	Page
I.	Amphibious Raid (Heliborne)	NFL Teams	Do not use CARDINALS, EAGLES, FALCONS, GIANTS, PANTHERS, RAVENS or SEAHAWKS	7-3
	Amphibious Assault	USMC Commandants	Do not use GRAY, GREENE, RUSSELL, SHEPHERD or WILSON	
II.	Amphibious Raid (LRHR)	NCAA Teams	Do not use bird or professional team names	7-4
III.	Amphibious Raid (Mechanized)	NBA Teams	Do not use HAWKS or KINGS	7-5
IV.	Amphibious Raid (Motorized)	NHL Teams	Do not use DUCKS, KINGS, PENGUINS, PANTHERS or RANGERS	7-5
V.	Forward Command Element (FCE) and Noncombatant Evacuation Operation (NEO)	American and European Countries	Do not use RUSSIA	7-6
VI.	Humanitarian Assistance Survey Team (HAST) and Humanitarian Assistance/Disaster Relief Operations (HADR)	Snacks	Do not use MARS	7-7
VII.	MAGTF CBRN CM	Greek and Roman Gods	Do not use MARS	7-8
VIII.	Mass Casualty Response	U.S. Presidents	Use only one ADAMS, BUSH, CLEVELAND, HARRISON, JOHNSON and ROOSEVELT; Do not use FORD, LINCOLN, WASHINGTON or WILSON	7-8
IX.	MSOC - Direct Action (DA)	Types of Wood	Do not use CHESTNUT, CHERRY or WALNUT	7-9
X.	MSOC - Visit, Board, Search and Seizure (VBSS)	Breeds of Dogs	Do not use BRITNEY, RUSSELL or SHEPHERD	7-9
XI(a).	R&S Mission I	Rock Bands	Do not use EAGLES	7-10
XI(b).	R&S Mission II	Female Names		7-10
XI(c).	R&S Mission III	Musical Instruments		7-11
XII(a).	Tactical Recovery of Aircraft and Personnel (TRAP/Air)	MLB Teams	Do not use BLUEJAYS, CARDINALS, GIANTS, MARLINS, ORIOLES or RANGERS	7-11
XII(b).	Tactical Recovery of Aircraft and Personnel (TRAP/Surface)	NJ Counties		7-12

Execution Checklists

I. Amphibious Raid (HELO)

EXECUTION CHECKLIST FOR [DTG] AMPHIBIOUS RAID (HELO) ISO [EXERCISE/OPERATION]										
DP	#	EVENT/SITUATION	RPT	CODEWORD	SCHED TIME	ACTUAL TIME	NET	FROM	TO	REMARKS
	1	FORCE LAUNCHED	M	BEARS			LFCMD3	AMC	LFOC	
	2	FEET DRY	M	BENGALS			LFCMD3	AMC	LFOC	
	3	ARRIVE LZ	M	BILLS			LFCMD3	AMC	LFOC	
	4	LZ SECURE	M	BRONCOS			MEUCMD1	MC	LFOC	
	5	INSERT COMPL	M	BROWNS			LFCMD3	AMC	LFOC	
	6	MOVING TO OBJ AREA	M	BUCCANEERS			MEUCMD1	MC	LFOC	
	7	RF/R&S L/U COMPL	M	CHARGERS			MEUCMD1	MC	LFOC	
	8	ORP ESTAB	M	CHIEFS			MEUCMD1	MC	LFOC	
	9	DEPARTING ORP	M	COLTS			MEUCMD1	MC	LFOC	
	10	CAS ON STATION	M	COWBOYS			LFCMD3	EFL	LFOC	
	11	COMMENCED ACTIONS ON THE OBJ	M	DOLPHINS			MEUCMD1	MC	LFOC	
	12	OBJ SECURED/COMMENCING SSE	M	FORTY-NINERS			MEUCMD1	MC	LFOC	
	13	CAS OFF STATION	M	JAGUARS			LFCMD3	EFL	LFOC	
	14	SSE COMPL/SPOTREP TO FOLLOW	M	JETS			MEUCMD1	MC	LFOC	
	15	MOVING TO EXTRACT POINT	M	LIONS			MEUCMD1	MC	LFOC	
	16	MACO COMPL/READY FOR EXTRACT	M	PACKERS			MEUCMD1	MC	LFOC	
	17	COMMENCING EXTRACT	M	PATRIOTS			LFCMD3	AMC	LFOC	
	18	EXTRACT COMPL	M	RAIDERS			LFCMD3	AMC	LFOC	
	19	FEET WET	M	RAMS			LFCMD3	AMC	LFOC	
	20	FORCE RECOVERED	M	REDSKINS			PHONE	MC	LFOC	
	21	MISSION ACCOMPLISHED	M	SAINTS			PHONE	MC	LFOC	
	22	AS NEEDED		STEELERS						
	23	AS NEEDED		TEXANS						
	24	AS NEEDED		TITANS						
	25	AS NEEDED		VIKINGS						

BRIEF BY EXCEPTION (Applicable to ALL Execution Checklists)

DP	#	EVENT/SITUATION	RPT	CODEWORD	SCHED TIME	ACTUAL TIME	NET	FROM	TO	REMARKS
	26	TIME CHANGE		ROLEX						
	27	IN CONTACT (GROUND)		EARTHQUAKE						
	28	IN CONTACT (AIR)		HAIL						
	29	IN CONTACT (IDF)		SNOWSTORM						
	30	AIRCRAFT/VEH DOWN (MECH)		DASH/VEH # BENT						
	31	AIRCRAFT/VEH DOWN (ENEMY)		DASH/VEH # DOWN						
	32	ABORTING MISSION		ABORT X 3						
	33	REQUEST TRAP FORCE		TRAP						
	34	PLANNED L/U DID NOT OCCUR		BAD DATE						
	35	EXECUTING EMERG ASSAULT		GERONIMO						
	36	INDIV/MATERIAL NOT FOUND		DRY HOLE						
	37	IED/BOOBY TRAP FOUND		RED ROCKET						
	39	MISSION COMPROMISED (CIV)		SPOOKED						
	40	MISSION COMPROMISED (ENEMY)		HAUNTED						
	41	SECURITY SITUATION UNSTABLE		CLUSTER						
	42	REQUEST REINFORCEMENT		KITCHEN SINK						
	43	L/U WITH REINFORCEMENT COMPLETE		HANDSHAKE						
	44	REQUEST MEDEVAC (x # PAX)		CASEVAC #						
	45	REQUEST EMERG EXTRACT		BUGOUT						
	46	EXECUTING E&E (TO POINT #)		HAIL MARY #						
	47	AT E&E POINT #		END ZONE #						
	48	SUSTAINED SIM CASUALTY (x #)		CHERRYPICKER #						
	49	CASEVAC LAUNCHED								
	50	CASEVAC ON-STATION								
	51	CASEVAC RETURNED TO BASE								

II. Long Range Helo Raid (LRHR)

EXECUTION CHECKLIST FOR [DTG] LRHR ISO [EXERCISE/OPERATION]										
DP	#	EVENT/SITUATION	RPT	CODEWORD	SCHED TIME	ACTUAL TIME	NET	FROM	TO	REMARKS
	1	MMT LAUNCHED	M	AGGIES			LFCMD3	AMC	LFOC	
	2	MMT FEET DRY	M	AZTECS			LFCMD3	AMC	LFOC	
	3	MMT ARRIVE DZ/LZ	M	BADGERS			LFCMD3	AMC	LFOC	
	4	MMT DZ/LZ SECURED	M	BEARCATS			MEUCM D1	MMT	LFOC	
	5	MMT INSERT COMPL	M	BEAVERS			LFCMD3	AMC	LFOC	
	6	MMT OPERATIONAL	M	BLAZERS			MEUCM D1	MMT	LFOC	
	7	FARP LAUNCHED	M	BLUE DEMONS					LFOC	
	8	FARP ARRIVE ISB	M	BLUE DEVILS			MEUCM D1	FARP	LFOC	
	9	FARP/SUPPORT CRAFT L/U COMPL	M	BLUE RAIDERS			MEUCM D1	FARP	LFOC	
	10	FARP DEPART ISB	M	BOBCATS					LFOC	
	11	FARP ARRIVE FARP	M	BOILERMAKERS			MEUCM D1	FARP	LFOC	
	12	FARP/MMT L/U COMPL	M	BRUINS			MEUCM D1	FARP	LFOC	
	13	FARP OPERATIONAL	M	BUCKEYES			MEUCM D1	FARP	LFOC	
	14	RF LAUNCHED	M	BUFFALOES			LFCMD3	AMC	LFOC	
	15	RF FEET DRY	M	BULLDOGS			LFCMD3	AMC	LFOC	
	16	RF ARRIVE FARP	M	CHIPPEWAS			LFCMD3	AMC	LFOC	
	17	RF/FARP L/U COMPL	M	COMMODORES			MEUCM D1	MC	LFOC	
	18	RF DEPART FARP	M	CORNHUSKERS			LFCMD3	AMC	LFOC	
	19	RF ARRIVE LZ	M	COUGARS			LFCMD3	AMC	LFOC	
	20	RF LZ SECURE	M	CRIMSON TIDE			MEUCM D1	MC	LFOC	
	21	RF INSERT COMPL	M	CYCLONES			LFCMD3	AMC	LFOC	
	22	RF MOVING TO OBJ AREA	M	DEMON DEACONS			MEUCM D1	MC	LFOC	
	23	RF/R&S L/U COMPL	M	FIGHTING ILLINI			MEUCM D1	MC	LFOC	
	24	RF ORP ESTAB	M	FIGHTING IRISH			MEUCM D1	MC	LFOC	
	25	RF DEPARTING ORP	M	FRIARS			MEUCM D1	MC	LFOC	
	26	RF CAS ON STATION	M	GAMECOCKS			LFCMD3	EFL	LFOC	
	27	RF COMMENCED ACTIONS ON THE OBJ	M	GATORS			MEUCM D1	MC	LFOC	
	28	RF OBJ SECURED/COMMENCING SSE	M	GOLDEN BEARS			MEUCM D1	MC	LFOC	
	29	RF CAS OFF STATION	M	GOLDEN FLASHES			LFCMD3	EFL	LFOC	
	30	RF SSE COMPL/SPOTREP TO FOLLOW	M	GOLDEN GOPHERS			MEUCM D1	MC	LFOC	
	31	RF MOVING TO EXTRACT POINT	M	GOLDEN KNIGHTS			MEUCM D1	MC	LFOC	
	32	RF MACO COMPL/READY FOR EXTRACT	M	GREEN WAVE			MEUCM D1	MC	LFOC	
	33	RF COMMENCING EXTRACT	M	HAWKEYES			LFCMD3	AMC	LFOC	
	34	RF EXTRACT COMPL	M	HILLTOPPERS			LFCMD3	AMC	LFOC	
	35	RF RETURN FARP	M	HOKIES			LFCMD3	AMC	LFOC	
	36	RF DEPART FARP	M	HOOSIERS			LFCMD3	AMC	LFOC	
	37	RF FEET WET	M	HORNED FROGS			LFCMD3	AMC	LFOC	
	38	RF RECOVERED	M	HOYAS			PHONE	MC	LFOC	
	39	RF MISSION ACCOMPLISHED	M	HUSKIES			PHONE	MC	LFOC	
	40	SUPPORT CRAFT ARRIVE FARP	M	LOBOS			MEUCM D1	FARP	LFOC	
	41	FARP CLOSE-OUT COMPL	M	LONGHORNS			MEUCM D1	FARP	LFOC	
	42	FARP/MMT DEPART FARP	M	MEAN GREEN			MEUCM D1	FARP	LFOC	
	43	FARP/MMT ARRIVE ISB	M	MINERS			MEUCM D1	FARP	LFOC	
	44	FARP/MMT DEPART ISB	M	MOUNTAINEERS					LFOC	
	45	FARP/MMT FEET WET	M	MUSTANGS					LFOC	
	46	FARP/MMT RECOVERED	M	NITTANY LIONS			PHONE	FARP	LFOC	
	47	FARP/MMT MISSION ACCOMPLISHED	M	ORANGEMEN			PHONE	FARP	LFOC	
	48	AS NEEDED		RAGIN CAJUNS						
	49	AS NEEDED		RAZORBACKS						
	50	AS NEEDED		REBELS						
	51	AS NEEDED		RED RAIDERS						

III. Amphibious Raid (Mech)

EXECUTION CHECKLIST FOR [DTG] AMPHIBIOUS RAID (MECH) ISO [EXERCISE/OPERATION]										
DP	#	EVENT/SITUATION	RPT	CODEWORD	SCHED TIME	ACTUAL TIME	NET	FROM	TO	REMARKS
	1	AAV'S LAUNCHED	M	BOBCATS			BOAT B	LSD	TACLOG	
	2	AAV'S FEET DRY	M	BUCKS			BOAT B	LSD	TACLOG	
	3	AAV'S ARRIVE BLS	M	BULLS			BOAT B	LSD	TACLOG	
	4	BLS SECURE	M	CAVALIERS			MEUCMD1	MC	LFOC	
	5	M1A1'S LAUNCHED	M	CELTICS			BOAT B	LSD	TACLOG	
	6	M1A1'S FEET DRY	M	CLIPPERS			BOAT B	LSD	TACLOG	
	7	MECH FORCE INSERT COMPL	M	GRIZZLIES			MEUCMD1	MC	LFOC	
	8	MOVING TO OBJ AREA	M	HEAT			MEUCMD1	MC	LFOC	
	9	RF/R&S L/U COMPL	M	HORNETS			MEUCMD1	MC	LFOC	
	10	ORP ESTAB	M	JAZZ			MEUCMD1	MC	LFOC	
	11	DEPARTING ORP	M	KNICKS			MEUCMD1	MC	LFOC	
	12	CAS ON STATION	M	LAKERS			LFCMD3	EFL	LFOC	
	13	COMMENCED ACTIONS ON THE OBJ	M	MAGIC			MEUCMD1	MC	LFOC	
	14	OBJ SECURED/COMMENCING SSE	M	MAVERICKS			MEUCMD1	MC	LFOC	
	15	CAS OFF STATION	M	NETS			LFCMD3	EFL	LFOC	
	16	SSE COMPL/SPOTREP TO FOLLOW	M	NUGGETS			MEUCMD1	MC	LFOC	
	17	MOVING TO EXTRACT POINT	M	PACERS			MEUCMD1	MC	LFOC	
	18	MACO COMPL/READY FOR EXTRACT	M	PISTONS			MEUCMD1	MC	LFOC	
	19	M1A1'S COMMENCING EXTRACT	M	RAPTORS			BOAT B	LSD	TACLOG	
	20	M1A1'S EXTRACT COMPL	M	ROCKETS			BOAT B	LSD	TACLOG	
	21	M1A1'S RECOVERED	M	SEVENTY-SIXERS			BOAT B	LSD	TACLOG	
	22	AAV'S FEET WET	M	SPURS			BOAT B	LSD	TACLOG	
	23	AAV'S RECOVERED	M	SUNS			BOAT B	LSD	TACLOG	
	24	MISSION ACCOMPLISHED	M	THUNDER			MEUCMD1	MC	LFOC	
	25	AS NEEDED		TIMBERWOLVES						
	26	AS NEEDED		TRAIL BLAZERS						
	27	AS NEEDED		WARRIORS						
	28	AS NEEDED		WIZARDS						

IV. Amphibious Raid (Motor)

EXECUTION CHECKLIST FOR [DTG] AMPHIBIOUS RAID (MOTOR) ISO [EXERCISE/OPERATION]										
DP	#	EVENT/SITUATION	RPT	CODEWORD	SCHED TIME	ACTUAL TIME	NET	FROM	TO	REMARKS
	1	MTVR'S LAUNCHED	M	BRUINS			BOAT B	LPD	TACLOG	
	2	MTVR'S FEET DRY	M	CANADIENS			BOAT B	LPD	TACLOG	
	3	MOTOR FORCE INSERT COMPL	M	CANUCKS			MEUCMD1	MC	LFOC	
	4	MOVING TO OBJ AREA	M	CAPITALS			MEUCMD1	MC	LFOC	
	5	RF/R&S L/U COMPL	M	COYOTES			MEUCMD1	MC	LFOC	
	6	ORP ESTAB	M	DEVILS			MEUCMD1	MC	LFOC	
	7	DEPARTING ORP	M	FLAMES			MEUCMD1	MC	LFOC	
	8	CAS ON STATION	M	FLYERS			LFCMD3	EFL	LFOC	
	9	COMMENCED ACTIONS ON THE OBJ	M	HURRICANES			MEUCMD1	MC	LFOC	
	10	OBJ SECURED/COMMENCING SSE	M	ISLANDERS			MEUCMD1	MC	LFOC	
	11	CAS OFF STATION	M	LIGHTNING			LFCMD3	EFL	LFOC	
	12	SSE COMPL/SPOTREP TO FOLLOW	M	MAPLE LEAFS			MEUCMD1	MC	LFOC	
	13	MOVING TO EXTRACT POINT	M	MIGHTY			MEUCMD1	MC	LFOC	
	14	MACO COMPL/READY FOR EXTRACT	M	NORDIQUES			MEUCMD1	MC	LFOC	
	15	MTVR'S COMMENCING EXTRACT	M	NORTH STARS			BOAT B	LPD	TACLOG	
	16	MTVR'S EXTRACT COMPL	M	OILERS			BOAT B	LPD	TACLOG	
	17	MTVR'S RECOVERED	M	PREDATORS			BOAT B	LPD	TACLOG	
	18	CAAT/LAR COMMENCING EXTRACT	M	RED WINGS			PHONE	TACLOG	LFOC	
	19	CAAT/LAR EXTRACT COMPL	M	SABRES			PHONE	TACLOG	LFOC	
	20	CAAT/LAR RECOVERED	M	SENATORS			PHONE	TACLOG	LFOC	
	21	MISSION ACCOMPLISHED	M	SHARKS			MEUCMD1	MC	LFOC	
	22	AS NEEDED		STARS						
	23	AS NEEDED		THRASHERS						
	24	AS NEEDED		WHALERS						
	25	AS NEEDED		WILD						

V. FCE/NEO

EXECUTION CHECKLIST FOR [DTG] FCE/NEO ISO [EXERCISE/OPERATION]										
DP	#	EVENT/SITUATION	RPT	CODEWORD	SCHED TIME	ACTUAL TIME	NET	FROM	TO	REMARKS
	1	FCE LAUNCHED	M	ALBANIA					LFOC	
	2	FCE FEET DRY	M	ARGENTINA					LFOC	
	3	FCE ARRIVE LZ/BLS	M	AUSTRIA					LFOC	
	4	FCE INSERT COMPL	M	BAHAMAS					LFOC	
	5	FCE/CONSUL L/U COMPL	M	BARBADOS			MEU CMD1	FCE	LFOC	
	6	FCE MOVING TO OBJ AREA	M	BELARUS			MEU CMD1	FCE	LFOC	
	7	FCE OPERATIONAL	M	BELGIUM			MEU CMD1	FCE	LFOC	
	8	NEO FORCE LAUNCHED	M	BELIZE					LFOC	
	9	NEO FEET DRY	M	BOLIVIA					LFOC	
	10	NEO ARRIVE LZ/BLS	M	BOSNIA					LFOC	
	11	NEO LZ/BLS SECURE	M	BRAZIL			MEU CMD1	MC	LFOC	
	12	NEO INSERT COMPL	M	BULGARIA					LFOC	
	13	NEO MOVING TO OBJ AREA	M	CANADA			MEU CMD1	MC	LFOC	
	14	NEO/FCE L/U COMPL	M	CHILE			MEU CMD1	MC	LFOC	
	15	NEO CAS ON STATION	M	COLUMBIA			LF CMD3	EFL	LFOC	
	16	NEO COMMENCED ACTIONS ON THE OBJ	M	COSTA RICA			MEU CMD1	MC	LFOC	
	17	NEO OBJ SECURED/COMMENCING ECC	M	CROATIA			MEU CMD1	MC	LFOC	
	18	NEO CAS OFF STATION	M	CUBA			LF CMD3	EFL	LFOC	
	19	NEO ECC COMPL/SPOTREP TO FOLLOW	M	DENMARK			MEU CMD1	MC	LFOC	
	20	NEO REQUEST EXTRACT OF AMCITS	M	ECUADOR			MEU CMD1	MC	LFOC	
	21	NEO EVAC CRAFT LAUNCHED	M	ESTONIA					LFOC	
	22	NEO EVAC CRAFT ARRIVE LZ/BLS	M	FINLAND			MEU CMD1	MC	LFOC	
	23	NEO FIRST WAVE AMCITS DEPART	M	FRANCE			MEU CMD1	MC	LFOC	
	24	NEO LAST WAVE AMCITS DEPART	M	GERMANY			MEU CMD1	MC	LFOC	
	25	NEO COMPL/SPOTREP TO FOLLOW	M	GREECE			MEU CMD1	MC	LFOC	
	26	NEO MOVING TO EXTRACT POINT	M	GRENADA			MEU CMD1	MC	LFOC	
	27	NEO MACO COMPL/READY FOR EXTRACT	M	GUATEMALA			MEU CMD1	MC	LFOC	
	28	NEO COMMENCING EXTRACT	M	GUYANA					LFOC	
	29	NEO EXTRACT COMPL	M	HAITI					LFOC	
	30	NEO FEET WET	M	HONDURAS					LFOC	
	31	NEO FORCE RECOVERED	M	HUNGARY			PHONE	MC	LFOC	
	32	NEO MISSION ACCOMPLISHED	M	ICELAND			PHONE	MC	LFOC	
	33	ISB FORCE LAUNCHED	M	IRELAND					LFOC	
	34	ISB FEET DRY	M	ITALY					LFOC	
	35	ISB ARRIVE LZ/BLS	M	JAMAICA					LFOC	
	36	ISB LZ/BLS SECURE	M	KOSOVO			MEU CMD1	ISB	LFOC	
	37	ISB INSERT COMPL	M	LATVIA					LFOC	
	38	ISB MOVING TO OBJ AREA	M	LITHUANIA			MEU CMD1	ISB	LFOC	
	39	ISB/R&S L/U COMPL	M	LUXEMBOURG			MEU CMD1	ISB	LFOC	
	40	ISB ORP ESTAB	M	MACEDONIA			MEU CMD1	ISB	LFOC	
	41	ISB DEPARTING ORP	M	MALTA			MEU CMD1	ISB	LFOC	
	42	ISB CAS ON STATION	M	MEXICO			LF CMD3	EFL	LFOC	
	43	ISB COMMENCED ACTIONS ON THE OBJ	M	MOLDOVA			MEU CMD1	ISB	LFOC	
	44	ISB OBJ SECURED/SPOTREP TO FOLLOW	M	MONTENEGRO			MEU CMD1	ISB	LFOC	
	45	ISB CAS OFF STATION	M	NETHERLANDS			LF CMD3	EFL	LFOC	
	46	ISB OPERATIONAL	M	NICARAGUA			MEU CMD1	ISB	LFOC	
	47	ISB SUPPORT EVAC CRAFT ARRIVE	M	NORWAY			MEU CMD1	ISB	LFOC	
	48	ISB FIRST WAVE AMCITS ARRIVE ISB	M	PANAMA			MEUCMD1	ISB	LFOC	
	49	ISB LAST WAVE AMCITS ARRIVE ISB	M	PARAGUAY			MEU CMD1	ISB	LFOC	
	50	ISB FIRST WAVE AMCITS DEPART ISB	M	PERU			MEUCMD1	ISB	LFOC	
	51	ISB LAST WAVE AMCITS DEPART ISB	M	POLAND			MEU CMD1	ISB	LFOC	
	52	ISB OPS COMPL/SPOTREP TO FOLLOW	M	PORTUGAL			MEU CMD1	ISB	LFOC	
	53	ISB MOVING TO EXTRACT POINT	M	ROMANIA			MEU CMD1	ISB	LFOC	
	54	ISB MACO COMPL/READY FOR EXTRACT	M	SERBIA			MEU CMD1	ISB	LFOC	
	55	ISB COMMENCING EXTRACT	M	SLOVAKIA					LFOC	
	56	ISB EXTRACT COMPL	M	SLOVENIA					LFOC	

DP	#	EVENT/SITUATION	RPT	CODEWORD	SCHED TIME	ACTUAL TIME	NET	FROM	TO	REMARKS
	57	ISB FEET WET	M	SPAIN					LFOC	
	58	ISB FORCE RECOVERED	M	SURINAME			PHONE	ISB	LFOC	
	59	ISB MISSION ACCOMPLISHED	M	SWEDEN			PHONE	ISB	LFOC	
	60	AS NEEDED		SWITZERLAND						
	61	AS NEEDED		UKRAINE						
	62	AS NEEDED		URUGUAY						
	63	AS NEEDED		VENEZUELA						

VI. HAST/HADR

EXECUTION CHECKLIST FOR [DTG] HAST/HADR OPS ISO [EXERCISE/OPERATION]										
DP	#	EVENT/SITUATION	RPT	CODEWORD	SCHED TIME	ACTUAL TIME	NET	FROM	TO	REMARKS
	1	HAST LAUNCHED	M	ALMOND JOY					LFOC	
	2	HAST FEET DRY	M	BABY RUTH					LFOC	
	3	HAST ARRIVE LZ/BLS	M	BUGLES					LFOC	
	4	HAST INSERT COMPL	M	BUTTERFINGER					LFOC	
	5	HAST/USAID L/U COMPL	M	CARAMELLO			MEU CMD1	HAST	LFOC	
	6	HAST MOVING TO OBJ AREA	M	CHARMS			MEU CMD1	HAST	LFOC	
	7	HAST OPERATIONAL	M	CHEETOS			MEU CMD1	HAST	LFOC	
	8	SECURITY FORCE LAUNCHED	M	CHEEZIT					LFOC	
	9	SF FORCE FEET DRY	M	COMBOS					LFOC	
	10	SF FORCE ARRIVE BLS	M	DORITOS					LFOC	
	11	BLS SECURE	M	FUNYUNS			MEU CMD1	SFC	LFOC	
	12	HA FORCE LAUNCHED	M	GRANDMA'S			BOAT B	LPD	TACLOG	
	13	HA FEET DRY	M	HOT FRIES			BOAT B	LPD	TACLOG	
	14	HA ARRIVE BLS	M	JOLLY RANCHER			BOAT B	LPD	TACLOG	
	15	HA INSERT COMPL	M	KIT KAT			MEU CMD1	MC	LFOC	
	16	HA MOVING TO OBJ AREA	M	LAYS			MEU CMD1	MC	LFOC	
	17	HA/HAST L/U COMPL	M	M&MS			MEU CMD1	MC	LFOC	
	18	HA COMMENCED ACTIONS ON THE OBJ	M	MILK DUDS			MEU CMD1	MC	LFOC	
	19	HA COMPL/SPOTREP TO FOLLOW	M	MILKY WAY			MEU CMD1	MC	LFOC	
	20	HA MOVING TO EXTRACT POINT	M	MOUNDS			MEU CMD1	MC	LFOC	
	21	HA MACO COMPL/READY FOR EXTRACT	M	MR. GOODBAR			MEU CMD1	MC	LFOC	
	22	HA COMMENCING EXTRACT	M	MUSKETEERS			BOAT B	LPD	TACLOG	
	23	HA EXTRACT COMPL	M	NUTRAGEOUS			BOAT B	LPD	TACLOG	
	24	HA FEET WET	M	OH HENRY			BOAT B	LPD	TACLOG	
	25	HA FORCE RECOVERED	M	PAYDAY			MEU CMD1	MC	LFOC	
	26	SF OPS COMPL/SPOTREP TO FOLLOW	M	POP TART			MEU CMD1	SFC	LFOC	
	27	SF MOVING TO EXTRACT POINT	M	PRINGLES			MEU CMD1	SFC	LFOC	
	28	SF MACO COMPL/READY FOR EXTRACT	M	RAISINETS			MEU CMD1	SFC	LFOC	
	29	SF COMMENCING EXTRACT	M	REESE'S						
	30	SF EXTRACT COMPL	M	ROLO						
	31	SF FEET WET	M	RUFFLES						
	32	SF FORCE RECOVERED	M	SKITTLES				SFC	LFOC	
	33	HA MISSION ACCOMPLISHED	M	SNICKERS			MEU CMD1	MC	LFOC	
	34	AS NEEDED		STARBURSTS						
	35	AS NEEDED		TWIX						
	36	AS NEEDED		TWIZZLER						
	37	AS NEEDED		WHOPPERS						

VII. CBRN

EXECUTION CHECKLIST FOR [DTG] MAGTF CBRN CM OPS ISO [EXERCISE/OPERATION]										
DP	#	EVENT/SITUATION	RPT	CODEWORD	SCHED TIME	ACTUAL TIME	NET	FROM	TO	REMARKS
	1	FORCE LAUNCHED	M	APHRODITE					LFOC	
	2	FEET DRY	M	APOLLO					LFOC	
	3	ARRIVE LZ/BLS	M	ARES					LFOC	
	4	INSERT COMPL	M	ARTEMIS					LFOC	
	5	MOVING TO OBJ AREA	M	ATHENA			MEU CMD1	TC	LFOC	
	6	E-CBRN/MC L/U COMPL	M	BACCHUS			MEU CMD1	TC	LFOC	
	7	DECONTAMINATION SITE ESTAB	M	CERES			MEU CMD1	TC	LFOC	
	8	ASSESSMENT TEAMS LAUNCHED	M	CRONUS			MEU CMD1	TC	LFOC	
	9	CONTAMINATION FOUND + TYPE (CBRN)	M	DEMETER			MEU CMD1	TC	LFOC	
	10	ASSESSMENT COMPL/ID TEAM LAUNCHED	M	DIANA			MEU CMD1	TC	LFOC	
	11	AGENT IDENTIFIED	M	DIONYSUS			MEU CMD1	TC	LFOC	
	12	SOURCE LOCATED	M	HADES			MEU CMD1	TC	LFOC	
	13	CASUALTY FOUND	M	HEPHAESTUS			MEU CMD1	TC	LFOC	
	14	FIRST CASUALTY ARRIVE DECON SITE	M	HERA			MEU CMD1	TC	LFOC	
	15	LAST CASUALTY ARRIVE DECON SITE	M	HERMES			MEU CMD1	TC	LFOC	
	16	SSE COMPL/SPOTREP TO FOLLOW	M	HESTIA			MEU CMD1	TC	LFOC	
	17	TEAM DECONTAMINATION COMPL	M	JUNO			MEU CMD1	TC	LFOC	
	18	DECON SITE CLOSE-OUT COMPL	M	JUPITER			MEU CMD1	TC	LFOC	
	19	MOVING TO EXTRACT POINT	M	MERCURY			MEU CMD1	TC	LFOC	
	20	MACO COMPL/READY FOR EXTRACT	M	MINERVA			MEU CMD1	TC	LFOC	
	21	COMMENCING EXTRACT	M	NEPTUNE					LFOC	
	22	EXTRACT COMPL	M	PLUTO					LFOC	
	23	FEET WET	M	POSEIDON					LFOC	
	24	FORCE RECOVERED	M	SATURN			PHONE	TC	LFOC	
	25	MISSION ACCOMPLISHED	M	URANUS			PHONE	TC	LFOC	
	26	AS NEEDED		VENUS						
	27	AS NEEDED		VESTA						
	28	AS NEEDED		VULCAN						
	29	AS NEEDED		ZEUS						

VIII. Mass Casualties

EXECUTION CHECKLIST FOR [DTG] MASS CASUALTY OPS ISO [EXERCISE/OPERATION]										
DP	#	EVENT/SITUATION	RPT	CODEWORD	SCHED TIME	ACTUAL TIME	NET	FROM	TO	REMARKS
	1	FORCE LAUNCHED	M	ADAMS					LFOC	
	2	FEET DRY	M	ARTHUR					LFOC	
	3	ARRIVE LZ/BLS	M	BUCHANAN					LFOC	
	4	INSERT COMPL	M	BUSH					LFOC	
	5	MOVING TO OBJ AREA	M	CARTER			MEU CMD1	TC	LFOC	
	6	MASCAS/MC L/U COMPL	M	CLEVELAND			MEU CMD1	TC	LFOC	
	7	MASCAS SITE ESTAB	M	CLINTON			MEU CMD1	TC	LFOC	
	8	CASUALTY FOUND	M	COOLIDGE			MEU CMD1	TC	LFOC	
	9	FIRST CASUALTY ARRIVE MASCAS SITE	M	EISENHOWER			MEU CMD1	TC	LFOC	
	10	LAST CASUALTY ARRIVE MASCAS SITE	M	FILLMORE			MEU CMD1	TC	LFOC	
	11	TRIAGE COMPL/SPOTREP TO FOLLOW	M	GARFIELD			MEU CMD1	TC	LFOC	
	12	REQUEST EXTRACT OF PAX	M	GRANT			MEU CMD1	TC	LFOC	
	13	EVAC CRAFT LAUNCHED	M	HARDING					LFOC	
	14	EVAC CRAFT ARRIVE LZ/BLS	M	HARRISON			MEU CMD1	TC	LFOC	
	15	FIRST WAVE PAX DEPART	M	HAYES			MEUCMD1	TC	LFOC	
	16	LAST WAVE PAX DEPART	M	HOOVER			MEUCMD1	TC	LFOC	
	17	EVAC COMPL/SPOTREP TO FOLLOW	M	JACKSON			MEUCMD1	TC	LFOC	
	18	MASCAS SITE CLOSE-OUT COMPL	M	JEFFERSON			MEUCMD1	TC	LFOC	
	19	MOVING TO EXTRACT POINT	M	JOHNSON			MEUCMD1	TC	LFOC	
	20	MACO COMPL/READY FOR EXTRACT	M	KENNEDY			MEUCMD1	TC	LFOC	
	21	COMMENCING EXTRACT	M	MADISON					LFOC	
	22	EXTRACT COMPL	M	MCKINLEY					LFOC	
	23	FEET WET	M	MONROE					LFOC	
	24	FORCE RECOVERED	M	NIXON			PHONE	TC	LFOC	
	25	MISSION ACCOMPLISHED	M	PIERCE			PHONE	TC	LFOC	
	26	AS NEEDED		POLK						
	27	AS NEEDED		REAGAN						
	28	AS NEEDED		ROOSEVELT						
	29	AS NEEDED		TAFT						

IX. Direct Action

EXECUTION CHECKLIST FOR [DTG] DIRECT ACTION ISO [EXERCISE/OPERATION]										
DP	#	EVENT/SITUATION	RPT	CODEWORD	SCHED TIME	ACTUAL TIME	NET	FROM	TO	REMARKS
	1	FORCE LAUNCHED	M	ASH					LFOC	
	2	FEET DRY	M	ASPEN					LFOC	
	3	ARRIVE LZ/BLS	M	BEECH					LFOC	
	4	LZ/BLS SECURE	M	BIRCH			MEU CMD1	MC	LFOC	
	5	INSERT COMPL	M	CEDAR					LFOC	
	6	MOVING TO OBJ AREA	M	CYPRESS			MEU CMD1	MC	LFOC	
	7	DA/R&S L/U COMPL	M	DOGWOOD			MEU CMD1	MC	LFOC	
	8	ORP ESTAB	M	ELM			MEU CMD1	MC	LFOC	
	9	DEPARTING ORP	M	FIR			MEU CMD1	MC	LFOC	
	10	CAS ON STATION	M	HICKORY			LFCMD3	EFL	LFOC	
	11	COMMENCED ACTIONS ON THE OBJ	M	HOLLY			MEU CMD1	MC	LFOC	
	12	OBJ SECURED/COMMENCING SSE	M	JUNIPER			MEU CMD1	MC	LFOC	
	13	CAS OFF STATION	M	MAGNOLIA			LFCMD3	EFL	LFOC	
	14	HVI KILLED/MATERIAL DESTROYED	M	JACKPOT			MEUCMD1	MC	LFOC	
	15	HVI CAPTURED/MATERIAL RECOVERED	M	MOSS			MEUCMD1	MC	LFOC	
	16	SSE COMPL/SPOTREP TO FOLLOW	M	MAPLE			MEUCMD1	MC	LFOC	
	17	MOVING TO EXTRACT POINT	M	OAK			MEUCMD1	MC	LFOC	
	18	MACO COMPL/READY FOR EXTRACT	M	PALM			MEUCMD1	MC	LFOC	
	19	COMMENCING EXTRACT	M	PINE					LFOC	
	20	EXTRACT COMPL	M	REDWOOD					LFOC	
	21	FEET WET	M	SEQUOIA					LFOC	
	22	FORCE RECOVERED	M	SPRUCE			PHONE	MC	LFOC	
	23	MISSION ACCOMPLISHED	M	SYCAMORE			PHONE	MC	LFOC	
	24	AS NEEDED		TUPELO						
	25	AS NEEDED		WILLOW						
	26	AS NEEDED		YUCCA						
	27	AS NEEDED								

X. Maritime Raid Force

EXECUTION CHECKLIST FOR [DTG] MRF ISO [EXERCISE/OPERATION]										
DP	#	EVENT/SITUATION	RPT	CODEWORD	SCHED TIME	ACTUAL TIME	NET	FROM	TO	REMARKS
	1	CCOI LOCATED	M	AFGHAN			PHONE	PHIBRON	LFOC	
	2	FORCE LAUNCHED	M	AKITA					LFOC	
	3	HQ ON SUPPORT SHIP/MEU SUPPORTED CMDR	M	BEAGLE			MEUCMD1	MC	LFOC	
	4	SUPPORT SHIP IN POSITION	M	BLOODHOUND			PHONE	PHIBRON	LFOC	
	5	DIVERSION COMPLETE	M	BOXER			LFCMD3	EFL	LFOC	
	6	SNIPERS IN POSITION	M	BULLDOG			LFCMD3	EFL	LFOC	
	7	SNIPER SHOTS COMPLETE	M	COLLIE			LFCMD3	EFL	LFOC	
	8	AE INSERT COMPLETE	M	DACHSHUND			MEUCMD1	MC	LFOC	
	9	KEY SPACES SECURED/SPOTREP TO FOLLOW	M	DALMATIAN			MEUCMD1	MC	LFOC	
	10	SHIP SECURED/COMMENCING SSE	M	DINGO			MEUCMD1	MC	LFOC	
	11	SSE COMPL/REQUEST PRIZE CREW	M	DOBERMAN			MEUCMD1	MC	LFOC	
	12	TURNOVER COMPL/MIOC SUPPORTED CMDR	M	GREAT DANE			MEUCMD1	MC	LFOC	
	13	AE MACO COMPL/READY FOR EXTRACT	M	GREYHOUND			MEUCMD1	MC	LFOC	
	14	AE COMMENCING EXTRACT	M	HOUND					LFOC	
	15	AE EXTRACT COMPL	M	HUSKY					LFOC	
	16	AE RECOVERED	M	MALAMUTE			PHONE	AEC	LFOC	
	17	DETAINEES/CARGO TO SHIP'S CO	M	MASTIFF			PHONE	AEC	LFOC	
	18	HQ MACO COMPL/READY FOR EXTRACT	M	PITBULL			MEUCMD1	MC	LFOC	
	19	HQ COMMENCING EXTRACT	M	POINTER					LFOC	
	20	HQ EXTRACT COMPL	M	RETRIEVER					LFOC	
	21	HQ RECOVERED	M	ROTTWEILER			PHONE	MC	LFOC	
	22	MISSION ACCOMPLISHED	M	SETTER			PHONE	MC	LFOC	
	23	AS NEEDED		SHEEPDOG						
	24	AS NEEDED		ST. BERNARD						
	25	AS NEEDED		TERRIER						
	26	AS NEEDED		WOLFHOUND						

XI(a). R&S I - Rock Bands

EXECUTION CHECKLIST FOR [DTG] R&S ISO [EXERCISE/OPERATION]										
DP	#	EVENT/SITUATION	RPT	CODEWORD	SCHED TIME	ACTUAL TIME	NET	FROM	TO	REMARKS
	1	TEAM LAUNCHED	M	AC/DC						
	2	FEET DRY	M	AEROSMITH						
	3	ARRIVE DZ/LZ/BLS	M	ALLMAN BROTHERS						
	4	DZ/LZ/BLS SECURE	M	BEATLES			MEU CMD1	TL	SARC	
	5	INSERT COMPL	M	BLACK SABBATH						
	6	MOVING TO OBJ AREA	M	BOSTON			MEU CMD1	TL	SARC	
	7	ORP ESTAB	M	CREAM			MEU CMD1	TL	SARC	
	8	DEPARTING ORP	M	DEF LEPPARD			MEU CMD1	TL	SARC	
	9	COMMENCED ACTIONS ON THE OBJ	M	DOORS			MEU CMD1	TL	SARC	
	10	L/U COMPL	M	FLEETWOOD MAC			MEU CMD1	TL	SARC	
	11	MOVING TO EXTRACT POINT	M	GRATEFUL DEAD			MEU CMD1	TL	SARC	
	12	MACO COMPL/READY FOR EXTRACT	M	LED ZEPPELIN			MEU CMD1	TL	SARC	
	13	COMMENCING EXTRACT	M	LYNYRD SKYNYRD			MEU CMD1	TL	SARC	
	14	EXTRACT COMPL	M	MOODY BLUES			MEU CMD1	TL	SARC	
	15	FEET WET	M	PINK FLOYD			MEU CMD1	TL	SARC	
	16	TEAM RECOVERED	M	ROLLING STONES			PHONE	TL	SARC	
	17	MISSION ACCOMPLISHED	M	RUSH			PHONE	TL	SARC	
	18	AS NEEDED		STYX						
	19	AS NEEDED		THE WHO						
	20	AS NEEDED		VAN HALEN						
	21	AS NEEDED		ZZ TOP						

XI(b). R&S II - Female Names

EXECUTION CHECKLIST FOR [DTG] R&S ISO [EXERCISE/OPERATION]										
DP	#	EVENT/SITUATION	RPT	CODEWORD	SCHED TIME	ACTUAL TIME	NET	FROM	TO	REMARKS
	1	TEAM LAUNCHED	M	AVRIL						
	2	FEET DRY	M	BRANDI						
	3	ARRIVE DZ/LZ/BLS	M	BRITNEY						
	4	DZ/LZ/BLS SECURE	M	CANDACE			MEUCMD1	TL	SARC	
	5	INSERT COMPL	M	COURTNEY						
	6	MOVING TO OBJ AREA	M	DARLENE			MEUCMD1	TL	SARC	
	7	ORP ESTAB	M	DIANA			MEUCMD1	TL	SARC	
	8	DEPARTING ORP	M	ELIZABETH			MEUCMD1	TL	SARC	
	9	COMMENCED ACTIONS ON THE OBJ	M	GINA			MEUCMD1	TL	SARC	
	10	L/U COMPL	M	GRETA			MEUCMD1	TL	SARC	
	11	MOVING TO EXTRACT POINT	M	JENNIFER			MEUCMD1	TL	SARC	
	12	MACO COMPL/READY FOR EXTRACT	M	JESSICA			MEUCMD1	TL	SARC	
	13	COMMENCING EXTRACT	M	KATY			MEUCMD1	TL	SARC	
	14	EXTRACT COMPL	M	LITA			MEUCMD1	TL	SARC	
	15	FEET WET	M	MELISSA			MEUCMD1	TL	SARC	
	16	TEAM RECOVERED	M	NICOLE			PHONE	TL	SARC	
	17	MISSION ACCOMPLISHED	M	REBECCA			PHONE	TL	SARC	
	18	AS NEEDED		SHERYL						
	19	AS NEEDED		SUE						
	20	AS NEEDED		TAYLOR						
	21	AS NEEDED		TINA						

XI(c). R&S III - Musical Instruments

EXECUTION CHECKLIST FOR [DTG] R&S ISO [EXERCISE/OPERATION]										
DP	#	EVENT/SITUATION	RPT	CODEWORD	SCHED TIME	ACTUAL TIME	NET	FROM	TO	REMARKS
	1	TEAM LAUNCHED	M	BASSOON						
	2	FEET DRY	M	CELLO						
	3	ARRIVE DZ/LZ/BLS	M	CLARINET						
	4	DZ/LZ/BLS SECURE	M	CORNET			MEUCMD1	TL	SARC	
	5	INSERT COMPL	M	CYMBALS						
	6	MOVING TO OBJ AREA	M	DRUM			MEUCMD1	TL	SARC	
	7	ORP ESTAB	M	FLUTE			MEUCMD1	TL	SARC	
	8	DEPARTING ORP	M	GUITAR			MEUCMD1	TL	SARC	
	9	COMMENCED ACTIONS ON THE OBJ	M	HARP			MEUCMD1	TL	SARC	
	10	L/U COMPL	M	HORN			MEUCMD1	TL	SARC	
	11	MOVING TO EXTRACT POINT	M	MANDOLIN			MEUCMD1	TL	SARC	
	12	MACO COMPL/READY FOR EXTRACT	M	OBOE			MEUCMD1	TL	SARC	
	13	COMMENCING EXTRACT	M	ORGAN			MEUCMD1	TL	SARC	
	14	EXTRACT COMPL	M	PIANO			MEUCMD1	TL	SARC	
	15	FEET WET	M	PICCOLO			MEUCMD1	TL	SARC	
	16	TEAM RECOVERED	M	TAMBOURINE			PHONE	TL	SARC	
	17	MISSION ACCOMPLISHED	M	TIMPANI			PHONE	TL	SARC	
	18	AS NEEDED		TROMBONE						
	19	AS NEEDED		TRUMPET						
	20	AS NEEDED		TUBA						
	21	AS NEEDED		VIOLIN						

XII(a). TRAP (Air)

EXECUTION CHECKLIST FOR [DTG] TRAP (AIR) ISO [EXERCISE/OPERATION]										
DP	#	EVENT/SITUATION	RPT	CODEWORD	SCHED TIME	ACTUAL TIME	NET	FROM	TO	REMARKS
	1	FORCE LAUNCHED	M	ANGELS			LFCMD3	AMC	LFOC	
	2	FEET DRY	M	ASTROS			LFCMD3	AMC	LFOC	
	3	ARRIVE LZ	M	ATHLETICS			LFCMD3	AMC	LFOC	
	4	LZ SECURE	M	BRAVES			MEUCMD1	MC	LFOC	
	5	INSERT COMPL	M	BREWERS			MEUCMD1	MC	LFOC	
	6	MOVING TO OBJ AREA	M	CUBS			MEUCMD1	MC	LFOC	
	7	CAS ON STATION	M	DIAMONDBACKS			LFCMD3	EFL	LFOC	
	8	RADIO L/U ESTAB	M	DODGERS			MEUCMD1	MC	LFOC	
	9	PERSONNEL/MATERIAL SECURED	M	EXPOS			MEUCMD1	MC	LFOC	
	10	CAS OFF STATION	M	INDIANS			LFCMD3	EFL	LFOC	
	11	MOVING TO EXTRACT POINT	M	MARINERS			MEUCMD1	MC	LFOC	
	12	MACO COMPL/READY FOR EXTRACT	M	METS			MEUCMD1	MC	LFOC	
	13	COMMENCING EXTRACT	M	NATIONALS			LFCMD3	AMC	LFOC	
	14	EXTRACT COMPL	M	PADRES			LFCMD3	AMC	LFOC	
	15	FEET WET	M	PHILLIES			LFCMD3	AMC	LFOC	
	16	FORCE RECOVERED	M	PIRATES			PHONE	MC	LFOC	
	17	MISSION ACCOMPLISHED	M	RAYS			PHONE	MC	LFOC	
	18	AS NEEDED		RED SOX						
	19	AS NEEDED		REDS						
	20	AS NEEDED		ROCKIES						
	21	AS NEEDED		ROYALS						

XII(b). TRAP (Surface)

EXECUTION CHECKLIST FOR [DTG] TRAP (SURFACE) ISO [EXERCISE/OPERATION]										
DP	#	EVENT/SITUATION	RPT	CODEWORD	SCHED TIME	ACTUAL TIME	NET	FROM	TO	REMARKS
	1	Force Launched	M	Atlantic			PHONE	TACLOG	LFOC	
	2	Feet Dry	M	Bergen			PHONE	TACLOG	LFOC	
	3	Arrive Bls	M	Burlington			PHONE	TACLOG	LFOC	
	4	Bls Secure	M	Camden			MEUCMD1	MC	LFOC	
	5	Insert Compl	M	Cape May			MEUCMD1	MC	LFOC	
	6	Moving To Obj Area	M	Cumberland			MEUCMD1	MC	LFOC	
	7	Cas On Station	M	Essex			LFCMD3	EFL	LFOC	
	8	Radio L/U Estab	M	Gloucester			MEUCMD1	MC	LFOC	
	9	Personnel/Material Secured	M	Hudson			MEUCMD1	MC	LFOC	
	10	Cas Off Station	M	Hunterdon			LFCMD3	EFL	LFOC	
	11	Moving To Extract Point	M	Mercer			MEUCMD1	MC	LFOC	
	12	Maco Compl/Ready For Extract	M	Middlesex			MEUCMD1	MC	LFOC	
	13	Commencing Extract	M	Monmouth			PHONE	TACLOG	LFOC	
	14	Extract Compl	M	Morris			PHONE	TACLOG	LFOC	
	15	Feet Dry	M	Ocean			PHONE	TACLOG	LFOC	
	16	Force Recovered	M	Passaic			PHONE	MC	LFOC	
	17	Mission Accomplished	M	Salem			PHONE	MC	LFOC	
	18	As Needed		Somerset						
	19	As Needed		Sussex						
	20	As Needed		Union						
	21	As Needed		Warren						

Chap 8

I. Abbreviations & Acronyms

60'S 60mm Mortar (Range 70 to 3,500m)
81'S 81mm Mortar (Range 90 to 5,800)

A

AAA Anti-Aircraft Artillery
AAV Amphibious Assault Vehicle
ACE Aviation Combat Element (of the MEU / MAGTF)
ACU Assault Craft Unit (LCAC or LCU)
ADAL Authorized Dental Allowance List
ADC Air Defense (Commander)
ADEX Air Defense Exercise
AFL Assault Flight Leader
AIG Address Indicator Group
AIMD Aircraft Intermediate Maintenance Department
ALCE Advance Liaison Command Element (Same As FCE)
ALO Air Liaison Officer
ALPHA APLHA Call sign for theater Officer in tactical command
AMAL Authorized Medical Allowance List
AMC Air Mission Commander
AN/PPN-19 Beacon for NGF
AOA Amphibious Objective Area
AOR Area of Responsibility
APB Air Planning Board
APZ Asset Protection Zone
ARG Amphibious Ready Group
ASCM Anti-Ship Cruise Missile
ASE Air Support Element (DASC Component) or Aircraft Survivability Equipment (T/M/S)
ASLT Air Support Liaison Team (DASC Component)
ASROC Anti-Submarine Rocket
ASW Anti-Submarine Warfare (Commander)
AT-4 Anti-Tank Weapon (84mm) (Range 300m)
ATO Air Tasking Order
AUTODIN Automated Digital Network
AWACS Airborne Warning & Control System
AWACS Airborne Warning And Control System (USAF)

B

BALD EAGLE Company-Sized Reinforcement/ Assault Force
BARCAP Barrier Combat Air Patrol
BAS Battalion Aid Station
BDA Battle Damage Assessment
BES Beach Evacuation Station
BHA Bomb Hit Assessment
BLS Beach Landing Site
BLT RECON Battalion Reconnaissance Detachment (23 Men)
BLT Battalion Landing Team
BMD Ballistic Missile Defense
BMNT Begin Morning Nautical Twilight
BMU Beach Master Unit
BOG Beach Operations Group
BP Battle Position
BRAVO OSCAR Call sign for Amphibious Warfare Commander
BUMP PLAN Actions taken to identify who goes/ remains behind if a transport (air or surface) does not function
BUU Basic User Unit (PIRs)

C

CAP Combat Air Patrol
CAS Close Air Support
CASEVAC Casualty Evacuation
CAT Crisis Action Team
CAT Crisis Action Team
CATF Commander Amphibious Task Force
CBU Cluster Bomb Unit
CCIR Commander's Critical Information Requirements
CCOI Critical Contact of Interest
CENTCOM US Central Command (Middle East)
CI Counterintelligence
CIC Combat Information Center
CIEA Classification Identification and Engagement Area
CIWS Close-In Weapons System
CLF Commander Landing Force
CLZ Craft Landing Zone for LCAC
COBRA AH-1W/Z
COI Contact of Interest
COLT Combat Observation Laser Team
COM Chief of Mission (Ambassador/Ranking Us Official; Term Associated In NEO Operations)
COMSEC Communications Security
CP Contact Point
CQ Carrier Qualification

CRRC Combat Rubber Raider Craft (Inflatable/17 Knots)
CRRC Combat Rubber Raider Craft (Inflatable/17 Knots)
CRTF Casualty Receiving and Treatment Facility
CRTS Casualty Receiving and Treatment Ship
CSAR Combat Search And Rescue
CSMO Close Station March Order
CVOA Carrier Operation Area
CWC Composite Warfare Commander

D

DAR Designated Area for Recovery
DASC Direct Air Support Center
DCA Defensive Counter-Air
DCS Defense Communications System (DOD Controlled)
DCT Digital Communications Terminal (AN/PSC-2)
DDG Guided Missile Destroyer
DEP Defense Of The ESG Posture
DESRON Destroyer Squadron
DLQ Deck Landing Qualification
DNBI Disease/Non-Battle Injuries
DOW Died of Wounds
DR Disaster Relief
DSN Defense Switching Network (Formerly AUTOVON)
DTAMS Digital Terrain Analysis Mapping System
DTG Date Time Group

E

E&E Escape and Evasion Plan
E&R Escape and Resist
EBFL Extended Boom Fork Lift
ECC Evacuation Control Center
ECM Electronic Countermeasure
EEFI Essential Elements of Friendly Information
EEIR Enemy Essential Information Requirements
EENT End Evening Nautical Twilight
EENT End Evening Nautical Twilight
EFL Escort Flight Leader
ELINT Electronic Intelligence
EMCON Emission Control
EMERGENCY ASSAULT Immediate or hasty offensive action to counter enemy activity
EMI Electromagnetic Interference
ESF Expeditionary Strike Force
ESG Expeditionary Strike Group
EUCE End User Computing Equipment
EVAC Evacuation

F

FAC Fast Attack Craft
FAC Forward Air Controller
FAC Forward Air Controller
FAC(A) Forward Air Controller (Airborne)
FARP Forward Arming and Refueling Point
FAX Facsimile
FCE Forward Command Element
FCT Firepower Control Team
FDC Fire Direction Center
FEZ Fighter Engagement Zone
FFG Guided Missile Frigate
FFIR Friendly Forces Information Requirements
FIAC Fast Inshore Attack Craft
FiST Fire Support Team
FLIR Forward Looking-Infrared
FLTBCST Fleet Broadcast
FLTSATCOM Fleet Satellite Communications
FMO Fleet Marine Officer
FO Forward Observer (For Artillery And Mortars)
FSC Fire Support Coordinator
FSCC Fire Support Coordination Center
FST Fleet Surgical Team
FST Fleet Surgical Team

G

GAIL Glide Angle Indicator Light
GCCS Global Command and Control System
GCE Ground Combat Element (of the MEU / MAGTF)
GO/NO-GO Criteria used to decide whether to abort the launch of the mission prior to launch
GOPLAT Gas Oil Platform
GPS Global Positioning System
GREENCROWN Call Sign for ADC
GVS-5 Hand Held Laser Range Finder

H

HA Humanitarian Assistance
HARRIER AV-8B
HASE Humanitarian Assistance Survey Element
HAST Humanitarian Assistance Survey Team
HDC Helicopter Direction Center
HDC Helicopter Direction Center
HEALT Helicopter Employment Assault Landing Table
HET Human Intelligence (HUMINT) Exploitation Team
HLZ Helicopter Landing Zone
HM Hospital Man (Corpsman)
HMH Marine Heavy Helicopter Squadron (CH-53E)

HMLA	Marine Light/Attack Helicopter Squadron(AH-1W/Z or UH-1N/Y)
HMMWV	High Mobility, Multipurpose-Wheeled Vehicle
HRST	Helicopter Rope Suspension Training
HS	Helicopter Antisubmarine Warfare Squadron
HSL	Helicopter Antisubmarine Squadron Light
HST	Helicopter Support Team
HUC	Heliborne Unit Commander
HUEY	UH-1N/Y

I

I&W	Indications and Warnings
IAC	Integrated ASW Course
IAD	Integrated Air Defense
IAS	Intelligence Analysis System
ICAO	International Civil Aviation Organization
ICE PACK	Call sign for TACRON
IED	Improvised Explosive Device
IFF	Identification, Friend or Foe
IFR	Instrument Flight Rules
INMARSAT	International Maritime Satellite Organization
IO	Information Operations
IOS	Intelligence Operations Server
IP	Initial Point
IPL	Imagery Product Library
IR	Information Requirements
ISB	Intermediate Staging Base
ITG	Initial Terminal Guidance
ITT	Interrogator Translator Team
IWC	Information Warfare Commander

J

JAC	Joint Analysis (Intelligence) Center Moles Worth Uk
JAVELIN	Anti Tank Weapon, (127mm) (Range 75m to 2,500m)
JDISS	Joint Deployable Intelligence Support System
JEZ	Joint Engagement Zone
JFIC	Joint Forces Intelligence Command
JIC-A	Joint Intelligence Center-Afloat
JOTS	Joint Operational Tactical System
JTAC	Joint Terminal Air Controller
JTAR	Joint Tactical Air Request

K

KIA	Killed in Action

L

LAAD	Low Altitude Air Defense
LAMPS	Light Airborne Multipurpose System (SH-60B Seahawk Helicopter)
LAR	Light Armored Reconnaissance
LARC	Lighter Amphibious Re-Supply Cargo Vehicle
LAV-25	Light Armored Vehicle W/ 25mm Chain Gun
LAV-L	Light Armored Vehicle – Logistics
LCAC	Landing Craft Air Cushion
LFOC	Landing Force Operations Center
LGB	Laser Guided Bomb
LGB	Laser Guided Bomb
LOCE	Linked Operations-Intelligence Centers, Europe
LOS	Line-of-Sight

M

M2	50 Caliber Machine Gun (Range 2,000m)
M777	Lightweight Howitzer, (155mm) (Range 24-40Km)
MACG	Marine Air Control Group
MACO	Marshaling Area Control Officer
MAGTF	Marine Air-Ground Task Force
MANPAD	Man Portable Air Defense
MARCENT	Marine Component Central Command
MATV	MRAP All-Terrain Vehicle
MC	Mission Commander
MC&G	Mapping, Charting, and Geodesy
MCA	Mission Coordination Airspace
MED EVAC	Medical Evacuation
MEWSS	Mobile Electronic Warfare Support System
MINIMIZE	Condition imposed to reduce communication traffic
MK 19	40mm Automatic Grenade Launcher (Range 1,600m)
MMART	Mobile Medical Augmentation Readiness Team
MOUT	Military Operations in Urban Terrain
MRAP	Mine Resistant Ambush Protected
MRC	Medical Regulating Center
MRCO	Medical Regulating Control Officer
MRT	Medical Regulating Team
MS	Master Station (PIRs)
MSE	Major Subordinate Element
MULE	Modular Universal Laser Equipment (AN/PAQ 3)

N

NAVCENT	Navy Component Central Command
NAVSTAR	Navigation System Using Timing and Ranging
NGF	Naval Gun Fire
NIST	National Intelligence Support Team
NO COMM PLAN	Signals to be used if voice/ data communications are inoperable
NOE	Nap of The Earth Flying (Cobras/ Hueys)

NOFORN	No Foreign Dissemination
NOTAL	Not to All
NTDS	Naval Tactical Data System (Synonymous W/CDS and TDS)
NVG	Night Vision Goggle
NVG/NVD	Night Vision Goggle/Night Vision Device

O

OMC	Ordnance Maintenance Company
OPSEC	Operational Security
OTH	Over-The-Horizon

P

PCRTS	Primary Casualty Receiving and Treatment Ship
PGM	Precision Guided Munitions
PHROG	CH-46E
PIR	Priority Information Requirements
PLA	Plain Language Address
PLAD	Plain Language Address Directory
PLRS	Position Location Reporting System
PTP	Pre-Deployment Training Plan

R

RADBN DET	Radio Battalion Detachment
RCA	Riot Control Agent
RF	Radio Frequency
RFC	Raid Force Commander
RGR	Rapid Ground Refueling
RHIB	Rigid Hull Inflatable Boat
ROE	Rules of Engagement
ROE	Rules of Engagement
RP	Rendezvous Point
RRC	Rigid Raider Craft (30 Knots)
RRT	Radio Reconnaissance Team
RW CAS	Rotary Wing Close Air Support

S

SACC	Supporting Arms Coordination Center
SACC	Supporting Arms Coordination Center
SAFE	Selected Area for Evasion
SALT	Supporting Arms Liaison Team
SAM	Surface to Air Missile
SARC	Surveillance and Reconnaissance Center
SATCOM	Satellite Communications
SAW	Squad Automatic Weapon (M249 (5.56mm)
SCC	Sniper Control Center
SCRTS	Secondary Casualty Receiving and Treatment Ship
SDLM	Scheduled Depot Level Maintenance
SFCP	Shore Fire Control Party
SFL	Strike Flight Leader
SHF QUICKSAT	Super High Frequency Satellite Terminal
SHITTER	Ch-53E
SIGINT	Signal Intelligence
SKID	Huey And Cobra A/C
SMAW	Shoulder-Launched, Multipurpose Assault Weapon (83mm) (Range 500m)
SPARROWHAWK	Platoon Size Reinforcement/ Assault Force
SPECAT	Special Category
SSIC	Standard Subject Identification Code
STA	Surveillance and Target Acquisition
STEL	Secure Telephone (Using Stu III Over SHF Circuit)
STP	Shock Trauma Platoon
STX	Situational Training Exercise

T

TAC(A)	Tactical Air Coordinator (Airborne)
TACC	Tactical Air Control Center
TACP	Tactical Air Control Party
TAFDS	Tactical Air Fuel Dispensing System
TAMPS	Tactical Aircrew Mission Planning System
TAOC	Tactical Air Operations Center
TARPS	Tactical Aerial Reconnaissance Photo System
TBFDS	Tactical Bulk Fuel Dispensing System
TDS	Tactical Data System
TERF	Terrain Flight
TIPS	Tactical Information Processing System
TOP	Transportation of Personnel
TOPO	Topographic Support Team
TOT	Time on Target (ACE) or Transportation of Things (CLB)
TOW	Wire-Guided Anti-Tank Weapon (5 Inch) (Range 3,750m)
TRAP	Tactical Recovery Of Aircraft and Personnel
TRP	Target Reference Point

U

UAS	Unmanned Aerial Systems
UAV	Unmanned Aerial Vehicle

V

VBSS	Visit, Board, Search, Seizure
VFR	Visual Flight Rules
VMA	Marine Attack Squadron (AV-8BII/II+)
VMGR	Fixed Wing, Marine Air-Refuel/Transport (KC-130J) Squadron
VSTOL	Vertical/Short Takeoff and Landing

W

WIA	Wounded an Action
WNINTEL	Warning: Intelligence Material or S Sources Involved

Z

ZIPLIP	Brevity Conditions (I, II, III)
ZIPPO (Brief)	Zone Inspection, Planning, Preparing, and Operation
ZULU	Time Zone for Greenwich Mean Time or UTC

II. Glossary

Ref: MCRP 5-12C, Marine Corps Supplement to the DoD Dictionary of Military and Associated Terms (Nov '11) and MSTP Pamphlet 5-0.2, OPT Leader's Guide (Jul '09).

A

asymmetrical threat—The potential of attack from unconventional, unexpected, innovative or disproportional means.

attack by fire—The use of fires (direct and indirect) to engage the enemy from a distance to destroy, fix, neutralize, or suppress.

attack guidance matrix (AGM)—A list of targets that can be attacked along with specifics such as when, how, and priority of attacks as well as desired effects on each attack.

B

battle damage assessment (BDA)—(See JP 1-02 for core definition. Marine Corps amplification follows.) The timely and accurate estimate of the damage resulting from the application of military force. Battle damage assessment estimates physical damage to a particular target, functional damage to that target, and the capability of the entire target system to continue its operations.

battlespace—The environment, factors, and conditions that must be understood to successfully apply combat power, protect the force, or complete the mission. This includes the air, land, sea, space, and the included enemy and friendly forces; facilities; weather; terrain; the electromagnetic spectrum; and the information environment within the operational areas, areas of interest, and areas of influence.

be prepared mission—A mission, assigned to a unit, that might be executed.

block—1. A tactical mission task that denies the enemy access to an area or prevents his advance in a direction or along an avenue of approach. It may be for a specified time. 2. An obstacle effect that integrates fire planning and obstacle effort to stop an attacker along a specific avenue of approach or to prevent him from passing through an engagement area.

branch(es)—A contingency plan or course of action (an option built into the basic plan or course of action) for changing the mission, disposition, orientation, or direction of movement of the force to aid success of the operations based on anticipated events, opportunities, or disruptions caused by enemy actions. (MCRP 5-12C)

bypass—1. To maneuver around an obstacle, position, or enemy force to maintain the momentum of advance. Previously unreported obstacles are reported to higher headquarters. Bypassed enemy forces are reported to higher headquarters. 2. A tactical mission task in which the commander directs his unit to maneuver around an obstacle, position, or enemy force to maintain the momentum of the operation while deliberately avoiding combat with an enemy force.

C

centers of gravity (COG)—Those characteristics, capabilities, or localities from which a military force derives its freedom of action, physical strength, or will to fight. (JP 1-02)

clear—1. To remove enemy forces and eliminate organized resistance in an assigned zone, area, or location by destroying, capturing or forcing the withdrawal of enemy forces that could interfere with the unit's ability to accomplish its mission. 2. To eliminate transmissions on a tactical radio net in order to allow a higher-precedence transmission to occur. 3. The total elimination or neutralization of an obstacle that is usually performed by follow-on engineers and is not done under fire.

close operations—Military actions conducted to project power decisively against enemy forces that pose an immediate or near term threat to the success of current battles or engagements. These military actions are conducted by committed forces and their readily available tactical reserves, using maneuver and combined arms. See also deep operations; rear operations.

commander's battle-space area evaluation (CBAE)—A methodology that supports the entire planning and decision-making process by aiding the commander in the visualization, development, assessment, integration, translation, and final transmission of knowledge to the staff and planning team. (MCRP 5-12C)

commander's critical information requirements (CCIR)—Information regarding the enemy and friendly activities and the environment identified by the commander as critical to maintaining situational awareness, planning future activities, and facilitating timely decision-making. Note: CCIR(s) are normally divided into three primary subcategories: priority intelligence requirements, friendly force information requirements, and essential elements of friendly information. (MCRP 5-12C)

commander's intent—(See JP 1-02 for core definition. Marine Corps amplification follows.) A commander's clear, concise articulation of the purpose(s) behind one or more tasks assigned to a subordinate. It is one of two parts of every mission statement which guides the exercise of initiative in the absence of instructions.

commander's planning guidance (CPG)—Directions and/or instructions that focus the staff's course of action development during the planning process.

constraint(s)—(See JP 1-02 for core definition. Marine Corps amplification follows.) Something which must be done that limits freedom of action. Constraints are included in the rules of engagement, commander's guidance, or instructions from higher headquarters. See also restraint(s).

course of action (COA)—1. A plan that would accomplish, or is related to, the accomplishment of a mission; 2. The scheme adopted to accomplish a task or mission. It is a product of the Joint Operation Planning and Execution System concept development phase. The supported commander will include a recommended course of action in the commander's estimate. The recommended course of action will include the concept of operations, evaluation of supportability estimates of supporting organizations, and an integrated time-phased data base of combat, combat support, and combat service support forces and sustainment. Refinement of this data base will be contingent on the time available for course of action development. When approved, the course of action becomes the basis for the development of an operation plan or operation order. (JP 1-02)

critical vulnerability (CV)—An aspect of a center of gravity that if exploited will do the most significant damage to an adversary's ability to resist. A vulnerability cannot be critical unless it undermines a key strength. (MCRP 5-12C)

D

decision point (DP)—(See JP 1-02 for core definition. Marine Corps amplification follows.) An event, area, or point in the battlespace where and when the friendly commander will make a critical decision.

decision support template (DST)—(See JP 1-02 for core definition. Marine Corps amplification follows.) A staff product initially used in the wargaming process that graphically represents the decision points and projected situations and indicates when, where, and under what conditions a decision is most likely to be required to initiate a specific activity (such as a branch or sequel) or event (such as lifting or shifting of fires).

decisive force—Combat power applied that results in the conclusive imposition of will on an adversary.

deep operations—Military actions conducted against enemy capabilities that pose a potential threat to friendly forces. These military actions are designed to isolate, shape, and dominate the battlespace and influence future operations. See also close operations; rear operations.

defeat—To disrupt or nullify the enemy commander's plan and overcome his will to fight, thus making him unwilling or unable to pursue his adopted course of action and yield to the friendly

defensive operations—Operations conducted to defeat an enemy attack, gain time, economize forces, and develop conditions favorable to offensive and stability operations. The three types of defensive maneuver are area, mobile, and retrograde.

delay—A form of retrograde in which a force under pressure trades space for time by slowing the enemy's momentum and inflicting maximum damage on the enemy without, in principle, becoming decisively engaged.

deny—To hinder or prevent the enemy from using terrain, space, personnel, supplies, or facilities.

design—The conception and articulation of a framework for solving a problem.

destroy—1. To physically rendering an enemy force combat ineffective unless it can be reconstituted. 2. In the context of defeat mechanisms, to apply lethal combat power on an enemy capability so that it can no longer perform any function and cannot be restored to a usable condition without being entirely rebuilt.

disengage—To break contact with the enemy and move to a point where the enemy cannot observe nor engage the unit by direct fire.

disrupt—1. To integrate fires and obstacles to break apart an enemy's formation and tempo, interrupt his timetable, or cause premature commitment or the piecemealing of his forces. 2. A tactical mission task in which a commander integrates direct and indirect fires, terrain, and obstacles to upset an enemy's formation or tempo, interrupt his timetable, or cause his forces to commit prematurely or

E

essential elements of friendly information (EEFI)—(See JP 1-02 for core definition. Marine Corps amplification follows.) Specific facts about friendly intentions, capabilities, and activities needed by adversaries to plan and execute effective operations against our forces.

essential task—(See JP 1-02 for core definition. Marine Corps amplification follows.) Specified or implied tasks that define mission success and apply to the force as a whole. The mission statement is derived from the essential tasks.

event template—(See JP 1-02 for core definition. Marine Corps amplification follows.) A model against which enemy activity can be recorded and compared. It represents a sequential projection of events that relate to space and time on the battlefield and indicate the enemy's ability to adopt a particular course of action. It is a guide for collection and reconnaissance and surveillance planning.

exploit—To take full advantage of success in battle and follow up initial gains to disorganize the enemy in depth.

F

fix—To prevent the enemy from moving any part of his forces, either from a specific location or for a specific period of time, by holding or surrounding them to prevent their withdrawal for use elsewhere.

follow—The order of movement of combat, combat support, and combat service support forces in a given combat operation.

friendly force information requirement (FFIR)— (See JP 1-02 for core definition. Marine Corps amplification follows.) Information the commander needs about friendly forces in order to develop plans and make effective decisions. Depending upon the circumstances, information on unit location, composition, readiness, personnel status, and logistic status could become a friendly force information requirement.

G

guard—To protect the main force by fighting to gain time while also observing and reporting information.

I

implied tasks—(See JP 1-02 implied task for core definition. Marine Corps amplification follows.) Tasks derived from a mission order that, while not specifically stated, must be completed to accomplish the overall mission. See also specified tasks.

infiltration—A form of maneuver in which friendly forces move through or into an area or territory occupied by either friendly or enemy troops or organizations. The movement is made, either by small groups or by individuals, at extended or irregular intervals. When used in connection with the enemy, it implies that contact is to be avoided.

intelligence preparation of the battlespace (IPB)—The systematic, continuous process of analyzing the threat and environment in a specific geographic area.

intelligence requirements (IRs)—(See JP 1-02 intelligence requirement for core definition. Marine Corps amplification follows.) Questions about the enemy and the environment, the answers to which a commander requires to make sound decisions.

interdict—To divert, disrupt, delay or destroy the enemy's surface military potential before it can be used effectively against friendly forces.

J

Joint Operation Planning and Execution System (JOPES)—A continuously evolving system that is being developed through the integration and enhancement of earlier planning and execution systems: Joint Operation Planning System and Joint Deployment System. It provides the foundation for conventional command and control by national- and theater-level commanders and their staffs. It is designed to satisfy their information needs in the conduct of joint planning and operations. JOPES includes joint operation planning policies, procedures, and reporting structures supported by communications and automated data processing systems. JOPES is used to monitor, plan, and execute mobilization, deployment, employment, and sustainment activities associated with joint operations. (JP 1-02)

L

latest time intelligence is of value (LTIOV)—The time by which information must be delivered to the requestor in order to provide decisionmakers with timely intelligence.

limited scale raid (LSR)—The capability to conduct short-duration strikes and small-scale offensive action, using tactics such as precision raid, ambush, and direct assault using close-quarter battle skills. Tactical recovery of aircraft and personnel is an example of a limited scale raid operation.

littoral—(See JP 1-02 for core definition. Marine Corps amplification follows.) A zone of military operations along a coastline, consisting of the seaward approaches from the open ocean to the shore, which must be controlled to support operations ashore, as well as the landward approaches to the shore that can be supported and defended directly from the sea.

M

main battle area—(See JP 1-02 for core definition. Marine Corps amplification follows.) That portion of the battlespace in which the commander conducts close operations to defeat the enemy. Normally, the main battle area extends rearward from the forward edge of the battle area to the rear boundary of the command's subordinate units.

main effort—The designated subordinate unit whose mission at a given point in time is most critical to overall mission success. It is usually weighted with the preponderance of combat power and is directed against a center of gravity through a critical vulnerability.

marshalling area—(See JP 1-02 for core definition. Marine Corps amplification follows.) 1. The general area in which unit preparation areas and departure airfields may be located and from which air movement is initiated. 2. In amphibious operations, the designated area in which, as part of the mounting process, units are reorganized for embarkation; vehicles and equipment are prepared to move directly to embarkation areas; and housekeeping facilities are provided for troops by other units.

military operations on urbanized terrain (MOUT)—All military actions that are planned and conducted on a topographical complex and its adjacent natural terrain where man-made construction is the dominant feature. It includes combat in cities, which is that portion of military operations on urbanized terrain involving house-to-house and street-by-street fighting in towns and cities.

N

neutralize—To render the enemy or his resources ineffective or unusable.

noncontiguous area of operations—An area of operations where one or more of the commander's subordinate forces' area of operations do not share a common boundary.

O

observe, orient, decide, act (OODA) loop—A conceptual model of the time-competitive decision cycle of observe-orient-decide-act (OODA). In military operations, the side that can consistently observe, orient, decide, and act more quickly than the other gains a significant operational and tactical advantage. This cycle is critical to generating tempo.

occupy—To move onto an objective, key terrain, or other manmade or natural terrain area without opposition, and control the entire area.

offensive operations—Operations conducted to take the initiative from the enemy, gain freedom of action, and generate effects to achieve objectives. The four types of offensive operations are movement to contact, attack, exploitation, and pursuit.

on-order mission—A mission to be executed at an unspecified time in the future.

operational planning team (OPT)—A group built around the future operations section which integrates the staff representatives and resources. The operational planning team may have representatives or augmentation from each of the standard staff sections, the six warfighting functions, staff liaisons, and/or subject matter experts. (MCRP 5-12C)

P

parallel planning—Planning by parallel chains of command refers to the planning procedures resulting from the close and continuous coordination necessary between corresponding naval and troop echelons.

penetrate—To break through the enemy's defense and disrupt his defensive system.

phase—(See JP 1-02 for core definition. Marine Corps amplification follows.) A planning and execution tool that is used to divide an operation in duration or activity. A change in phase may involve a change in task or task organization. Phasing helps in planning and controlling and may be indicated by time, by distance, by terrain, or by occurrence of an event.

principles of war—The most important nonphysical factors that affect the conduct of operations at the strategic, operational, and tactical levels. The nine principles of war are mass, objective, offensive, security, economy of force, maneuver, unity of command, surprise, and simplicity.

priority intelligence requirement (PIR) —(See JP 1-02 for core definition. Marine Corps amplification follows.) An intelligence requirement associated with a decision that will critically affect the overall success of the command's mission.

protect—To prevent observation, engagement, or interference with a force or location.

pursuit—An offensive operation designed to catch or cut off a hostile force attempting to escape, with the aim of destroying it.

R

raid—(See JP 1-02 for core definition. Marine Corps amplification follows.) 1. An attack, usually small scale, involving a penetration of hostile territory for a specific purpose other than seizing and holding terrain. It ends with a planned withdrawal upon completion of the assigned mission. 2. In amphibious operations, conducted as an independent operation or in support of other operations, such as another landing, land operations, or air or naval operation. When required, they are conducted by stealth or appropriately supported so that they resemble the early stages of an amphibious assault, except they include a provision for withdrawal. 3. In artillery operations, the movement of an artillery unit (or portion of that unit) to a designated firing position to attack a high-payoff target with artillery fires followed by the immediate withdrawal to a safe location. See also limited scale raid.

restraint(s)—(See JP 1-02 for core definition. Marine Corps amplification follows.) 1. Things that a commander is prohibited from doing that may limit freedom of action. 2. Things that a command prohibits its subordinates from doing. Restraints are included in the rules of engagement, commander's guidance, or instructions from higher headquarters. See also constraint(s).

S

screen—1. A security element whose primary task is to observe, identify, and report information, and only fight in self-protection. 2. A form of security operation that primarily provides early warning to the protected force.

secure—To gain possession of a position or terrain feature, with or without force, and to prevent its destruction or loss by enemy action. The attacking force may or may not have to physically occupy the area.

seize—(See JP 1-02 for core definition. Marine Corps amplification follows.) To clear, occupy, and control a designated area.

shaping—The use of lethal and nonlethal activities to influence events in a manner that changes the general condition of war to an advantage.

situation template—(See JP 1-02 for core definition. Marine Corps amplification follows.) A series of projections that portray, based on enemy doctrine, the most probable disposition and location of enemy forces within constraints imposed by weather and terrain.

specified tasks—(See JP 1-02 for core definition. Marine Corps amplification follows.) Those tasks delineated in the mission order received from higher headquarters. See also implied tasks.

supporting effort—Designated subordinate unit(s) whose mission is designed to directly contribute to the success of the main effort.

T

target precedence list—The commander's list of types of mobile potential targets arranged in the order in which they are to be attacked. It establishes target priorities for reactive targeting.

target selection standards (TSS)—A list of requirements (time, location accuracy, posture) that must be met before attacking a specific target.

V

visit, board, search, and seizure (VBSS)—Maritime boarding actions and tactics, designed to capture enemy vessels, to combat terrorism, piracy and smuggling, and to conduct customs, safety, and other inspections, as employed by modern navies, marine and maritime services, and military and police forces.

W

warfighting functions—The six mutually supporting military activities integrated in the conduct of all military operations. The six warfighting functions are command and control, fires, force protection, intelligence, logistics, and maneuver. See also command and control; fires; force protection; intelligence; logistics; maneuver.

wargaming—A step-by-step process of action, reaction, and counteraction for visualizing the execution of each friendly course of action in relation to adversary courses of action and reactions. It explores the possible branches and sequels to the primary plan resulting in a final plan and decision points for critical actions.